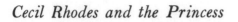

Cecil Rhodes and the Princess

By the same Author

LADIES IN THE VELDT

Cecil Rhodes
and
The
Princess

by BRIAN ROBERTS

J. B. LIPPINCOTT COMPANY
PHILADELPHIA AND NEW YORK

For Theo Aronson

Contents

Part One

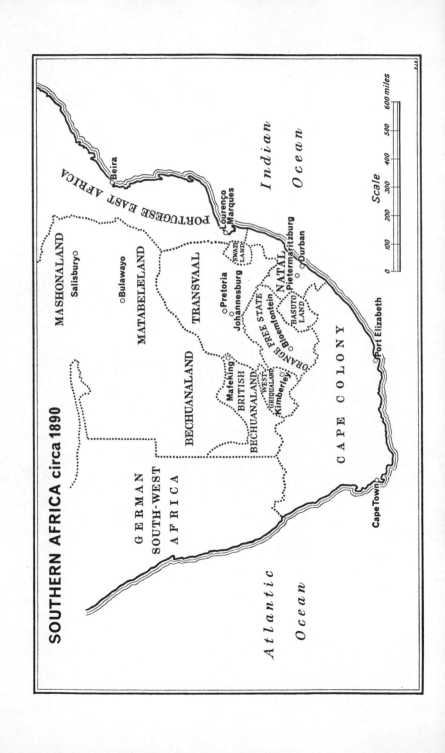

SOUTHERN AFRICA circa 1890

Atlantic
Ocean

CapeTown○

GERMAN
SOUTH-WEST
AFRICA

BECHUANALAND

BRITISH
BECHUANALAND

Mafeking○

WEST
GRIQUALAND
Kimberley○

CAPE COLONY

MASHONALAND
Salisbury○

○Bulawayo

MATABELELAND

TRANSVAAL

Pretoria○
Johannesburg○

ORANGE FREE STATE
Bloemfontein○

BASUTO
LAND

NATAL
Pietermaritzburg
Durban○

PORTUGUESE EAST AFRICA

○Beira

Lourenço
Marques○

SWAZI
LAND

Indian
Ocean

Port Elizabeth○

Scale

0   100   200   300   400   500   600 miles

CHAPTER ONE

The Boy from the Vicarage

IN HIS last will and testament Cecil John Rhodes instituted what will probably be his most lasting memorial: the Rhodes scholarships. By means of these scholarships Rhodes hoped to ensure that a never-ending stream of bright, healthy young men, nurtured beneath the spires of Oxford and a-glow with Anglo-Saxon ideals, would emerge to influence history and guide a less enlightened world to sanity and stability. This was a vision which, in one form or another, had dominated his life. The Rhodes Scholars, therefore, were to be the heirs, not only to his fortune, but to his dreams.

According to the terms of his will, the selection of a scholar was to depend upon: 'his literary and scholastic achievements; his fondness of and success in manly outdoor sports such as cricket, football and the like; his qualities of manhood, truth, courage, devotion to duty, sympathy for the protection of the weak, kindliness, unselfishness and fellowship; and his exhibition during schooldays of moral force of character and of instincts to lead and take interest in his schoolmates . . .' As a picture of a budding head prefect—a clean-cut all-rounder with a sense of responsibility, justice and fair play—this description would be difficult to better; but as a blueprint for future leaders of nations or men of destiny it is too simple-minded by half. What makes it more remarkable is that it is not a hastily assembled set of maxims, thrown together to evaluate the worth of schoolboys, but the result of a lifetime's reflection on the moral and intellectual potential of men. Nothing, in fact, illustrates better Rhodes's own limitations in matters of human relationship than does this naïve assessment of what makes for superiority in men.

As critics of the scholarships have pointed out, it is rarely the

3

upright, unselfish, sports-loving paragons who influence history. More often than not the Empire-makers of this world look back on an adolescence marred by their feeling of isolation, their egocentricity, their inability to adjust to their surroundings and, in many cases, their physical deficiencies. Rhodes should have known this. He had studied the great and the powerful all his life; his heroes were the Roman Emperors, Napoleon and Bismarck. But he did not need to look so far to discover such an elementary truth: he could have found an equally striking example in himself. It is extremely doubtful whether Rhodes would have qualified for one of his own scholarships.

He was not a particularly dull boy but his 'literary and scholastic achievements' left a great deal to be desired. He is said to have had a reasonable grasp of French, the classics and religious knowledge, but he was surprisingly weak in mathematics. A thorough, conscientious worker, he once won a small classical scholarship and a silver medal for elocution; the two awards marked the extent of his academic attainments. They would hardly have singled him out as a Rhodes Scholar. An even greater question mark hangs over his ability to fulfil the other requirements. He was certainly no sportsman. At the age of thirteen he did, it is true, make the school cricket XI—there is a photograph at Rhodes House, Oxford, to prove it—but how keen the competition was and how well he acquitted himself is not known. Certainly, once he had left school he showed little interest in sport; like most of his contemporaries he rode and he shot but he did both badly. In the two games specifically mentioned in his will—football and cricket—he displayed in adulthood little or no interest. But it is in the final requirements for the scholarship awards—those calling for fellowship, manliness, leadership and interest in others—that he misses out altogether. Try as they might, even his most sympathetic biographers cannot disguise the fact that he was a moody, solitary, not very robust boy, who was given to fits of violent temper (he once had difficulty in restraining himself from hurling a textbook at his teacher) and who had very few friends. There was something about him that froze any attempt at intimacy: from his earliest days he was known to his school-fellows simply as Rhodes; only his family called him Cecil. 'A slender, delicate-looking, but not delicate boy,' was how he was described, '. . . possessing a retiring nature, and a high proud spirit.' This is not the stuff of which the gregarious Rhodes Scholars are made.

He was probably happiest when he was alone. It allowed him to indulge his daydreams. 'Fantastical' was how he described these dreams but, from what one can gather of them, they appear to have been strangely prosaic for one so young; there is no suggestion of gallantry about them—no visions of shining armour or feats of self-sacrifice: his head might have been in the clouds but his feet seem to have remained firmly on the ground. The story is told that, when he was out riding one day, another boy pointed to a pretty girl leaning over a gate, but the gaze of the youthful Rhodes went over the girl's head; he merely remarked that the farm was well cultivated but badly managed. That was the way his mind worked. People interested him very little and girls least of all.

His family background might have had something to do with his remoteness. Details of his early life are few and have been assumed by most of his biographers to fit into the conventional pattern of similar Victorian childhoods. But there is reason to doubt this. On the surface, life at the Bishop's Stortford vicarage —where he was born on 5th July, 1853—seems simple enough, but in one important respect the Rhodes family was unusual and their oddity should not be ignored.

The Rev. Francis William Rhodes, Cecil's father, was a man of stern, no-nonsense, Christian principles. His sermons, it is said, lasted precisely ten minutes and were more notable for soundness of doctrine than for originality of thought. He had been married twice. His first wife died in childbirth two years after their marriage, leaving him one child, a daughter, and nine years had elapsed before he had married Louisa Peacock, Rhodes's mother. The second Mrs Rhodes was thirty at the time of her marriage and, for the next twenty years, her life was given over to repeated pregnancies and to the care of her children. There were eleven children altogether—nine of whom were boys—the fifth son being Cecil. Two of the boys (born before Cecil) died early. Of the remaining nine children only one married. A large family of bachelors and spinsters might be an odd coincidence, but the proportion of eight out of nine seems too high to be entirely a matter of chance. To say, as it has been said, that the boys were too adventurous to settle down does not explain this peculiarity. Their restless natures do not make them unique; it is their united resistance to marriage that makes them exceptional. No profound knowledge of psychology is needed to appreciate the effects of early environment on a child's mental and emotional development: family tensions, possessiveness, lack of affection—all these things can contribute to a child's subsequent attitudes and particularly his sexual attitudes. A disturbed childhood does not necessarily produce the same aberration in each child but it leaves its mark—and a mark there seems to have been on the Rhodes family. It is admitted that Rhodes's father was a severe man, who was regarded as eccentric by the servants, and that his mother was pitifully overworked—worn out by child-bearing and child-rearing; the children, in fact, seem to have confided more in their maternal aunt, Sophy Peacock, than in their parents. Shadows might well have been cast over that seemingly peaceful English vicarage. Certainly, where sexual matters were concerned, Cecil Rhodes never quite shook off the influence of his father's puritanism. In later life he was to turn his back on the Church, to become an agnostic, to involve himself in some questionable transactions and to discard the orthodox Christian teachings of his childhood—but the very mention of sex would cause him to blush and change the conversation.

Even among his widely varying brothers and sisters, Cecil was something of an odd man out. They regarded him with respect but treated him with suspicion; 'long headed Cecil' is how one of his brothers referred to him. The nearest to him in temperament was his sister Edith; but even she was not allowed to come too close. In later years, when she came to stay with him at Groote Schuur, he was forced to send her packing; he said the house was not big enough for them both. His two elder brothers, Herbert and Frank, were educated at Winchester and Eton respectively but during Cecil's schooldays the family had grown larger than their father's purse and the third surviving son completed his education at the local grammar school. It had been their father's hope that his sons would follow him into the Church; he saw his seven sons as 'the angels of the Seven Churches'. But instead of angels they became soldiers, farmers and adventurers.

Cecil, it is true, did toy with the idea of taking orders. On leaving school he studied at home under his father and became concerned about his future career. He wrote to his Aunt Sophy and told her that he was torn between becoming a barrister or a clergyman; he was more inclined towards the Law but thought a clergyman's life was probably more pleasant. Come what may, he was determined to go to University. But this was not to be; at least, not yet. Soon after he left school he fell ill and, upon being examined by the family doctor, was found to be tubercular. The doctor advised that he should leave England for a while and, as his brother Herbert had recently emigrated to South Africa and was sending home enthusiastic reports concerning his prospects as a cotton grower in Natal, it was decided that Cecil should join him there.

He set sail for South Africa at the end of June 1870, shortly before his seventeenth birthday. History was to be influenced, not by a scholarship to Oxford, but by a sickly boy's lungs.

*

Of the seven Rhodes brothers, Herbert, the eldest, was undoubtedly the most erratic. Never staying in one place for long, seldom completing any task he undertook, he seemed to be driven on to an ever-shifting rainbow's end. Described as 'tall, lean, hatchet-faced', he combined an extraordinary physical strength and love of adventure with an unfortunate lack of tenacity or sense of purpose. It was this rainbow-chasing that had lured him to Natal and started him on his career as a cotton planter.

By the late 1860s, the lush and fertile colony of Natal had been open to white settlers for little over quarter of a century. With few roads, no railway, only a handful of small towns and a scattering of isolated farms, the colonists were ever-conscious of their precarious position at the tip of Africa. To the north of the colony lay the land of the Zulus, and the war-like propensities of this warrior tribe did little to allay the settlers' fears. Emigrants were needed desperately and, in order to attract enterprising young men from Europe, the Natal Land and Colonization Company were offering suitable settlers a free grant of fifty acres, with the option of purchase of a further 100 acres for £120, payable over a period of twelve years.

For men of sturdy ambition and few means, it was a tempting

7

offer and one which Herbert, with his irrepressible optimism, was unable to resist. He had applied for a farm and, upon arrival, had been given a grant of land in the luxuriant Umkomaas Valley, a few miles from the colonial capital of Pietermaritzburg. Here he had joined a group of men very much after his own heart. Full of the self-confidence of new arrivals, these farming pioneers had ignored the warning of older colonists and were attempting to introduce cotton-growing into the colony. It was, as they soon found out, an extremely chancy undertaking. In spite of Natal's promising climate, the sub-tropical insects, droughts and the planters' lack of experience put each new crop in jeopardy. Herbert's first year was disastrous.

Nothing daunted, he was soon pursuing a more attractive venture. His arrival in Natal had coincided with a cataclysmic event in southern Africa. In March 1869, the discovery of a huge diamond near the Orange River, lying to the west of Natal, confirmed previous suspicions as to the mineral potential of the region. Towards the end of the year more diamonds were found in a neighbouring river and bands of prospectors began to invade the sparsely populated and hitherto neglected area. Among the first to arrive was a party organized and equipped in Natal and, needless to say, the ever-hopeful Herbert Rhodes was among their number. He had by no means given up hopes of his cotton plantation but, if there was an easier way to make a fortune, he was not one to let it pass without investigation.

Herbert was still away on his expedition to the diamond diggings when Cecil arrived at Durban on the 1st September, 1870. The voyage had taken seventy-two days and had not only improved his health but, apparently, had helped to relax his previous reserve. In a letter to his mother he told of how he had joined in the nightly sing-songs in the deckhouse and had danced with delight at the sight of the whales, porpoises and flying fish which followed the ship.

Although Herbert had not been at the docks when he landed, he had arranged for Cecil to be met and lodged with Dr Sutherland, the Surveyor General of Natal. Both the doctor and his wife were delighted with their youthful, mild-mannered and rather solemn guest. Mrs Sutherland found him 'very quiet and a great reader' and her husband was so struck by his earnestness that he saw him achieving his vaguely-held ambition to become a clergyman and ending his days in an English parsonage. Such are the first recorded impressions of Cecil John Rhodes in Africa.

There is a photograph of Rhodes, taken shortly before he left England, which gives one an idea of how he must have appeared to the Sutherlands. Wearing a stiff white collar, cravat and braided jacket, with his thick auburn hair brushed neatly from a broad forehead, he looks like a typical middle-class youth of his day. One has seen the face many times before. Pale and rather uncertain-looking, he could have been a solicitor's clerk starting his first job or a clerical student about to enter a seminary. There is nothing to distinguish him from a thousand other young men; his nose is rather large, his expression fixed and his mouth down-curving above a somewhat receding chin. It is a plain and, above all, very ordinary face. There could have been little about him to hint at his future greatness. Indeed Herbert, with his aura of derring-do, must have seemed a far likelier candidate for setting a continent on fire. With his serious, methodical ways Cecil was a dull contrast to his more colourful brother; but, as the Sutherlands were to discover, those unspectacular qualities were to prove more durable than Herbert's vivacity.

When Herbert finally turned up in Pietermaritzburg, the two brothers set off to renew the battle against the rankness of the Umkomaas Valley. Life on the cotton plantation was hard but, as far as Cecil was concerned, exhilarating. Free from the restraints of conventional society, no longer plagued by his failure to outshine his fellow students, he could shake off his previous inhibitions and broaden his horizons. The outdoor work suited him; it freed his mind and toughened his body; he could think, he could plan, he could be a man among men. From now on he was to reverence manual labour: it became a cardinal tenet in the schoolboyish philosophy that guided him through life. Those who worked by the sweat of their brow were decent chaps; the rest were loafers. It was as simple as that.

Domestic arrangements on the Rhodes's plantation were crude. The brothers lived in two huts, sleeping in one and using the other as a sitting-room-cum-store. They were looked after by an African servant and, when the food became inedible, they would ride over to an adjoining farm where, Rhodes was to claim later, they 'could always be sure of a square meal'. Occasionally Herbert would take a day off for a game of cricket

9

and on Sundays they were both to be seen at church in Pieter-maritzburg. Cecil, for all his new-found love of the outdoors, had still not abandoned the idea of becoming a clergyman and spent his spare time studying, with a view to entering University. His fixation concerning the uselessness of sedentary loafers was tempered only by his respect for education and the advantages of a profession.

And it was in Natal that he made the first real friend of his own age: Henry Caesar Hawkins. Young Hawkins, the son of a local magistrate, had come out to Natal with his family after leaving an English public school and, like Rhodes, he hankered after a University education. 'The lads,' explains one of Rhodes's biographers almost apologetically, 'without being bookworms, had been soundly educated, and were keen on retaining what classical knowledge they possessed. In their spare moments they studied together, and formed many plans for the future.' The most important of these plans was to make enough money to return to England and enter Oxford without having to rely on outside assistance. It was an ambition which only one of them was to realize.

Altogether it was not a bad life. Work, study, friends and the feeling of being master of one's own fate, all contributed to Rhodes's growing self-confidence. In March 1871, his ego was to receive a further boost when he was left to manage the plantation on his own. Herbert's restlessness had once more got the better of him and he left Cecil to supervise the cotton picking while he went to try his luck at the diamond diggings for a second time. There can be no doubt that the seventeen-year-old Cecil felt more than equal to the task. He had learnt a great deal during his stay in South Africa and, of his many new accomplishments, he was particularly proud of his ability to handle African labourers. Shortly after arriving on the plantation, he was writing home to explain how easy it was to get the 'Kaffirs' to work if you lent them money when they needed it. He found that a loan to pay the annual hut-tax was a good investment; it not only secured the farm labour but helped one's reputation. His days in Natal are always cited as the time when he 'came to understand the native'. On a certain level this is probably true. It is equally true, on the same superficial level, that he had been given an early lesson in the practice of power.

He had discovered that men could be bound by purse strings; and the longer the strings, the more securely they were tied— both physically and mentally.

The cotton crop was reasonably satisfactory. At the annual show of the Pietermaritzburg Agricultural Society, on 25th May, 1871, Rhodes's cotton entry was the only one from the Umkomaas Valley and it came near to carrying off the top honours. 'Mr Rhodes,' states a Press report of the show, 'came close behind the winner of the £5 money prize . . . he showed about half a bale of cotton prepared with the McCarthy gin, which would most certainly have taken the best prize had there been the requisite quantity.' It was a minor triumph which he was to translate into a major symbol. In later years, when anyone told him that something was impossible, he would reply: 'Ah, they told me I couldn't grow cotton.'

He was not to have the opportunity of improving his showing. Although he had started negotiations to lease a farm of his own, he was not destined to stay in Natal. South Africa was in the grip of diamond fever. New finds had been made away from the rivers and the drift of prospectors had become a rush. From all over the colony young men were flocking to the diamond fields: Herbert had gone in March and Henry Hawkins had left in June. As soon as the cotton harvest had been gathered in July (and sold for a poor price) Cecil prepared to join his brother at the diamond diggings. His short association with Natal was over. It had been a memorable few months. The excited young man who packed his ox-wagon in Pietermaritzburg in October 1871 was a very different person from the subdued youth who had arrived there a year earlier. He had come a long way in a very short time: he was healthier, more assured, more purposeful; he had worked at his first job, earned his first money, made his first friends and shouldered his first responsibilities. He had acquitted himself well and could afford to be a little smug.

It is also worth noting that while he was in Natal, he had made his first public speech. Unfortunately, it was not recorded. The occasion was the annual dinner held by the Pietermaritzburg Agricultural Society on their show-day—the show at which Rhodes had almost walked off with the cotton prize. The dinner was a dull affair (even the chairman had refused to oblige with his customary song in spite of several requests) and the speeches

11

received scant attention from the Press. It is a pity because, in view of Rhodes's later reputation, a report of his speech might have made amusing reading. As it is, one is left with the tantalizing 'Captain Bond proposed the toast of "The Ladies" and Mr Rhodes replied'.

*

Life at the diamond diggings threw him somewhat off balance. Once again he was forced to withdraw from the crowd. It was perhaps inevitable. In Natal he had found a friendly, open-hearted community; like any pioneer society, the colonists tended to stick together and to welcome additions to their ranks. As a young man and a prospective settler, Rhodes was received without question and made to feel at home; the challenges he had to meet were the challenges of nature; he did not feel himself to be in competition with his fellow men. Things were very different at the diamond fields.

It was a tough, brash, mixed-bag of individualists, drawn from every quarter of the globe, who flocked to Griqualand West in the early 1870s. James Anthony Froude, who visited the settlement two years after Rhodes arrived there, described them as: 'Diggers from America and Australia, German speculators, Fenian head-centres, ex-officers of the Army and Navy, younger sons of good family who have not taken to a profession or have been obliged to leave; a marvellous motley assemblage, among whom money flows like water from the amazing productiveness of the mine.' They lived in tents and covered wagons—pitched along rutted, dust-choked roads; they drank in rickety canvas-framed hotels and they slept in the makeshift coloured brothels. It was like an army camp that had discarded its discipline and assimilated its followers. The diggers worked hard, played hard and put their faith in a turn of the soil and a strong right arm. They were quite a new breed to Rhodes: their like was not to be met in Bishop's Stortford or even Pietermaritzburg. He viewed them with suspicion and held himself aloof. It was during his early days at the diamond fields, he would say in later years, that he learned the value of doing a good day's work and keeping his own counsel.

His initiation into this strange new world was not helped by his being thrown upon his own resources almost from the start.

Hardly had he arrived when Herbert, running true to form, disappeared down country to inspect the cotton plantation in Natal before leaving on a visit to England. Cecil, knowing little of diamonds and scarcely acclimatized to his surroundings, found himself in sole charge of his brother's three claims—claims which it was estimated were then worth £5,000. Given the moral climate of the camp, his inexperience and an inborn scepticism, it is not surprising that he found it necessary to play a cool game.

But if he was chary of the diggers, they were equally uncertain about him. Young as he was, he did not seem to fall into any of their familiar categories. He was not a rake or a chancer, nor was he excessively prim and earnest; and yet, there was something about him that just did not fit. Descriptions of him as a young digger always depict him as moody, taciturn, rather calculating and decidedly touchy. He is remembered as: 'A tall gaunt youth, roughly dressed, coated with dust, sitting moodily on a bucket, deaf to the chatter and rattle about him, his blue eyes fixed intently on his work or on some fabric of his brain.' Or: 'A compound of moody silence and impulsive action. He was hot and even violent at times, but in working towards his ends he laid his plans with care and circumspection.' W. C. Scully, claimed by Rhodes's biographers to have been one of his close friends at this period, does not, in fact, seem to have found him a very easy companion. 'I received several kind favours at his hands, but we never became really intimate,' he says. 'He was even then somewhat intolerant of discussion.' And Louis Cohen, admittedly a biased witness, is nevertheless in agreement with the rest when he says: 'The silent, self-contained Cecil John Rhodes . . . I have many times seen him in the Main Street, dressed in white flannels, leaning moodily with hands in his pockets against a street wall. He hardly ever had a companion, seemingly took no interest in anything but his thoughts.' Most of these recollections of the young Rhodes were written many years later and pictured him through a haze of his subsequent reputation; inevitably they are coloured by hindsight and his air of solitary preoccupation is attributed to the broodings of the budding genius. But there could be a much simpler explanation. A genius is also human and it is equally possible that he was just a lonely, sensitive youth, somewhat out of his depth, and on his guard against a world which he did not yet fully understand. He would not be the first young man to try to impress a crowd of assertive strangers by adopting a pose of silent, inscrutable superiority: such poses are the refuge of the young introvert. He was, after all, still in his teens.

The more one reads of these early days, the more difficult it is to escape the impression of Rhodes as a nervous exhibitionist. Herbert shared a mess with a group of young men—sometimes known as the Twelve Apostles—which Cecil joined and remained with after Herbert had left. Here, one would have thought, he could have relaxed and enjoyed the communal life. He had all day for musing while working his claims and it would have been natural to welcome the novelty of company and to join in discussions of the day's events. But this does not seem to have been the case: the picture of the abstracted youth persists. 'I can very clearly picture Cecil Rhodes in one of his characteristic attitudes,' writes one of his mess-mates. 'After dinner it was his wont to lean forward with both elbows on the table and his mouth slightly open. He had a habit, when thinking, of rubbing his chin gently with his forefinger. Very often he would sit in the attitude described for a very long time, without joining in whatever conversation happened to be going on. His manner and his expression suggested that his thoughts were far away, but occasionally some interjection would indicate that, to a certain extent, he was keeping in touch with the current topic.' If the conversation bored him, he had other ways of drawing attention to himself. 'As I search my memory for the Rhodes of the early seventies,' runs another account, 'I seem to see a fair young man, frequently sunk in deep thoughts, his hands buried in his trousers pockets, his legs crossed and possibly twisted together, quite oblivious of the talk around him; then without a word he would get up and go out with some set purpose in his mind which he was at no pains to communicate.'

Such behaviour, coupled with his outbursts of violent temper (an association which he formed with a boy of his own age, Christiaan Maasdorp, was more remarkable for the number of black eyes it produced between them, than for any semblance of friendship), seems to speak as much of a frustrated personality trying to assert itself by resorting to histrionics as it does of the vague yearnings of adolescent genius. The two interpretations could, of course, complement each other: it is the age factor that seems to indicate the emphasis.

But he could be sociable when he wished. After Herbert's departure, Cecil went into partnership with C. R. Rudd— another English youth sent out to South Africa for his health— and the two young diggers worked at the Rhodes's claims and devised various schemes for improving their capital, including setting up an ice-plant from which they supplied the thirsty camp with cold drinks. It was a partnership which, starting as a purely business arrangement, was to blossom into a firm friendship; and while they do not appear to have been particularly close friends, their relationship was one of the few that survived intact from Rhodes's beginnings in the diamond industry. If Rudd had a fault as a partner, it was that the state of his health prevented his joining in the toast that invariably concluded any business transaction. This was left entirely to Rhodes who was a match for any of the hard-drinking miners. That was one of the puzzling things about him. He could swear and drink with the best of them and was even known to join in an occasional practical joke. Yet he lacked any sense of camaraderie.

It was probably these drinking bouts that later caused him to write to Dr Sutherland in Natal saying that he had been subjected to too much 'lust of the flesh' at the diamond fields to hold out much hope of becoming a village parson. Certainly, the lust to which he was referring could not have been the one that must have sprung immediately to the good doctor's mind. There was nothing like that about young Rhodes. Wine, yes; but women never. It was another of his peculiarities. To be one of the boys it was necessary to have an eye for the girls and this is where Rhodes drew another anti-social line. He made no pretence about it: women simply did not interest him. Admittedly he was to be seen at the camp dances, but he went solely to dance and nothing more. Always picking the ugliest girls in the room as partners, he must have been a godsend to many an unfortunate wall-flower, even if his insistence that he was only dancing 'for the exercise' was hardly flattering. 'I do not believe,' remarked the acidulous Louis Cohen, 'if a flock of the most adorable women passed through the street he would go across the road to see them.' What could one make of a chap like that?

He still continued his studies with young Hawkins who had preceded him to the diamond fields, and his determination to go to University was as resolute as ever. As his clerical ambitions retreated before the temptations of Mammon, so did his attraction to the legal profession reassert itself. A University education, he was heard to say, would help him in any career and if he went on to eat his dinners at the Inns of Court, the position of a barrister would always be useful. The sight of Rhodes seated amidst the dust and clatter of the diggings, his attention divided between his African labourers and his inevitable textbooks, was to become a familiar one at the camp. 'To all appearances,' it was said, 'he seemed to have no other object in life than his books and the successful working of his diamond claim.'

As time went by, he did find a few congenial companions with whom he could unbend. There was, for instance, John Xavier Merriman, son of the Archdeacon of Grahamstown; a young man some twelve years Rhodes's senior who had recently been elected to the Cape Parliament and who was then trying his luck at the diamond fields. Rhodes found him a 'pleasant young fellow' and Merriman was impressed by Rhodes's practical ability; the two of them would often ride into the veld discussing the classics, history and South African politics. Merriman was later to say that they had come to an agreement that the only intellectual pursuit open to a colonist was an active interest in public affairs; it was an agreement which they both took to heart, although with differing results. There was also J. B. Currey, Government Secretary to the first Lieutenant-Governor of Griqualand West. Currey had arrived at the diamond fields with his wife, and Rhodes, welcoming a breath of domesticity amid the rough and tumble of camp life, formed a lasting friendship with the entire Currey family. J. B. Currey, although much older than Rhodes, was to be one of the pall-bearers at his funeral and his son, Harry Currey, was to become one of Rhodes's private secretaries.

These friendships did little to dispel the image of the solitary young digger that Rhodes had created for himself. When all is said and done, the impression that remains is of a self-absorbed youth riding about the camp on his shaggy Basuto pony, followed by his most constant companion—a tail-less mongrel which, it is said, looked more like 'an exaggerated guinea-pig' than a dog.

*

A diamond claim was thirty-one feet square. When Cecil Rhodes arrived at Colesberg Kopje (or the New Rush, as it was called) where Herbert had established himself, the little hillock was divided into six hundred claims. In an unusually long letter to his mother, Rhodes described the diggings as they appeared from the opening of his tent. It was, he said, like looking out at an immense number of ant-heaps, covered with black ants. The ants, however, were human beings. In order that she should understand how the diggings were operated, he told her to imagine her garden divided into thirty-one-foot squares and she would then appreciate the difficulties involved in removing the soil from the claims so that it could be sorted. Each claim holder had to allow enough undug ground at the edge of his claim so that the roads leading to the circumference of the diggings could be established. Along those roads—which became more and more precarious as the diggers burrowed deeper, and often caved in completely—mule carts trundled, taking loads of soil to the sorting tables where it was sieved and raked over in order to uncover the diamonds. There was a great variation in both the quality and quantity of the diamonds that were found in each claim but Cecil was able to inform his mother that he was soon averaging £100 a week.

His letter—one of the first he wrote from the diamond fields—is a curious example of his relationship with his family. A long, matter-of-fact description of his new life, it reads more like a company report than a youthful letter home; it contains nothing of a personal nature, no inquiries about his family or intimate news of himself, and it is signed abruptly, 'Yrs. C. Rhodes'. It seems a strange letter for a son to write to his mother. What it does reflect, however, is his business-like approach to his new undertaking. He surveys the scene, weighs up his chances and estimates his profits. It was an approach that was to stand him in good stead when pitted against the impatient, get-rich-quick philosophy of some of the other diggers. To take full advantage of the new industry that was developing, needed a cool head, patience and clear thinking, and these, as far as business was concerned, were qualities that young Rhodes possessed to the full.

Most of his day was spent at the sorting table, supervising the sifting of the soil and keeping his eye on his African labourers. There was a brisk trade in illicit diamonds and the temptations that such easily acquired wealth held for the raw tribesmen were enormous. The majority of the Africans had trekked to the diggings from far and wide with one purpose in mind—to earn enough money to buy a gun and ammunition; and as one diamond was often all that was necessary to obtain firearms, a claim-holder needed all his wits about him to prevent the best of his finds being spirited away. The simple requirements of the Africans presented other problems as well. Once having procured his gun, a labourer was liable to disappear overnight, heading straight back to his kraal and leaving the claim-holder short-handed or, as was sometimes the case, without any workmen at all. When this happened to Rhodes, both he and Rudd would strip off their shirts and set to work loading the bags and buckets themselves and hauling them to the sorting tables. According to J. G. McDonald, it was while engaged on such manual work that Rhodes broke the little finger of his right hand which, never being properly set, made it impossible for him throughout his life to give a proper grip when shaking hands.

The combination of good management and hard work boosted his reputation as a practical digger. He was already spoken of as a shrewd business man and the term 'Rhodes's luck' became a by-word throughout the camp. Everything he touched seemed to turn out well and nobody doubted that, young as he was, he was able to look after his own interests. When Herbert Rhodes returned after a year's absence, he brought his brother Frank with him and the two of them discovered Cecil down in the claim with a lawyer, measuring the ground, and threatening to sue a neighbour who, he said, was encroaching on his property. The situation, not an unusual one as far as Cecil was concerned, came as an eye-opener to the newly-arrived Frank. 'I know,' he wrote home, 'that Father will be horrified at the idea of Cecil going to law.'

It was shortly after Herbert and Frank arrived that Cecil fell ill. Life at the diamond fields, despite a sparkling atmosphere, was certainly no rest cure. The hot days and cold nights, appalling sanitary conditions, lack of fresh vegetables, vicious dust storms and an incessant plague of flies, made it as unhealthy as it was uncomfortable. In the summer the camp was rife with diarrhoea, dysentery, enteric fever and typhus. One would have thought that it was the last place to strengthen a young convalescent; and yet Rhodes does not seem to have suffered unduly. Descriptions of his physical appearance at this time tend to differ. One account has him as 'a slender stripling, showing some traces of the delicacy that had sent him to the Cape'; but another says 'he was a fresh looking young fellow, with plenty of spirit and energy and a person one would not think was ever a consumptive subject'. Whatever the truth might be, the fact remains that it was neither consumption nor camp fever that caused his first illness in South Africa. It was the first murmuring of the disease that was to overshadow his life: in the winter of 1872 he suffered a slight heart attack. It was largely a matter of overwork and, nursed by the Currey family, he seems to have recovered fairly quickly. As soon as he was well enough, it was decided that he should have a short break from the diggings. Rumours of gold finds were beginning to drift in from the Transvaal and Herbert, as restless as ever, was anxious to investigate them. By going with him, Cecil would have an opportunity of recuperating.

Leaving Frank in charge of the claims, the two brothers set off along the Missionaries' Road into Bechuanaland and then turned eastwards to the Murchison Range where Herbert hoped to find his gold. The more sentimental of Rhodes's biographers are inclined to read a great deal into this lonely trek across the highveld. Just as Natal is supposed to have given him a deep understanding of the Africans, so this journey is said to have given him a profound knowledge of the Transvaal Boer. He is pictured outspanning his cart at isolated farmsteads, listening to the solemn, pipe-puffing patriarchs on the stoeps and sipping coffee with their wives in the kitchens. The Boers were noted for their hospitality and he may well have done all these things but, like most that is written in a romantic vein about Rhodes, the assumed significance of these overnight stops must be taken with a pinch of salt. It would have taken longer than a few weeks to arrive at an understanding of a people as complex as the

Transvaal Boers and, as the future was to show, there was a great deal about them that he never did appreciate.

Indeed, the only existing evidence of his thoughts on this trip shows that his mind was occupied with problems far removed from the pastoral life of the Transvaal farmers. He was thinking of his own country and of that country's mission in the world. For it was on this journey that he made his first will. Writing on an odd scrap of paper, the younger digger bequeathed his small fortune to the Secretary of State for the Colonies; the money was to be used for the purpose of extending the British Empire. It was, perhaps, no mere coincidence that this first tangible evidence of his faith in his country's mission should have been written in the Transvaal. The association of the British Empire with the Boer Republic remained permanently in his mind and eventually became a dangerous obsession.

As a gold prospecting expedition, the journey proved disappointing. The rumours had been more exciting than the finds and by the time the Rhodes brothers arrived, most of the miners had already packed up and moved on. This did not deter Herbert. No sooner had they arrived back at the diamond fields than he was preparing for another expedition. This time his never-failing optimism was to carry him out of Cecil's life. Selling up his share of the diamond claims, he set out on a series of wanderings that were to last another six years and end only in a ghastly accident in which he was burnt to death in his hut in Nyasaland in 1879. It seems tragically appropriate that such a smouldering, fitful life should have ended in a burst of flame.

The Transvaal trek did produce some positive results. It restored Cecil's health, enabled him to buy a 3,000-acre farm, and helped him arrive at a decision about his future. The time had come, he felt, to put some of his vague plans into action. Frank was due to return to England to take up a commission in the cavalry and Cecil decided to go with him. They left the Cape towards the end of July 1873. Cecil was now twenty years of age and was going at last to Oxford.

CHAPTER TWO

The Girl from the Castle

CECIL RHODES started his new way of life by matriculating at Oxford in October 1873. In that same month, in a different country and under very different circumstances, the life of a fifteen-and-a-half-year-old girl underwent an even greater transformation. She was Ekaterina Adamevna Rzewuska, the only daughter of Count Adam Rzewuski, an exiled Polish nobleman living in Southern Russia; and the occasion was her marriage to Prince Adam Karl Wilhelm Radziwill, another Polish exile, who lived with his family in Berlin. The wedding took place in a small Russian Orthodox church on the Rzewuski estate of Werchownia near Kiev. It was a very quiet affair. The nervous and bewildered bride was given away by her father and the ceremony was witnessed by the bridegroom's brother and his two sisters; no other member of either family appears to have been present. From now on the bride was to be known as the Princess Catherine Maria Radziwill, but never for one moment did she forget—or allow anyone else to forget—that she was by birth a member of the proud, passionate and decidedly aristocratic Rzewuski clan. 'We came,' she would say, 'of a strong, clever, brave race, famous for personal courage and remarkable intelligence.' Many of the things she said about herself are open to doubt but at least this arrogant and seemingly pretentious claim does appear to be well-founded.

By any standards the Rzewuskis were a remarkable family. They could trace their antecedents back to the former Kings of Poland; members of the family had played leading roles in various Polish revolutions; a relation of Count Adam Rzewuski had married King Louis XV of France and his uncle, Wenceslaus, had spent years in the desert, living the life of a Bedouin, and becoming a great friend of the famous Lady Hester Stanhope.

The marital ramifications of the family were spread far and wide and there was hardly a country in Europe where Catherine could not claim a distinguished relative.

Her grandfather, Count Adam's father, was a former Polish Ambassador to Denmark who, on marrying his own niece, settled on the family estate of Pohrebyszcze (an estate brought into the family by a distant marriage to a member of the Radziwill family). From this marriage were born three sons and four daughters who, in various ways, more than lived up to the romantic Rzewuski tradition. The eldest son Henry, for instance, distinguished himself as a novelist of no mean talent, earning a reputation as the Polish Sir Walter Scott; Caroline, the eldest daughter, left her first husband to marry a general, joined the religious crusade of the Russian mystic, Julie de Krudener, and, on the death of the general, finally settled in Paris as the wife of Jules Lacroix, a brother of the famous bibliophile, Jacob. But perhaps the most notable of these Rzewuski children was the second daughter, Evelina, who not only enhanced the Rzewuski tradition but, by her high-spirited and unorthodox personality, added to the picturesque annals of literature. Married first to an elderly Polish nobleman, Count Wenceslaus Hanski, she started an anonymous correspondence with Honoré de Balzac which, after a series of romantic meetings and the death of her husband, led to her marriage to the famous novelist and her installation in Paris as the celebrated Mme de Balzac. If Catherine Radziwill's behaviour in later years was to strike people as somewhat bizarre, it is not difficult to trace its origins: the female Rzewuskas were not noted for their conformity.

Count Adam Rzewuski's career, if not as intellectual as that of his novel-writing brother, was no less colourful than that of his sisters. Born on Christmas Eve 1801, he was educated at a Jesuit college and then entered the Military Academy at Vienna. At the age of twenty he was admitted as an officer in a Russian cavalry regiment and from that time on identified himself entirely with Russia and its causes. In 1825 his father died and on his elder brother—the literary Henry—declining the inheritance, Adam took possession of the Rzewuski estates and became virtually the head of the family. While still a young man, he married the elderly Mme Gerebtsoff, a one-time favourite of

Tsar Alexander I. Despite the fact that his wife was some twenty-two years older than himself and had a daughter who was a year his senior, the marriage seems to have been a complete success. It was largely due to the influence of Mme Gerebtsoff that he won for himself a prominent position at the court of the autocratic Tsar Nicholas I. His loyalty to Nicholas was unquestioning and when, in 1830, the Polish nationals rose in rebellion against the Tsar's reactionary régime, Adam Rzewuski acted as an agent for the Russians in their brutal suppression of his countrymen. It was an act of treachery which his fellow Poles never forgave or forgot, but one which was in accord with his fanatical pro-Russian sympathies. He turned his back on his Polish origins completely and thought of himself exclusively as a Russian. It was an attitude which he was to pass on to his daughter. 'Personally,' Catherine was to write, 'I have no sympathy with the Polish cause . . . I am essentially a Russian in opinions, ideas, affections; I love my country with a passionate devotion, and would not belong to any other.'

Tsar Nicholas was delighted with the loyal and dashing Adam Rzewuski. He singled him out for special favours at court and entrusted him with a number of diplomatic missions. In 1851, he was sent to Spain to explore the possibility of re-establishing relations between the Government of Russia and that of the voluptuous Queen Isabel II; and, like many another handsome man, he appears to have caught the Spanish Queen's roving eye. His stay in Madrid was 'rather longer than he intended' and when he returned to St Petersburg he carried with him a souvenir of Queen Isabel's liberal affections in the form of a painting of the Madonna by Murillo.

Mme Gerebtsoff died a few months after his return from Spain and two years later, shortly before the outbreak of the Crimean War, he married Mlle Daschkoff, the twenty-three-year-old daughter of a former Russian Secretary of State for Justice and, according to her daughter, 'one of the loveliest women at the Russian Court'. The Daschkoffs were a truly Russian family, supremely proud of their Tartar origins. In later years Catherine—always eclectic where the virtues of her ancestors were concerned—was quick to claim these origins as her own. 'I am afraid,' she would say, 'that the Tartar blood which is in me has got the upper hand of the Polish.'

But Catherine was never to know this lovely mother of hers. The marriage, which lasted five years, was fraught with disaster. During its early stages, Adam Rzewuski was away fighting in the Crimea and shortly after he returned to take up the position of Military Governor of St Petersburg, Tsar Nicholas died and Rzewuski suffered the 'fate which overtakes all the favourites of a reign when it passes away'. The new and comparatively liberal Tsar, Alexander II, disliked him and he was forced to retire from the court and divide his time between his country estate and his town house in St Petersburg. But for his young wife the greatest sorrow of the marriage was her apparent inability to have a child. She longed passionately to provide her husband with the heir which had been denied him by his elderly first wife; but when, after five years, a child was born to her, it was a daughter and the mother's strength proved unequal to the long-awaited event. Catherine was born in St Petersburg on 30th March, 1858, and five days later her mother died. 'She passed away in full consciousness of her approaching end, with a resignation which can be called heroic, thanking her husband for the years of happiness he had given to her, and reconciled to the will of the Almighty.' Thus, thirty years later, Catherine wrote of her mother whose death haunted her childhood and marked the first tragedy of her ill-starred life.

*

Pohrebyszcze, the home of the Rzewuski family, was completely cut off from the outside world. The estate—45,000 acres of cornfields—was like a little kingdom: hereditary, self-contained and feudal. Over this huge domain the Rzewuskis ruled with all the autocratic disdain for liberal thought which typified nineteenth-century Russia. Their power was absolute and unchallenged. When one of the two thousand serfs married, he would bring his bride to pay homage to his master; the couple would lie full length in front of the Count and, after striking the ground three times with their foreheads, would kiss their overlord's feet. Servants had been known to wish a new Count 'a happy reign'. If the Rzewuskis were noted for their arrogance, there can be no doubt that they had every opportunity to display it.

No master of Pohrebyszcze was more arrogant than Count

Adam Rzewuski. By the time Catherine was born he was approaching sixty and all traces of his former *élan* had long since vanished. His fall from favour at Court and the virtual collapse of his military career seem to have embittered him and turned him into a martinet. When Catherine was two years old he married for the third time but, although his new wife immediately provided him with the long awaited son, the marriage seems to have done little to soften his harsh, uncompromising nature. More and more he withdrew from the world of affairs and took refuge in the reflected lustre of his heroic ancestors, treating those he considered beneath him with an ill-disguised contempt. 'Rzewuski,' it was said, 'will always shake hands with you, but then he has got such a damned way of making you feel he is going to wash them afterwards.' Even Catherine, who adored him, found it hard to paint him in attractive colours. She claims he was thoughtful and sympathetic towards others, but these qualities, if he possessed them, were not obvious outside his family. 'He was disliked by many people,' Catherine admits. 'His independence, the fearlessness with which he used to express his opinions made him dreaded by high and low.' He was hardly an ideal confidant for a motherless girl.

Catherine grew up with few companions, in an atmosphere of macabre legends and spine-chilling superstitions. The castle at Pohrebyszcze was a crumbling and sinister fortress, complete with creaking drawbridge, underground passages and gloomy vaults. In the surrounding park a brick column marked the spot where three hundred Cossacks had been put to death on a single day, and the nights were said to echo with the rattling of ghosts. A final gruesome touch was the ever-present threat of the family curse. It was believed that many years earlier, when the Rzewuskis had lived in Poland, a member of the family had walled up his own mother in a tower in order to obtain his inheritance, and the curse of the old woman had descended upon the entire family. So strong was this belief that one of Count Adam's cousins (who was said to have found the bones of his incarcerated ancestress) had sold the Polish castle in an attempt to escape the curse. His cowardice does not appear to have been rewarded. 'The prediction,' says Catherine, 'has been strangely fulfilled, for scarcely a member of my family has died in his or her bed, and certainly misfortune has dogged their footsteps.'

Catherine's family was so obsessed with the occult that it is difficult to picture her childhood other than in the terms of the eerie romanticism with which nineteenth-century novelists imbued Eastern Europe. It carried with it an aura of vampire bats, werewolves, gaping coffins and fear-ridden peasants. One of Catherine's earliest memories could have come straight from the pages of Mary Shelley or Bram Stoker. In 1863, when she was five years old, her father had been called out of retirement to help put down a second violent uprising of the Poles against their Russian masters. Count Rzewuski had been given a command on the Austrian frontier and had taken with him his wife, his daughter Catherine, and his two-year-old son. While they were lodging at a small house in the town of Oustiloug, the little boy was taken ill and died in a fit of convulsions. The day of his funeral happened to follow a skirmish between the Russian troops and the insurgents and as the funeral procession was slowly making its way to the church, with the coffin being borne on the shoulders of Count Rzewuski and his staff, it was met by a party of Cossacks escorting some Polish prisoners. At the sight of the cortège, the prisoners stopped and one of them, recognizing the traitorous Rzewuski, began shouting curses at him, saying that his child's death was God's punishment for betraying his countrymen. 'One of the Cossacks of the escort, indignant at this piece of brutality,' says Catherine, 'lifted his whip and was going to strike the man on the mouth, when my father raised his voice, and in a sharp ringing tone ordered him to desist. The Pole was suddenly cowed, and with a brusque movement took off his cap that he had up to that time kept on his head. My father turned round, and after gravely saluting with his sword the long line of prisoners, gave the order for the procession to resume its march.' There was, it would seem, more than a whiff of the haughty Count Dracula about Count Adam Rzewuski.

But her childhood was not all gloom. Other sons were later born to Count Rzewuski and his third wife and Catherine took a protective delight in her new young brothers. There were also trips to Kiev, where the grain from the estate was sold and provisions were bought for the year; visits to her sharp-tongued grandmother in St Petersburg and to relatives in Warsaw. Above all there was the excitement of the great religious feast days, particularly Christmas, when Count Rzewuski celebrated his own birthday as well. Preparations for this event started long before December. Her parents' secret shopping expeditions to Kiev were spread over a number of weeks and secrecy ended only when the children were allowed to accompany the head forester to select a Christmas tree from the surrounding woods. On the day itself peasants would arrive from miles around with presents of butter and eggs for the Count and his family. In the afternoon came the highspot of the day when the children were admitted into the dining-room to inspect the tree which had been decorated behind closed doors, by the housekeeper. That evening the family would sit down to an enormous dinner, served at an immense table covered by a gleaming white cloth under which hay had been spread as a reminder of the Bethlehem stable. The day ended with a little ceremony peculiar to the Rzewuskis. A small donkey was led into the dining-room and made to stand opposite the Christmas tree while it was fed with carrots. This was supposed to bring the family luck throughout the year.

In 1866 Catherine was in St Petersburg to see the beautiful Princess Dagmar of Denmark married to Alexander, the heir to the Russian throne. 'It was the first time I had witnessed a pageant of this kind . . .' she remembered, 'and could not sleep for excitement.' The following year she was taken to Paris for the great 1867 Exhibition, presided over by the Emperor Napoleon III and the lovely Empress Eugénie (whom her father remembered as a girl in Spain), and, although Catherine was not impressed by the Exhibition, she burst into tears at the sight of Marie Antoinette's cell in the Conciergerie.

But Paris was to mean more to her than exhibitions and morbid sightseeing; it was to play an important part in her worldly education. For in Paris lived her two delightful aunts: the raddled and socially-conscious Mme Lacroix and the fat, independent and warm-hearted Mme de Balzac. These two Rzewuska sisters, Caroline and Evelina, were totally dissimilar but equally fascinating.

The ageing Mme Lacroix (Aunt Caroline) was an important figure in the social life of Paris. Rouged, bewigged and swathed in velvets and satins, she prided herself on meeting at least twenty celebrated persons each day and her influence as a match-maker among the European aristocracy was so active that she had earned for herself the rather dubious reputation of a 'matrimonial agent'. At her Aunt Caroline's house in the Rue d'Anjou St Honoré, young Catherine was able to catch a glimpse of the glittering society which characterized the French Second Empire. One of the most interesting personalities at Aunt Caroline's receptions was her brother-in-law, Jacob Lacroix, the elderly librarian of the Arsenal, who took a great interest in Catherine and, she says, gave her 'the first encouragement I ever got to try my hand at literary work'.

Mme de Balzac (Aunt Evelina) was far removed from the social whirl. Her seventeen-year-long affair with Honoré de Balzac had ended when the great novelist died six months after their marriage. Having forfeited her inheritance in order to marry Balzac, the impoverished Evelina lived on in her husband's house, rarely going out and meeting only a few literary friends. Balzac had died in 1850, eight years before Catherine was born, and by the time Catherine came to know her aunt, Evelina was established as the mistress of Jean Gigoux, a French portrait painter, a liaison which lasted until her death. Life in Paris had freed Evelina from all the rigidities of her severe Russian upbringing and made her more tolerant, more liberal and more compassionate than any member of her family. She had never shared her brother's reactionary pro-Russian sympathies and in later life she became an ardent, anti-clerical Republican with 'a strong tendency to socialism'. In every respect she was the antithesis of all that Count Adam Rzewuski stood for and, although brother and sister were devoted to each other, it is not surprising to find Catherine remarking that her father was never 'in sympathy' with Mme de Balzac's 'mind or her intellect'. There was a great deal of the Benthamite radical about Evelina de Balzac; she judged people on their value to society and made happiness her criterion. 'If I had my way,' she once said to Catherine, 'I would bring children up to respect happiness just as one brings them up to respect religion.' Naïve as this might have been, there is much to recommend it when set against her brother's unenlightened philosophy.

Contact with her Aunt Evelina was to bring a new sense of purpose into Catherine's life. Madame de Balzac taught her the value of thinking for herself and of standing by her own decisions;

she transformed the natural Rzewuski arrogance into a fiercely-held independence of spirit. If this sometimes resulted in an ill-advised stubbornness, it was, none the less, responsible for Catherine's resilience in the face of adversity. Catherine recognized this herself. 'I owe to her all the good that is in me,' she wrote; 'I am certainly indebted to her for any power of resistance I may possess. But for her lessons and example it is probable I would have been a different being from the one I have become, and though perhaps I might have been a better, I certainly should have been a weaker one. She taught me that though circumstances may break a human creature, they ought not to be able to make her bend under them, when any vital principle is at stake.'

But what Catherine perhaps valued most during these early years was her aunt's warmth and understanding. When Count Adam Rzewuski married for the third time, all mention of Catherine's mother was forbidden. Catherine longed for someone in whom she could confide; someone with whom she could discuss the mother she had never known. There was no one. Her mother's family had broken with Count Rzewuski when he married again, and on the occasions when Catherine was allowed to visit her grandmother, the taciturn old lady remained silent on the subject of her dead daughter. It was only Aunt Evelina who understood the lonely child's need and she became, says Catherine, 'the only being with whom I could talk of the beautiful young creature who had died giving me birth.'

Shortly after their return from Paris in 1867, Count Rzewuski withdrew yet further into his shell by selling his house in St Petersburg and retiring permanently to his country estate. For the next three years Catherine saw little beyond the vast confines of Pohrebyszcze. 'I was growing up,' she says, 'and had little time for anything else but the very severe course of studies to which I was subjected.' In 1870, however, the family went on holiday to Odessa so that Catherine could take advantage of the fashionable sea-baths, and it was while walking along the promenade of this seaside town that they heard of the French surrender at Sedan. Napoleon III had been defeated by the Prussians and the Second Empire had come to an end. Fast on the heels of this calamity came news of the siege of Paris and a letter from Aunt Evelina prophesying the revolutionary uprising, known as the Commune, which followed the armistice. Throughout the winter of 1870–71 they waited anxiously for news of Mme Lacroix and Mme de Balzac and as soon as the horrors of the Commune were over, they made straight for Paris. They found the French capital in ruins but the two Rzewuska sisters as whole-hearted as ever. Aunt Caroline was full of complaints about *des horreurs* which she had been forced to eat during the siege and Count Rzewuski was delighted to find that his sister Evelina's Rzewuska pride had overcome her sense of democracy during the Commune; when a Communard had forced his way into her house and addressed her as Citoy-enne, she had replied: 'Take off your hat, I am not used to people talking to me with their heads covered; and call me Madame, I am too old to be addressed as Citoyenne.'

To Catherine's delight, the next two years were spent in Paris and it was at this time, she says, that she first began to take an interest in politics. Despite Mme de Balzac's temporary lapse, she remained firmly entrenched in her liberal opinions and these opinions undoubtedly had a great influence on Catherine's political thinking. She was always to be torn between her naturally conservative instinct and her admiration for the political principles imbibed from her radical aunt. More often than not the end result was a vague compromise between prejudice and theory but, blurred as her views might be, she was never to lose her taste for politics.

If she had remained in Paris longer, her opinions might, perhaps, have had time to mature. But Count Rzewuski had other plans for her. In the spring of 1873 she returned to Russia. She had just turned fifteen and her childhood was over.

*

Youthful betrothals were by no means unusual in Russia or, for that matter, throughout Europe. Queen Victoria's eldest daughter, the future Empress Frederick, was officially engaged when she was fifteen years of age, and the Tsar Alexander II not only chose his own wife when she was fifteen, but started cultivating his future mistress when she was ten. It could, therefore, have caused no undue surprise when Catherine's father informed her that she was to be engaged to Prince Adam Karl Wilhelm Radziwill, generally known as Prince

Wilhelm Radziwill. Although this twenty-eight-year-old Prussian army officer was almost twice her age and was a complete stranger who spoke a language she did not understand, she appears to have accepted her betrothal as a matter of course. What did confuse the young bride-to-be was the haste with which her engagement was transformed into a marriage. She returned to Russia in the spring of 1873, her engagement became official in the autumn and the wedding ceremony was performed in October of the same year. 'I have often wondered,' she was to say, 'how my father, who loved me so tenderly, could have been party to such a hurried affair. The only explanation I can find is that he was getting on in years, and wished to see me settled before he died. He had begun at that time to suffer from the heart disease to which he eventually succumbed, which might have had some influence on the decision he came to. It is also likely that he was tempted by the great position he thought he had secured for me. If my father had any fault it was the pride of birth, and the determination that his daughter should follow in the steps of all his ancestresses, and add to the glory of the great alliances the family had been faithful to, ever since it began to play a part in the history of its country.'

Prince Wilhelm Radziwill, even by the standards of the ambitious Count, was undoubtedly a catch. Like the Rzewuskis, the Radziwills were a noble family of Polish origin, most of whom had cut their ties with Poland and settled in the capitals of Western Europe. Not only were they higher in the aristocratic hierarchy than the Rzewuskis but they were far more prolific, and through their numerous alliances, had gained an even greater international reputation; there were Radziwills in St Petersburg, Paris, Vienna and Berlin, and wherever they were established, they wielded considerable social power. Catherine's future husband was a member of the Prussian branch of the Radziwills; it was a particularly influential branch, closely connected with the Prussian royal family. His grandmother, Princess Anton Radziwill, had been born Princess Louise of Prussia (a niece of Frederick the Great) and, as a Royal Highness, had given the family quasi-royal rank. Nor was this the family's only tie with the Royal House, for one of Princess Anton's daughters—Princess Eliza Radziwill—had been the first love of the German Emperor, Wilhelm I, and although their marriage had been forbidden, the now ageing Emperor had never forgotten Eliza Radziwill and still looked upon her family 'with eyes different from those with which he looked upon the rest of the world'. Prince Wilhelm Radziwill's father (who had died during the recent Franco-Prussian War) had been a life-long friend of the German Emperor and the entire family enjoyed a privileged position at the Prussian Court. By linking Catherine with a dynasty which was rapidly becoming one of the most powerful forces in Europe, Count Rzewuski had every reason to think that his daughter's future was assured.

Catherine always claimed that she had no idea how the match was arranged. All she knew was that Prince Wilhelm Radziwill arrived at Pohrebyszcze, with his elder brother Prince Anton Radziwill, and at the end of a three days' stay was introduced to her as her future husband. 'I was not given the chance to say a single word,' she claimed. Nor, it seems, was Prince Wilhelm. The final negotiations were conducted entirely between her father and Prince Anton.

One cannot help suspecting that somewhere along the line old Mme Lacroix had had a hand in it; it was acknowledged that she had arranged the marriage of one member of the Radziwill family and it is highly unlikely that such an inveterate match-maker would ignore her own niece. Whoever was responsible, the arrangement was cold-blooded and cynical; Catherine got a title and Prince Wilhelm got a rich wife. Certainly Catherine had little, other than her dowry, to offer. By the prevailing standards, she would never have been considered pretty. Her sallow complexion and thick black hair were very different from the fashionable milk-white skins and red-gold coiffures of the reigning European beauties. For all that, a discerning suitor might have recognized in her gipsy-like features—high cheek bones, dark heavy-lidded eyes and sensuous mouth—the promise of a mature attraction which went deeper than superficial pretti-ness. Wilhelm Radziwill was given no opportunity to judge.

Before Catherine could be handed over to the Radziwills, there was an important formality to be observed. As the daughter of a nobleman living in Russia, it was necessary that she be presented to the Tsar before she was married so that her début into society could be recognized. Like everything to do with her unfortunate marriage, this Court presentation was arranged with more speed than taste. The receptions at the royal palaces took place only during the winter season and the impatient Count Rzewuski had no intention of delaying the marriage several months for the sake of a formality; instead, he seized upon the very first opportunity of approaching the Tsar. When the marriage negotiations were settled in August, it was learnt that the Tsar and his family would be passing through Kiev that month on their way to the Crimea. It was therefore arranged that Catherine should be rushed to Kiev and presented to her Sovereign, not in a royal drawing-room but in a railway station waiting-room.

Wearing an 'atrociously made' white muslin dress, the petrified Catherine was pushed into the presence of the tall, bewhiskered Alexander II and his pale, consumptive wife. It was a tense occasion for all concerned. Count Rzewuski had avoided the royal presence since his dismissal from Court and the Tsar was not one to forget an old enemy. The two men, however, seem to have risen to the occasion and managed to exchange a few polite words with a semblance of affability. Then, after Alexander had glanced at Catherine and remarked: '*Comme elle rapelle sa mère!*' and the Tsaritsa had muttered a polite greeting, the royal party moved on to the station platform. 'The whole ceremony lasted only a few minutes,' says Catherine. 'The Imperial couple entered their railway carriage, and the assembly dispersed with, on my part, a feeling of the intensest relief.' Her existence had been acknowledged by the Tsar of all the Russias and she was now considered fit to embark upon her adult life. It was not until some time later that the Tsar discovered the reason for this hasty presentation and when he did, he sent a sharp note to Catherine's father disapproving of the marriage. His concern was not for the young bride but for the fact that a young heiress had been lost to Russia.

The Tsar's disapproval came too late; by then Catherine had left the country. After their wedding at Evelina de Balzac's old estate of Werchownia on the 26th October, 1873, she and her husband spent a few days with her grandmother in St Petersburg and then went to Berlin where, she says, 'my new and real life began'.

They arrived in Berlin on a wet November evening and drove

straight to the Radziwill Palace. This palace, a huge, rambling old building, had been brought into the family by Prince Wilhelm's royal grandmother, Princess Louise of Prussia. After the death of the old Princess, the building had been divided between two of her sons—Prince Wilhelm's father, Prince Wilhelm-Frederick Radziwill, and his uncle, Prince Bogaslaw Radziwill—who had married two sisters of the Austrian nobility. Although both of Princess Louise's sons were dead when Catherine joined the family, their two widows and numerous children continued to share the palace, each family occupying half the State apartments. The rest of the building was crammed with other members of the Radziwill clan who were either too poor or too obstinate to give up their crowded quarters. On the evening that Catherine arrived, the entire family—brothers, sisters, uncles, aunts, nephews, nieces, cousins and grandchildren—were lined up in the great hall to welcome her. It was a formidable reception committee. To make matters worse, the introductions were hardly over when Catherine was informed that, in three days' time, her brother-in-law was giving a grand dinner party in her honour. 'To say I was dismayed would be using a feeble expression,' she wrote. 'I was a mere child and felt too frightened for words.'

*

When Catherine arrived in Berlin, the Prussian capital was in a state of transition. Three victorious campaigns in seven years—against Denmark in 1864, against Austria in 1866 and finally, against France in 1870—had established Prussia as the foremost German state and one of the most powerful countries in Europe. With the proclamation of Wilhelm I as German Emperor, in 1871, Berlin had acquired a new status, and its citizens, flushed with their recent victories and conscious of their new standing, were determined that their prim, provincial little city should be worthy of their imperial achievements. 'Berliners,' recalled a visiting Englishman, 'had always been jealous of Vienna, the traditional "Kaiser-Stadt". Now Berlin was also a "Kaiser-Stadt" and by the magnificence of its buildings must throw its older rival into the shade . . . So building and renovation began at a feverish rate.' Within a matter of a few years the city was transformed. The foul-smelling, open drains which flowed down every street disappeared, the cobbled roads were replaced by asphalt and new buildings seemed to spring up overnight. All the picturesque features of the eighteenth-century town were obliterated and replaced by a maze of porcelain plaques, glass mosaics 'and other incongruous details dear to the garish soul of the Berliners'. Above this brash, modern city, with its military monuments and belligerent statuary, rose the triumphant Prussian eagle and along its newly paved streets strutted the crop-headed, wasp-waisted army officers—twin idols of the aggressive new nation.

Impressive as all this might have been, it was merely a surface glitter. Essentially the Prussians were a narrow-minded, tight-lipped and tight-fisted people who found it difficult to acclimatize themselves to their newly-acquired grandeur. Their sudden rise to glory had been achieved only by practising the most rigid economy and behind Berlin's imposing façade there existed a frugal society hemmed in by self-imposed disciplines and hide-bound conventions. Nowhere was this stringent way of life more in evidence than in the Radziwill Palace.

When Catherine first saw the apartments that had been allotted to her she was appalled. Situated at the top of endless flights of stairs and known, euphemistically, as the *appartements aux fenêtres en mansarde*, they would, she says, have been more factually named 'the garret' anywhere else. Uncomfortable as they undoubtedly were, she was soon to discover that they were very much in tune with the bleak atmosphere of the palace. The Radziwill family lived in accordance with uncompromising routine; every hour of every day was mapped out on the lines laid down by Catherine's late father-in-law. Although this bigoted Prince had been dead for more than two years, the imprint of his personality was still very much in evidence. While he had lived, the domestic arrangements of the palace had been entirely under his control and no member of the household had been allowed to say or do a thing without his approval; he considered that women should be kept in the background and not be allowed to express an interest in anything but dress, children and gossip. 'He had not been liked in his family,' says Catherine, 'and, for my part, I was very thankful to have been spared acquaintance with him. But I found his influence still reigning in the house, and the sort of daily routine he had established was observed regularly as if he had still been there to see it was carried out.'

Following the Prussian custom, the family dined at five o'clock and after the meal retired to their rooms, reassembling in one of the State apartments at half past nine in the evening. These soirées, like everything else, were meticulously divided between the two main families living in the palace; one evening Catherine's mother-in-law, Princess Mathilde, would preside over the gathering and the next evening the entire ménage would transfer to her sister's apartments. Stiff, formal and deadly dull, these family get-togethers held very little to amuse a young girl and Catherine came to dread them. Tea would be served at a large round table and the women would sit at another table, plying their needles and discussing the latest piece of trivia regarding the health and doings of the royal family. No one would dream of leaving before the stroke of eleven when, after a dutiful round of good-nights, they were allowed to retire. Occasionally a visitor would put in an appearance—a visiting Polish nobleman, a member of the Prussian aristocracy or a distinguished Catholic politician—but even the presence of strangers did nothing to lessen the boredom; indeed, it often intensified the agony.

The most dreaded of visitors, as far as the younger members of the family were concerned, was the Empress Augusta who, during the winter season, would visit the Radziwill Palace twice a month. She came sometimes alone and sometimes accompanied by her daughter, the Grand Duchess of Baden. The very sight of the old Empress's carriage was enough to put the entire male population of the palace to flight. Unlike her husband, who found it difficult to remember that he was no longer King, but Emperor, the Empress Augusta was fully conscious of her new style and title. Catherine's first encounter with the Empress took place shortly after she arrived in Berlin. The Court had just returned to the capital from Baden-Baden and arrangements were immediately made for Catherine to be introduced to the Empress. It was her second presentation to royalty within a matter of months and she did not look forward to this occasion any more than she had welcomed her Russian début. What she feared most was that the Empress would address her in German and she would not be able to understand a word of what was said.

Much to her relief, she was accompanied by her French sister-in-law on her visit to the Royal Palace and the audience was conducted entirely in French. Not that she was given the opportunity of saying much. The Empress, in her chestnut wig and mass of youthful ribbons and laces, was an awesome sight but her strange appearance and harsh voice were offset by the fact that she expected little response from Catherine. After kissing the new bride and lecturing her on the excellence of the Radziwills, she plunged into the latest Court gossip with Catherine's sister-in-law. The following day Catherine was introduced to the Empress's eldest sister, the deaf Princess Charles of Prussia, and then to Prince Frederick and his wife, Queen Victoria's eldest daughter.

Catherine got on better with her husband's family than she had expected. Princess Mathilde, her mother-in-law, was a quiet, somewhat foolish woman of whom she became very fond and she had a great admiration for her elder brother-in-law, Prince Anton Radziwill, the nominal head of the family. Her favourite in the family, however, was Prince Anton's soignée French wife, Princess Marie Radziwill, a great niece of Talleyrand, who Catherine considered was 'possessed of the noblest qualities which can adorn a woman' and who was one of the most influential persons in Berlin. It was the assured Princess Marie who shepherded her through the stiff-necked Prussian society and eased her into the duties which all the Radziwill princesses were expected to perform at Court. The most important was attendance at *'les soirées de la Bonbonnière'*—the royal equivalent of the dreary Radziwill evenings—at which Catherine was expected to be present twice a week. 'There were rarely more than five or six people invited,' says Catherine. 'The Empress used to preside at one round table, whilst the Emperor, who usually appeared a little late, sat at the other. Tea, cakes, ices (always of the same kind), and roasted chestnuts, which were most difficult to eat on account of the gloves it was against etiquette to take off, were handed round in turns. Her Majesty, who usually worked at some kind of embroidery, directed the conversation in the channel she liked best, and it always took place in French. Any new book was discussed, as well as the current reviews, and not a little gossip took place before the King [sic] appeared. As it was nearly always the same people who met at these entertainments, one was pretty sure what was going to be related or said even before one entered the room. It would be a stretch of politeness to say these evenings were not dull, though they gave those who were invited to them the opportunity of hearing a great many things they would otherwise have known nothing about.' Although she was undoubtedly bored, Catherine was to remember these Court secrets and, even if she tended to exaggerate them, she was later able to put them to good use. Indeed, trading in secrets—particularly political secrets—was an accomplishment for which she had a decided talent.

But at this time the sedate and stuffy atmosphere of Berlin was almost unbearable. The Royal Palace, the Radziwill Palace, it was all very much of a muchness—polite conversation, subdued voices, an occasional snippet of gossip about people she did not know and was not interested in—it must have seemed a long way from the gay, worldly receptions she had glimpsed at Mme Lacroix's Parisian salon. To make matters worse, the prevailing gloom was intensified, soon after her arrival, by the death of the Emperor's aged mother, Elizabeth, the Queen Dowager. The whole Court was plunged into mourning and, to Catherine's dismay, she was obliged to set aside all her pretty trousseau to dress herself in black.

All her life Catherine was to remember the first Christmas she spent away from her own family as a very gloomy affair. With the entire household dressed in mourning, celebrations were kept to a minimum and the festivities were not enlivened by the arrival of the Empress on Boxing Day to distribute an embarrassing assortment of gifts. This ceremony, which took place each year, was dreaded by everyone. The Empress's idea of a suitable present was so outlandish that the recipients had difficulty in mastering their amazement in order to express their thanks. Catherine's husband had made up a little song for the occasion which began: '*Un vilain, vilain, vilain cadeau de la Reine.*' Catherine's first sample of the imperial largesse was, considering her chilly quarters, singularly inappropriate. 'I remember,' she says, 'having been scared by the sight of an appalling thermometer in green bronze representing the Column of Victory in Berlin, which in itself is a hideous monument. As my ill luck would have it, I was made the unhappy recipient of this monstrosity, and never could get rid of it in after life.'

By the time her birthday came round, in the following March, she had resigned herself to her dreary existence and was preparing for a new type of confinement. In theory she was already a woman and in fact she was about to become a mother: she was sixteen years of age and pregnant.

CHAPTER THREE

High Learning and High Finance

IT TOOK Cecil Rhodes eight years to obtain his pass degree at Oxford. He matriculated at Oriel College in October 1873 and graduated in December 1881. For the ambitious young Rhodes, however, there was far more to these student years than a mere course of academic studies.

He still retained his faith in the benefits of a University education and was convinced of the need to acquire professional status; but he could not ignore the fact that he had already embarked on a career. This career, although a far cry from the future he had once envisaged, was much too important for him to discard. The partnership of Rudd-Rhodes—diamond diggers, claim-holders and contractors—a small but going concern, must feature prominently in his plans and exert a definite influence on his University career. He thus found himself forced to lead an extraordinary double life. It was a life divided between high finance and high learning, conducted in two continents and involving, it is said, an outlay of some £2,000 in steamship fares alone. Few undergraduates, even among the heterogeneous products of Oxford, can have pursued their degrees in quite such an erratic, preoccupied and expensive fashion.

Nor were his frequent absences from Oxford occasioned solely by business concerns. In his second term at Oxford he caught a cold while rowing on the Isis and it affected his heart and lungs. The doctors gave him less than six months to live. The set-back meant a return to Africa where it took two years in the clear, invigorating air of the diamond diggings (now officially named Kimberley) to put him right. When one considers the profound effect that this division of interest and environment—this curious see-sawing from philosophy to materialism, from the cloisters to the mining office—was to have in moulding the man

40

who was Rhodes, it is impossible to ignore the importance of a physical defect in the creation of a genius and the life of a continent.

There can be no doubt that these years at Oxford and Kimberley were the most formative of Rhodes's life. They saw the uncertain youth replaced by the man of destiny. At Oxford he discovered the philosophical vehicle to which he could harness the fortune he was amassing in Kimberley. Each aspect of this double life was dependent on the other; without either, his subsequent career might well have been sterile or, at best, irresolute.

But it was a slow process, this dovetailing of his interests into their final form. For one thing Rhodes was not immediately at home at Oxford. He did not make friends any more easily at University than he had at the diamond diggings. In his early days at Oxford he was still something of an odd-man-out. Unlike most of his fellow undergraduates, he had not been to a public school and his late start, coupled with the constant interruptions to his studies, made him older than the majority of his contemporaries. Such distinctions tended to set him apart. Among those who did associate with him were a great many who considered him to be something of a bore. He had a tedious habit of starting a debate—quoting a phrase from the classics and getting others to discuss it—for the sole purpose of clearing his own mind and making sure he had a full grasp of an idea by examining it from all sides. It was a habit which was to persist throughout his life. To those who did not follow his method, it could be very tiresome.

This earnestness was one side of the coin; the other was hardly more endearing. His experience of the world had given him an air of vulgar boyishness, disconcerting to self-conscious youngsters trying to conceal their own youth. A friend, attending a drinking party, was amused to discover how much older in manner the other undergraduates were than Rhodes. 'They were,' he recalled, 'full of that spurious wisdom assumed by many young men as a defensive armour, an armour he did not require.' In a way, it was a reversal of his own attitude towards the older diggers. There was a certain vulgarity too, in the way he would fling a fistful of diamonds on to a table to convince his audience of the prospects awaiting an enterprising 'Oxford man' in Africa. It is no wonder that some of them regarded him as a rum sort of character.

But it would be a mistake to picture him at Oxford, as have some of his biographers, as the 'shy and solitary spirit', a latter-day Napoleon at Brienne. All his life he was to cherish his memories of Oxford; the love he felt for the University could not have been born in the heart of an estranged student. He did make friends. They were friends who stood, as he did, a little apart from the general run of undergraduates. 'He belonged to a set of men like himself,' remembered one of his tutors, 'not caring for distinction in the schools and not working for them, but of refined tastes, dining and living for the most part together, and doubtless discussing passing events in life and politics with interest and ability. Such a set is not very common at Oxford, living, as it does, a good deal apart from both games and work, but it does exist and, somehow, includes men of much intellectual power which bears fruit later.' At least two, Rochfort Maguire and Charles Metcalfe, were to join his African enterprises and remain loyal to him throughout his life. They were to be competent assistants and steadfast friends, and as such were to be valued by Rhodes: he rarely sought to cultivate the brilliant. Anyone as flamboyant as Oscar Wilde, one of the luminaries of Oxford at that time, would have terrified him. He would have had little time for Wilde's sparkling wit and even less for his literary aspirations. When one of his own friends announced that he wished to make his living by writing, he received no encouragement from the hard-headed diamond digger. 'Shouldn't do that,' he was told, 'it's not a man's work—mere loafing.'

But all these factors—his gaucherie, his insularity, his combination of seriousness and boyishness—were irrelevant when set against the true meaning of Oxford to his life. For Rhodes, Oxford was a point of departure. It was important for what it came to represent rather than for the education it gave him. Once he had matriculated he felt free to seek a new and more permanent goal in life. What was this to be? Of academic ambition he had none. He knew that he would obtain his degree eventually and that was all he wanted. His reading was spasmodic and undisciplined and he attended only a minimum of lectures. The formal requirements of his studies irked him.

'Now, Mr Butler,' he replied to a tutor who had remonstrated with him, 'you let me alone and I shall pull through somehow.' No, the significance of Oxford was due more to the intellectual stimulus received there than to the course of studies he was obliged to follow. The works of Aristotle, Gibbon's *Decline and Fall*, the *Meditations* of Marcus Aurelius—books which absorbed him—may or may not have been essential to his degree, but there can be no doubt as to the effect they had upon his evolving philosophy. Together with the plutocratic atmosphere of Kimberley, they coloured his thinking and played no small part in the formation of a vision that was to be the lode-star of his life.

Many years later, he confided to W. T. Stead the way his mind had been working during these years. At Oxford, he said, he had been profoundly impressed by a saying of Aristotle as to the importance of having an aim in life sufficiently lofty to justify spending one's entire life in endeavouring to reach it. He was aware that he had no such aim. On returning to Kimberley, he found himself unable to accept the object to which those about him had dedicated their lives. There was nothing lofty in the pursuit of money for its own sake. And so, says Stead, 'he fell a-thinking.' Life must have some purpose. What was that purpose? Religion? He had no religion. What remnants of Christianity had survived his life at the diamond diggings had finally been swept away when he read Winwood Reade's disturbing book, *The Martyrdom of Man*. Like many of his contemporaries, Rhodes had found this compound of Darwinian theory, comparative religion and literary skill difficult to refute. Even so, he was not prepared to accept Reade's atheistic conclusions entirely. He was prepared to give God a fifty-fifty chance of existing. At those odds it would be wise to accept the Deity's existence as a working proposition. But such a theory could not ally him to any particular religion. What then was the highest thing he could work for? His answer was a social trinity: Justice, Liberty, Peace. If there *were* a God, then these were the cornerstones upon which He would want human society to be based. How was such a society to be achieved? 'Mr Rhodes,' says Stead, 'had no hesitation in arriving at the conclusion that the English race—the English-speaking man, whether British, American, Australian or South African—is the type of race which does now, and is likely to continue to do in the future, the most practical, effective work to establish justice, to promote liberty, and to ensure peace over the widest possible area of the planet.' *Pax Romana* was dead; long live *Pax Britannica*! Cecil John Rhodes had found his mission in life.

For Rhodes, there seemed nothing illogical in the sudden jump from metaphysical speculation to patriotic prejudice; or in the fact that a problematical God should have been so capricious throughout history in selecting a chosen race. The achievements of the English-speaking race were self-evident and must, therefore, have been divinely inspired. This was the creed which the 'decent chaps' must uphold by 'man's work' and not sin against by 'loafing'.

The crudity, the *naïveté*, the underlying arrogance of Rhodes's thinking has since come in for a good deal of criticism. This is understandable. To a later generation, sickened by its accents of racial superiority, his creed carries sinister overtones; it conjures up a vision of a power-grasping megalomaniac. Some, indeed, have judged Rhodes entirely in these terms. This is unfair. The ingredients are there, it is true. Once started on his course he was bound to pursue it and it led him into some very questionable byways. The cynic of today might well find Rhodes's creed egocentric, but his motivations were far removed from the psychopathic dreams of later racialists. His vision was born in an atmosphere of high idealism. The world had much to learn about the brutalities that could distort such concepts. To Rhodes, at Oxford, in the 1870s, things looked very different.

British nineteenth-century imperialism was then in its first flush. From 1874 until 1880, Benjamin Disraeli, 'the first of our latter-day imperialists', was Prime Minister of Great Britain. These were the triumphant years in which Britain gained control of the Suez Canal and opened the way to mastery of Egypt and the Far East; in which a gratified Queen Victoria was proclaimed Empress of India; in which the lordly annexation of the Transvaal Republic was looked upon as a first step towards a great Confederation of South Africa; in which Disraeli pulled off a major diplomatic *coup* at the Congress of Berlin by bringing home his famous 'Peace with Honour' to a country which had already sung itself hoarse with its newly-coined 'jingo' threat to Russia: *We don't want to fight but by Jingo if we do, We've got the ships, we've got the men, we've got the money too.*' It was almost as though Britain were having greatness thrust upon her. And if this new blend of national self-righteousness with territorial aggrandisement was somewhat distasteful, it was certainly heady stuff and many a young man succumbed to it. To the patriotic Englishman, the future seemed as much a matter of inevitable responsibility as it did of inevitable dominance.

And what Disraeli was achieving politically, that high-minded but unorthodox socialist, John Ruskin, was expressing poetically. His famous inaugural lecture of 1870 left an indelible impression on a generation of undergraduates. Men who were at Oxford in the 'seventies, says one of them, learned to interpret imperialism through 'words of unsurpassable beauty, from John Ruskin'.

'There is a destiny now possible to us, the highest ever set before a nation to be accepted or refused,' the prophet had proclaimed. 'Will you youths of England make your country again a royal throne of kings, a sceptred isle, for all the world a source of light, a centre of peace; a mistress of learning and of the Arts, faithful guardian of time-tried principles? . . . This is what England must either do or perish: she must found colonies as fast and as far as she is able, formed of her most energetic and worthiest men; seizing every piece of fruitful waste ground she can set her feet on, and there teaching these her colonists that their chief virtue is to be fidelity to their country, and their first aim is to be to advance the power of England by land and sea . . . If we can get men, for little pay, to cast themselves against cannon-mouths for England, we may find men also who will plough and sow for her, who will behave kindly and righteously for her, and who will bring up their children to love her . . . You think that an impossible ideal. Be it so; refuse to accept it, if you will: but see that you form your own in its stead. All that I ask of you is to have a fixed purpose of some kind for your country and for yourselves, no matter how restricted, so that it be fixed and unselfish.'

None of Ruskin's disciples was to be more fixed in his purpose than Cecil Rhodes. He freely admitted how much his inspiration owed to this lecture. It was, indeed, an 'impossible ideal' that Ruskin had proposed, but it was one with a strong emotional appeal to romantic, idealistic youths; and Rhodes, for all his hard-headedness in business and politics, remained a romantic, idealistic youth throughout his life. Had his life been ordained differently, he might, in common with the majority of his contemporaries, have matured emotionally, married, and bestowed his name on a large Victorian family. As it was, his personality was never fully resolved; he used the British Empire as an emotional outlet and bequeathed his name to the centre of Africa.

There is, perhaps, no better illustration of his immature approach to the vision that dominated his life, than the first tangible evidence of it. In 1877 (he was twenty-four) he made his will. This was not the first will he had made; there was that earlier one—scrawled on a crumpled piece of paper in the Transvaal in 1872—and from this first will it is obvious that the idea had been germinating in his mind before he went to Oxford. The will of 1877, however, presents not only the results, but the drift of his subsequent reflections. It is an extraordinary document. Written in the same year in which the Transvaal was annexed, the will names the Colonial Secretary responsible for the annexation as one of the executors. The other was the Attorney-General for Griqualand West, Sidney Shippard. These two unsuspecting gentlemen were to be responsible for the establishment of a Secret Society, whose aim and object would be the extension of British rule throughout the world. No less. A clandestine and dedicated brotherhood was to bring the entire continent of Africa under its sway and to populate South America, the Holy Land, the seaboard of China and Japan, the Malay Archipelago, the islands of Cyprus and Candia, and any islands in the Pacific not possessed by Britain, with British settlers. As if this were not enough for any underground movement to be going on with, the Society was also instructed to recover the United States for Britain, consolidate the Empire and inaugurate a system of Colonial Representation in the Imperial Parliament for the foundation of 'so great a power as to hereafter render wars impossible and promote the best interests of humanity'. This was the result of a *mélange* of Aristotle and Gibbon, Ruskin and Winwood Reade. One cannot help wondering what the reaction of the two executors would have been had they ever been aware of the task bequeathed to them.

*

By the time he left Oxford, Rhodes had made great strides towards consolidating his position in Africa. The small diamond digging concern that he had left in the charge of Charles Rudd had grown enormously. Rudd, some nine years older than Rhodes, was an astute, practical businessman and it has been claimed that it was due largely to his level-headedness that the partnership prospered during these years. However, there can be no doubt that Rhodes played an essential part in the spectacular growth of their joint enterprise. During the long vacations from Oxford—which he invariably spent in Kimberley—and by means of a lengthy and regular correspondence, Rhodes was able to add his intuitive genius to Rudd's talent for organization.

In 1875, while Rhodes was convalescent in Kimberley after his early Oxford illness, the diamond industry experienced its first great slump. The rich-seeming yellow ground which had yielded such wealth, suddenly gave out and the diggers struck a layer of blue ground of unknown depth and potential. The rumour spread that the diamond-bearing soil had been exhausted and that nothing could be expected from the new substratum. This 'blue-ground scare' coincided with a world-wide trade depression; the price of diamonds dropped and many claim-holders regarded the double calamity as the beginning of the end for Kimberley. They gave up. Rhodes and Rudd, however, bought up the abandoned claims, contracted to pump out diggings that had been flooded, built up their capital and expanded their business. It was not done without sacrifice. Rhodes's funds were so tied up at Kimberley that, while he was at Oxford, he was often without money to pay his day-to-day expenses. But the gamble paid off. The blue ground proved rich beyond their wildest expectations and their joint initiative enabled them to take advantage of the opportunities that came their way. Slowly but surely they were able to squeeze out the smaller claim-holders until, in March 1881, nine months before Rhodes took his degree, they amalgamated their interests in De Beers mine with a rival combine and consolidated the De Beers Mining Company Limited. This company, formed with a capital of £200,000, was to spearhead Rhodes's drive for complete control of the diamond industry. The diamond industry, in turn, was to become the chief weapon in his campaign to ensure British rule throughout the world. His partners knew little of this. His society was still very secret.

It was at the beginning of 1881 also, that he was able to launch out in another direction. In April of that year he took his seat in the Cape Parliament. Political influence was as necessary to the furtherance of his schemes as was financial power and, by a characteristic stroke of luck, Rhodes was able to harness both assets simultaneously. The previous year the district of Griqualand West had been added to the Cape and in the ensuing elections Rhodes had stood as an independent candidate for Barkly West. This parliamentary division of the newly annexed territory was centred on the old river-diggings (the area where diamonds had first been discovered) and the electorate was predominantly Dutch. It says much for Rhodes's reputation in the district that not only did he win his seat but, despite subsequent Boer hostility, he retained it until the day he died.

If fortune seemed to smile upon his schemes during these opening months of 1881, his life was not without its anxieties. In fact his entry into Parliament was overshadowed by an un-precedented disaster. The times were hardly propitious to a budding Imperialist embarking upon his political career. Some two months earlier, British prestige in South Africa had been dealt a severe blow. On 27th February a small Boer force, determined to win back the independence which the annexation of the Transvaal had taken from them, scored a decisive victory over a British army contingent at the Battle of Majuba. At least one of the Imperial ambitions that had seemed so easily attainable when Rhodes was at Oxford—the Confederation of South Africa—was in the process of coming to grief. Nor was it without significance that on the very day that Rhodes made his maiden speech in the Cape Parliament, on 19th April 1881, Disraeli, that great champion of the British Empire, died.

The new Member of Parliament gave little indication of being disheartened by these portentous events. If anything, they could only have served to cement his determination. A new figure was needed on the Imperial scene and nowhere was he needed more urgently than in South Africa. It must have seemed very much a case of the time and place heralding the man.

Cecil Rhodes was far from being a natural politician. He

lacked the restraint, the imperturbable reserve and gravity of manner, that distinguishes the statesman, and his voice was too uncontrolled for him to be effective as an orator. His habit of sitting on his hands and rocking with laughter during debates was almost as embarrassing as the way in which his voice was apt to break into a shrill falsetto when he spoke. After his first speech to the House, the less discerning predicted that he would be a political failure. Others were not so sure. Despite his impetuous remarks, his awkward gestures, his unkempt appearance and his disregard for Parliamentary etiquette (the Speaker had repeatedly to remind him to address members by their constituencies and not their names) he spoke with a sweeping enthusiasm that was difficult to ignore. He was, said some, a man to watch.

Things, as far as Rhodes was concerned, were now under way. A mining magnate and a Member of Parliament, it only remained for him to get his pass degree before starting the serious business of reforming the world. He had a great deal on hand. If he was to give his full attention to the task he had set himself, it would be necessary for him to shed a few of his minor responsibilities. One of these responsibilities was his position as secretary to the De Beers Mining Company. He announced his intention to resign and the post was given to a young man named Neville Ernest Pickering.

*

In any biography of Rhodes, one can find, listed in the index, the name *Pickering, N.* The references that follow are usually short and scrappy. This is surprising as, almost without exception, Rhodes's biographers have freely acknowledged the importance of this young man in Rhodes's life. Pickering has been described as Rhodes's 'right-hand man'; he is said to have been 'probably the closest friend Rhodes ever had', and the one upon whom Rhodes bestowed 'more confidence than anyone else'. 'For him,' says Basil Williams, 'Rhodes had a romantic affection; he probably never loved anyone so well.' Indeed, the relationship between Rhodes and Pickering has been likened to that of David and Jonathan.

Yet, in spite of this importance of Pickering in Rhodes's life, details about him are vague. Not one of Rhodes's biographers has bothered to find out who he was or where he came from; for the most part they have been content to pay sentimental tribute to his memory and then to ignore him.

To a certain extent this neglect is understandable. When dealing with Rhodes the Empire-builder, the financial potentate and political strategist, there has been a tendency to brush aside details which seem to have no direct bearing on his public life. This is particularly true of the period during which he knew Neville Pickering. For these were the years in which Rhodes crossed the threshold of his public career, made his first real impact on the South African scene and formulated his plans for further conquests. It was in the early 1880s that he is said to have flattened his hand on a map of Central Africa and declared: 'All this to be painted red; that is my dream.' Set against such surging events, his friendship with an unknown young man does indeed appear to be of little consequence.

However, there is less excuse for ignoring the impact that this friendship had upon Rhodes as a man and the effect which it might well have had upon his future career. Had fate decreed otherwise, the name of Neville Pickering would have featured prominently, not only in the life of Rhodes but in the history of a continent. His significance lies in the part which he was cast to play as much as in the role he actually performed. It is by refusing to acknowledge that significance that Rhodes's biographers have been remiss. Those who have not hurried past the Pickering episode have simply paused to explain it away with evasive platitudes. One is left with the impression of a mating of rare souls; of two dedicated young men sharing a common ideal and working together in the harmony of high endeavour. 'Pickering,' says J. G. McDonald, 'was delicate and imaginative; and he shared to the full Rhodes's dreams of the future.' It is a touching, romantic picture but one which is open to question. Knowing too little, his biographers appear to have assumed too much.

The truth is that Neville Pickering was a very ordinary young man; perhaps the most remarkable thing about him was this ordinariness. Intelligent, lively and easy-going, he was, says one who knew him, 'beloved by both men and women alike'. As secretary of the De Beers Mining Company, he performed his duties with a business-like efficiency and was highly regarded by the directors for his 'strict probity and unfailing attention to duty'. But, such praiseworthy traits apart, there was little in his career, either before or after he arrived in Kimberley, to single him out from a thousand other conscientious young men in similar positions.

Christened Neville Ernest, he was the third and youngest son of the Rev. Edward Pickering of Port Elizabeth. His father had first come to South Africa with the British army when he was a young man and had returned in 1857 to take up the appointment of incumbent of St Paul's Church, Port Elizabeth. On taking up this appointment, Mr Pickering had brought with him his twenty-three-year-old wife, Frances, and four young children: two boys, Edward and William, and two girls, Mina and Ethel. Neville, the third son and last child, was born in St Paul's Rectory on 29th October, 1857, six months after the family arrived in South Africa.

The Rev. Edward Pickering appears to have been a lively and able parson. Some eighteen months after his arrival in Port Elizabeth, the Colonial Chaplaincy attached to St Mary's Church fell vacant and he was appointed to the post. He was also extremely active in helping to raise funds for the newly established Grey Institute, the school to which he sent all three of his sons. At the time the Pickering boys attended the 'Grey', the school was under the rectorship of the Rev. H. I. Johnson, a brilliant Cambridge scholar, stern disciplinarian and firm believer in the benefits of physical exercise. Of the three boys, Edward, the eldest, was undoubtedly the cleverest. He completely outshone his brothers. Neville Pickering was a bright, competent youngster but, apart from once coming second in his class prize list, does not appear to have distinguished himself in any way. His school attainments were not unlike those of Cecil Rhodes. He had a flair for languages—for English, French and Latin—but was hopeless at mathematics. When he left school in 1875, at the age of eighteen, he was apprenticed as a clerk to a leading firm of merchants in Port Elizabeth, Messrs Dunell Ebden and Company. He was to continue working for this firm until he was appointed secretary of De Beers in 1881.

When and how he first met Cecil Rhodes is not certain. It is possible that they knew each other before Pickering joined De Beers. The firm of Dunell Ebden, for whom Neville worked, was well known in Kimberley, having been the owner of the farm, *Vooruitzicht*, upon which the Kimberley and De Beers mines were discovered in 1871. The farm had actually been sold to the Cape Government for £100,000 in the year that Pickering joined Dunell Ebden in Port Elizabeth, but it seems likely that the firm retained some of its interests in the diamond fields and it might well have been these interests that first brought Rhodes and Pickering together. But their acquaintance could only have been slight. In the years that Pickering was employed in Port Elizabeth, Rhodes was fully occupied with his work in Kimberley and his studies at Oxford, and Pickering does not appear to have spent a great deal of time away from home. In fact, during his first months in Kimberley, Neville was to complain of feeling like an 'exile' after being separated from his family for so long.

From what probably started off as a casual business acquaintanceship, the intimacy between the two men developed with (as far as Rhodes was concerned) unprecedented speed. It was most likely in March 1881, when the mining concern was registered as a joint-stock company, that Rhodes relinquished the secretaryship of De Beers but, although appointed to the post, Pickering does not appear to have taken up his duties until the end of that year. The first public announcement of the new secretary was not made until November 1881 when N. E. Pickering was listed among those who were issued with a Diamond Broker's Licence during the month of October. One cannot be certain of the exact date on which the two friends set up house together but it seems to have been at the beginning of 1882, shortly after Rhodes had taken his degree at Oxford. They could thus have been friendly for a matter of months only.

For Rhodes, this sudden plunge into intimacy with a fellow human being was very much out of character. He had kept himself studiously aloof from his mess-mates in his early days at Kimberley and none of his friendships at Oxford strike one as having been particularly close. What, on the face of it, makes this sudden friendship even more surprising is the fact that the two young men were so dissimilar in status, personality and outlook. Rhodes, by the time they started living together, was a man of considerable standing; Pickering a mere secretary. Where Rhodes was moody, remote and difficult to get on with,

Pickering was uncomplicated, sociable and popular. The description of Rhodes's young friend as a sickly, sensitive youth is, as far as these early days are concerned, extremely difficult to accept. From the moment that Neville Pickering arrived in Kimberley, he threw himself into the social life of the town with gusto. If, in his quieter moments, he felt himself to be an exile, it was not from any lack of ability to make himself feel at home. In an account of his early life at the Diamond Fields, he talks of arriving at church with a girl on each arm, of having to make an effort to fit in all his duty calls and of the expense entailed in keeping up with the ceaseless round of entertainment. 'We have dinners and dances,' he says, 'one finds oneself in evening dress every night. It's ruination to health and pocket.' This is a very different person from Rhodes, who went to dances for the exercise and confined his sociability to the cementing of business deals.

The two of them shared a cottage facing the Kimberley Cricket Ground. For almost five years they lived there but, in all the written recollections of the mining town, there are few mentions of anyone visiting the Rhodes-Pickering *ménage*. Whatever entertaining they may have done was no doubt confined to the newly-built Kimberley Club. 'Our club is such perfection,' wrote the exuberant Neville to his brother. 'Electric bells wherever you like to touch. Velvet pile and turkey carpets to walk upon and then one loses oneself in a luxurious lounge.' This institution was to witness the birth of more than one of Rhodes's grandiose schemes.

But if the friends were rarely seen in their home, they were very much in evidence in the day-to-day life of the town. 'They shared the same office and the same dwelling-house,' says the journalist Ian Colvin, 'worked together, played together, rode together, shot together.' And it was while with Pickering that Rhodes developed one of his greatest assets: an hypnotic and persuasive charm—an ability, as he was to put it, to win people over 'on the personal'. It would be a mistake to attribute this personal magnetism entirely to Pickering's influence; there had been indications of it before the two friends met and it was something which Rhodes could switch on and off at will. Nevertheless, the warmth that this deep and personal friendship brought to Rhodes's hitherto lonely life undoubtedly helped melt away some of the more jagged edges of his personality. It was at this period of his life that he emerged as the great negotiator and drew some of the men who were to be his staunchest supporters to his side.

One of the most frequent errors made by Rhodes's biographers is in imagining Pickering to have been a good deal younger than Rhodes. More often than not he is referred to as Rhodes's 'young friend' or his 'youthful secretary'. It has even been suggested that Rhodes and Pickering belonged to different generations. That such a belief could be held by those who, at the same time, represent Pickering as Rhodes's alter-ego, is rather curious. There is, in fact, no truth in this alleged disparity of age between them. When Pickering was appointed secretary to De Beers, he was twenty-three years of age (it was an age that was to assume a strange significance in Rhodes's later life). At that time Rhodes was twenty-seven. It is not difficult, however, to appreciate how the error originated. In addition to their difference in worldly status, the cumbersome, solidly-jowled Rhodes always looked ten years older than he was. And then, beside the gregarious Pickering, Rhodes with his self-contained, brooding personality must, despite occasional outbursts of boyishness, have seemed like an irascible uncle. It was, very largely, the difference in temperament which gave rise to the legend of a difference in age. But it was this very difference that explains much of Rhodes's attachment to Pickering.

It was an attraction of opposites. Pickering was the type of young man whom Rhodes was to admire all his life; a type which he himself could never emulate. A photograph of Pickering taken in Kimberley shows an alert and fresh-faced youngster, not particularly handsome, but attractive, clean-cut and candid. It fits a contemporary description of him as a 'frank, sunny-tempered young Englishman'. Looking at it one feels that here is the prototype for the Rhodes scholars. And that is what he was. Not a dreamer, not a genius, but a sound, honest-to-goodness all-rounder of undeniable masculinity. If Rhodes expected too much from the scholarships he founded, perhaps his faith in them can be traced to the overwhelming trust he placed in this likeable, unassuming young man.

For trust him he certainly did. At no time in his life did

Rhodes place greater confidence in any single living person than he did in Neville Pickering. And this singular display of faith manifested itself not, as is commonly assumed, after years of close friendship, but within a few months of their sharing a cottage together. On 28th October, 1882, Rhodes made his third will. It was short and to the point. In it C. J. Rhodes, 'being of sound mind', leaves his worldly wealth to N. E. Pickering. He handed this in an envelope to Pickering with a covering note: 'My dear Pickering—Open the enclosed after my death. There is an old will of mine with Graham, whose conditions are very curious, and can only be carried out by a trustworthy person, and I consider you one.' The note is signed in the same stilted manner in which Rhodes always signed his letters to his mother: 'Yours, C. J. Rhodes'. In a postscript he added: 'You fully understand you are to use the interest of money as you like during your lifetime.'

At that time, Rhodes's income is estimated to have been in the region of £50,000 a year.

To Pickering, who had written to his brother a few weeks earlier welcoming a windfall of £142 as 'a most undeniable Godsend. I am grateful, altho I have not been sober since . . .', this promise of financial security must have seemed almost unbelievable.

Had Pickering ever had to refer to the 'curious conditions' of that older will, he would have had an even more profound shock. For he now replaced the Colonial Secretary and the Attorney-General for Griqualand West as Rhodes's executor. His was to be the task of extending the British Empire, of recovering the United States for Britain, and of sending British settlers into the heart of Africa, South America, the Holy Land, the Malay Archipelago, the islands of Cyprus and Candia, the seaboard of China and Japan . . .

*

With his entry into Parliament, Rhodes was once more forced to lead a double life. In Kimberley he was the mining magnate, working at De Beers and sharing a cottage with Neville Pickering. In Cape Town he was the 'young member for Barkly West', attending sittings in the House and sharing a *pied-à-terre* (rooms in Adderley Street) with the Marine Superintendent of the Docks and Harbour, Captain Penfold. The association of Rhodes and Captain Penfold seems to have been remembered mainly on account of the captain's often-repeated boast that he alone was able to ensure that the day-dreaming Rhodes kept his engagements on time and was suitably dressed. Even so, there were occasions when this self-appointed secretary-cum-valet slipped up. Rhodes was notoriously careless about his appearance and his informal dress in Parliament often shocked the more conventional members of the House. Once, while making a speech, he felt obliged to defend the shabby suit he was wearing. 'I am still in Oxford tweeds,' he announced, 'and I think I can legislate as well in them as in sable clothing.'

But such trivialities were usually beneath his notice. His mind was fully occupied with the great task he was now beginning to tackle. Inside and outside Parliament, he was busily making useful friends among the political *élite*. At Government House he cultivated the new Governor and High Commissioner, Sir Hercules Robinson, and the Imperial Secretary, Captain Graham Bower. At the Civil Service Club or at Poole's where he often had lunch, he struck up an acquaintance with many of the leading civil servants and politicians of the day. It was probably in the lobby of the House of Assembly that he now met for the first time Jan Hofmeyr, the great Afrikaner statesman, who would be his most important political ally for the next fifteen years. In Cape Town, also, were some of his old Kimberley friends: John X. Merriman, his early companion in the veld, and J. B. Currey, whose family had nursed him through his first heart attack. New acquaintances and old friends, he had a use for them all. The time had now come to put his plans into action and he would need all the support he could muster.

Almost from the moment Rhodes entered Parliament his eyes were turned northwards. 'I went down to the Cape Parliament,' he was to say, 'thinking in my practical way, "I will go and take the North" .' For one who had set his heart on winning the world it was a modest enough ambition. By 'the North' he meant, of course, the continent of Africa; but this, even for Rhodes, had to be regarded as a long-term objective. More immediately, the north was represented by Bechuanaland. This was the vast and largely barren land situated to the north of the Cape Colony and to the west of the Transvaal. In most respects it was an unpromising and unattractive prize; its fascination for Rhodes lay in the comparatively fertile territory that ran along its eastern border—the border it shared with the Transvaal. It was through this territory that missionaries, such as Livingstone and Moffat, had passed on their journeys into the heart of Africa; it was known, in fact, as the Missionaries' Road to the North. And where missionaries could go, so could trade, railways and of course, British settlers. It was essential to Rhodes's plans that this stretch of land be secured to the Cape. 'I look upon this Bechuanaland territory,' he was to announce in the Cape House of Assembly, 'as the Suez Canal of the trade of this country, the key of its road to the interior.' It was not a matter that could be left to the Imperial authorities; the humiliating capitulation of the British Government after the Battle of Majuba had shown that British interests in Africa were best served by those nearer at hand. 'We want to get rid of the Imperial factor in this question and deal with it ourselves,' declared Rhodes.

This was easier said than done. By the time he was ready to make his first move, this vital 'Suez Canal' was blocked. The Bechuanas were a quarrelsome people and were inclined to drag outsiders into their quarrels. Some of these outsiders were Boers from the Transvaal who, having got a foothold in Bechuanaland, were reluctant to move. They had, in fact, set up two small independent republics—Stellaland and Goshen—at the mouth of Rhodes's canal. Until they were removed, the 'North' was effectively sealed off. The first four years of Rhodes's political life were to be devoted to the removal of these obstructive republics.

The negotiations were both protracted and complicated. Nor were things helped when, in April 1884, Bismarck proclaimed a German protectorate over the ill-defined country to the west of Bechuanaland. The scramble for Africa among the countries of Europe was already under way and the need to safeguard British interests in Bechuanaland now became imperative. Whitehall, at last, was stirred into action. Although Bechuanaland was not under British jurisdiction, a British Deputy Commissioner was sent to the territory. This was the controversial missionary John Mackenzie whose high-handed attitude towards the Boers created such a commotion that he soon had to be recalled.

Rhodes, using his influence with the British High Commissioner, Sir Hercules Robinson, had himself appointed Deputy Commissioner in Mackenzie's place.

In August 1884 Rhodes set off to win over the truculent republics. In Stellaland his down-to-earth diplomacy met with almost immediate success. 'Blood must flow,' said Groot Adriaan de la Rey when Rhodes arrived. 'No, give me my breakfast, and then we can talk about blood,' replied Rhodes. By the end of the week Rhodes had become godfather to de la Rey's grandchild and had Stellaland in his pocket. Goshen proved a trickier problem. The Transvaal had already proclaimed a protectorate over the territory and although, in response to a British demand, they eventually withdrew their claim, Rhodes still felt the need for a show of force. Unable to get support from the Cape Parliament, he reluctantly fell back on the 'Imperial factor'. In January 1885, at Rhodes's request, Sir Charles Warren, with 4,000 troops, arrived in South Africa and proceeded to Bechuanaland. Rhodes, dressed in a ragged coat, dirty white flannels and a pair of old tennis shoes and accompanied by J. B. Currey's twenty-one-year-old son, Harry, joined the British troops soon after their arrival. He was present at Sir Charles Warren's meeting with Paul Kruger, the President of the Transvaal, a few days later. This took place at Fourteen Streams on the Vaal River and was one of the few times that Rhodes came face to face with the man who was to be his greatest adversary. Rhodes took little part in the discussions but he did not escape the eye of the wily old President. 'That young man will cause me trouble,' Kruger is said to have remarked, 'if he does not leave politics alone and turn to something else.'

The final result of the Bechuanaland negotiations was not what Rhodes had hoped for. He and Sir Charles Warren were soon at loggerheads and the territory was lost to the Cape. Despite Rhodes's protestations, Bechuanaland was divided into a Crown Colony and a British Protectorate. But if the area had not been freed of the 'Imperial factor', it was at least safeguarded from Germany and the Transvaal. With British authority established in the territory, Rhodes still had room to manœuvre. There was yet hope of opening his canal.

Busy as he was in Bechuanaland and Cape Town, Rhodes still found time to expand his diamond interests. De Beers, already one of the largest companies in Kimberley, was still growing apace. But Rhodes was not satisfied. It was his ambition to amalgamate the diamond mines; he would stop at nothing less than complete control of the industry. The demand for diamonds, he argued, was limited; unless there was some control of output, the markets would be flooded and the stones would lose their value. The way to control output was by limiting production and this could only be done by amalgamating the mines. He preached his doctrine of amalgamation to the financiers of Kimberley and one by one began to win them over. Perhaps his most important conquest was that of Alfred Beit, the shy but shrewd little German Jew who is said to have had one of the best financial brains in Kimberley. The story is told of an early encounter between them. One night Rhodes, having recently been introduced to Beit, stopped by to see him at his office. 'What is your game?' demanded Rhodes. 'I am going to control the whole diamond output before I am much older,' replied Beit. 'That's funny,' said Rhodes, 'I've made up my mind to do the same. We had better join hands.' And join hands they did. In Beit, Rhodes gained not only a brilliant financial adviser, but a staunch ally. Few men were as loyal to Rhodes as 'little Alfred'.

The main obstacle to the amalgamation was the Kimberley Central Mine. This organization was even more powerful than De Beers and the man behind it, Barney Barnato, was much richer than Rhodes. Barnato was one of the most colourful characters in Kimberley. Having started life as Barnet Isaacs in the slums of London, he had arrived in Kimberley in 1873 with sixty boxes of dubious cigars as his most tangible asset. An actor, conjurer and boxer, he had exhausted every means of making a living during his early days at the diamond diggings. Finally he had bought a horse and cart and set himself up as a 'kopje-walloper'—one of those hopeful bargainers who made the rounds of the sorting tables, buying up rough diamonds. The venture had prospered. Barney had a shrewd business sense and, with the help of his brother, succeeded in buying up, not only diamonds, but diamond mines as well. It was certainly not by accident that he now emerged as Rhodes's most influential rival. Barney Barnato was no fool; he too saw that amalgamation was inevitable but he had no intention of allowing Rhodes to dominate him. He felt himself to be in a position equal to, if not better than, that of Rhodes and was determined to take every advantage of it. The battle against Barnato for the control of the diamond industry was one of the toughest and most involved that Rhodes ever fought. In the end Barney, for all his shrewdness, was forced to capitulate. Rhodes had outmanœuvred him and he gave in gracefully. 'You can't resist him,' he is supposed to have said of Rhodes as he admitted defeat.

The amalgamation issue was still very much in the air, however, when a new and startling development occurred. In 1886, after years of rumours and false hopes, gold was discovered on the Witwatersrand in the Transvaal. At first Kimberley was sceptical. Stories of gold-bearing reefs were everyday fare and few had grown fat on them. More often than not, the quest for gold had proved more trouble than it was worth. Even now, as the stories became more frequent and some of the bolder spirits left for the Transvaal to investigate, the cynics continued to scoff. Rhodes was among them. He knew only too well how disastrous the gold fever that had infected so many diamond diggers could be. His brother Herbert had dissipated his life by chasing after each new cry of gold. Only by keeping faith with Kimberley had Rhodes been able to build up his own fortune, and Kimberley, at that particular time, was demanding all his attention. Not only was he deeply involved in his bid to win over the Kimberley Central Mine but he was troubled by a very real personal anxiety: Neville Pickering, his friend and heir, was seriously ill.

*

Two years earlier, on 26th June, 1884, Neville Pickering was thrown from his horse while riding in the veld. He crashed into a clump of thorn bushes and was badly cut and bruised, 'some of the thorns', it is said, 'entering below the knees of both legs'. It was only with the greatest difficulty that these thorns were extracted, leaving his legs poisoned and inflamed. But his injuries, although extensive, did not seem to be unduly serious and it was hoped that he would soon recover. Unfortunately, a few months earlier, he had contracted the dreaded 'Kimberley fever' and this appears to have left him too weak to withstand the after-effects of the accident. Within a couple of days of his fall he suffered a relapse; the poison from the thorns had entered his system and in addition his lungs had become affected. He was confined to bed for more than a month and when he did get up he was forced to hobble about on crutches. 'It will . . .' noted a local journalist, 'be some time yet before he will be able to resume that stately stride of his pedestrianizing.'

In fact, he was rarely to be seen about the streets of Kimberley again. His health had been permanently impaired and the next two years were spent in moving between Kimberley and the various places of convalescence recommended by his doctors. To one as active and high-spirited as Neville Pickering, this chronic invalidism must have been particularly hard to bear. The blow had been struck at a time when he was beginning to establish a reputation at De Beers as an able and reliable diamond-dealer. At the Annual General Meeting of shareholders, which had taken place a month before Pickering's accident, the Chairman had referred to him as 'certainly one of the best brokers for the Company's diamonds at Kimberley'. It was a reputation of which he was undoubtedly proud and the fact that he was now forced into semi-retirement could only have aggravated his physical condition. He rarely went to the office; his duties were handed over to the Acting Secretary, H. J. Feltham, and it was probably on Rhodes's insistence that, despite his frequent absences, his name still featured as the official Company secretary.

Throughout his friend's long and depressing illness, Rhodes's devotion was unquestioned. All that could be done to ease Neville Pickering's physical and mental suffering, he did. He nursed him, comforted him and obtained the best medical advice. Among the doctors called in to attend young Pickering was a popular and successful Scotsman—Dr Leander Starr Jameson. This short, perky and extremely able physician had arrived in Kimberley, at the age of twenty-five, some eight years earlier. It is said that his reason for coming to South Africa was the same as Rhodes's—to cure a weak lung. Having given up a promising career in London, he had quickly established himself as one of the leading medical practitioners on the diamond fields. He was known to the townsfolk of Kimberley as Dr Jim and his cheerful, easy-going manner, combined with a sound knowledge of medicine, had assured his success among the down-to-earth diggers and their families. He and Rhodes had known each other casually for some years but, according to Jameson's biographer, it was 'Neville's sickbed' that drew the men together and clinched their friendship. For Rhodes it was the beginning of a life-long and fateful association.

But nothing could help Pickering. He grew weaker by the month. It became obvious to everyone except himself that his case was hopeless. In the early part of 1886, when he was staying with his family in Port Elizabeth, he suddenly, and against all advice, made up his mind to return to Kimberley. It was a wilful and foolish decision.

Pickering arrived back in Kimberley at the time when stories of gold finds on the Witwatersrand were gathering momentum. A few Kimberley notables had already left for the Transvaal and among them was Dr Hans Sauer, an old acquaintance of Herbert Rhodes. It was when Dr Sauer returned with some rock samples that Rhodes decided to make some investigations of his own. On Sauer's first visit to Rhodes's cottage he was given a rather cool reception; he found Rhodes in bed and not particularly interested in the tale he had to tell. Returning the following day, at Rhodes's request, he was rather surprised to find Charles Rudd and two Australian miners awaiting him. The miners, who had brought gold-panning equipment with them, quickly confirmed that the rock samples were indeed gold-bearing and Rhodes immediately commissioned Sauer to leave for the Transvaal in order to secure claims for him. At the last moment, however, he appears to have changed his mind and when Sauer boarded the coach the following day, he found that two of his fellow passengers were Rhodes and Rudd. This was obviously a mission which Rhodes felt he should undertake personally.

When they arrived on the Witwatersrand Rhodes seemed to be out of his depth. He had made himself a diamond expert but of gold he knew nothing. Sauer, who had quickly set about securing options on various farms for the partners, was driven to despair by the hesitancy of Rhodes and Rudd. Other Kimberley capitalists were busily snapping up property on the Rand but in spite of Sauer's urgent requests for the partners to buy land, they seemed unable to make up their minds.

It was while Sauer was waiting for Rhodes's signature on deals he had made for two valuable farms that negotiations were interrupted in a dramatic fashion. A message arrived from

Kimberley to say that Neville Pickering had taken a turn for the worse; he was thought to be dying.

Rhodes immediately announced that he was leaving that night by coach for Kimberley. Sauer was staggered. 'What about the options?' he protested. 'You can't go now. You must wait.' But there was no question of waiting. 'I must go to my friend,' said Rhodes. 'Get me a seat quickly.'

The coach that evening was fully booked. This did not deter Rhodes. He was determined to waste no time in getting to Pickering's side. Climbing on to the roof of the coach, he completed the three hundred dust-choked miles to Kimberley propped up among the mail bags. The journey lasted for more than fifteen hours.

As it happened, his haste had not been strictly necessary. For almost two months longer Neville Pickering hovered between life and death. Rhodes never left his side. It was said that he was 'careless of anything but the wants and comforts of his friend'. At times he was joined by Neville's brother William, who was then the manager of a bank at nearby Dutoitspan. Together they sat and watched the life ebb from this once virile, active and light-hearted young man.

The end came on the morning of October 16th, 1886. Shortly after midnight, Rhodes became alarmed at the change in Neville's appearance; he sent William Pickering for the doctor. Jameson came at once but there was nothing he could do. It is said that once, before the end, Neville managed to stir himself and, turning to Rhodes, whispered: 'You have been father, mother, brother and sister to me.' At seven o'clock that morning he died in Rhodes's arms.

He was buried the same day. His hearse was followed to the Dutoitspan cemetery by 'upwards of fifty carts'. And at the short ceremony that followed, it was noticed that all the leading citizens of the town were gathered round the grave. 'It might be said of him,' commented the *Diamond Fields Advertiser* in its obituary, 'that he had not a single enemy and many warm-hearted friends.'

The chief mourner was his brother William, but the most conspicuous was undoubtedly Cecil Rhodes. Dressed in a crumpled old suit, passing from tears to hysterical laughter and burying his face in a large handkerchief, Rhodes hardly seemed to know where he was or what he was doing. As he turned from the grave, he came face to face with the sobbing Barney Barnato. 'Ah, Barney,' shrieked Rhodes in his high falsetto, 'he will never sell you another parcel of diamonds!'

Rhodes slept that night in Dr Jameson's cottage opposite the Kimberley Club. For years to come this was to be his Kimberley home. He never again lived in the house he had shared with Neville Pickering.

*

Many years later Sir David Harris, one of the Kimberley pioneers, was to recount a strange incident which he witnessed shortly after Neville Pickering's funeral. He was passing the board-room at De Beers and happened to notice two men sitting at a table. Their attitudes were identical: each was supporting his head with one arm—the elbow on the table and the hand covering the eyes—while the other arm lay flat along the table-top. Between them was a gold watch which they were pushing from one to the other. Looking close, Sir David recognized the men as William Pickering and Cecil Rhodes. As they pushed the watch backwards and forwards, they would each shake their heads in turn and say: 'No, you are his brother' and 'No, you are his greatest friend.'

'And I give you my word,' the astonished Sir David was to claim, 'they were both crying.'

In years to come it would be difficult to associate Cecil Rhodes with tears. For with the death of Pickering there died in Rhodes much of a warmth and tenderness that had been characteristic of his short-lived friendship. From now on, where personal relationships were concerned, Rhodes was to be a man on his guard. Others would come close to him but none would succeed in disarming him to the extent that Neville Pickering had done. In his short but incisive study of Rhodes, William Plomer has speculated on this change in Rhodes's personality. 'There seems,' he says, 'to be some reason to think that the shock of losing this young man who had so enchanted him was an emotional one, and it may possibly have had something to do with his tendency to cultivate more and more a hardness and even brutality of manner which, it was supposed by some, was not really natural to him but served to hide his susceptibilities.'

This was more than Rhodes's less critical admirers were prepared to allow. To them the friendship between Rhodes and Pickering was something of an embarrassment; it did not fit their preconceived notion of a man of destiny. They did their best to gloss over it with fine words and high-flown phrases—but it was impossible to ignore it altogether.

It has been said that by neglecting the options secured for him by Sauer and by returning to Pickering's side, Rhodes lost the opportunity of controlling the goldfields on the Witwatersrand. Dr Sauer, in his autobiography, records that Rhodes promised to wire him about the options but that, once back in Kimberley, he allowed his business affairs to slide. In a man as purposeful as Rhodes, such an emotional aberration was difficult to account for. That he considered Pickering more important than the chance of dominating the goldfields was an undeniable, if disturbing, fact; it needed considerable dexterity on the part of Rhodes's champions to explain it away. There could, it was claimed, be only one explanation: it was an illustration of his essential nobility; a man who could put a friendship before a fortune must have strength of character beyond that of ordinary mortals.

But was Rhodes's action really so noble? Or was it simply natural? The plain fact of the matter is that he loved Pickering and loving him, wanted to be near him at a time when he was ill. Had he done as much for any woman, there would have been no need to transform him into a demi-god in order to explain an act of love. Indeed, one can imagine the incident being magnified out of all proportion instead of being hastily dismissed. But Pickering was a man, and as a man could not be considered in such simple terms; Rhodes might transcend common humanity but he could not be allowed to transgress a conventional code of behaviour. It therefore became necessary to interpret a human weakness, calling for compassion, as a superhuman strength, defying credibility. To the complexities of Rhodes's many-sided character was added the suggestion of an emotional response that could only be described as Olympian.

In truth, such reasoning seems to have been not only unconvincing but, in some respects, unnecessary. A recent study of Rhodes's activities on the Witwatersrand has shown that, far from neglecting his interests in the goldfields during the last weeks of Pickering's illness, he was in constant touch with his agents in the Transvaal. This does not necessarily detract from his devotion to Pickering or from the fact that he might well have sacrificed a second fortune. One of the incredible features of the fortunes made out of gold and diamonds in South Africa is the extent to which the making of them depended on sheer luck. And in this respect Rhodes's luck was usually phenomenal. Had he stayed longer in the Transvaal, his luck might have worked for him there in the same way that it had worked for him in Kimberley. He gave it very little opportunity and it was not something that could be transmitted to subordinates by telegram.

But there can be no doubt about his love for Pickering. He made him heir to his entire fortune and if he did not actually sacrifice a second fortune for his sake, he was perfectly prepared to do so. His attachment to the young man was an emotional one but there is no reason to think that it was expressed in any way other than by an obvious and open devotion. The suggestion that 'ugly rumours' concerning their relationship circulated Kimberley seems to be without foundation. It is true that Rhodes was reputed to dislike feminine company and tended to shun conventional society but his aloofness was more than offset by Pickering's popularity. Any rumours that may have been spread must have started much later and were probably coloured by hindsight. The most pertinent question posed by their friendship is whether it would have endured. Judged by future events, there is reason to think that Neville Pickering, had he lived, might have found it impossible to meet the demands made upon him by Rhodes's possessiveness. For, despite his affectionate loyalty, Pickering could not have viewed the friendship in quite the same terms as did Rhodes. Indeed, the difference in temperament which had first drawn them together might, in the end, have separated them.

There is a legend in the Pickering family that Neville, at the time of his death, was engaged to a certain Maud Christian of Port Elizabeth. The truth of this story is difficult to ascertain. There is no indication that Miss Christian was sent for when Neville was dying and there is no mention of an engagement in Pickering's obituaries in the Kimberley or Port Elizabeth papers. But Miss Christian, who married Sir William Solomon (a future Chief Justice of South Africa), always wore a ring on her engagement finger which had been given to her by Neville Pickering. When she died, she left this ring to Neville's niece. It would seem that if the engagement were indeed a fact, it was not made public. It could be possible, also, that Rhodes was unaware of it.

As later events were to show, the prospect of his close friends marrying was one which Rhodes found impossible to contemplate. When obliged to face the situation, his rage was monumental. One such scene took place some time after Neville Pickering's death. The young man concerned had been Rhodes's companion for a number of years. 'Everyone knew he was engaged—except Rhodes,' says a friend of them both. 'When the news was broken, there followed an amazing scene. Rhodes raved and stormed like a maniac. His falsetto voice rose to a screech as he kept screaming: "Leave my house! Leave my house!" No small schoolboy, or even schoolgirl, could have behaved more childishly than he did.' In this case there was a temporary reconciliation but the friendship was terminated shortly after the young man married.

Whether the same thing would have happened with Neville Pickering it is not possible to say. It was never put to the test. There is always the chance, moreover (as often happens in relationships such as this), that as Pickering matured and grew older, he would have lost his attraction for Rhodes; it was towards the qualities of youth and enthusiasm and virility that Rhodes was always drawn. By dying in his twenties, Pickering ensured that his image—for Rhodes—remained untarnished; nothing, not marriage, nor middle-age, nor disillusion, could spoil it now.

With the Pickering family Rhodes remained friendly for the rest of his life. It was Neville's brother, William, who took over the post of Acting Secretary to De Beers and he worked for the company all his life, eventually becoming a highly esteemed director. Another brother, Edward, was taken under Rhodes's protection when his shipping firm, Pickering and Toft, was made the agent for De Beers in Port Elizabeth. This firm was destined to play a significant part in one of Rhodes's more disastrous ventures.

Rhodes never found anyone to replace the dead Neville Pickering. But he was to spend the rest of his life searching.

CHAPTER FOUR

Berlin Society

PRINCESS CATHERINE RADZIWILL was to look back on her years in Berlin with loathing. The longer she lived there, the more unbearable did the German capital seem to become. In time the boredom of her first few months in the Radziwill Palace gave way to more active emotions: frustration, resentment and an almost neurotic desire to free herself from her restrictions.

The atmosphere of the palace itself was claustrophobic; if Catherine so much as moved a chair from one of the rooms, she would be sharply rebuked; the furniture, she would be told, had been arranged by her dead father-in-law and to interfere with it was an insult to his memory. Admittedly, the palace was a beautiful building: an imposing front court opened out on to the Wilhelmstrasse and behind stretched a garden which was said to be 'almost like a park'; inside, although the living quarters left much to be desired, the state rooms were magnificent. Having come into the Radziwill family through their Hohenzollern ancestress, Louise of Prussia, it was, in every respect, a home fit for a princess. 'But to me,' complained Catherine, 'it always appeared a prison, and in reality it was nothing else, because getting away from it, even for a walk, was a feat.' The women of the household were not allowed to be seen in the streets without their husbands and, as their husbands were rarely at home, they were obliged to confine their walking to the palace grounds. Here they could roam where they wished but, for all the park-like spaciousness of the garden, the setting remained familiar and they could expect to meet only each other. At times, while pacing the well-worn garden paths, Catherine was to feel more like a convent schoolgirl than a young married woman; or, in her more depressed moments, like an inmate of a strictly guarded asylum.

Such outings as were allowed her were hardly more stimulating. Shut in a closed carriage and accompanied by the other
Radziwill princesses, she was permitted to make certain, carefully prescribed social calls. The women whom she could meet,
the length of the call and the degree of familiarity entered upon,
depended entirely upon the rank, title and respectability of the
family concerned. Any suggestion of a spontaneous, intimate
friendship with a girl of her own choosing was out of the
question. The chance of her finding such a friend among the
young women of Berlin's *haut monde* was, in any case, highly
unlikely. For her, the gilded salons of the German capital were
little more than a carpeted desert inhabited by hostile, moronic
and incomprehensible creatures. In a long career of vitriolic
comment, she was rarely to equal the scorn and condemnation
which she lavished on the ladies who comprised the Radziwill
circle. 'For the most part the high-class Berlin woman neither
reads, works, nor has any occupation,' runs a typical observation. 'She passes her time in chattering, dressing and undressing,
and seeking who will help her in these things. She has neither a
serious idea in her head, nor a worthy thought in her heart. Her
preferences are vulgar, and she has no influence. She is wanting
in grace, education and tact. She is noisy, and unfortunately for
her, she tries to imitate the Frenchwoman of the "fast" school.
It is difficult, if not impossible, to talk with a Berlin fashionable
lady, so ignorant is she of what is going on, so absorbed in
herself, or in the actions and gestures of her rivals.'

Nor were her husband's family safe from her strictures. There
were over thirty people living in the Radziwill Palace; they
were all related, all full of their own importance, and all,
according to Catherine, equally difficult to get on with. They
were, she claimed, as different from the Rzewuskis as 'earth is
from heaven'. They lacked any semblance of intellectuality, they
were continually quarrelling among themselves and the palace
was a hot-bed of intrigue, rivalry and malicious gossip. Apart
from religion, the only thing that united the family was their
consciousness of being distantly related to the Prussian royal
family. With them, as with the people who visited them, says
Catherine, 'it was nothing but rank and rank, and a morbid
dread of not being recognized'. Undoubtedly the resentment
which she came to harbour against the Radziwills coloured

Catherine's judgment of them. Her own feuds with various members of the household did much to disrupt the domestic harmony of the palace and added to the tensions about which she complained so bitterly. There can be little doubt, however, that her accusations of stifling formality and petty snobbery were justified. Even those who were deceived by the placid front presented by the Radziwills could not ignore their overweening pomposity. 'They were all very united and happy together,' remarked one family acquaintance, 'but rather dull and stiff, also a little pretentious.'

*

Strangely enough, the one member of the family whom Catherine came to admire—her French sister-in-law, Princess Marie Radziwill—was the one who appeared to outsiders to be largely responsible for the family's stuffy reputation. She was said to have a 'waspish tongue' and to be a 'terrible stickler for etiquette and tradition'; in later years she became a formidable *grande-dame* and Berlin society was said to 'stand in awe of her sharp judgments and severe criticisms'. For Catherine, however, she was always to remain 'one of the persons I respect most in the world, and certainly one of the few really remarkable women in Europe'. In fact, Catherine's admiration was such that the caustic wit which Princess Marie employed with such effect might well have served as a model for Catherine's own acidulousness towards Berlin society. But she lacked her sister-in-law's detachment. Catherine's nature was far too passionate and impulsive to allow her to carry off a role that called for disdainful indifference.

Her first two years in Berlin were unfortunate. To her loneliness and feeling of estrangement was added a very real tragedy. Her first child was born on 7th December, 1874, and died shortly afterwards. The loss was a sad one, but she was not allowed to brood over it for long. That winter, she admits herself, 'was one of the most brilliant which had been known at the Prussian Court, and entertainment followed entertainment'. In June of that same year she accompanied her husband, Prince Wilhelm, to Warsaw where the Tsar of Russia was attending some manœuvres. The Polish capital was *en fête*. Prince Wilhelm, as German representative at the Russian military display, was much sought after and the young couple were plunged into another round of balls and parties. For Catherine the weeks that followed had an almost dream-like quality about them. 'The aspect of the illuminated town,' she was to remember, 'the brilliant uniforms, lovely jewels and dresses, the beauty of the women, all contrived to make the scene like one of those of which one reads in the *Arabian Nights.*' From Warsaw they went on to spend a few weeks with Catherine's family in Russia.

Shortly after their return to Berlin, on 5th April, 1876, their second child, a daughter, Louise—known to the family as Loulou—was born. They were back in Russia later that year, this time for a longer stay. After visiting Moscow they went on to Pjatino, an estate on the Volga which Catherine had inherited as part of her dowry. The estate was situated a few miles from the small town of Simbirsk where a little boy, Vladimir Ilich Ulyanov, was then growing up. In years to come Simbirsk was to be renamed Ulyanovsk in honour of this boy, while St Petersburg was to take its new designation, Leningrad, from the name by which he became known to the world.

For the next two years the Radziwills were to be on the move between Russia, Poland and Germany; and for most of that time Catherine was pregnant. On 30th January, 1877, a second daughter, Wanda, was born at Chocieozewice in Poland and a third daughter, Gabrielle (Ella), was born in Berlin on 14th March, 1878. If the young mother was bored with the sameness of her existence, it was certainly not for lack of occupation.

Child-bearing suited Catherine. Far from taxing her energies, the birth of four children in little over five years left her looking radiant. By the time her third daughter was born she was nineteen years old. She had lost all that thin, sallow gawkiness of childhood and had matured into an undeniably lovely young woman. The Rzewuska duckling had emerged as a Radziwill swan. Graceful and assured, she had a voluptuousness which gained still more distinction when set against the heavily Teutonic looks prevalent at the Prussian Court. Berlin in the 1870s, says Lord Frederic Hamilton, was not remarkable for its show of feminine beauty. 'I retain very pleasant recollections of my Berlin dancing partners,' he says. 'They were bright cheery girls with the most stupendous appetites, who danced beautifully.' But he had to admit that there were only 'three or four very beautiful women'. Among this handful he considered Catherine to be outstanding. 'Princess Wilhelm Radziwill, a Russian,' he says, 'was, I think, the loveliest human being I have ever seen.' He was forced to add, however, that 'she was much dreaded on account of her mordant tongue'.

These were early days. Time was to sharpen that tongue to such an extent that few would be aware of her beauty.

*

Once Bismarck had succeeded in establishing the new German Empire, he found himself faced with a new and, to some extent, unlooked for opponent—the Catholic Church. In many of the German territories which had not previously been united to Prussia, the Church exercised profound influence and considered itself above the jurisdiction of the State. This was a situation which the Iron Chancellor was not prepared to tolerate. The Catholics of Germany had always been suspected of siding with Austria against Prussia; their clergy were known to be active among the industrial working-class, agitating for reforms; and, more important than anything else, Bismarck saw in the Church a challenge to his personal supremacy throughout the Empire. Thus it was that the great struggle between Church and State, known as the *Kulturkampf*, was launched.

Having failed in his attempts to subordinate the Catholic clergy to the State through the Minister of Education and Worship, the Chancellor hit out at the Catholic laymen and politicians. In a speech to the Upper House of the German Parliament, some two months before Catherine first arrived in Berlin, he had fulminated against the 'party within the Catholic Church who were striving for temporal power'. That party, he had no doubt, was guided by members of the Radziwill family who exerted a sinister influence at Court and who had infiltrated their minions into the governing bureaucracy. Their aim, he said, was the furtherance of Polish national ambitions rather than to obtain religious independence. 'The beginning of the *Kulturkampf* was decided for me preponderantly by its Polish side . . .', Bismarck was to write. 'Since the solidification of the Radziwill influence upon the King and the establishment of the "Catholic section" in the Ministry of Public Worship, statistical data proved beyond doubt the rapid progress of the Polish nationality.' The 'Catholic Section', he maintained, had 'become a body in the heart of Prussian bureaucracy defending Roman and Polish interests against Prussia'.

The repeated attacks which Bismarck was to make upon the Radziwills were not aimed directly at Catherine's side of the family. Her father-in-law, Prince Wilhelm-Frederick, had been a close friend of the Prussian monarch and her brother-in-law, Prince Anton, was known to be a particular favourite of the old Emperor; even Bismarck was wary of moving too openly against such influential foes. In any case, he considered both of them to be 'soldiers too honest to take part in Polish plots against the King and State'. He admitted also that 'the ladies in the Radziwill family were friendly to Germany'. The real driving force behind the ecclesiastical intrigues, he maintained, came from the other half of the Radziwill Palace. It was first directed by Prince Bogaslaw (the uncle of Catherine's husband) and later by his son, Prince Ferdinand. But once Bismarck began to take action against the Radziwill influence, such distinctions were swept aside and the entire family suffered. Catherine had a taste of this persecution a few months after her arrival in Berlin. On coming down to dinner one evening, she and the other women of the household were confronted by the police. Both Catherine's husband and her brother-in-law were away at the time and when the frightened women wanted to know the reason for the intrusion, the police said they had orders to take possession of certain rooms used by Prince Anton Radziwill's secretary, von Kehler—a zealous Catholic who had previously been employed by the Foreign Office. There was nothing that the women could do but stand by while the palace was searched. 'Doubtless, under the pretence of searching through von Kehler's desk,' says Catherine, 'the police had the expectation of discovering some incriminating document belonging to my brother-in-law or my cousin . . . [the raid] vividly expresses the methods of the man.'

The *Kulturkampf* issue was the predominant political concern of the Radziwills. It was responsible for many of the quarrels that sprang up amongst them and added considerably to the tension under which they lived. As far as Catherine was concerned, it gave her an added reason for resenting her husband's family. For she had no time for the Poles or their religion. She had married into a Polish Catholic family, her children were brought up as Catholics, but she considered herself a Russian and a member of the Orthodox Church. 'I do not understand them,' she was to say of Polish Catholics, 'and the way in which religion is used by them for the furtherance of their political animosities is profoundly repugnant to me. I do not understand God being invoked in order to spread one's hatreds and revengeful feelings.' As for the feud with Bismarck, she refused to be drawn into the intrigues of her husband's family. During her early years in the Radziwill Palace, she claims that the family tried to mould her according to their own beliefs but they had reckoned without the anti-clerical teaching of Mme de Balzac. 'I had been taught,' says Catherine, 'to consider the influence of the clergy in private life, as well as in politics, as an evil which ought to be fought against with energy.'

If she is to be believed, her contempt for the war which the Radziwills were waging even went as far as taking her into the enemy camp. She was to give various versions of her friendship with Prince Bismarck and his wife; each slightly different from the others. But it would seem that when she was presented to the Bismarcks at a ball, they remembered having known her father when the Chancellor had been Prussian Ambassador at St Petersburg. Princess Bismarck asked Catherine to call on them but she was terrified to do so lest the Radziwills found out. After much scheming she eventually managed to make the call and from then on remained on friendly terms with the Bismarck family. 'By some miracle,' she says, 'the Radziwills never suspected such was the case. To tell the truth, the idea that I could have done such a thing was something so monstrous in their opinion that it never entered their minds.'

That this friendship remained intact is, in view of Catherine's later activities, extremely doubtful. The political opinions she was to express concerning the Chancellor would hardly have endeared her to the Bismarck family. These opinions, however, had nothing to do with the *Kulturkampf*. They sprang mainly from her friendship with Crown Princess Victoria. The admiration which Catherine was to profess for this English-born, liberal-minded Princess surpassed all her other enthusiasms. It was to be a recurring theme in her writings until the day she died. Long after she had disowned most of her former connections, she clung to the memory of this 'noble, courageous woman'.

The wife of the heir to the Imperial crown of Germany was the eldest daughter of Queen Victoria. From childhood she had been trained by her father, the Prince Consort, to respect the principles of constitutional monarchy and to champion a liberal approach to government. Together with her husband, Crown Prince Frederick, she had struggled to maintain her progressive opinions in the face of the authoritarian régime upheld by Bismarck. The conflict between the Crown Prince and Princess and the Iron Chancellor was one of the most significant features of the German Court. Those who sided with the heir to the throne and his wife were very much in the minority, but it was a minority to which Catherine was proud to belong. For Catherine the Crown Princess personified all the virtues instilled into her as a child: the pride of the Rzewuskis and the intellectual aspirations of Mme de Balzac. Not only did she regard Princess Victoria as a fellow exile—a civilized foreigner amid the barbarians of Berlin—but she was able to take advantage of the opportunities which the Crown Princess's receptions offered to meet people whom she could admire. If there was to be any hope for German society, she considered that it must come from the 'universal genius' who was destined to rule over it.

At times, however, Catherine's political opinions must have startled even the progressive Crown Princess. Despite her complaints of a lack of freedom, Catherine appears to have spent a great deal of time at the Reichstag. Her knowledge of the main political parties, if not profound, was certainly extensive. Listening to the debates from a seat in the diplomatic box, she found the parliamentary proceedings a source of much amusement. For the three 'great' parties—the Conservatives, the National Liberals and the Centre—she had nothing but contempt. In her opinion they were little more than puppets manipulated by the cynical Chancellor for his own convenience. None of them, she claimed, was 'strong enough to hold its own against any force, least of all against Prince Bismarck'. What praise she had was confined entirely to the small Socialist party. Although hopelessly idealistic, they were sincere, determined and honourable. Their leader, Herr Bebel, was a working-class man of conviction and integrity and his speeches were among the few that could really affect her. 'Never has a political party better defended a desperate cause,' she wrote, 'never has a handful of men given proof of more indomitable courage and energy . . . All that is sweet and mystic in the German nature is concentrated in them.' These were hardly opinions likely to win her friends in conventional society nor, for that matter, to smooth her path with the Radziwills. This might, of course, have been why she adopted them.

Nor did her views on international affairs do anything to enhance her popularity in the patriotic German capital. Her approach to European politics was simple. The interests of Russia must take precedence over all else. Never did she forget, or allow anyone else to forget, that she was Russian born, bred and biased. So often did she force this down everyone's throat that it is difficult to find even a casual mention of her at this time which does not acknowledge the fact that she was 'a Russian'. And at no time were her pro-Russian sympathies more in evidence than during the Russo-Turkish War of 1877.

When war was declared in April 1877, Catherine followed the Russian advance with enthusiasm. It was an enthusiasm which was not shared by all her associates. Her friend the Crown Princess, for instance, was inclined to agree with the attitude of her mother, Queen Victoria, and her mother's Prime Minister, Lord Beaconsfield—the former Benjamin Disraeli, who saw Russia's advance as a threat to Constantinople and to the balance of power in the Near East. A British fleet was ordered to the Dardanelles and the Russian troops were brought to an abrupt halt. This was a bitter pill for Catherine. She was loud in her condemnation of British interference and, more particularly, in her scorn for the British Prime Minister. 'He represented to my imagination everything that was bad, mischievous and destructive . . .' she was to say. 'I detested him as a *parvenu*, and a man to whom my country had owed some of its bitterest humiliations.'

A Congress was held the following year in Berlin to decide the outcome of the war. As a Russian and one of the German capital's reigning beauties, Catherine found herself thrust unexpectedly into the limelight. At the balls, the dinners and the receptions held to entertain delegates to the Congress, she was in demand both as a hostess and a guest. And nowhere was her presence considered more essential than at the functions attended by her *bête-noir*—the ageing, but still susceptible Lord Beaconsfield.

She was introduced to him at the Austrian Embassy. He entered the room looking bent and sphinx-like. Smothering her resentment, Catherine asked him what he was thinking about. 'I am not thinking,' he replied, 'I am enjoying myself.' From that moment she was completely captivated. 'My prejudice melted like snow in springtime,' she said. 'A more fascinating man than Lord Beaconsfield never breathed.' That evening, seated between the beautiful blonde wife of the Austrian Ambassador and the vivacious Catherine, the old statesman was equally enchanted. 'Austria feasted us,' he wrote to Lady Bradford, 'and I sate between the Countess Karolyi and the Princess Radziwill, who is not twenty and has [had] four children. She is pretty with the oriental Polish eye, very chattery and amusing.' The evening, he noted in his diary, was 'very successful'.

When confronted by a powerful and stimulating personality, all Catherine's acerbity tended to evaporate. She could then be extremely charming.

*

On the 4th July, 1880, Catherine gave birth to a son. He was born in Berlin and christened Raphaël Nicholas Demetrius Hugues Adam Waclaw. To the family he was known as Nicholas.

Shortly after the birth of this, their fifth, child, the young parents set off on a long tour of Europe. For some months Prince Wilhelm Radziwill had been unwell and the doctors had advised an extended holiday. After visiting Venice and Corfu, they went on to Constantinople. Here they stayed for some weeks and Catherine was able to add the British Ambassador and his wife, Lord and Lady Dufferin, to her growing circle of English acquaintances. On the day the Radziwills arrived in Constantinople, Catherine and Lady Dufferin were invited to visit the harem of a Turkish official. The two young women hardly knew each other and the visit turned out to be more embarrassing than interesting. They were bombarded with questions regarding their own married lives and, many years later, Lady Dufferin was to remember being amused when one of the ladies of the harem, 'hearing that Princess Radziwill had married at fifteen, asked her whether it was a love match!' In Constantinople, also, Catherine met Donald Mackenzie Wallace, the correspondent of *The Times* of London, whom she was later to claim as one of her dearest friends. Both the Dufferins and Mackenzie Wallace knew Russia well—Lord Dufferin having been Ambassador at St Petersburg and Mackenzie Wallace being the author of a classic study of the country—and Catherine felt immediately at home with them. In fact, these early friendships marked the beginnings of the ardent Anglophilism that was to have a profound influence on her later life.

From Constantinople the Radziwills went on to Russia, spending the winter in St Petersburg, where they were presented to the new Tsar, Alexander III, and the summer on their Pjatino estate. They returned to Berlin for the winter of 1882 but were back in Russia the following year for the Coronation of Alexander III.

Catherine claimed that these frequent journeys to Moscow and St Petersburg were among the few joys of her dreary Berlin existence. Once she had crossed the border into Russia, she felt able to relax and enjoy the freedom denied her in Germany. But this freedom would seem not to have been without its own anxieties. On her journey to Moscow for the Tsar's Coronation, for instance, she travelled in the same train as the French delegation; Mme Waddington, wife of the French Ambassador Extraordinary to Moscow, has left a revealing account of Catherine's approach to her native land. In a letter from Warsaw, dated 17th May, 1883, Mme Waddington writes: 'I had a little talk with Princess Wilhelm Radziwill, who is starting for the Coronation. It seems she has splendid jewels, and was rather bothered to know how to carry them. She has got them all on, in little leather bags around her waist, and thinks she won't be very comfortable all night, with pins, brooches, etc., running into her.' Evidently Catherine's lack of confidence in the honesty of her countrymen was not shared by Mme Waddington, who adds: 'She was horrified when I told her where mine were.'

It was while she was in Russia, in the spring of 1882, that Catherine heard of the death of her aunt, old Mme de Balzac.

She felt the loss keenly. 'Her disappearance put an end to a chapter in my life . . .,' she wrote. 'With her passed away ideas and opinions which are no longer heard, and with her death a great light went out.' The debt which Catherine owed to her Aunt Evelina was very real. She had constantly looked to Mme de Balzac for advice and guidance, both as a child and as a young married woman. Incessant as her jauntings about eastern Europe appear to have been, they had not prevented her from fitting in an occasional trip to Paris. These visits had been a source of great comfort: they had brought her into contact with a set of people whom she would never otherwise have met. It is quite possible to imagine Catherine leading a very different sort of life had she not come under the influence of Mme de Balzac and her circle. Despite her protestations to the contrary, she might well have succumbed to the intrigues, the gossip and the petty snobberies of the German Court. She would always have been a forceful, astringent and no doubt tactless princess, but she would have been very little else. It was Evelina de Balzac who stimulated her political interests, awakened her literary ambitions and encouraged her in her intellectual pretensions. It was probably through her aunt, too, that she was first introduced to that coterie of Parisian journalists whose influence was to transform her life.

Exactly when Catherine first met Mme Juliette Adam is not certain. It was probably in the late 1870s. It was after the fall of the French Second Empire that the fiery Mme Adam really came into her own. Together with her second husband, Edmond Adam, she had dedicated herself to the establishment of a French Republic and throughout the Empire had worked for the overthrow of Napoleon III. Her salon was regarded as the headquarters of Republican intrigue—her most notable protégé being Léon Gambetta, the future Prime Minister. With the collapse of the Bonaparte régime, Mme Adam had emerged as a real force in the political and literary life of France. She was considered to be the 'Queen of the Third Republic' and it is said that 'no political measure was undertaken by any member of the government of that day without her having been consulted about its opportuneness'. According to Catherine, Léon Gambetta once claimed that had it not been for Mme Adam 'he would certainly never have reached the political eminence on which he found himself'. Chauvinistic and bitterly resentful of the humiliation suffered by her country during the Franco-Prussian War, Juliette Adam detested Germany and the Germans and was reputed to favour an alliance with Russia. Catherine must have warmed to her immediately. Her admiration for Juliette Adam was certainly unstinting. 'An exception she has always stood amongst women, and an exception she will remain . . . ,' she was to write of her friend, 'a noble, beautiful creature.'

It was not until after the death of Mme de Balzac that the friendship between Catherine and Juliette Adam took a fatal turn, as far as Catherine was concerned. In October 1879 Mme Adam had launched her influential magazine, *La Nouvelle Revue*. This was a literary journal with an unmistakable political bias, designed to promote the work of the editress's protégés ('she was the literary godmother of Pierre Loti and Paul Bourget') and further her political ambitions. Well known for her interest in foreign affairs, it came as no surprise to her readers when, in 1884, Mme Adam announced a new series of articles devoted to the social and political life of the various European capitals. The articles were to be written by an elderly Russian diplomat and would start with a study of Berlin society. A few eyebrows might have been raised had it been known that the new contributor was neither an elderly diplomat nor, for that matter, a man. In fact, Count Paul Vassili did not exist outside the imagination of his creator—the twenty-six-year-old Princess Catherine Radziwill.

Whether or not the idea for the articles originated with Catherine, one does not know. But there is plenty of evidence to show that she flung herself wholeheartedly into the spirit of the scurrilous series. Nothing could have better suited her particular talent for vilification. Under a pledge of secrecy, she was given *carte blanche* to pay off old scores and to air her opinions before a wide and influential public. The readers of *La Nouvelle Revue* were to be treated to several weeks of sensational revelations.

The articles were written in the form of letters from Count Vassili to a young friend who was due to arrive in the German capital. The tone of the series was obvious from the very outset.

'My Dear Young Friend,' runs the first letter, 'I have your

letter, dated the 18th instant, informing me you have entered the Diplomatic Service and become an *attaché* at Berlin. The first half of your news is good, and I heartily congratulate you upon it; I cannot say so much for the second. Berlin is not the best place in which to begin your career . . . Berlin Society does not welcome foreigners; men of high position are exceedingly reserved; the women are either prudes or dissolute; the young men, for the most part scamps . . . Berlin is essentially provincial. Gossip and scandal are more than usually prevalent, and intrigues are very numerous. Society there is most intolerant, and has constantly some new story to revel in: it has no literature, little education, and not the least interest in anything that does not immediately concern it . . .'

There are twenty-three 'letters' altogether, each written in the same derogatory vein. Starting with the royal family, they range over the entire spectrum of Berlin's social life. Princes, nobles, politicians, military leaders, diplomats, merchants and journalists are all paraded in grotesque caricature. The Court, the *haut-monde*, the middle classes, the Catholics and the Jews, all come in for their share of libellous comment. From this wholesale slaughter of German manners and morals, one or two are singled out for particularly vicious and sustained attacks. High on this list of special targets is the Empress Augusta—'intriguing, false and affected . . . she has no dignity, no notion of propriety'; the Empress's friends and followers—'vain, interested flatterers'; and the Empress's arch-enemy, Prince Bismarck—'his elastic conscience knows no scruples; his soul has no ambition except for absolute power over men.' What she calls 'The Great World of Berlin' is dismissed as boorish, self-indulgent and completely immoral. 'In Berlin,' she says, 'adultery flourishes like a plant in favourable soil . . . Most married women either have a lover or mean to have one. Vice is not reprobated, virtue is rated superfluous.' And so it goes on. Personalities, groups, classes and institutions are all tarred with the same malicious smears and feathered with accusations.

Appreciating the outcry which these letters were bound to produce, she was careful to cover her tracks by mild attacks on her friends as well. Of the Crown Princess, for instance, she says: 'She does not cultivate the spirit of consistency . . . She seems to despise the obligations of fidelity in friendship.' And she was even more severe with her favourite sister-in-law, Princess Marie Radziwill. 'Her greatest fault,' she says, 'is a constant preoccupation about her rank and position in the world . . . she is a cold woman, who loves domination above everything.' In view of these women's reputations in Berlin, Catherine could have been a good deal harder on them both. More interesting is the carefully considered sketch which she draws of herself. After dealing with Princess Marie, she goes on to talk about her 'sister-in-law'. 'This sister-in-law is a Russian and still young,' she observes. 'She is pretty, elegant but, like many of her compatriots, affected, haughty, a coquette in head rather than heart, jealous of the homage addressed to her, but treating men as if they were made only for her amusement and pastime. She loves none, neither is she herself beloved. They say, however, that she is intelligent, and that her conversation can be interesting, but few persons are in a position to pass judgment on this point as she is extremely reserved.' Considering the picture she had painted of Berlin, this pretty, intelligent young woman, who is much sought after but who keeps herself aloof, emerges, for anyone who cared to think about it, as a rather superior being. Such foibles as she might have spring from the fact that she is a Russian which, in any case, is infinitely preferable to being German.

The articles created a greater sensation than even Catherine could have anticipated. Hardly had the series come to an end than the letters were published in book form, translated into several languages and quickly reprinted in new editions. It was the book rather than the *Nouvelle Revue* articles that set Berlin by the ears. Few Berliners read French literary journals, but the book, with its intriguing title, *Berlin Society*, quickly found a wide and avid readership. Some were amused by it, others found it too distorted to be taken seriously, but a vast majority were profoundly shocked by its scandalous and unmitigated invective. The German Empire had been established for little more than a decade and its leading citizens were still extremely sensitive on matters affecting their newly-won dignity. That a book such as this should be circulating Europe was considered an insult, not only to those whom it attacked personally, but to the national pride. It was the accusation of decadence and immorality that caused the greatest offence. The most widely discussed letter, in fact, was one in which no actual names were mentioned. It referred to the 'Three Sisters' who presided over a salon which was little better than a brothel. 'People go there,' it was said, 'to play, smoke, dance, or flirt, as they please . . . Glasses of beer are handed round; the young officers unbutton their tunics . . . The reign of liberty is complete.' Although they were not named, everyone recognized the three women concerned as the Countess Perponcher and her sisters, Frau von Prillwitz and the Countess Dantelmann: three frivolous, empty-headed but eminently respectable ladies. They were, said one of their outraged friends, 'kind-hearted, amiable women, and the exact opposite of the description of them in the French skit'. Be that as it may, the rumours had been started and it was to take the unfortunate sisters many years to live down the accusations.

But if the identity of the 'Three Sisters' was obvious, that of the author, Count Paul Vassili, was a little more difficult to uncover. That the author was using a pseudonym was apparent; no outsider could have had access to the secrets revealed concerning the Imperial family, but Count Vassili was not known to the German Court circle. Whoever had written the letters was close to the throne. Who could it be? Several people were suspected but eventually all evidence seemed to point in one direction: M. Auguste Gerard, the Empress's reader. Had not the letters concentrated on the Empress and her friends? Was not M. Gerard a Frenchman? The letters had first appeared in *La Nouvelle Revue* which was edited by Juliette Adam; was it a coincidence that M. Gerard had been recommended to the Empress by none other than Mme Adam's friend, Léon Gambetta? It was surely 'characteristic of German *naïveté* and French astuteness that the Empress Augusta chose a Frenchman to read to her, thereby making him her intimate'. It could be nobody else. M. Gerard, when accused of being the infamous author, vehemently protested his innocence. But nobody believed him. Even the bewildered Empress, who was reluctant to accept that she could be so betrayed, was at last forced to regard her reader as the culprit. M. Gerard was dismissed. In fact, the incident did the poor man little real harm. On returning to France, he entered the Diplomatic Service and eventually became an Ambassador. His resentment of his unjust treatment, however, remained a perpetual grievance. Whenever he came into contact with Germans, he would renew his protestations of innocence— but to little effect. 'When I met him in Paris,' says Prince von Bülow, 'he began to talk spontaneously about the *"Société de Berlin"*, and gave me his word of honour *propio motu* that he had nothing to do with this pamphlet. I could not take this *Foi d'honnête homme* of his *au sérieux*.'

Catherine, of course, said nothing. She was to remain silent on the identity of Count Paul Vassili for a very long time. It was more than thirty years before she was 'happy to relieve . . . poor M. Gerard' of his burden.

*

But it was impossible for Catherine to remain completely undetected. Her reputation counted against her. She had enemies in high places. That the author of *Berlin Society* had made a point of attacking the Empress was no accident. From the time of Catherine's arrival in Berlin she had been treated with marked coolness by the ageing Empress. Her Russian nationality had not endeared her to Augusta who, although partly Russian herself, could not forget that her grandfather, Tsar Paul, had been murdered by Catherine's countrymen. To this natural antipathy had been added the fact of Princess Radziwill's outrageous behaviour. The Empress was an inveterate gossip and little happened in Berlin without her knowing about it. What she saw and heard of Catherine was far from reassuring.

The sardonic wit, the flirtatiousness and the unorthodox political views for which Catherine had become notorious, could only have increased the Empress's dislike. And to make matters worse, Catherine seemed to go out of her way to antagonize Augusta. Shortly after the publication of *Berlin Society*, for instance, she had been involved in an unbecoming incident at a State banquet. The dinner had been given to honour the Prince of Wales and his eldest son, the Duke of Clarence, who were visiting the German capital. Catherine was seated next to the Duke of Clarence and was entertaining him by poking fun at an elderly guest sitting opposite them. The young couple giggled so much during the meal that the butt of their jokes finally leaned across to ask them what they found so amusing. What could have been an embarrassing situation was averted by the Crown Princess who, at that moment, rose to lead the ladies from the table. The reason for their hilarity must have been quite obvious to those sitting near them and the incident was no doubt reported to the Empress. Augusta could hardly have been amused. The man Catherine had chosen as her victim was the Grand Duke of Weimar—the Empress's brother.

But even this incident paled beside Catherine's later conduct in the Empress's own drawing-room. It was at a concert arranged by the Imperial couple for a gathering of friends. In the middle of the performance the Empress happened to glance across the room to where Catherine was sitting. She saw an astonishing sight. One of the Emperor's aides-de-camp was leaning over Catherine's chair and quite openly fumbling with her skirt. Augusta's horror can be imagined. Next day a note from the Empress arrived at the Radziwill Palace and Catherine was summoned for a 'severe scolding'. Her excuse that she was suffering from a cold and that the gentleman had been helping her to search for a handkerchief was regarded as rather a poor one.

But it was neither Catherine's acid tongue nor her coquetry that brought matters to a head; what appears to have caused her downfall was her fatal inability to learn from past mistakes. That she should have welcomed the opportunity to contribute articles to *La Nouvelle Revue* is understandable. But having seen what damage had been done by those articles to an innocent courtier, she should have fought shy of involving herself further. But no. The series, as far as Juliette Adam was concerned, had been a great success, and other contributors had followed Catherine. Using the same pseudonym they had written studies of London, Madrid and Vienna.

It was then decided to include St Petersburg. The survey of the Russian capital was undertaken by Countess Yuliana Glinka, aided by the enthusiastic Catherine. It was not a very satis-factory arrangement. Set against Catherine's Berlin studies, the St Petersburg articles proved comparatively tame. The malice, the sneers and the innuendoes were still there, but much of the bite had gone out of them. It requires a certain amount of con-viction on the part of the writer for vilification to make its mark and, in Catherine's case, this was lacking in the attack on the Russian capital. The articles, like those on Berlin, were eventually published in book form but with nothing like the success of *Berlin Society*.

As far as Yuliana Glinka was concerned, the articles were only too effective. Secrets in St Petersburg were not as easy to keep as they were in Berlin. The unfortunate Mme Glinka was not only unmasked but, at the Tsar's order, her estates in Russia were confiscated and she was sent into temporary exile. And it is possible that word concerning Catherine's connection with *La Nouvelle Revue* was passed from the Russian Court to the Royal Palace in Berlin. This seems to be the most likely explanation for Catherine's subsequent fate.

Precisely what happened to Catherine after the publication of the St Petersburg series in *La Nouvelle Revue* is difficult to say. This was a period of her life about which she did not care to talk. If she mentioned it, she did so in the vaguest possible terms. And few others were able to throw any light on the matter.

The surface events of these years are easy enough to follow. In the winter of 1885–86, an epidemic of measles spread throughout Berlin society. Catherine was amongst the first to succumb. She was seriously ill and, according to her own account, 'very nearly died'.

Soon after she had recovered, she and her husband closed their Berlin home and left Germany for good. Catherine claimed that the reason for this was that Prince Wilhelm was ill with malarial fever and that the doctors had advised him to spend the following winter in a warm, dry climate. If this is true, then Prince Wilhelm's illness, for all its seriousness, was most convenient. It is quite likely that the illness was a diplomatic one.

After leaving Germany, they went to Russia where they remained throughout the following summer. At the end of the year they travelled to Egypt, taking the children with them, and the fact that they spent the winter of 1886 in Cairo does seem to bear out the claim that Prince Wilhelm was under doctor's orders. At that time Cairo was becoming fashionable and Catherine thoroughly enjoyed her first experience of the African continent. She made several new English friends and, like many jaded Europeans, fell under the spell of the desert.

They made excursions up the Nile and found the temples, the mosques and the monuments of Egypt 'wonderful and interesting', although Catherine confessed to a disappointment in the Pyramids and to an aversion to the broken-nosed Sphinx.

In June 1887, Catherine returned to Russia with the children while her husband went back to Germany to settle up his affairs. The Egyptian climate apparently restored Prince Wilhelm sufficiently for him to withstand a European winter, for the family was still in Russia when Catherine's father died the following April. It was her father's death, says Catherine, 'and some complications which followed upon it connected with the disposal of his property [that] obliged us to settle in Russia'.

This was her side of the story. But there was more to it than she cared to admit. The decision to settle in Russia had been arrived at long before her father died. The sudden departure from Germany was occasioned as much by the anger of the Empress Augusta as by the illness of Prince Wilhelm. Somehow or other the old Empress had discovered that Catherine was the author of *Berlin Society* and had made it quite clear that Princess Radziwill was *persona non grata* at the German Court. For a woman in Catherine's position, this made it virtually impossible for her to live in Berlin. Her unfortunate husband was obliged to resign his commission in the German army and to follow his wife and family into exile.

The affair was kept very quiet. The Empress's friendship with the Radziwills ensured that Catherine's disgrace was not mentioned beyond the family circle. Berlin society remained convinced that M. Gerard was the author of the infamous book and Catherine's disappearance was explained away (probably at her own instigation) as a political move on the part of Prince Bismarck. However, there is very little reason to believe that Bismarck would have troubled himself with Catherine's petty intrigues. His feud with the Radziwill family was more intense than any annoyance he may have felt with Catherine's slanders but he never went as far as to expel a Radziwill from Germany. In any case, Catherine was allowed back into the country and the only place where she was not received was at Court.

She never openly admitted her expulsion from Court but many years later she once hinted at it. 'The Empress,' she said, 'disliked me, and made no bones about it. I was far too independent for her, and when I had committed what was in her eyes the inexcusable crime of having written a book, a most innocent book by the way, she made no secret of her antagonistic feelings in regard to my unfortunate person.'

The only book Catherine wrote while she was living in Berlin was the 'innocent' *Berlin Society*, and she never lived in Germany again.

CHAPTER FIVE

'I'll Take Their Country . . .'

To the north of Bechuanaland, at the outlet of Rhodes's 'Suez Canal', lay Matabeleland. Originally an off-shoot of the Zulu nation, the Matabele were, after the subjugation of the Zulus in 1879, the most formidable black race in southern Africa. Earlier in the century they had been led to the high, fertile plateau which lies between the Limpopo and Zambesi rivers by the leader and founder of their nation, Mzilikazi. By the 1880s they had been settled there for some forty years.

During his lifetime, Mzilikazi—the Path of Blood—had ruled his people in the iron-handed manner of Shaka, the powerful Zulu king whom he had served as a high-ranking young warrior. His had been a régime of autocratic cruelty and bloodshed, supported by his ability to satisfy the warlike propensities of his followers. For the Matabele, like the Zulus, were in essence one huge army and their way of life was that of battle and plunder; even their name was derived from their method of fighting—Matabele, *Those who hide behind the long shields*. Every young man was a soldier who established his manhood in battle; the nation was governed by a hierarchy of warriors, dominated by the Paramount Chief; the land they occupied was ruled by right of conquest and their defeated foes were treated as slaves. Leadership was hereditary only in as much as it depended upon the talent for survival of one of Mzilikazi's many contending sons. The fact that Mzilikazi had some three hundred wives and a regrettable tendency to rid himself of possible heirs made the right of succession far from predictable. After Mzilikazi's death, it was largely power politics that established his son, Lobengula, as leader of the nation in 1870. For those who look for some meaning in the

89

workings of fate and the coincidences of history, there may be some significance in the fact that the year that brought Lobengula to power was the same year that brought Cecil Rhodes to Africa.

In the manner of authoritarian régimes, the Matabele had imposed a semblance of peace throughout the territory in which they had settled. It was the peace which invariably accompanies tyranny: it depended entirely on the absence of effective challenge. The original inhabitants of the country, the comparatively placid Mashona and Barotse, had been quickly subdued and had long since accepted their vassalage. The only threat to the supremacy of the Matabele was that of the white races in the south. Mzilikazi had done his best to safeguard himself against any such threat. In his tempestuous drive northwards from Zululand, he had clashed with the Boers in the Transvaal and it was not an experience he wished to repeat. His attitude to the white man had been wary rather than hostile; he had remained friendly with the missionaries and had been careful to circumscribe the activities of any white visitors to Matabeleland. This was the policy which his son Lobengula tried to continue. He was not to be as fortunate as his father.

By all accounts, Lobengula was an impressive man. He was over six feet tall, bronze, muscular and, despite a considerable paunch, a dignified and undeniably majestic-looking person. He is said to have been more intelligent than his father; not so great a warrior, but a shrewd and talented politician. Together with Rhodes and Kruger, he is often cited as one of the truly distinguished men of nineteenth-century Africa. His misfortune was not that he lacked ability but that the time and place in which he lived did not allow him to reap the fruits of his genius.

Shortly after Lobengula assumed the leadership of his people, the mineral potential of southern Africa was confirmed. First came the diamonds at Kimberley and then the gold in the Transvaal: it was therefore inevitable that the fortune-seekers should look further north. Gold, in fact, had been discovered on the borders of Matabeleland before Mzilikazi died and it was not long before the handful of missionaries and traders visiting Lobengula's royal kraal at Gubulawayo were joined by a new breed of white man: concession-hunters asking permission to mine the new King's lands. The more strongly the gold-fever raged in the south, the more persistent did the concession-hunters in Matabeleland become. Lobengula was not interested in the precious metals himself but he knew the dangers of allowing Europeans into his domains. He became alarmed at the unending demands of these newcomers who, he was to tell the British High Commissioner for Bechuanaland, 'come in here like wolves without my permission and make roads into my country'. How long he could have withstood the individual claim-seekers it is impossible to say. There is a chance that he could have bargained with them and still retained control of his country. The encroachment would have been gradual and with the fortune-hunters divided amongst themselves, it would have been possible for the astute King to have played them off against each other. He might even have been forced to yield to the demands of his bloodthirsty warriors who were anxious to deal with the intruders by the traditional method of the Matabele. Whatever solution he might eventually have arrived at, it is not unreasonable to suppose that he might have prevented, during his own lifetime at least, the wholesale occupation of his dominions by white settlers. But this was not to be. In the final analysis, Lobengula's fate was sealed, not merely because he was an obstacle to the search for gold, but because his burly figure obscured a vision. When, in Kimberley, Cecil Rhodes had planted his hand on a map of Africa and declared: 'All this to be painted red; that is my dream,' it is possible that his palm had rested on Matabeleland.

*

Rhodes was undoubtedly aware of the activities of the concession-hunters at Lobengula's kraal. With Bechuanaland once secured to British interests, Matabeleland was his next objective, and anything that happened there was of concern to him. But he does not seem to have been unduly perturbed by the fact that individual fortune-hunters, or even representatives of syndicates, were invading his north. At the stage when the trek northwards was beginning to gather momentum, Rhodes was fully occupied with his own concerns in Kimberley and on the Witwatersrand; the amalgamation of the diamond mines had reached a crucial point and he was still striving to make good his initial losses on the goldfields of the Transvaal. This was more than enough to be going on with and he could have had no wish to add to his responsibilities. In any case, the problem of Matabeleland did not appear to be pressing. By that time he had gained sufficient experience in manipulating capitalist enterprise to know that, when faced with a divided opposition, he was in a position to choose his own time to step in and take over. He might even have been prepared to play a much longer waiting game had he not been challenged by more formidable opponents.

The threat which propelled him into action came not so much from the scramble for wealth as from the scramble for Africa. The mineral potential of Matabeleland had proved to be more than a magnet for private speculators: it had awakened the territorial ambitions of Lobengula's neighbours. To the west the Germans, now firmly established as a colonial power in southern Africa, were showing an unmistakable interest in Matabeleland. To the east the Portuguese, occupying the seaboard, attempted to stake their claim in central Africa by issuing, in the year 1887, a map showing Lobengula's territory as a Portuguese possession. In that same year the Transvaal entered the arena by sending an emissary to the Royal kraal at Gubulawayo for the purpose of negotiating a treaty of friendship and protection with the Matabele monarch. These overtures were merely tentative moves but they were ominous enough to alarm Rhodes. He was prepared to deal with the concession-hunters in his own time but the interference of foreign powers was quite another matter. It was the sort of thing that could easily get out of hand.

On hearing of the Transvaal's diplomatic mission to Lobengula, he immediately hurried south and urged the British High Commissioner, Sir Hercules Robinson, to declare a protectorate over Matabeleland and its subject state, Mashonaland. A similar move had safeguarded Bechuanaland two years earlier and there seemed to be no reason why it should not be repeated. But Sir Hercules was hesitant. It was one thing for the enthusiastic Rhodes to expect nations to fall into his lap at the stroke of a pen but quite another for Her Majesty's representative in South Africa to explain away such actions to the British Government. The Colonial Office, as Sir Hercules well knew, had little appetite for African possessions at that time and, with Bechuanaland scarcely digested, could hardly be expected to swallow another huge slice of the trouble-fraught continent. Yet it was impossible to refuse Rhodes entirely. At times like this, when he set out to get his own way—to win someone over 'on the personal'—Rhodes's powers of persuasion were prodigious. The poetic grandeur of his vision, his irrepressible enthusiasm and engaging candour, the very single-mindedness of his arguments, could mesmerize the most hard-headed of men; few were known to resist him for long. Sir Hercules was no exception. Although he would not annex Lobengula's territory outright, he was prepared to take an option on it. At Rhodes's suggestion, he sent a despatch to Gubulawayo asking the Matabele monarch not to enter into any treaty with a foreign power or to part with any land without the sanction of the British High Commissioner. To this Lobengula agreed. On 11th February, 1888, a treaty of 'peace and amity' between Victoria, the Great White Queen of England, and Lobengula, the Mighty Elephant of Matabeleland, was signed at Gubulawayo. It was not quite what Rhodes had hoped for but it was enough.

Even before he heard that Lobengula had signed the treaty, Rhodes set about putting himself in direct control of the situation. Experience had shown him that he could not leave the business of Empire-building to the Imperial Factor, nor could he rely upon any assistance from the Cape Government. Only Cecil John Rhodes was capable of conquering Africa, but in order to do so, it was essential that he have a free hand. Having done what he could to stave off foreign intruders, he now proceeded to clear the field of private speculators. On his return to Kimberley after his interview with Sir Hercules Robinson, he and Alfred Beit sent a representative to Lobengula's kraal with the object of obtaining a gold-mining concession; unfortunately, the man chosen for the job fell ill and was forced to return without accomplishing anything. Rhodes then paid a flying visit to England to investigate the financial backing of the other concession-hunters in Matabeleland and to find out how they stood with the British Government. Satisfied that he could deal with any rivals, he hurried back to Africa and despatched a second mission to Lobengula. This time he was taking no chances. He chose as his agents three healthy, capable and reliable men: Charles Rudd, his business partner from early Kimberley days, Rochfort Maguire, a lawyer whom he had befriended at Oxford, and F. R. Thompson, a former compound manager of De Beers who knew the languages and customs of Africans. It was a delegation designed to meet every eventuality. To add extra weight, Sir Hercules Robinson was persuaded to provide Rhodes's envoys with an official introduction to the Matabele king.

Their task was not simple. Unlike their avaricious but less ambitious rivals, they had not come in search of a likely spot to dig in Lobengula's territory. What they wanted was a monopoly: the exclusive right to all the metals and minerals in the King's domain. And this is what they obtained. It took them three months to pull off the deal; three months of suspense during which they were watched over by the King's disgruntled warriors and confined to the royal goat kraal.

They were helped by the gifts they had brought and the bribes they were able to pay. They were also helped by Rhodes's name, for Lobengula knew of the powerful white chief who ruled at Kimberley—from which his warriors returned with guns and ammunition. But they were helped, most of all, by the timely arrival of a representative of the Great White Queen. It happened that Rhodes's friend, Sir Sidney Shippard, the administrator of Bechuanaland, was on a mission in Matabeleland and decided to call at the royal kraal. He was accompanied by two of Lobengula's trusted missionary friends. As was often the case, the advent of a sympathetic British official proved opportune for Rhodes. No record was kept of the talks between Sir Sidney Shippard and Lobengula, but shortly after Sir Sidney's departure, the long-awaited concession was granted.

On 30th October, 1888, Lobengula agreed to give Rhodes's agents 'exclusive charge over all metals and minerals' in his kingdom. He also gave them the right to expel all other claimants to 'land, metals, minerals or mining rights'. In return for this monopoly, the holders of the concession were to pay the King £100 on the first day of each lunar month and supply him with a thousand Martini-Henry rifles and a hundred thousand cartridges. The promise of an armed steamboat on the Zambesi was thrown in for good measure. That Lobengula appreciated the implications of the document to which he affixed his elephant seal, is extremely doubtful. He must have imagined the white men would dig their holes and he would be left to rule his subjects as he had always done. It was a relief to have put an end to the constant stream of petitioners to his kraal and he is reported to have expressed the wish that not more than ten men would come and dig as a result of the concession. How wrong he was. But he realized his mistake too late.

The King was given no time to change his mind. Within a few hours, Rudd was on his way to Kimberley. On his journey south he met with near disaster. Separated from his party, he was lost in the Bechuanaland desert and nearly died of thirst. He was forced to bury the concession in an ant-bear hole and recovered it only when he was rescued by a band of Bushmen. When the concession reached Cape Town, Sir Hercules Robinson gave it his blessing and forwarded it to the Colonial Office. It would, noted Sir Hercules in all seriousness, 'check the inroad of adventurers' and 'secure the cautious development of the country with a proper consideration for the feelings and prejudices of the natives'. Lobengula was not the only one to be fooled.

With the concession secured, the African chessboard had been simplified. Rhodes could now think in terms of checkmate; his pawns had cornered the black King and he was now prepared to bring the white Queen into action. He had been considering the plan for some months. In March 1888 he had finally succeeded in amalgamating the diamond mines. The trust deed of the new company went far beyond the necessities of a financial organization. Its purpose was clearly political. When legal opinion was sought by some of the more apprehensive shareholders, it was authoritatively stated that: 'The powers of the Company are as extensive as those of any Company that ever existed.' De Beers Consolidated Mines, said a lawyer, would be 'empowered to annex a portion of territory in Central Africa, raise and maintain a standing army and undertake warlike operations'. He compared the new venture with the old East India Company; all that it lacked was a Royal Charter. Rhodes's next move was to obtain the Royal Charter.

He arrived in London in March 1889 and set to work immediately. His first concern was to eliminate, once and for all, any possible claims of rival concessionaires. This he achieved by a process of incorporation and, when this was not possible, by outright purchase of all existing concessions granted by Lobengula. Next he set about cultivating influential supporters.

Among these was W. T. Stead, the editor of the *Pall Mall Gazette* and one of the most powerful journalists of his day. Stead, who had been suspicious of Rhodes's activities in Bechuanaland, approached his first interview with Rhodes in a cautious mood. He came away completely captivated. 'Mr Rhodes is my man!' he wrote joyously to his wife. 'I have just had three hours talk with him . . . His ideas are federation, expansion, consolidation of the Empire.' The fact that Rhodes had offered him £20,000 for a share in the *Pall Mall Gazette* might have had something to do with his enthusiasm, but from then on Stead became one of Rhodes's most devoted disciples. Others were not quite so susceptible but there was sufficient support in Britain to ensure the success of Rhodes's application for a Charter. Lord Salisbury, the Prime Minister, was persuaded that some sort of action was advisable in Central Africa and that the existence of a Chartered Company would be the cheapest way for Britain to establish a foothold there. The Duke of Abercorn agreed to accept the Chairmanship of the Company and the Duke of Fife, son-in-law of the Prince of Wales, became a director. Smiled upon by the Government and blessed by the aristocracy, the new enterprise could discount all opposition. Soon after Rhodes arrived back in Cape Town it was announced that Her Majesty Queen Victoria had been pleased to grant a Royal Charter of Incorporation to the British South Africa Company.

It is from this period of his life that the most telling criticism of Rhodes can be dated. His bid for financial and political supremacy in Africa has been described as unscrupulous, callous, shabby and contemptible. He is said to have tyrannized his enemies and deceived his friends. In amalgamating the diamond mines he resorted to tactics which even his admirers are at a loss to defend: he tricked his opponents into submission and brought ruin to many of the smaller business men in Kimberley. He bamboozled Lobengula by pretending to seek mining rights when, in fact, his intention was to rob the King of his country and, at the same time, he allowed Lord Salisbury to believe that Lobengula had agreed to the occupation of his territories. Accompanying his every move there are stories of bribery, double-dealing and sharp practice. His more virulent critics have even hinted at murder. It has been said that he was

responsible for the death of the Boer emissary who was am-
bushed and killed on his way back from Lobengula's kraal in
1887. There is little evidence to support such an accusation but
many people, including President Kruger, are reported to have
believed it.

It is easy to understand how the theory arose that after
Neville Pickering's death Rhodes became hardened and more
ruthless. The time factor supports it. Pickering died towards
the end of 1886 and the relentless drive northwards started in
1887. To accept such an explanation as the sole cause of the
change in Rhodes's personality would, of course, be an over-
simplification, but it may have played a part. With Pickering's
death Rhodes lost not only his friend but his heir. From now on
there would be no one person left to further his vision; it would
be passed on to an impersonal group of trustees. His individual
task became more urgent. And he knew that his time was short.
'Everything in the world is too short,' he said to Lord Rosebery.
'Life and fame and achievement, everything is too short.'

But there was more to it than that. Rhodes's dream of extending the British Empire was older than his friendship with Pickering and he would have pursued it whatever happened. It was the
nature of the quest rather than the nature of the man that produced the latter-day Rhodes. Empires, as he was the first to
admit, are rarely established by philanthropists. 'Pure philanthropy is all very well in its way,' he said, 'but philanthropy plus
five per cent is a good deal better.' It was cynicism, but
cynicism with a motive. 'Money is power,' he remarked on
another occasion, 'and what can one accomplish without power?
. . . Ideas are no good without money.' His idea, rightly or
wrongly, was to spread British civilization and bring peace to
the world. It was a question of cause and effect; a matter of
means to an end. To achieve his Utopia, he needed money and
he needed power. But the power he sought can only be obtained
at the expense of others and is rarely wielded by saints. Men
like Rhodes must always wear their haloes crooked.

*

When Charles Rudd had set out from Lobengula's kraal to
deliver the signed concession to Rhodes, he had left his two
companions, Maguire and Thompson, at Gubulawayo. 'Nature,'

Rhodes was fond of saying, 'abhors a vacuum.' It was a maxim which his lieutenants had taken to heart. A vacuum at Gubulawayo would be extremely inadvisable at such a time. The concession-hunters who were still crowding the royal kraal were hardly likely to accept Rhodes's monopoly without putting up a fight. Lobengula might always be persuaded to change his mind. It did not take long for their fears to be realized. The King was told that he had been deceived, that he had given his country away, that the white men would be able to dig anywhere, even in his kraal. Lobengula began to have second thoughts and Maguire and Thompson found themselves regarded as hostages.

When rumours of what was happening in Matabeleland reached Rhodes, he decided to act. It was obvious that, without Rudd, Maguire and Thompson were not astute enough to deal with the situation. He wanted to send Rudd back to Gubulawayo but Rudd was ill. He would have liked to go himself but there was the Charter to consider. At last he decided to send his most trusted confidant: the energetic Dr Jameson. To persuade Jameson to accept the mission was not easy. It is said that the little doctor was reluctant to leave his patients in Kimberley. He knew all about Rhodes's plans for the British Empire; he found them exciting and inspiring, but he was a professional man and he had his responsibilities. Rhodes wore him down. It may have been Rhodes's persuasiveness; it may have been, as is claimed by Jameson's biographer, that the doctor was unable to ignore an appeal to his sense of duty; or it may simply have been that Jameson was lured on by the prospect of adventure. The expedition would be a bit of a gamble and Dr Jim could seldom resist a gamble. He went. He met Lobengula and charmed him in his breeziest bedside manner. The promised rifles and ammunition were delivered and the King was placated. Jameson returned to Kimberley in triumph.

For a while all seemed well. But not for long. Maguire became bored with the goat kraal and left. The concession-hunters continued to work on Lobengula. There was an ugly incident when the King executed an *induna* (head man) who had advised him to sign the concession. Thompson fled. Rhodes was faced with a vacuum at Gubulawayo when he could least afford one. He had just returned from obtaining his Charter and was poised to move northwards. Once again Jameson was sent off to deal with Lobengula. This time he took his medicine chest along. First he gave the gouty old King some morphia injections and then announced that the men would be coming to start digging. Under the spell of Jameson's good-natured chaff and pain-relieving drugs, Lobengula agreed to honour his contract. On 10th December, 1889, he gave his permission for Rhodes's men to enter his territory; not into Matabeleland itself, but into his vassal state of Mashonaland. 'Jameson;' Rhodes was to say, 'I am more indebted to him than to any man in South Africa.' Their first joint venture had paid off and Rhodes was never to forget it.

They were an incongruous pair, these two friends—the big, bovine-looking Rhodes, with his lumbering gait, flaccid face and heavy-lidded blue eyes, and the slim, doe-eyed and nimble little Jameson. The difference between them, not only in looks but in personality, has frequently been commented on. More often than not, it has been used to explain the tie which bound them. Their natures, it has been said, complemented each other perfectly and their friendship became 'as strong as a marriage bond'. It is a view which is easy to understand. Jameson was indeed the opposite of Rhodes in many respects. Where Rhodes was ponderous, calculating and earnest, Jameson was sharp, impulsive and sophisticated. Unlike Rhodes, he had an easy social manner, a quick wit and a great deal of sympathy with the views of others. He was easy to get on with, a good mixer and very popular. These were qualities which Rhodes always found attractive. But there was more to it than a mere attraction of opposites. The two of them had a great deal in common. They were the same age and they came from similar backgrounds; both were products of large middle-class families. They were both life-long bachelors: women played no part in Rhodes's life and, as far as one can gather, very little in Jameson's. They had both been brought to South Africa by tubercular lungs and both suffered ill health for most of their lives. Neither had made much of a mark at school and neither was particularly interested in organized sport. Like Rhodes, Jameson would have been a poor candidate for a Rhodes scholarship.

Yet despite all this—despite the attraction and the sympathy, despite the closeness and durability of their relationship—one must question whether this friendship was as all-absorbing as it is sometimes made out to have been. Subsequent events were to highlight the comradeship between Rhodes and Jameson and their relationship was to be talked about in dramatic and often romantic terms. As a result, it is often assumed that Jameson replaced Pickering in Rhodes's life. This is very doubtful. There are many similarities between the two friendships and they were both important in Rhodes's life, but they were conducted on different emotional levels. Rhodes never, for instance, made Jameson his heir and only on his deathbed did he include Jameson as one of his trustees. Pickering, on the other hand, became Rhodes's legatee after they had known each other for a comparatively short time. It has been said that Rhodes was wary of handing such a trust on to Jameson because he considered him unstable. But this was claimed only after Jameson had plunged them both into disaster. Had Rhodes not had faith in Jameson's judgment in these early days he would surely never have trusted him with such vital and delicate missions. There is reason to suppose that Jameson had more of the makings of an Empire-builder than did Pickering but the fact remains that Rhodes never made him his heir. And there were to be other examples of the dissimilarity between these two friendships. Perhaps the most striking is Rhodes's behaviour at a time of crisis in both relationships. When Pickering had needed him, he had hurried back to Kimberley; when Jameson needed him, Rhodes made so little effort that he had finally to be fetched by a servant. Jameson was a boon companion, a brother even, but he never aroused a compulsive emotional response from Rhodes.

Perhaps Jameson was too independent to allow himself to be taken over completely. He withstood Rhodes's blandishments for longer than most and when he agreed to undertake the mission to Lobengula, he did so on his own terms. He was quite prepared to come back to his medical practice in Kimberley and even when he had become more deeply involved in Rhodes's plans, he tended to regard himself simply as a doctor on temporary leave. For Rhodes, this was hardly good enough; his demands tended to be exclusive. 'I must not only have you, but I must have your heart as well!' he was to say to a young man whom he employed. 'If your best is to be given to me, my interests must be your interests.' It took Jameson a long time before he was prepared to go that far. In the often emotive language of Rhodes's detractors, Jameson has been described as 'Rhodes's tool'. But Jameson was never a passive instrument; he was, as time would show, quite capable of making his own decisions.

At the time that Jameson made his first trip to Gubulawayo, he and Rhodes had been living together for over two years. They shared a little corrugated-iron roofed cottage opposite the Kimberley Club. One of them was a millionaire and the other a successful doctor, but they still lived the lives of impoverished diggers. The cottage was sparsely furnished and always untidy; there were two bedrooms containing little more than truckle-beds, and a sitting-room which looked, according to one astonished visitor, 'like that of an undergraduate at college'. Most of their meals were eaten at the Club across the road.

For all its unpretentiousness, the cottage was to become one of the sights of Kimberley. It was here that Rhodes, after an all-night session, had finally won over Barney Barnato in their battle for the diamond mines; it was here that the campaigns for obtaining first the Concession and then the Charter had been planned; and it was here that Rhodes now began to make his preparations for the advance into Lobengula's territory.

It was decided that the pioneer column should be made up of young men recruited from every district in South Africa. They were to be paid at the rate of seven and sixpence a day while on the march and rewarded with a grant of 3,000 acres of farm-land and fifteen gold claims when they reached their destination. Preferably they should be unmarried. The main difficulty would be their route. In order not to alarm Lobengula unduly, Rhodes wanted the column to avoid Matabeleland entirely and to head straight for Mashonaland. This meant that not only would they have to make a road as they went but that they would be travelling through hundreds of miles of completely wild country. Lobengula had given permission for Rhodes's men to enter Mashonaland but it was known that his young warriors were spoiling for a fight; there was always the possibility that they might get out of control. It was therefore essential that the column be accompanied by an armed escort. Rhodes was assured that 2,500 men would be needed. The cost of the expedition would be prohibitive; it would swallow most of the Chartered

Company's available capital even before the development of the country was begun. Things seemed to have reached a deadlock.

Rhodes broke it in a characteristic fashion. One morning, shortly before Christmas 1889, he crossed to the Kimberley Club for his breakfast. As he made his way through the dining-room, he noticed a young man sitting alone. He recognized him vaguely as the representative of a company with whom he had recently had some dealings. He sat down opposite him and ordered his bacon and eggs. Then, without bothering to say good morning, he launched into the story of his troubles. What did the young man think of the military estimate of 2,500 men? How many men did *he* think would be necessary? The young man was Frank Johnson. He was twenty-three years old. His only experience of the issues involved sprang from the fact that he had once paid a visit to Mashonaland and had served briefly as a quartermaster-sergeant in the Bechuanaland Police Force under the command of Colonel Sir Frederick Carrington. It was this same Colonel Carrington who had given Rhodes the estimate of 2,500 men. Not every day does a quartermaster-sergeant get asked to comment on the decision of his former commanding officer. Young Johnson was flattered. He decided to cheer Rhodes up. 'Two thousand five hundred men!' he exclaimed. 'Absurd.' With a mere two hundred and fifty men he could walk through the country. Rhodes said nothing. He went on eating his bacon and eggs. Then he looked up. 'Do you mean that?' he asked. Johnson was somewhat taken aback. He had hardly given the problem any thought. His suggested 250 men had been an automatic reduction of the 2,500. 'I might just as easily have said twenty-five men as two hundred and fifty,' he later admitted. But he was unwilling to retract and decided to bluff it out. When he replied that he had meant what he said, Rhodes immediately asked him what a force of 250 men would cost. Johnson, of course, had no idea, but said that if he were given some paper and a room in Rhodes's cottage, he would work out an estimate. Rhodes complied.

The calculation took Johnson four hours. He claims that the estimate he produced for Rhodes was £87,500. Rhodes was delighted. Carrington's proposal had been in the region of a million sterling. Knowing next to nothing about Johnson, Rhodes there and then offered the young man complete command of the expedition. But Johnson was not looking for a job. He had certain reservations about the Chartered Company and, in any case, was leaving that night for the Cape. He turned down the offer. Rhodes was flabbergasted. Here he was, presenting an unknown young man with the chance of a lifetime—the chance to add a new country to the Empire—and it was being refused! The discussion grew more and more heated until finally Rhodes, in a fit of temperament, slammed out of the room. That same evening, Johnson caught his train to Cape Town.

But Rhodes had no intention of leaving the matter there. He had been much impressed by this young man and his simple mathematics. For the next few days he went round Kimberley showing Johnson's estimate to his friends. Not surprisingly, they told him he was mad even to consider it. But at the end of the week he sent a cable to Johnson asking him to be on Cape Town station early the following morning in order to meet the Kimberley train. Johnson met the train from which Rhodes emerged puffing with impatience. 'Where can we talk?' he asked. Johnson suggested the Government Avenue in the Botanical Gardens. For over two hours they paced up and down under the great oaks lining the Avenue, with Rhodes alternating between bribes and appeals to duty and Johnson raising objections to certain members of the board of the Chartered Company. At last Rhodes won. Johnson agreed to accept the job on contract. In nine months he promised to hand over Mashonaland to Rhodes fit for civil government. With the matter settled, they went off to Poole's Club for their second breakfast together. A new nation was about to be born. Heralded by the clatter of breakfast cups, it was to be delivered by an inexperienced young man who had happened to catch the eye of its creator.

*

According to Frank Johnson, he was to be responsible for recruiting the young men who were to form the Pioneer Column. Rhodes's only stipulations were that the corps should be made up largely of South Africans and that it should comprise a cross-section of artisans and tradesmen so that, on arrival in Mashonaland, the skills required for establishing a civil settlement would be available. Butchers, bakers, builders and blacksmiths: these were the men to whom priority should be given.

Selection was no easy matter. The proposed expedition fired the imaginations of adventurous and impoverished young men throughout the country. Applications came in by the thousand. Johnson was left to sort them out. To add to his worries he was continually pestered by candidates whose only qualification was the influence which their families had with Rhodes. After a number of these place-seekers had been turned down, Rhodes sent for Johnson and demanded to know the reason. Somewhat heatedly, Johnson told him that to include such men would cost more than had been allowed for in his original estimate. Rhodes saw his point. There were, however, twelve young men whom Rhodes had personally selected and who he was determined should be included in the column. Having listened to Johnson's objections, he merely scribbled a note agreeing to the extra cost involved and later sent Johnson a list of the chosen twelve. It was inevitable, of course, that these favoured few should have been dubbed 'the twelve apostles'. But they were also given other names. Sometimes they were known as 'Rhodes's Angels' and sometimes as 'Rhodes's Lambs'.

Among the twelve were two young men in whom Rhodes was particularly interested. They were Troopers Bob Coryndon and John Grimmer. Both were Kimberley men: Coryndon had been born in Kimberley and Grimmer had been brought to the diamond diggings at the age of five. Each in his own way was exceptional and each was to play an important role in Rhodes's life. Coryndon was intelligent, able and adventurous and was to distinguish himself in the furthering of Rhodes's schemes in the north. Grimmer was frank, manly, a good shot and a rugged individualist who was destined to occupy a special place in Rhodes's heart. Of the two, it was Grimmer whom Rhodes had singled out as his particular favourite.

Jack Grimmer—or Johnny, as Rhodes liked to call him—was the son of Dr Irving Grimmer. He was born at Colesberg in the Cape in 1867 and his father was one of the early pioneers of Kimberley. Brought up amid the rough and tumble of the diamond fields, his education appears to have been scrappy and when still young he started work at the Dutoitspan Mine. After gaining some experience in the mines, he was eventually taken on at De Beers where his eldest brother had been working for some time. It was while he was employed by De Beers that he first came to Rhodes's notice. Rhodes's interest in the young man was immediate. A short account of Grimmer's life merely states that: 'Mr Rhodes first made his acquaintance in Kimberley, and took a great fancy to him.' But there is a more romantic account of their first meeting. It is said that Rhodes was one day standing on the veranda of the De Beers office, which looked on to the Company's stables, when he noticed young Grimmer trying to mount a rearing horse. The youngster was thrown to the ground several times but at last managed to get astride the animal and bring it under control. Rhodes is reported to have been completely fascinated by the struggle and, when it was over, to have turned to a friend and said: 'That boy has grit, I must speak to him.'

The story has a faintly familiar ring about it—it smacks of the Empress and the stable boy—but it may well have been true. Certainly there was little about Jack Grimmer, other than his obvious virility, to attract immediate attention. He was a hefty young man with an honest, good-natured but somewhat stolid face. People meeting him for the first time invariably commented on his singular lack of animation; it was said that he was 'undemonstrative and phlegmatic' and that he had a taciturn, 'seemingly brusque' manner. Nor does he seem to have distinguished himself at De Beers. He worked as a clerk but had little aptitude for office work.

When the call went out for young men to join the Pioneer Column, Jack Grimmer was among the first volunteers. He went straight to Rhodes to offer his services. The story is told that Rhodes teased him by at first refusing to consider his application. 'No,' he is reported to have said, 'I only want men with beards.' Then, having watched Grimmer's face fall, he laughed and said: 'I think you will probably do very well.' There could, of course, have been no question of his being turned down on account of his age. In 1890, when the Pioneer Column was being mobilized, Jack Grimmer was twenty-three. He was the same age as Neville Pickering had been when he was appointed secretary to De Beers, and the same age as Frank Johnson when he was given command of the Mashonaland expedition.

On 27th June, the Chartered Company's force set off. The

column was led by the hunter Frederick Selous, commanded by Frank Johnson and accompanied by Dr Jameson. Dr Jim had at last committed himself irrevocably to Rhodes. The Pioneers were on the march for over two months. They hacked their way through dense bush, waded across swamps, bridged rivers and marked a new road on their maps. Towards the end of August they emerged on the open plains of Mashonaland and on 11th September came in sight of their destination. Tents were pitched, guns were fired and the flag was hoisted. They named the place Fort Salisbury after the British Prime Minister and an express letter was sent to Rhodes. 'When at last I found they were through to Fort Salisbury,' he said, 'I do not think there was a happier man in the country than myself.'

He was happy but it was no more than he had expected. For Frank Johnson the expedition was to be followed by a bewildering anti-climax. After Fort Salisbury had been established, Johnson and Dr Jameson embarked on a perilous journey down the Pungwe River in order to explore the route to the coast through Portuguese East Africa. When at last they reached Cape Town, Johnson's first thought was to see Rhodes. Not unnaturally he expected to be congratulated on his singular achievement. Rhodes was not in Cape Town so Johnson caught the train to Kimberley. He had not gone far when he received a message to say that Rhodes was travelling back to the Cape on the same line. In order that they could meet, it was arranged that the two trains should be halted at a convenient siding. To Johnson's amazement the meeting, which should have been historic, fell completely flat. Rhodes greeted him as if he had been away on a short holiday. 'You've got back,' he said. 'You're looking well.' Nothing more. 'He never even mentioned the country which I had obtained for him,' says Johnson. 'Yet, I think, that was so typical of the man. The job he had ordered had been carried out, and there was nothing more to be said about it.'

In a way, Johnson was right. The casual manner was typical of Rhodes in certain circumstances. But it was very different from his attitude towards many another young man. Perhaps it was the penalty which Johnson had to pay when Rhodes discovered that he was married. 'Johnson,' he used to say, 'was lost before I first knew him.'

A year after the flag had been hoisted at Fort Salisbury Rhodes paid his first visit to Mashonaland. He travelled there by way of the East Coast route that had been pioneered by Jameson and Johnson. On arriving by sea at Beira in Portuguese East Africa, his luggage was seized for inspection by the Portuguese officials. He was outraged. He considered it an unforgivable impertinence. 'I'll take their —— country from them!' he shouted as he stamped down the gang-plank. This attitude, too, was becoming typical.

*

The reason for Rhodes's tardy appearance in Mashonaland was his new and unexpected involvement in the politics of the Cape.

The Cape Parliament was a factional body, made up of small, indeterminate and ever changing groups. The only party with any real semblance of unity was the Afrikander Bond, which, led by the shrewd Jan Hofmeyr, represented moderate Dutch farming interests. But although it could claim thirty-three out of the seventy-four seats, the Bond could not command a parliamentary majority. More often than not, government of the Cape depended on compromise rather than policy. Even a minor crisis could put the office of Prime Minister in jeopardy. One such crisis arose while the Pioneer Column was being mobilized. It concerned railway construction. Rhodes was vitally interested in the railways of South Africa (he intended to build a railway line from the Cape to Cairo) and he saw in the proposed legislation a threat to his schemes. He hurried from Kimberley to Cape Town to vote against the Government. This was the first time he had taken his seat in Parliament since his re-election in 1888 but such was his reputation in the Colony when the Government duly fell that it was he who now became Prime Minister of the Cape. He alone could command the necessary support. Jan Hofmeyr offered him the tentative backing of the Bond and some of the ablest Parliamentarians agreed to serve under him. Inevitably, his Cabinet was known as the 'Cabinet of all the Talents'.

What a man this was! One may not admire his methods or agree with his scale of values; one might consider him intolerant, ruthless and egocentric—a man obsessed by his own interpretation of the world and its destiny—but one must stand aghast at his achievements. Consider what he had done in twenty years; the twenty years when most men are struggling to find their feet. He had arrived in South Africa an ailing, inconspicuous lad. He had neither name nor influence to help him. He had educated himself. He had built up one of the largest financial empires in the world. He had organized the conquest of a country. He had become Prime Minister. He was thirty-seven years old.

There was to be no suggestion of his being a nominal Prime Minister; a name for the Ministry and nothing more. He was to serve the Cape well despite his preoccupation with the north. During his terms of office much was done to build up and expand the Colony. Support from Hofmeyr and the Bond was essential and he secured it by championing the farmers. He pioneered agricultural reforms that were to have a lasting and beneficial effect on the productivity of the Cape. By introducing Arab stallions and Angora goats and by the implementation of his unpopular but effective Scab Act, he strengthened the livestock; he imported the American ladybird and saved the orange crop from insect pests; he threw his weight behind the wine trade and pressed for Colonial Preference at Westminster. With the gesture of a tyrant, he annexed Pondoland to the eastern Cape: 'That,' he said to a local Pondo chief, as a Maxim gun mowed down a field of mealies, 'is what will happen to you and your tribe if you give us any further trouble.' The chief was impressed and so was the Bond; even farmers can appreciate the advantages of territorial expansion when it includes the farm next door.

It was the Premiership which brought Rhodes into close alliance with the Bond and cemented his friendship with Jan Hofmeyr. He addressed Bond meetings, he got into the habit of going for early morning rides with Hofmeyr in order to discuss the day's parliamentary business and he was said to favour Bond candidates whenever a post fell vacant in one of his many concerns. All this brought him a good deal of criticism. Some of his supporters thought that he was too deeply in the pocket of the Bond, that his sympathies were becoming too Dutch. But he brushed such talk aside. A united South Africa was what he wanted—'the government of South Africa by the people of South Africa, with the Imperial flag for defence'—and this Hofmeyr was prepared to support.

The responsibilities of office added considerably to Rhodes's many burdens. For all his diverse talents, his mental energy and his inexhaustible enterprise, it became physically impossible for him to cope with the demands made upon him. The time had come for him to employ a responsible private secretary who could take some of the load from his shoulders. A suitable young man for the post was already in his employ and, shortly after assuming the Premiership, Rhodes made him his personal assistant. The young man was Henry L. Currey, the son of J. B. Currey, the friend of Rhodes's early Kimberley days.

Harry Currey was an efficient, intelligent young man with a talent for organization and a gift for caustic comment. Rhodes had taken an interest in him from the time that he was twenty-one. It was Harry Currey who, on leave from the Cape Public Service, accompanied Rhodes to Bechuanaland at the time when Rhodes was clearing the Boer Republics from his 'Suez Canal'. Two years later, when Currey was twenty-three, Rhodes decided to employ him full time. It was shortly after Neville Pickering's death when Rhodes, with the help of Alfred Beit, was busy securing what gold claims were still available on the Witwatersrand. He was about to launch the Goldfields Company (which later became the Consolidated Goldfields of South Africa) and needed a secretary for the enterprise. At that time Harry Currey was still working as a civil servant in the Cape; he had no experience of the goldfields and knew nothing about goldmines; it was enough that he was the right age and had won Rhodes's approval. Rhodes sent for him, asked him how much he was being paid in the Cape Public Service and immediately offered him three times as much. Not surprisingly, the young man leapt at the offer. For all his lack of experience, he quickly made his mark on the Rand and won the respect of his associates. He was thus a logical choice when Rhodes needed someone to take charge of his personal concerns and of the routine business of the Chartered Company.

There were to be other changes in the life of the new Prime Minister. From the time that Rhodes had arrived in South Africa, he had never had a comfortable home of his own. Rich as he was, he had been content to pig it in the tin-roofed cottages of Kimberley and to share rooms when he was in Cape Town. His meals were eaten at his club and the only servant he employed was Tony de la Cruz, a coloured man from Portuguese East Africa, who served him faithfully as a valet and general factotum. Now all this was to be changed. For a long time he had been unhappy with his lodgings in Cape Town (he believed the rooms to be haunted and refused to sleep there alone) and in any case, he considered them as unsuitable for a Prime Minister of the Cape. He decided to find a more fitting home.

The place he chose was a rambling old two-storied house, known as 'The Grange', and built on the lower slopes of Devil's Peak, at Rondebosch, just outside Cape Town. It was a place of historic interest, dating back to the days of the Dutch East India Company, when it had been used as a granary. Originally a delightful, whitewashed barn with muscular gables and a high-pitched thatched roof, it had lost much of its pristine charm by the time Rhodes became interested in it. A succession of owners and a series of shoddy conversions had effectively camouflaged the dignified simplicity of the original buildings. After renting it for two years, Rhodes was to buy the house and commission Herbert Baker, an unknown young architect whom he met casually at a dinner party, to restore its original architectural character. Working from a water-colour sketch of the old granary and from his own detailed knowledge of Cape Dutch architecture, Baker faithfully restored the house and, at the same time, founded his reputation as one of the leading architects of his day. Given back its original name Groote Schuur—Great Granary—it was to become one of the show places of the Cape and one of the few personal possessions in which Rhodes took a real delight.

When Rhodes first moved into the house, however, it was ill-equipped and bleakly furnished and its new tenant had neither the time nor the experience to cope with the business of home making. He handed the domestic arrangements over to Harry Currey. 'Let's try on £250 a month,' he said; 'let me know if you need more.' Generous as it was, this monthly allowance does not seem to have included the stocking of the cellar; this was something which Rhodes organized. He was also prepared to lend a hand with the selection of the household staff. He did so in typically unorthodox fashion. Currey was to tell the story of how the butler was acquired. The young man was an

Inniskilling Dragoon 'whom Rhodes's quick eye for a likely lad spotted amongst the Mess waiters' when he and Currey were guests of the nearby Wynberg garrison. The fortunate young waiter was somehow released from military service and became one of Rhodes's most valued servants.

The fact that Rhodes employed only male servants at Groote Schuur was taken as a further example of his hatred for women. As an answer to the accusation, it has been claimed that at one time a few of the servants had been allowed to have their wives living with them but 'the breath of scandal caused Rhodes to clear every woman, white and coloured, off the place'. How true this was is difficult to say; the source is none too reliable. In any case, as far as most people could remember, Groote Schuur was as free of feminine residents as a monastery. The myth of Rhodes's misogyny grew.

For Harry Currey, life with 'the great man', as he called Rhodes, was an exciting experience. These were the peak years of Rhodes's career. Success was his plaything and the world his nursery. Groote Schuur was besieged by the high and the mighty and England waited breathlessly for his coming. A visit to England at the beginning of 1891 crowned Currey's role as a private secretary. Then it was that he saw Rhodes at his most expansive: it was a time of great gestures, high living and staggering largesse.

Alfred Beit joined their ship at Madeira and the Duke of Abercorn was waiting, at one o'clock on a bitter winter's morning, to greet them at the station when they arrived in London. The following morning Lord Rothschild was announced. From then on the stream of visitors to the Westminster Palace Hotel was unending. Currey found that his days were divided between warding off the various 'odd fish' trying to gain Rhodes's ear, and amusing the celebrities who crowded the 'great man's' office. One of the most impressive visitors was Charles Stewart Parnell, leader of the Irish Nationalist Party. In 1888 Rhodes had promised Parnell a donation of £10,000 for his party funds in order, it is said, to win the Irish Party over to the idea of Imperial Federation. The donation was to be paid in two instalments of £5,000 each. Rhodes had paid the first half by cheque and it was left to Currey to implement payment of the second half. The way in which this sizeable sum was handed over is an interesting example of Rhodes's private financial transactions. 'One morning,' says Currey, 'Rhodes said to me, "Make out a cheque for £5,000, go and cash it, and bring the money to me here as soon as you can." I asked to whom the cheque was to be made out and he said "To Bearer" and in the counterfoil insert "For Self". I went off with the cheque to Hoares Bank . . . Without blinking an eyelid the teller required [*sic*], "How would you like it, sir?" and when a little taken aback I replied, "Well, in hundreds, please," he tossed me a bundle of fifty notes without even troubling to count them. That evening the money was handed to Parnell.'

While they were in London a command came for Rhodes to dine and sleep at Windsor. This led to a domestic crisis. Rhodes had no Court dress and no idea of what he should wear. After some hurried consultations, a Bond Street tailor was called in. Not until a few minutes before Rhodes's train was due to leave Paddington Station did a messenger come panting along the platform with a suitcase containing a suitable wardrobe. It was then discovered that he had not enough money on him to buy his train ticket. This was one of Rhodes's idiosyncrasies. He would gaily send his secretary to cash a cheque for £5,000 but, like royalty, never carried any ready cash on his person; more often than not, whoever happened to be with him at the time would have to provide him with funds which he invariably forgot to pay back. On this occasion Harry Currey was able to buy him a return ticket and give him a further two sovereigns as pocket money. The story goes that these two sovereigns mysteriously disappeared while he was at Windsor and he had to borrow more money from a fellow guest.

It may have been on this visit to Windsor that the Queen asked him what he was doing and he replied: 'I am doing my best to enlarge Your Majesty's dominions.' Legend records another exchange between Queen Victoria and Cecil Rhodes. Victoria, having heard of his reputation as a woman-hater, taxed him about it. 'How,' replied Rhodes courteously, 'can I hate a sex to which Your Majesty belongs?' His charm seems to have allayed the Queen's fears for when it was later suggested to Queen Victoria that Rhodes was indeed a woman-hater, she replied: 'Oh, I don't think that can be so, because he was very civil to me when he came here.'

The London visit came to an end and so did Harry Currey's career as a private secretary. The one event followed shortly after the other. On his return from England, Currey became engaged to be married. For some time the news of the betrothal was kept from Rhodes. When Currey at last announced that he was to be married, all hell broke loose. This was the occasion on which Rhodes stormed up and down the room screaming, 'Leave my house! Leave my house!'

The subject of Currey's engagement was not mentioned again until some days later when it was broached by Rhodes in a more subdued but equally curious fashion. It was late one evening; Currey was working in a room just off the dining-room and Rhodes was entertaining a guest in the drawing-room. Quite unexpectedly Rhodes left his guest and came into the dining-room to have a talk with Currey. He asked him when he was getting married and then, to the young man's amazement, said that he thought he was doing the right thing. He pointed out, says Currey, that 'we only live once, and that if one met a nice girl who could be a friend and a companion it was the right thing to try and marry her. In my case I had done the proper thing. For himself he said that he would miss me very much, that we always got on "exceedingly well" and that had I not proposed to get married we should doubtless have continued to live together until one or other of us died. He did not know or care whom he would get to succeed me . . .' As always when making a point, Rhodes went on for some time in the same vein. 'Then,' says Currey, 'he talked a good deal about his income, both present and prospective, and what he intends to do with it.' It was a puzzling conversation. Writing to his father the following day to describe the incident, Currey is clearly at a loss as to what to make of his moody, unpredictable employer. 'I feel that neither I nor any living man will ever "know" him,' he concludes. 'He does not want any living man to know him. His life and his interests seem mapped out in squares; and the man who is concerned with Square No. 6 must know nothing of Square No. 7.'

But was Rhodes's behaviour as inexplicable as it seemed to his secretary? To the uninvolved, his intention seems as obvious as his tactics were clumsy. First there were the conventional platitudes about Currey's forthcoming marriage. These were followed by an emphasis on their broken association and Rhodes's own loneliness. Then the conversation was switched to Rhodes's immense wealth and his grandiose schemes. It was all a matter of comparison. What was the companionship of a 'nice girl' when set against the life-long friendship with a wealthy man of destiny such as himself? When it was put like this, surely no young man in his right senses would sacrifice a glittering career for the sake of prosaic domesticity. 'I have never met anyone in my life,' Rhodes once said, 'whom it was not as easy to deal with as to fight.' He had tried fighting with Currey and he had failed. Was he now trying to make a deal with him? It is freely admitted that Rhodes considered every man to have his price and that even his most important opponents could be 'squared' as he put it. 'Can't you square the Pope?' he asked Parnell when he heard that the Irish leader was opposed by the priests. Money, position and influence; many a young man would have given his right arm for the opportunities that were now being paraded before Rhodes's secretary.

That Rhodes had not been sincere in his apparent approval of Currey's decision to marry, was made startlingly clear on the day of the wedding. The ceremony had just been performed. The guest of honour was Cecil John Rhodes. Chairman of De Beers Consolidated Mines, Chairman of the Consolidated Goldfields of South Africa, Prime Minister of the Cape, founder of a nation, guest of the Queen, host to the famous and one of the world's wealthiest men, Rhodes marched up to the nervous young bride and announced: 'I am very jealous of you.' And he was not joking.

After his marriage Harry Currey gave up his post as private secretary but continued in Rhodes's employ. On the surface, things seemed to continue as before. But not for long. There was a final quarrel and the two separated. With a fine sense of loyalty, Currey refused to speak of this last decisive quarrel but it was thought to have been caused by Rhodes's tendency to nepotism. Currey later became active in politics and gave his support to Rhodes's liberal opponents.

On the subject of his relationship with Rhodes, Currey always remained silent. 'Rhodes was in many ways a great man,' he was to write half a century later. Then he crossed out 'great' and substituted 'big'. 'But,' he continued, 'has any big man friends?

Does he not so give himself to his "cause" that there is no room left in his heart for people?'

Perhaps there had been room in Rhodes's heart for Harry Currey. If so, then it was something which Currey did not recognize. How could he? It was due to a deep-seated emotional need which Rhodes himself probably did not fully appreciate. How else can one explain the extraordinary demonstrations that preceded their parting? Was it the annoyance, the disappointment, the inconvenience of losing a valued secretary? Surely not. It is true that Rhodes was subject to violent outbursts of temper over trivialities but, provided they did not interfere with his plans, he quickly recovered and behaved reasonably. Nor was he likely to be seriously inconvenienced by Currey's departure. There were any number of talented, well-qualified civil servants at hand who would have been only too eager to take over a private secretary's duties. Indeed, Rhodes could have afforded an army of them. Had he not said himself that he did not care who replaced Currey?

No, there was more involved than the loss of a secretary. This was a case where Rhodes's emotions were engaged; frustrated emotions which became violent for the want of a conventional outlet. He had come to depend on this secretary for more than his correspondence. He had adopted Currey, shared his home with him, made him part of his life. Currey was always there, he could be confided in and he made no demands. In fact, one suspects that in Harry Currey Rhodes sought a second Neville Pickering. How could Currey have known what this implied?

*

'I'll take their —— country from them!' Rhodes had shouted in Beira in 1891. It was no idle threat. The idea of taking over Portuguese East Africa was very much in his mind just then. Earlier that same year he had met President Kruger in Pretoria and had suggested that if the Transvaal would work with him, they could take over Delagoa Bay in the province of Lourenço Marques and thus give the Transvaal an outlet to the sea. President Kruger later professed himself to have been horrified at the idea of seizing a neighbouring territory. But Rhodes had gone even further. Unknown to the Boer President, he had made an offer to buy from the Portuguese, not only Delagoa Bay but the entire province of Lourenço Marques. The Portuguese had turned down the offer. All that Rhodes could do was ensure that the Portuguese made no encroachments in Mashonaland and, for the time being, he let the matter rest; he no doubt believed that he would be able to deal with the Portuguese in his own good time. But these overtures are an indication of the direction in which his mind was working. The annexation of countries was becoming second nature to him. He had secured Bechuanaland, occupied Mashonaland and his eyes were already turned further north towards Uganda. It was all a matter of choosing the right moment and of employing the most effective methods.

But before he could move into any new territory, there was a problem to be settled nearer home. Lobengula was proving a troublesome neighbour. Friction was inevitable. Although the Matabele King had reluctantly resigned himself to the white settlers in Mashonaland, it was impossible for him to admit any curtailment of his power over the Mashona themselves. To acknowledge such a loss of authority would have been an affront to the traditions of the Matabele and would have lowered him in the eyes of his own people. The Mashona, he insisted, were his 'dogs' and he continued to regard them as such. In the frequent disputes over cattle raids between the Matabele and the Mashona, the King's warriors did not hesitate to pursue their enemies into Mashonaland and there punish them. This was all very well, but the Mashona were nominally under the protection of the Chartered Company. Labour was short and the white settlers did not relish the idea of having their employees slaughtered before their eyes. And there was more to it than that. The settlers had found that this new country fell far short of their expectations. 'Mashonaland, so far as is known, and much is known,' declared Lord Randolph Churchill, who visited the territory in 1891, 'is neither an Arcadia nor an El Dorado.' The grass upon which Lobengula's cattle grazed began to look much greener than the settlers' own.

Things came to a head with a particularly bloody massacre at Fort Victoria in July 1893. Dr Jameson, who was now acting as the administrator of Mashonaland, arrived on the scene to find the road littered with the corpses of butchered Mashona and the white inhabitants in a state of panic. The time had obviously come to take decisive action. Jameson telegraphed to Rhodes, who wired back: 'Read Luke xiv 31.' This, Jameson found, read: 'Or what king, going to make war against another king, sitteth not down first, and consulteth whether he be able with 10,000 to meet him that cometh against him with 20,000?' When Jameson replied that he had read the text and it was 'all right', Rhodes, complaining of the expense, sold some 50,000 Chartered shares to raise the necessary funds, and prepared for war. Volunteers were raised for the campaign with a promise of a farm of 6,000 acres and twenty gold claims. Three months later they moved against Lobengula.

It was a short war; hardly a war at all, in fact. Jameson moved his men off in the middle of October and by 4th November the white troops were marching into Lobengula's ruined and deserted kraal. Any suggestion that the war was intended simply as a punitive measure was quickly forgotten. Within a month of occupying Lobengula's capital, the European settlement of Bulawayo was fully marked out.

For Lobengula, defeat was quickly followed by death. After he had fled from the royal kraal, Jameson sent word that if he returned he would be 'kindly treated'. But by then the King had no faith in the cheery little doctor. He spurned the offer as 'a trap'. Shortly afterwards it was learned that Lobengula was dead. The cause of his death is not certain: it was thought to be small-pox but the more sentimental put it down to a broken heart. In either case, he had long since passed the stage where Dr Jameson's remedies could prove effective. Right up to the end the old King had tried to negotiate a peace with the white men. He had no quarrel with the Chartered Company and his *impis* had always been instructed that no white person should be harmed in their raids on the Mashona. One of the King's last acts had been to ensure the safety of two white traders at his kraal. It would, of course, be ridiculous to weep over the passing of the bloodthirsty Matabele régime but, on the other hand, there is little to be said for those who overthrew this savage nation.

Rhodes now had both Mashonaland and Matabeleland: two territories which were to bear his name. That the new country should be called after its founder was inevitable and there had been various suggestions as to the form this name should take. 'Rhodesland' had been considered and so, in all seriousness, had

'Cecilia'; but for some time it had been commonly known by the name which was finally adopted: Rhodesia. When, at the beginning of 1895, this name was officially recognized, Rhodes was jubilant. 'Has anyone else had a country called after their name?' he exclaimed. 'Now I don't care a damn what they do with me!' He spoke too soon. In a few months he would be very concerned about what was to be done with him.

Already he had embarked upon a course of action which was to threaten his entire career. Foolhardy in retrospect, it was, in essence, simply a new approach to an old problem. It concerned the unification of South Africa. Unless it were achieved, Rhodes's empire would be built on uncertain foundations and all his other schemes in Africa would be jeopardized. From the time he had assumed the Premiership of the Cape he had worked patiently at welding the four states of South Africa—the two British colonies, the Cape and Natal, and the two Boer Republics, the Orange Free State and the Transvaal—into a single political entity. It was a formidable undertaking.

At first he attempted to tackle the problem diplomatically. A union which entailed the breaking down of racial as well as territorial barriers could only be achieved gradually. To start with it was necessary to dispel the antagonisms which existed between the English and Dutch in southern Africa and to strengthen the economic ties between the British colonies and the Boer Republics. With these objectives in mind, he had set about cultivating the Afrikander Bond in the Cape and, at the same time, pressing for a common railway system and a customs union for the four states. As was to be expected, his motives came under suspicion. It was thought that he was out to destroy his neighbours in the same way as he had destroyed his rivals at Kimberley. To amalgamate with Rhodes was regarded as the first step into oblivion.

But, whatever their merits or defects, his schemes were destined to fail. He might make some progress with Natal and the Orange Free State, but there was never a hope of making any headway with the Transvaal as long as the ageing Paul Kruger presided at Pretoria. At every turn Rhodes was to find his plans frustrated by the shrewd and implacably hostile old President. And there seemed to be nothing he could do about it. Practised as he was in the art of dealing with rival financiers, of squaring civil servants and buying off political opponents, he was quite helpless when faced with a nationalistic bigot like himself. For this is what Kruger was. Unalike as they were in every other respect, the one thing that Cecil Rhodes and Paul Kruger could be said to have in common was their fanaticism.

If Rhodes considered the British to be mankind's favoured race, Kruger was equally convinced that the Boers were the elect of God. Inspired by a crude, unyielding Calvinism and reared in the isolation of the veld, the Boers of the Transvaal were a very different breed from the Dutch colonists of the Cape. Their outlook was as narrow as their experience of life outside their own country was limited. They viewed the world across the pages of the Old Testament and equated themselves with the Children of Israel—God's Chosen People. For them British rule in the Cape represented the bondage from which they had fled, when Kruger was a child, and the Transvaal was the Promised Land to which they had been Divinely led. It was a land which they held as a sacred trust. Kruger was determined that it should remain inviolate. He had no intention of tying his country to the neighbouring British colonies and certainly wanted no dealings with Rhodes, whom he is said to have regarded as 'the foul fiend himself'.

In his desire for independence, however, the Boer President was faced with a problem of geography. The Transvaal was an inland country and it was essential that it obtain an outlet to the sea. Only by securing a seaport could Kruger hope to free himself from dependence on the British colonies. The situation had been made even more precarious by Rhodes's activities. With the annexation of Bechuanaland to the west and the development of Rhodesia to the north of the Transvaal, the Boers were rapidly being encircled. Any fears they may have had on this score were fully confirmed when all chance of their reaching the eastern seaboard through Swaziland was foiled by the British annexation of the coast line up to Portuguese East Africa. 'Now,' said Kruger, 'they have shut me up in a kraal'. His only hope lay in the railway that had been built between Pretoria and Delagoa Bay: better the Portuguese than the British. Rhodes, of course, was fully aware of the importance of Delagoa Bay to the Transvaal. Had he not dangled it before the old President at the time when he was trying to buy it from Portugal? If he had succeeded either in luring the President into his net or in purchasing the seaport, his Transvaal problem would have been solved: Kruger would have been at his mercy. But Portugal would not sell and Kruger would not bite. The railway line between Portuguese East Africa and the Transvaal went ahead and with its completion the Boer President began using it as a weapon to free himself from the British colonies. It posed a very real threat to Rhodes's dream of a United States of South Africa.

And other threats began to loom. The more Kruger became shut up in his kraal, the more necessary it became for him to find allies who might come to his rescue. He began to look to the country that Rhodes feared most: Germany. 'I know I may count on the Germans in the future,' said Kruger at a banquet in Pretoria, and went on to refer to Germany preparing his stripling Republic for the time when it would wear 'larger clothes'. To Rhodes this was a matter of great concern. Bechuanaland was still his 'Suez Canal' and an alliance between the Germans to the west of it and the Boers to the east could jeopardize all his achievements. Obviously he would have to do something about President Paul Kruger.

An excuse to take action against the Government of the Transvaal was not difficult for him to find. There was a substantial body of Transvaal residents who were as anxious as he to see the downfall of the Kruger régime. These were the gold-miners of the Witwatersrand; the 'Uitlanders' as all foreigners were called in the Transvaal. From the time these fortune-hunters had invaded his country in 1886, Kruger had viewed them with suspicion. Much as he welcomed the new wealth which the discovery of gold had brought to his depleted exchequer, he had no intention of allowing it to corrupt his people. Whatever happened, the Boer nation must retain its independence: the burghers must be free to pursue their God-appointed mission. The new-found riches must be handled with caution and the forces of Mammon kept at bay. The miners could dig for gold, enrich themselves and pay their taxes, but they could be allowed no say in the government of their adopted country. They must abide by the laws of the Transvaal but they could not make them. His stand was both a matter of principle and politics. Not only did he fear the influence of the Uitlanders but he was alarmed at their numbers. Within a very short time the mining community had grown to such a size that, if equal franchise were granted, the newcomers could easily outvote the Transvaal burghers.

The restrictions which Kruger imposed on the mining community were harsh, unimaginative and frustrating. Instead of heeding the advice given to him by President Brand of the Free State to 'make friends with his Uitlanders', he seemed to go out of his way to make life as difficult as possible for the miners. Not only did he exclude them from the Transvaal Volksraad but, in his efforts to control their activities, left them very little say over their own affairs. Johannesburg, a rapidly developing town which had been founded by the predominantly English-speaking Uitlanders, continued to be treated as a mining camp administered by a handful of Boer officials. Local government was incompetent and often dishonest, taxation was heavy and the only instruction available in the State schools was conducted in Dutch. The efficiency of the mines suffered from the fact that monopolies and concessions for such vital commodities as dynamite and coal were farmed out to Dutch and German adventurers. The cost of living in Johannesburg rose, the crime rate soared, the expense of operating the mines increased and the grievances of the Uitlanders were multiplied by the day. In vain did they protest against the unfair treatment to which they were subjected. Kruger treated their demands with contempt. 'Their rights!' he is said to have exclaimed. 'Yes, they'll get their rights—over my dead body.'

Faced with this intransigent attitude, it became increasingly obvious to the miners that they could not expect an improvement of their lot until they had a voice in the central Government of the Transvaal. They began to agitate for the vote. This change of tactics got them no further. In 1893, a petition which they presented to the Volksraad was scornfully dismissed. The following year, a disorderly Johannesburg audience retaliated by openly insulting the Boer President when he came to address them. Further unseemly incidents followed and resentment mounted on each side. Some of the Uitlanders began to talk about revolt. Kruger, they argued, would only see reason if a gun was held to his head and the time was approaching when it would be necessary to do just that.

Things had reached this stage when Rhodes decided to step in. Although he was the head of one of the biggest mining concerns on the Rand, he had, until now, kept somewhat aloof from the squabbles between Kruger and the Uitlanders. The idea of supporting the miners in their quarrel did not occur to him, so it is said, until some time in September 1894. During that month he and Jameson were touring Rhodesia in the company of John Hays Hammond, an American mining engineer from Johannesburg. Hammond had been taken along in order to give an opinion on the mineral potential of the Chartered Company's lands, but the main topic discussed appears to have been the resentment which the Uitlanders harboured against the Transvaal Government. It was a subject in which Hammond was well versed. 'Unless a radical change is made,' he said, 'there will be a rising of the people of Johannesburg.' Whether or not this was the first time Rhodes had entertained the thought, there can be no doubt that the idea of a revolution in the Transvaal appealed to him. Not only would it put an end to Kruger's stranglehold on the mining industry but it would also stop his interference in Rhodes's schemes for a united South Africa. All things considered, it was the quickest and easiest solution to a great many of his problems.

At the end of the year Rhodes and Jameson visited London. While they were there Rhodes saw Lord Rosebery, Prime Minister in the tottering Liberal Government. Among the things they discussed was the possibility of the Bechuanaland Protectorate being transferred to the Chartered Company. Later these talks were to assume a sinister significance. The suspicion that the British Government was privy to Rhodes's plans for taking over the Transvaal can be dated from this time.

There was no doubt concerning Rhodes's involvement with the projected rising on the Rand. From the time he entered upon the scene, the Uitlanders' vague threats began to take on a definite shape. A plan was evolved and organization went ahead. The first concern was to arm Johannesburg. This had to be done in a way which would not arouse the Boers' suspicion. The actual ordering of guns and ammunition presented no problems. Bought by Rhodes and Alfred Beit, the arms arrived at the Chartered Company's depot in Cape Town as equipment for the Company's police. To get them to Johannesburg was more difficult. First they were sent to Kimberley where they were stored at De Beers and then concealed in the false bottoms of oil drums and bags of coke. Thus disguised, they were transferred by rail to Pickering and Co. of Port Elizabeth, a firm which acted as agents for De Beers and was owned by Neville Pickering's eldest brother, Edward. From here the railway trucks were diverted to the Johannesburg line and, upon arrival at the Rand, were unloaded at various mines and the arms hidden underground.

Equipping a citizen force with arms, however, was not enough to ensure the success of the rising. Although the Uitlanders far outnumbered the Boers, they were mostly miners and business men with little experience of fighting. Matched against the Boers, who were renowned for their marksmanship and guerrilla tactics, their superior numbers would count for little. Rhodes had no intention of leaving the rebellion to a crowd of enthusiastic amateurs. What is more, he was not at all certain how far he could trust the Uitlanders to fall in with his schemes. There would be no advantage in swopping Kruger for an equally obstinate mining magnate. It was clearly necessary for him to have his own man on the spot to influence the Uitlanders from the outset. He needed a man who would have played a conspicuous part in the rebellion and won for himself a reputation which could not be challenged; a man such as Jameson who was already something of a popular hero after his successes in the Matabele campaign. With Jameson established among the triumphant Uitlanders, Rhodes could appear on the scene and dictate the final settlement. It was therefore decided that the Uitlanders should be assisted by an outside force; a force which would be sufficiently well equipped and well led to play a decisive role in the insurrection.

As it happened, it was possible to place such a force on the border of the Transvaal without arousing undue suspicion. Towards the end of 1895, the Chartered Company was ceded a strip of Bechuanaland for the purpose of building a railway line to connect the Cape with Rhodesia. As soon as possession of this strip was confirmed, Dr Jameson, assisted by some army officers, started to muster an armed corps in Bechuanaland, ostensibly to guard the railway construction from marauding tribesmen. This was a rather weak excuse for the presence of such a large body of men, but it was hoped that Jameson would not be there long enough for his activities to be disputed.

The plot was by no means confined to South Africa. Once again Rhodes had his eye on the power of the Imperial Factor. When the time came for him to go to Johannesburg after the rebellion, he intended to have the British High Commissioner in tow. This would give his settlement a semblance of legality. For this reason he had arranged for his old friend, Sir Hercules Robinson, to be reappointed as High Commissioner at Cape Town. As soon as the arming of the Uitlanders was under way, Sir Hercules was informed that momentous events were afoot in the Transvaal. Precisely how much the High Commissioner was told was later to become a matter of some speculation. An even bigger question mark was to arise over the extent to which the Colonial Secretary, Joseph Chamberlain, was involved in the affair. There is no doubt that Chamberlain knew something of Rhodes's plans. Information had been passed to the Colonial Office by Rhodes's agents in London. The most active of these agents was another of Rhodes's doctor friends, Dr Rutherfoord Harris. Rhodes and the doctor had known each other for some years.

Rutherfoord Harris, an unpopular, bumptious, and somewhat sinister man, had been employed as the South African Secretary of the Chartered Company and was now acting as a highly placed odd-job man for Rhodes. He has been described as Rhodes's 'evil genius'. Certainly he was an unfortunate choice for the delicate mission with which he was now entrusted. It was he who had been delegated by Rhodes to negotiate with the Colonial Office for the transference of Bechuanaland to the Chartered Company. At first it was hoped that the entire Bechuanaland Protectorate would be divided between the Cape Government and the Chartered Company—with the Company taking the biggest slice. But the Colonial Office was hesitant. The need for a strip along the eastern border of Bechuanaland—to accommodate Rhodes's railway—was recognized, but Chamberlain postponed his decision on the rest of the Protectorate. In the course of his negotiations, Harris had four interviews with Mr Chamberlain and, together with other agents of the Chartered Company, discussed the matter with various Colonial Office officials. Exactly what was said at these talks remains a mystery. The connection between the negotiations for Bechuanaland and the unrest in the Transvaal has, in fact, produced one of the most tantalizing questions ever posed concerning the activities of Cecil Rhodes. It is fairly certain that Chamberlain and his officials knew something of what was planned; but how much was said by Rhodes's agents and how far Chamberlain committed himself to the plot remains a mystery.

Part of the answer was contained in certain telegrams which Harris and others sent to Rhodes at this time. It is possible that these telegrams distorted Chamberlain's views. Harris, for instance, had a tendency to interpret conversations to suit his own ends and his wording of telegrams was often equivocal. The messages sent to Rhodes by his agents at this time were to be the subject of considerable debate. So potentially explosive were they that eight of the most vital telegrams were later suppressed by Rhodes and at least one of them disappeared completely. The mystery of the 'missing telegrams' and the part played by Joseph Chamberlain in Rhodes's conspiracy has never been satisfactorily solved.

From the very beginning the proposed rebellion seemed destined to fail. It was too hastily conceived and too glaringly obvious. The over-all plan was sketchy and uninspired, it contained no safety valves and, most disastrous of all, lacked any semblance of co-ordination. With Rhodes in Cape Town, Jameson in Bechuanaland and the Uitlanders in Johannesburg, there was no central point of control and communication between the three centres was restricted to vaguely coded telegrams: little or no allowance was made for emergency action. The entire affair was like an elaborate schoolboy prank, thought up on the spur of the moment and carried through regardless of the consequences.

What made Rhodes agree to such a madcap scheme? Opinion varies. Some put it down to his increasing arrogance. They say that success had gone to his head and, urged on by the sycophants who surrounded him, he had become convinced of his own infallibility. Old friends who met him at this time were shocked by the contemptuous way in which he dismissed even a hint of opposition. 'Newspapers,' he is said to have shouted; 'do you think I care a continental fig what the newspapers may say? I am strong enough to do what I choose in spite of the whole pack of them.' It was the conventional voice of the dictator. Others attribute his outbursts to his failing health. At this time he is said to have become haggard-looking, his hair was turning grey and he had lost weight. His fear of a further heart attack had made him neurotic. All too conscious that his life might be cut short, he was willing to take further risks in order to complete his great task. This, it is said, was the root cause of his growing impatience and displays of petulance. Whatever the reason, the result was disastrous.

The rising was planned for the end of December 1895. Jameson had been provided with an undated letter calling for him to rescue the 'thousands of unarmed men, women and children of our race . . . at the mercy of well armed Boers'. It was intended that he should date the letter at the appropriate time and ride in. But as the day for the rising drew nearer some of the Uitlanders began to have second thoughts. They did not think themselves sufficiently prepared; the arms that had been smuggled into Johannesburg fell short of what they had expected; Jameson's force was smaller than had been promised; there were arguments as to what flag should be raised if the rebellion was successful . . .

The telegraph wires between Johannesburg and Cape Town buzzed with frantic messages. It was decided to postpone the rising. Messengers were sent to stop Jameson. But by then things had gone too far. The little doctor refused to be put off. He was tired of the endless dithering. 'I received so many messages from day to day,' he was later to say, 'now telling me to come, then to delay starting, that I thought it best to make up their minds for them, before the Boers had time to get together.' Assuring his subordinates that the venture had the blessing of the Imperial authorities, he sent a last telegram to Rhodes, cut the telegraph wires and, on Sunday, 29th December, led his force across the Transvaal border. He was much too late. The Boers had assembled and were waiting for him at Doornkop, some twenty miles outside Johannesburg. After a short fight he surrendered and he and his men were taken to Pretoria as prisoners.

In Cape Town, Rhodes had received Jameson's last telegram and immediately drafted a reply telling the doctor that he was not to move. But it was Sunday and the telegraph office was closed for the afternoon. By the time Rhodes's reply was transmitted, Jameson had cut the wires.

The realization that he had been too late to stop the raid stunned Rhodes. 'Old Jameson has upset my apple cart . . .' he told a visitor. 'I thought I had stopped him . . . poor old Jameson. Twenty years we have been friends, and now he goes in to ruin me.' The following day he handed in his resignation as Prime Minister of the Cape. For six days he was 'worried to death' and hardly slept. But at last he pulled himself together. He was determined, whatever else happened, to keep the Chartered Company afloat.

After paying a hurried visit to Kimberley, he sailed for England on 15th January, 1896.

CHAPTER SIX

The Brilliant Years

For Princess Catherine Radziwill, life in St Petersburg, where she made her headquarters during the 1880s, was a far cry from her existence in Berlin. In the first place, the city itself was so different. Whereas Berlin was a provincial town in the process of being transformed into an Imperial capital, St Petersburg had been especially designed as the principal city of a great empire. Tsar Peter the Great, in his determination to open a window from Russia on to the western world, had chosen the flat marshlands where the river Neva flowed into the Baltic Sea and there raised a city that was undeniably western in character. With its huge baroque palaces, its sweeping boulevards, its formal gardens, its ornamental bridges and its wide balustrated quays, it was the epitome of an Imperial capital. In atmosphere too, it was quite different from Berlin. Where Prussian society was narrow and insular, the St Petersburg *haut monde* was sophisticated, Frenchified and cosmopolitan. The season, beginning on New Year's Day and lasting until Lent, was a round of balls, receptions, visits to the opera and the ballet and, for the men, the less edifying delights of the gambling clubs and the gipsy cafés. In place of the formal old Emperor Wilhelm and the punctilious Empress Augusta, were the massive Tsar Alexander III and the beautiful Empress Marie Fedorovna—sister of the no less lovely Princess of Wales. As the Empress Augusta had set the tone of the stuffy Prussian Court, so did the elegance, the vivacity and light-heartedness of the Empress Marie Fedorovna affect the life of the Russian Court. Of the stolid self-consciousness of the German capital, there was hardly a trace in St Petersburg.

Catherine later claimed that returning to Russia gave her not only a sense of freedom but a feeling of security. 'I was related

to half of St Petersburg society,' she says, 'and found myself at
once among my own, and protected on all sides by the great
social position of my family. I had plenty of money, and we
bought a very pretty house, where we began to see and entertain
our friends as much as we liked. Very soon I made a great
position for myself, and had a salon which became the meeting
place of a set of intelligent and clever people . . . Those years
were the brilliant ones of my life.'

Outwardly the pattern of these 'brilliant years' followed that
of most Russian aristocrats. Life was centred on the winter
season in St Petersburg, while the summer months were spent
at fashionable European resorts. In the autumn and early winter
there would be a brief respite while the wealthy Russians rested
at their country estates. For Catherine this period of temporary
retirement meant a rather dreary few months at Pjatino, her
estate on the Volga. It was at Pjatino that her second son and
fifth child was born on 21st January, 1888, a couple of months
before her father died. The birth of this boy, Michel-Casimir,
completed the Radziwill family. Catherine took only a per-
functory interest in her children. She was content to leave their
upbringing to her long-suffering husband and his family. As
soon as her daughters were old enough, they were sent to
Vienna to complete their education in the care of Prince Wilhelm
Radziwill's eldest sister, Princess Mathilde Windisch-Graetz.
In later years the three girls were to regard Vienna as their
home and to remember their mother with understandable
prejudice. Of all the children Nicholas, the elder son, was
Catherine's favourite, but even he saw little of his mother during
these early years in Russia.

Her attitude towards her family is well illustrated by her
departure from Pjatino immediately after the birth of her
youngest child. Leaving the infant in his father's care, she set off
at once for St Petersburg. The season had just started and she
was not going to allow the birth of a child to spoil her fun.
During the winter season of 1888, no one was more active in
St Petersburg than the carefree Princess Radziwill.

The attractions of the Russian capital were not, of course,
entirely social. Catherine was by no means averse to drawing-
room gossip but, as had been the case in Berlin, the political
scene aroused her real interest. Affairs of state would always

129

assume more importance in the life of Princess Radziwill than the affairs of her neighbours. Politics was her particular forte and political intrigue her fatal weakness.

In St Petersburg she was well placed for exercising her political talents. She was able to count some of the most influential ministers in the Russian Government among her friends. This not only added to her importance but had a distinct effect on her political views. Whereas in Berlin she had championed the opposition parties and given the impression of being a crypto-socialist, in St Petersburg she emerged as a convinced supporter of Alexander III's autocratic régime. This switch in her political sympathies was not entirely due to her new friends; it was largely the result of a personal prejudice and a deep sense of family loyalty. For it had been the relatively liberal Alexander II—the 'Tsar-Liberator'—who had expelled her father from the Russian Court, and Catherine was prepared to give her support to anyone who opposed the former Tsar's policies. Her allegiance to the 'Tsar-Liberator's' son was therefore automatic. Alexander III was convinced that his father had been assassinated by Russian liberals and that the only way to rule the Russian Empire was by restoring the absolutism of his grandfather, Nicholas I. Throughout his thirteen-year reign, the Tsar Alexander III dedicated himself to crushing all opposition to autocracy. There was no parliament, political opponents were sent to Siberia, a heavy censorship was imposed on the Press and political discussion reduced to a minimum.

Catherine accepted this reactionary régime with all the enthusiasm she had previously shown for German socialism. She considered Alexander III to be 'conscientious, straightforward, honest and kind' and was convinced that his firm guidance was responsible for saving Russia from chaos. She refused to admit that the Tsar's iron-fisted rule had killed political discussion in Russia.

In some respects her indulgence towards the Russian autocracy is surprising. Her own experience had shown her how dangerous outspoken criticism of the régime could be. In the early years of Alexander III's reign her friend and collaborator, Yuliana Glinka, had been exiled from Russia for her part in the writing of *St Petersburg Society*. And on at least one other occasion, during her visit to Russia in 1881, shortly after

Alexander III's accession to the throne, Catherine had cause for alarm over a political indiscretion. On that occasion, at a ball in Moscow, her partner, Prince Alexander of Battenberg, who was disliked by the Tsar, had severely criticized the Russian Government. Catherine had passed on the gist of this conversation to Donald Mackenzie Wallace, the correspondent of *The Times* of London, whom she had recently met in Constantinople. 'One may imagine my horror,' she says, 'when a month or two afterwards, I found in *The Times* the whole account of my conversation with Prince Alexander, accompanied by the remark that the story had come from a Russian lady. I nearly had a fit.' Fortunately for her, the identity of the Russian lady was never discovered but Prince Alexander never forgave her for discrediting him even further in the eyes of the Tsar. 'I must confess,' says Catherine, 'he had reasons for being angry, for I certainly ought not to have mentioned to anyone what he told me, and I could not defend my conduct. But the adventure was a lesson to me, and after that I held my tongue whenever I was made the recipient of confidences.'

But the lesson was one which she was incapable of learning. She could never resist making use of this kind of secret. No sooner was she established in St Petersburg than she was up to her neck in further intrigue. The little comedy which followed her return to the Russian capital in 1888 provided a good illustration of her brand of political activity.

Arriving in St Petersburg, she put up at the fashionable Hotel de l'Europe. The season was well under way and the hotel was full of distinguished visitors. Prominent among them was Mme Olga Novikoff, an influential Russian journalist who was noted for her pro-British sympathies. Mme Novikoff had spent a great many years working for an alliance between Britain and Russia. She was well known in London, where she wrote under the pseudonym 'O.K.', and numbered several British statesmen —including Mr Gladstone—among her personal friends. When Catherine met her at the Hotel de l'Europe, Mme Novikoff was actively engaged in one of her many attempts to improve the relationship between the British and Russian Governments. To assist her in her schemes, she had enlisted the support of W. T. Stead who, besides being a friend of Cecil Rhodes, was a keen advocate of the Russo-British alliance. Stead was also staying at the Hotel de l'Europe and Mme Novikoff introduced him to Catherine. They appear to have made a considerable impression on each other. The famous English journalist was intrigued by Catherine's story. 'She was then virtually under sentence of banishment from Berlin by decree of Prince Bismarck, who regarded her as an enemy by no means to be despised,' he was later to recall. 'She had written a novel which made no small sensation at the time, owing to the side-lights which it threw upon the inside track of German politics . . . and was recognized both in St Petersburg and Berlin not only as a lady of great personal charm, but as a political personage of no small influence.' Catherine found Stead interesting for quite different reasons. Mme Novikoff had given her no indication of what Stead was doing in St Petersburg and the Princess suspected that his presence at the Hotel de l'Europe boded ill for the plot which she herself was busy hatching.

Catherine's current activities were again closely allied to those of her old friend Mme Juliette Adam. Between them, the two women were hoping to pull off a diplomatic *coup* of considerable importance. With a fervour which matched that of Mme Novikoff, Princess Radziwill, the supporter of Imperial Russia, and Mme Adam, the champion of Republican France, were working for a *rapprochement* between their two countries. The idea of a Franco-Russian alliance was one which Juliette Adam had cherished since the foundation of the Third French Republic. She saw in such an alliance the solution to Republican France's isolation in Europe and a safeguard against the perennial threat of German aggression. The negotiations upon which she and Catherine were embarked, however, had originated from a source which many French Republicans regarded with grave suspicion. They had been instigated by the supporters of that popular, if over-rated, darling of the French right wing— General Boulanger. It was one of Boulanger's followers, Lucien Millevoye, who had approached Mme Adam with a scheme for a Franco-Russian alliance. According to Catherine, the liberal Mme Adam had no idea that Millevoye was acting for the conservative Boulangists, and had agreed to assist him in the cause of Republican France. Be this as it may, Millevoye found a valuable ally in Juliette Adam. Not only was she able to offer him Princess Radziwill's assistance in St Petersburg, but she provided him with 'certain political documents calculated to help him in his perilous adventure'. In order that these documents could be taken to Russia without arousing suspicion, a third woman was brought into the affair. This was the beautiful Maud Gonne, a fiery Irish patriot who was later to achieve fame by relentlessly opposing British domination in Ireland. Miss Gonne had her own reasons for accepting the mission. 'It was certainly against the whole English diplomacy,' she says, 'so I did not hesitate and that night I started for St Petersburg with the documents sewn into my dress.'

On her arrival in the Russian capital, Maud Gonne joined the other political agents staying at the Hotel de l'Europe. Following her instructions, Miss Gonne immediately arranged to meet Catherine. 'Princess Radziwill,' she afterwards wrote, '[was] a charming and beautiful Pole who had dabbled a little in politics and, in spite of being the mother of eight [sic] children, looked surprisingly young. We liked each other and she took me to parties with her.' But Catherine had other uses for the lovely Miss Gonne. Still suspecting that W. T. Stead might be on the track of their own secret negotiations, Catherine asked her new friend to talk to the English journalist and try and find out what he was doing in Russia. The result of Maud Gonne's discreet inquiries was somewhat unexpected. Stead was unable to resist a beautiful young woman. Instead of confiding his political secrets to the inquisitive Irish girl, he mistook her intentions entirely and wrote her a 'very amorous letter'.

By now the suspicions of Mme Novikoff had been aroused. The attentions paid by Princess Radziwill and Miss Gonne to Stead, her protégé, had not escaped the astute Mme Novikoff. Soon after receiving Stead's amorous letter, Maud Gonne was surprised, on returning from a party, to find Mme Novikoff waiting for her in her hotel room. This was hardly the hour for a polite social call. It was not until the following morning that Miss Gonne discovered the real reason for Mme Novikoff's visit. To her amazement Stead came stamping into her room to accuse her and Mme Novikoff of making fun of his love letter. He told her that Mme Novikoff had quoted extracts from the letter and he was convinced that Maud Gonne had shown it to her. Maud Gonne realized that while Mme Novikoff had been waiting, she had opened her writing desk and read her letters.

As soon as the truth dawned on her, Maud Gonne pushed the protesting Stead out of her room and hurried off to find Princess Radziwill. 'I had to warn Catherine,' she says, 'that Mme Novikoff was working for an English alliance and was responsible for Stead.'

Mme Novikoff's intervention had come too late. By this time Maud Gonne's mysterious documents were in the hands of the Russian Government. 'Through an introduction which I procured for her,' says Catherine, 'the documents were handed over to M. Pobedonosteff, the Procurator of the Holy Synod, and by him put under the eyes of Alexander III. The result was the despatch, some time later, of the Russian squadron to Toulon.' Maud Gonne was equally convinced of the success of her mission. She says that the safe delivery of the documents was responsible for paving the way for the Franco-Russian Entente two years later which marked the beginning of an alliance which was to change the whole of European diplomacy. Only Juliette Adam appears to have been disappointed with the outcome of these negotiations. 'Mme Adam,' says Catherine, 'was furious when she heard that Millevoye, instead of pleading the cause of the Republic, had tried to put forward that of General Boulanger.'

But what is particularly interesting about this conspiratorial escapade, is the light which it throws on Princess Radziwill's world. With secret documents sewn into dresses, writing-tables being rifled and women darting in and out of hotel rooms, it contains all the ingredients of a French farce. Yet there can be no doubt that the incidents took place. At least four of those involved—Catherine, Stead, Maud Gonne and Mme Novikoff—have referred to them, independently of each other, in their memoirs. This odd mixture of high politics and low comedy was to be repeated in many of Princess Radziwill's later activities. Only by an understanding of this world of theatrical intrigue is it possible to appreciate the often extraordinary behaviour of the Princess and her apparent lack of concern for accepted values.

*

In the year 1891 Catherine and her husband spent eight months on Jersey after the illness of their elder son Nicholas had made it necessary for them to escape the rigours of the long

Russian winter. It was probably during this stay that a friendship developed between the Radziwill family and Prince Gebhard
Blücher von Wahlstatt. Prince Blücher, a descendant of Marshal
Blücher of Waterloo fame, was then a man in his middle fifties.
Two years earlier he had married for a second time and was
living on the island of Herm with his wife and one-year-old
son, Lothair. He was a rich, pompous and incredibly mean man
who had quarrelled with everyone. 'Amongst my father's most
marked and unusual oddities,' recalled his eldest son, 'was a feud
with the whole world which even extended to his ancestors . . .
his feuds, amassing money, and escaping taxation became the
three ruling passions of his life.' It was to escape taxation that
Prince Blücher had moved from Germany—where Catherine
had first met him—and taken up residence in the Channel
Islands. Despite all Prince Gebhard's unprepossessing qualities,
the Radziwills seem to have got on well with the Blücher family.
The friendship which now developed was to have a lasting effect
on the lives of Catherine's children.

The stay on Jersey was important to Catherine for another
reason. It was during the months that she spent in the Channel
Islands that she paid her first visit to England. She already
numbered a great many English people among her friends and
regularly read the English newspapers but had never before
visited the country. Surprisingly, she has little to say about
these visits to England in 1891. Apart from recording that 'we
often went to London', her only written impression was of a visit
she paid to Lord and Lady Salisbury at Hatfield House. She first
met Lord Salisbury when he accompanied Disraeli to the Berlin
Conference and, in 1884, while on holiday in Dieppe, she appears
to have made friends with Lady Salisbury. Meeting them now
at Hatfield House was, she claims, a significant experience for
her. 'They belonged to that rare type, which disappears every
day,' she wrote, 'of the real Grand Seigneurs, invariably cour-
teous, invariably amiable, invariably kind and invariably interesting. The very air one breathed had something different from
that of other places.' By the time she came to write this account,
she would have an ulterior motive for emphasizing her friendship with Lord and Lady Salisbury. Her familiarity with Hatfield
House might not have been as close as she later liked to pretend.
However, it seems reasonably certain that she visited the

Salisburys from time to time, and her admiration for them was probably quite genuine.

Two years later she paid a more eventful visit to England. In 1893 her eldest daughter Louise was presented at the Court of St Petersburg. 'And,' says Catherine, 'we thought it to her advantage to take her to England, thus giving her the opportunity of spending a season in London.' Catherine and Louise arrived in London in April 1893 and remained there for three months. The visit was a great success; more so for Catherine than for the seventeen-year-old Louise.

Much of their time was spent sightseeing. British politics were, of course, an added attraction and Catherine speaks of her meetings with various Liberal politicians. Her English friends were mostly Conservatives but it was the ruling Liberal party which interested Princess Radziwill. She was forced to admit that she found Gladstone, whom she met at a dinner at the Russian Embassy, disappointing. She thought him colourless when compared with her memories of Disraeli. 'And yet,' she says, 'as a whole, I found myself far more in sympathy with Mr Gladstone's opinions.' It was a further example of her unresolved political views. A socialist sympathizer in Berlin, an ardent Imperialist in St Petersburg, she was, it would seem, a Liberal in London.

For all her cultural and political preoccupations, Catherine did not neglect the real purpose of her London visit. Her daughter was introduced to English society at the customary round of balls and visits. The climax of this London season was a garden party at Marlborough House in honour of the marriage of the Duke and Duchess of York—the future King George V and Queen Mary. There was also a reception at the Russian Embassy to mark the occasion which was attended by the bridegroom's cousin, the future Tsar Nicholas II. Princess Radziwill and her daughter were not invited to the wedding itself. They watched the procession from a balcony in Clarges Street; Catherine had no idea of the strange circumstances in which she would next meet the royal bride and groom.

The visit confirmed her Anglophilism. From now on she was to be an unquestioning admirer of all things English. 'Personally, I love England,' she declared. 'After my own native Russia, it is the country I care for most.'

The following season in St Petersburg was overshadowed by the illness of the Tsar. The first Court Ball of 1894 had to be postponed because of Alexander's inability to appear in public. When it took place a few weeks later, everyone was struck by 'the haggard looks of the unfortunate Emperor'. Catherine and her husband had decided to further their eldest daughter's education by taking her to Italy that year. For Prince Wilhelm and his daughter the months in Rome were a delight. As representatives of the staunchly Catholic Radziwill family, they were treated with deference and were fully at home in the clerically dominated city. Catherine, on the other hand, found the religious atmosphere oppressive. She associated Catholicism with all that she had found objectionable in the Radziwill Palace in Berlin. Her attitude towards the ceremonies of the Church was one of cynical disdain. On the day they arrived in Rome, the Radziwills were given tickets for St Peter's where Pope Leo XIII was to say a special Mass. The occasion was a ceremony for the canonization of a new saint. 'As I watched that silent, haughty, hieractic figure,' says Catherine of the Pope, 'I suddenly understood what I had not been able to comprehend until then, the power wielded by the Church of Rome, simply through its immobility, and its stagnation into paths which the human mind has left long ago.'

Strangely enough, she applied none of this criticism to the mysticism which pervaded the Holy Church of Russia. Her approach to religion was like her approach to politics: she accepted what suited her and was quite capable of championing both sides of any argument simultaneously.

From Rome they travelled to London by way of Florence and Paris. In England they took a house at Sevenoaks in Kent for the months of July and August. According to Catherine they were again invited to Hatfield House as well as to the Rothschilds' at Waddesdon Manor. It was while they were in Scotland, in September, that they learned that Tsar Alexander's condition had become quite hopeless. They made immediate preparations to return to Russia but by the time they reached Berlin the Tsar was dead.

There can be no doubt that Catherine felt the death of Alexander III very keenly. Her admiration for the burly, autocratic Tsar was quite unfeigned. His power, his purposefulness, even his ruthlessness were qualities which appealed to her, regardless of political principles. In his death she saw the passing of an era for Russia.

In a way, the Tsar's death marked the end of a phase in her own life. St Petersburg was never the same for her. Once Alexander III had gone, her sense of security in the Russian capital seemed also to disappear. Unconsciously, she began to look beyond Russia for a new hero whom she could respect and support.

*

A few days after the funeral of Alexander III, his son, the new Tsar Nicholas II, was married to Princess Alix of Hesse. The wedding ceremony was conducted in the Winter Palace in St Petersburg on 14th November, 1894.

Catherine and her second daughter, Wanda, were among the many guests invited to witness the marriage of the new ruler of Russia to his young German bride. In years to come Princess Radziwill would write countless descriptions of this ill-fated wedding ceremony. She always paid tribute to the grandeur of the occasion and praised the bearing of the new Tsar and the breathtaking beauty of his bride. Her glowing accounts were written with a purpose. She aimed to give the impression that she had approached the reign of Nicholas II with high expectations. But, in fact, she seems to have been prejudiced against the new Tsar and his wife long before they ascended the throne. There was something almost pathological about Catherine's detestation of them. The Emperor and Empress were, it is true, destined to become extremely unpopular with Russian society, but Catherine's hostility towards them was excessive by any standards. Forgetting her admiration of Alexander III's autocratic rule, she blamed his son entirely for the suppression of liberal opinion in Russia and, at the same time, derided him for being a weak and vacillating sovereign. Her contempt for Nicholas II was surpassed only by her loathing for his German-born wife. She claimed that together Nicholas and Alexandra were the sole cause of the downfall of the Romanov dynasty and the collapse of Imperial Russia. It was an opinion shared by many other Russians.

For Catherine's daughter Wanda, the royal wedding had a

double significance. She was seventeen years old and this was her first appearance at the Russian Court; it was also the only state occasion she would attend as a single girl. Shortly before the Tsar's wedding, her own marriage had been decided upon. The sight of the royal bride and groom, however, could hardly have been reassuring for the inexperienced young Wanda. There could have been no comforting comparisons between the glamour of the ceremony in the Winter Palace and the prospect of her own wedding. Whatever the new Tsar's failings might have been, there was no doubt about his physical attractions. Wanda could look forward to no such romantic match. The man she was to marry was almost three times her age and far from attractive. In six months' time, having bowed to her parents' decision, she was to become the wife of the elderly Prince Gebhard Blücher von Wahlstatt.

Catherine was to lay the blame for a great many of her misfortunes on her hasty marriage to an older man. If this was indeed the case, it makes the match which she organized for her daughter an even more cynical arrangement than most *mariages de convenance*. Prince Blücher was a decidedly disagreeable man, almost sixty years old. His second wife had died in March 1894 after five years of marriage, and within seven months of her death it had been arranged that he should marry the seventeen-year-old Wanda. It was certainly an illustrious match but even the most sanguine of parents must have known that it held little prospect of happiness for the young bride. Catherine refused to admit this. 'Tradition says that a mother-in-law never finds anything kind to say about her son-in-law,' she wrote. 'Perhaps, therefore, I ought to say something cutting about mine; but speaking quite truly I cannot. My daughter is married to Prince Blücher, and her happiness—which I believe is very great and real—inspires me with respect.' It was a respect, however, which was notably absent in most of Catherine's references to Prince Blücher. Her daughter's husband came in for more than his share of Princess Radziwill's caustic comments.

Wanda was married to Prince Blücher in St Petersburg on 6th May, 1895. After the wedding the newly married couple left Russia and divided their time between their house on the island of Herm and the Blücher estates at Radun in Silesia—present-day Czechoslovakia. It was on the island of Herm, two years later, that Wanda's first child, a daughter, was born, making Catherine a grandmother at the age of thirty-nine.

But if Catherine was satisfied with the match which she had arranged for her daughter, she was becoming more and more discontented with her own marriage. By sharing Catherine's banishment from the Court of Berlin, Prince Wilhelm had ruined his own career. When he left Germany in 1887, he had been a major in the Prussian army. By voluntarily resigning his commission, he had put an end to all hopes of the steady promotion he could otherwise have expected. Although not an ambitious man, he would inevitably have benefited from his family's military prestige in Germany. In Russia he appears to have lost all taste for soldiering. He had an estate of his own at Kudice, near Minsk, and was made a gentleman-in-waiting to Alexander III, but he continued to regard Germany as his real home. 'He never got used to life in St Petersburg which was so different from that which he had lived in Germany,' says Catherine. 'He spent most of his time at his club and left me very much to myself.' The aimless existence which Prince Wilhelm was forced to lead put a further strain on his far from ideal marriage. He shared none of Catherine's interests in politics and seemed to go out of his way to dissociate himself from his wife's enthusiasms. But there seems to be no truth in Catherine's claim that he was 'a brute and treated her badly'. If anything, the boot seems in fact to have been very much on the other foot. Catherine's eldest daughter Louise described her father as a timid, reserved man, completely dominated by her mother. 'She treated him like a *moujik*,' Louise told a friend.

Whatever the cause of the rift in the marriage, there was little hope of reconciliation. Wanda's wedding seems to have been the last occasion on which the family was together. From now on Catherine spent more and more of her time in England and France, while Wilhelm returned as often as he could to his family in Berlin, or paid long visits to his sister's home in Vienna.

The break-up of her marriage merely added to Catherine's disenchantment with St Petersburg. She was, of course, quite capable of living a life of her own in the Russian capital but many changes were taking place there. With the death of Alexander III, Catherine lost much of her former influence in Court circles. Some of her important friends were replaced and others died soon after Nicholas II ascended the throne. And then the shift in the hierarchy had brought many of those who disliked her into prominence. For, as in Berlin, her inability to check her acid tongue had earned her many enemies. 'I was supposed,' she admits coyly, 'to be in possession of a sharper tongue than was really the case, which at times amused me greatly, at others annoyed me. But I was young and careless in many ways.'

Not the least among those whom she had offended was Alexander III's sister-in-law, the Grand Duchess Vladimir, who, it is said, 'would not look at her'. Always a social and political force, the Grand Duchess Vladimir was now in a position to assert herself as never before. The death of Alexander III had brought her own family into the limelight. Until Nicholas II produced an heir, only his younger brother Michael stood between the Grand Duke and the throne. This, in theory, gave the Grand Duchess Vladimir the rank of the third most important woman in Russia and, in practice, made her the uncrowned Empress in St Petersburg. For when the new young Empress showed no inclination to take her place as the leader of society, her prerogatives were quickly usurped by her husband's ambitious aunt. All this put Princess Radziwill's nose sadly out of joint.

Catherine had, in fact, good reason to assume that her 'brilliant years' in St Petersburg had ended with the death of Tsar Alexander III.

＊

Princess Radziwill spent most of the next two years drifting about Europe. Now that she had been obliged to abandon her position in St Petersburg, she began to seek other ways in which to carve out a political niche. The most obvious course was to exploit her influential connections and devote herself to political journalism. Most of her time was spent in either Paris or London where she was well known in journalistic circles. In Paris she could count on the support of Mme Adam and in London, through her old friend Donald Mackenzie Wallace of *The Times*, she was introduced to various leading newspaper men.

Her unattached and seemingly aimless existence did not pass

without comment. It was probably during these years that much scandal was spread about her. However, many of the stories appear to owe more to imagination than to fact. She was said, for instance, to have associated not only with royalty and states-men, 'but also with socialist agitators, artists, circus riders, authors and journalists'. This is misleading. She did, indeed, associate with authors and journalists and more than probably knew a few artists. Some of her friends may have shown socialist sympathies in the same way that her aunt, Mme de Balzac, had prided herself on her radical opinions. But when 'circus riders' are included in this otherwise acceptable list, it gives all her friends a decidedly disreputable look. There seems no evidence to support the unlikely theory that her friends were chosen indiscriminately. This would have been very much out of charac-ter for a woman of Catherine's intelligence and interests. Her behaviour was unorthodox by the standards of the day but it was never skittish. Her journalistic contacts were not those of the gutter press but of the civilized *Nouvelle Revue* and the highly respectable *Times*.

Her interest in the newspaper world was not, however, entirely intellectual. Now separated from Prince Wilhelm, she needed to earn her own living. Only thus could she hope to achieve complete independence from her husband. There was little hope of her receiving help from anyone else. After her father's death, Pohrebyszcze and the Rzewuski fortunes had been divided between her younger brothers. She had her own property at Pjatino but had no desire to live there and the estate yielded little in the way of income. For a while she may have hoped for some assistance from her daughter's rich husband but any such hopes were short-lived. Like the rest of Prince Blücher's family, she was quickly made to realize that her elderly son-in-law gave away very little.

Catherine seems to have spent much of her time with Wanda and her husband during the early years of their marriage. The island of Herm, situated between Paris and London, provided her with a convenient headquarters. But she must have found her visits to the Channel Islands somewhat trying. Her pompous son-in-law, who, according to his own son, 'was obsessed by delusions of grandeur' and insisted on being addressed as Your Serene Highness, would almost certainly have disapproved of her journalistic activities. She, on the other hand, was highly critical of his extreme meanness and intense religiosity.

She must soon have realized that her type of journalism offered few rewards to the newcomer. Formerly, her strength had been in her ability to provide her readers with a glimpse behind the scenes at the courts of Berlin and St Petersburg. Although she still moved in influential circles, the information she was able to gather was no more revealing than that available to any well placed journalist. There was no lack of political writers and her chosen field was one where a woman invariably found herself at a disadvantage: the world of politics was still very much a man's world. A few women had, it is true, managed to overcome the prejudice against their sex and establish themselves as political journalists but these were mainly women who had some cause to champion. Catherine's approach to politics lacked this necessary spark. Essentially, she was a commentator rather than a crusader. Unlike her friend Juliette Adam, Catherine had neither a political conviction nor a politician to inspire her. In the overcrowded world of European journalism, she was simply one more enthusiastic amateur. She had a flair for intrigue and a ready pen; all she now needed was an opportunity to exercise her undoubted talents.

A possible solution to her problem presented itself, in an unexpected way, a few months after her daughter's marriage to Prince Blücher. At the beginning of 1896 Catherine, like most Russian aristocrats, was busy preparing for the Coronation of Nicholas II, due to take place in Moscow that May. Before returning to Russia for this important event, she paid a short visit to London. She was in the British capital at the beginning of February and was quickly caught up in the political excitement accompanying the news of Dr Jameson's raid into the Transvaal. Her association with the staff of *The Times* placed her in an excellent position to follow the effect of this news on British public opinion. For, of all English newspapers, none was more involved in the South African fiasco than *The Times*. Some of *The Times*'s correspondents had played a part in the conspiracy preceding the raid and their activities had been supervised by Moberley Bell, the newspaper's energetic manager. Both Moberley Bell and his wife were friends of Catherine's and between them had provided the Princess with many useful contacts. 'Moberley Bell went everywhere, and knew every-body,' wrote Catherine, 'and entertained everybody of note at dinners which were as amusing as they were execrable. He invited about three times as many as his rooms could contain, but no one ever dreamed of refusing, for there one would meet all the leading men and politicians in England.'

Cecil Rhodes arrived in England on 4th February, 1896. A few days later he was invited to dine at Moberley Bell's home. It was one of the few engagements he accepted on this troubled visit to London. He found himself seated next to Princess Catherine Radziwill. She, recognizing the possibilities of the situation, set out to make the most of her heaven-sent oppor-tunity. On this occasion there were no sharp-tongued comments. The Princess was at her scintillating best.

CHAPTER SEVEN

Alarms and Excursions

R HODES hardly noticed her. At least, that is what he claimed. And it is probably true. He might have been susceptible to a title but there was little reason for him to be unduly impressed by an obscure Continental Princess. On his rare visits to the British capital, he was relentlessly pursued by a horde of *grandes dames* who would go to almost any lengths to entice him to their tables. His wealth, his power and, perhaps most challenging of all, his reputation as a misogynist made him a tantalizing prize for the lion–hunting hostesses of May-fair. Challenged by his apparent indifference, they vied with each other to claim his acquaintance and his acceptance of an invitation to dine was regarded as something approaching intimacy. He was flattered, fawned upon and gushed over. It made little impression on him. If reports were true, he was not above treating some of his more shameless pursuers with an ill-concealed contempt. 'It's rare sport being cornered by some fat bediamonded duchess,' he is supposed to have said to E. H. Pearson. 'I tell her what I think of her. She smiles and shakes her head. I go one better and give out a few oaths. She begins to gush. I blaspheme. She laughs. I become Rabelaisian. She guffaws. I curse. She fawns. There is no limit to her endurance.' But he was not always so rude. At times he was extremely gratified by the attentions of the aristocracy but certainly not during his brief visit in 1896. Catherine could hardly have chosen a less auspicious occasion to bring herself to his notice. Still recovering from the shock of the disastrous Jameson Raid, it is unlikely that he was in a mood to respond to the social chatter of a chance dinner companion. He had far weightier things on his mind: his entire future was at stake.

For a week Rhodes busied himself with the work of the

Chartered Company. His one concern was that his precious Charter should not be abrogated. This is what his opponents were demanding, both in the House of Commons and in the Press. But he had good reason to hope that all would be well. Opinion in England, though officially frowning, was inclined to be indulgent towards him. The reason for this was due, in part, to a feeling of resentment towards the German Emperor. When the news of the Raid had reached Europe, the Kaiser had sent a telegram to President Kruger, congratulating him on maintaining his independence against 'armed bands'. A large section of the British public had taken exception to this foreign interference and, to show their displeasure, tended to rally in support of Rhodes. Rhodes was later to thank the Kaiser for his timely intervention. 'I was a naughty boy,' he explained archly, 'and you tried to whip me. Now my people were quite ready to whip me for being a naughty boy, but directly *you* did it, they said, "No, if this is anybody's business, it is ours." The result was that Your Majesty got yourself very much disliked by the English people, and I never got whipped at all.'

Even so, Rhodes could not rely on public indignation to save his Charter. Popular support was one thing but official leniency quite another. The Government might be forced to take action against him.

But he was not without influence in high places. The day he arrived in England, his solicitor, Mr Bourchier Hawksley, called at the Colonial Office to start negotiations on his behalf. The outcome of these and subsequent talks was to provide Rhodes with an important weapon. Despite the fact that the negotiations were carried on through the medium of his very respectable legal adviser, they were to be regarded by many as little short of blackmail.

Mr Hawksley had, or would shortly have, in his possession a dossier of telegrams that had been sent to Rhodes when Dr Rutherfoord Harris had been securing the important railway strip in Bechuanaland. Some of these telegrams appeared to point directly at Joseph Chamberlain's involvement in the preparations for the Raid. If they were made public the Colonial Secretary would probably be forced to resign. Hawksley had been anxious that the telegrams should be placed on record in order to clear Rhodes and Jameson of some of the blame for the

Raid. Rhodes thought otherwise. The telegrams could be put to much better use.

If Chamberlain would help him, Rhodes would be willing to suppress the more incriminating telegrams. What Rhodes was hoping for was that Chamberlain would be able to stop an official Inquiry—such as was being demanded by the opponents of the Chartered Company—into the Raid. But if the Colonial Secretary was unable to avoid setting up a Committee of Inquiry, Rhodes would insist that Chamberlain use his influence to protect the Charter. At all costs, the Charter must be safeguarded.

Although no definite bargain was struck, this is what seems to have been tacitly understood between Rhodes and the Colonial Secretary.

Other considerations were, of course, involved. Rhodes may well have been concerned about the national disgrace that would follow a disclosure that the British Government had been connected in any way with his schemes. And Chamberlain, although he could not promise to stop an Inquiry, was ready to meet Rhodes on the question of the Charter. He did not feel that the Government could accept responsibility for Rhodesia. There seems to be little doubt that the unspoken bargain influenced both sides. When Rhodes himself called to see Chamberlain on the 6th February, no mention was made of the incriminating telegrams but he came away from the interview slightly more hopeful that the Charter would be saved. He felt obliged, however, to hand in his resignation as a director of the Chartered Company.

Having done this, he left at once for Africa; not for the Cape, where his career lay in ruins, but for Rhodesia where he hoped to make a fresh start. Travelling via Egypt and the east coast of Africa, Rhodes reached Beira on 20th March, 1896. He was greeted, within a few days of his arrival, by news of a most frightening nature. On 24th March, the Matabele had murdered an isolated group of white settlers just outside Bulawayo. It was the signal for a serious rising among the Africans of Rhodesia; a rising which had been threatening for some months.

For the Matabele the coming of the white man had brought nothing but disaster. They had been deprived of their traditional territory, their king was dead and their *impis* had been put to flight. They were now a defeated nation living in a

147

country occupied by the enemy. As such, they had suffered all the humiliations of a proud and conquered people. They had been herded into reserves after the Matabele War and their chiefs had been stripped of much of their former authority. They were treated with studied insolence by some of the Chartered Company's officials. The young warriors were dragooned into forced labour for the mines and, when an African police corps was raised, they found themselves at the mercy of those whom they had once regarded as their vassals. It was hardly to be expected that such a lordly and arrogant race as the Matabele would submit to this servitude. To their bitter resentment was added a series of natural disasters. The harrowing drought of 1893 was followed, at the beginning of 1896, by a widespread and fatal attack of *rinderpest*, the most dreaded of all cattle diseases: their herds were decimated and the reserves impoverished. Looking for portents which would herald the destruction of the white invaders, the witch-doctors found one in an eclipse of the moon at the end of February.

The time for rebellion seemed right and the circumstances favourable. Not only had Jameson drained the Chartered Company's white police force for his ill-fated raid, but the news of his capture by the Boers augured well for the Matabele's own chances of success. Their *impis* massed and once again the fearful sound of Matabele war-cries was heard throughout Rhodesia.

It is said that the weeks following the outbreak of the rebellion were the finest of Rhodes's life. Perhaps they were. A column was marching from Salisbury to Bulawayo and he insisted on joining it. He was accompanied by the burly Charles Metcalfe, a friend of his Oxford days whom he now employed as his railway engineer, and Jack Grimmer, his favourite Rhodesian 'Angel'. Still weak from a bout of malaria, Rhodes was ill equipped, both physically and mentally, for the perilous march which lay ahead. He was not a brave man. This is something which even his most staunch admirers admit. 'Mr Rhodes,' says T. E. Fuller, one of the least critical of his biographers, 'as a rule, preferred a sheltered position when danger was about, and would rather escape an ordinary peril than face it.' And, on referring to this march, Rhodes himself was to admit that he was 'in a funk all the time', but that, like many another honest hero, he was 'more afraid to be thought afraid'. There can be no doubt, however, that he acquitted himself superbly. Armed with only a hunting crop, he led the most dangerous of reconnoitring expeditions; conspicuous in his white flannel trousers, he was to be seen in the forefront of every battle.

There was more than a hint of desperation about Rhodes's attitude. It was as though he had made up his mind either to die a hero or to emerge triumphant. Only thus could he restore his shattered image. At first he would hear of no compromise with the Matabele. Even those who threw down their arms and surrendered, he wanted shot.

By the time he reached Bulawayo, however, he had become more temperate. The politician took over from the avenger. A bloodstained victory would do little to restore his reputation. If he was regarded as an irresponsible adventurer who had schemed to overthrow the legitimate Government of the Transvaal, would the hammering of primitive tribesmen be considered the act of a prudent and mature statesman? How much better it would be if the instigator of the infamous Jameson Raid now became the wise and moderate pacifier of the Matabele. The enemy had already been taught a salutary lesson. They had been defeated on all fronts and forced to flee into the hills. The time had come to negotiate an honourable peace.

But it would not be easy. Safe in the rocky fastnesses of the Matopo Hills, the Matabele were wary of exposing themselves to the messengers of the white man. They had been tricked too often. At last, however, a reliable intermediary was found. An African scout from Tembuland in the Cape, named John Grootboom, undertook the difficult task of sounding out the rebels. He returned to report that certain chiefs were ready to meet Rhodes. They were preparing for his arrival. He was to come unarmed and accompanied by not more than four or five men.

The risks involved in agreeing to this proposal were enormous. Although he had no official position in the country—having resigned from the board of the Chartered Company—Rhodes was still regarded by the Africans as the most important white man in the land which now bore his name. By going unprotected to a secret *indaba* with the hostile chiefs, he would be placing himself completely at their mercy. Even a more civilized foe would have been prepared to take advantage of such a valuable hostage. But Rhodes did not hesitate. Once again his new-found courage astonished his companions. 'I believe they mean well,' he said and, rejecting all suggestions of an armed patrol, he chose his companions. The chiefs had asked that Johan Colenbrander, a former agent of Rhodes's whom they trusted, should act as interpreter; John Grootboom was taken along to act as a guide. To complete the party Rhodes selected Vere Stent, a newspaper correspondent who was to record the proceedings, and Dr Hans Sauer, the friend of his early gold-prospecting days.

They set off on a fine winter's morning. Threading their way through the ochre-coloured grass, they headed towards the distant hills. 'We talked very little,' says Vere Stent. 'Must I confess it?—we were all a little nervous.' For part of the way they were accompanied by Jack Grimmer and J. G. McDonald, one of Rhodes's young estate agents. After they had gone a few miles, Grimmer and McDonald off-saddled and the rest of the party rode on towards a small clearing at the foot of the hills. Here, Rhodes gave the order to dismount and shortly afterwards they spotted the huge white flag which preceded a small pro-cession of Matabele warriors. 'Yes, yes, there they are,' whispered Rhodes. 'This is one of those moments in life that make it worth living! Here they come!' He seemed, says Stent, 'the calmest man of the five'.

The Matabele formed a semicircle facing the white men and Rhodes, at Colenbrander's prompting, welcomed them with a peace greeting. 'The eyes are white,' he said in Zulu. 'The eyes are white, oh chief, oh great hunter,' replied the men. A spokes-man for the Matabele then launched into a long oration. He outlined the history and the struggles of his people and detailed their grievances against the Chartered Company. Rhodes heard him out and then replied. He acknowledged the wrongs the Matabele had suffered and promised that such things would come to an end. 'But why,' he asked, 'did they kill women and children?' At this the Matabele became restless. They all started to talk and make angry gestures. One of the chiefs silenced them and their spokesman replied. The Europeans, he said, had first killed their women and children. 'I shouldn't go on with the subject,' whispered Colenbrander to Rhodes. 'It is quite true. Some women were shot by cattle collectors.'

The *indaba* continued until the sun began to set. Then, with Rhodes promising justice for the future, the meeting broke up. 'The eyes are white,' chorused the chiefs. 'The eyes are white,' replied Rhodes.

A week later there was a second *indaba*. Some of the chiefs wished to see Sir Richard Martin, the Queen's representative, but Sir Richard would not move without an armed escort. Rhodes went again. Dr Sauer had left by this time but his place was taken by Grimmer and McDonald. With the party also were two incredibly brave women. Johan Colenbrander's spirited wife and her sister had ridden into the camp and insisted on attending the *indaba*. This time things were a little more difficult. There are conflicting accounts of what happened. McDonald claims that it resulted in a glorious triumph for Rhodes. Stent, writing nearer the event, says that it ended on a somewhat uncertain note. In any case, there seems to be little doubt of Rhodes's growing confidence that he could deal with the situation peacefully.

The following day he moved his camp away from the military columns and set about reaching the refractory chiefs who had refused to come to the *indabas*. To win them over would take time and he would need patience. But he appears to have regarded the outcome of these negotiations as the touchstone of his future career and applied himself to the task with surprising vigour. The after-effects of malaria, from which he had suffered on the march to Bulawayo, and the strain of the months following the Jameson Raid, were no longer evident. His life had taken on a new sense of purpose and with it had come a rejuvenating and seemingly inexhaustible vitality. 'Mr Rhodes's physical strength and power of endurance were phenomenal at this time,' says Philip Jourdan, a young man who had recently arrived in Rhodesia. 'Sometimes the morning ride extended from five a.m. until twelve noon . . . but Mr Rhodes never seemed to feel the strain of a long ride in the least, but hurried through his breakfast, and immediately afterwards commenced talking to the chiefs, which he kept up right through the terrible heat till four in the afternoon. Then the horses were saddled again and he rode till dusk. After dinner the chiefs turned up again, and sometimes he chatted with them until late into the night.'

For Jourdan, the sight of Rhodes in the saddle was a revelation in more ways than one. It was all part of the bewildering new life he was experiencing in Rhodesia. Until a few weeks earlier Philip Jourdan had journeyed little further than the Cape and his horizons had been bounded by the staid precincts of the Cape Parliament. Then, suddenly and out of the blue, he had received instructions to resign his post as a civil servant and to travel north in order to become Rhodes's private secretary. Not a young man given to compulsive action, he had nonetheless obeyed the command without question. For Philip Jourdan, this was the chance of a lifetime. It was something about which he had dreamed for years.

*

Since the departure of Harry Currey, Rhodes had been without a full-time private secretary. Nominally, the post had been filled by his two favourite Rhodesian 'Angels'—Johnny Grimmer and Bob Coryndon, but they could hardly be called secretaries. Essentially young men of action, they had been very reluctant to exchange their saddles for office chairs. 'That's not my job, sir,' Coryndon is supposed to have said when Rhodes had asked him to act as his secretary. 'If you want to use me, think of something I'm suited for.' Grimmer's attitude had been much the same but, in his slap-happy fashion, he had agreed to help Rhodes out. The result was chaotic. A young man of few words, Grimmer seems to have tackled his secretarial duties with typical abruptness. An example has been given of his method of dealing with Rhodes's correspondence:

> Dear Sir,
> In reply to your application Mr Rhodes says no.
> Yours faithfully,
> John R. Grimmer.

That the recipients of this sort of answer should have been outraged is hardly surprising. What many of them found equally incredible, however, was the lighthearted manner in which Rhodes reacted to their protests. Confronted by a glaring *faux pas* committed by his secretary, he was apt to brush it aside with an indulgent chuckle. This was the period when Rhodes was still Prime Minister of the Cape, and it became a matter of some concern that a man in his position was prepared to allow his private affairs to be so appallingly mismanaged. Political associates complained and friends expostulated but it made no difference; he steadfastly refused to hear a word against Grimmer. A civil servant has recorded a scene in the Prime Minister's office in Cape Town that must, one feels, have been typical of many similar incidents. 'On one occasion,' says the observer, 'he [Rhodes] was perusing some documents I had brought him, when a friend of his came in with a letter in his hand and asked Rhodes why the devil he had been sent a letter like that, and why he had such a god-forsaken ass of a private secretary who could not even write decent English.

' "Ah!" exclaimed Rhodes, "but you've never seen him handle mules."

'The reply so astonished the visitor that after gazing at Rhodes for a few seconds he turned and went out without saying another word. Rhodes smiled.'

Rhodes may have been amused, but it was a situation which even he could not tolerate indefinitely. Although there was no question of his dismissing Johnny Grimmer, it became obvious that he would have to employ a more efficient secretary. He was able to solve the problem when a special Prime Minister's Department was established at the House of Assembly. The new office was placed under the capable direction of W. H. Milton (later Sir William Milton) who acted as Rhodes's parliamentary secretary, and a chief clerk was appointed to handle the Prime Minister's personal affairs. This chief clerk, who, in effect, was to become his private assistant, was chosen by Rhodes himself. The young man he appointed was Philip Jourdan, a junior civil servant whom he had long since singled out as a likely candidate for the post of his confidential aide.

Philip James Jourdan was a South African of Huguenot descent. His family had been settled in the Cape for many years and he had been born in the beautiful Hex River Valley of the Cape Province. Shy, unassuming and conscientious, he was quite unlike any of the other young men for whom Rhodes displayed a particular liking. His appearance reflected his manner; with his soft, gentle features, which even the heavy moustache of the period did little to strengthen, he gave an impression of quiet efficiency. Never very healthy, he was the type of youngster who arouses the protective instinct in both men and women. It was unusual for Rhodes to be attracted by such refined and delicate qualities but that he was immediately drawn to this modest civil servant, there can be no doubt.

Jourdan had first come to Rhodes's notice in 1890. These had been the hectic days in which Rhodes had returned to Parliament to unseat the Government and assume the Premiership of the Cape. At that time Jourdan had just become a junior clerk at the House of Assembly and worked in an office leading off the Assembly Chamber. Whenever Rhodes entered the House he would stop at this office in order to leave his hat and coat there. 'He seemed to have a liking for young men,' said Jourdan, 'and, although I was only a youngster, twenty years of age, he always had a kind word for me on going into or coming from the House.' For a time their acquaintanceship was confined to these casual greetings. Then, on a never-to-be-forgotten day, Rhodes stopped for a longer chat. He questioned Jourdan closely about his background and private affairs. He wanted to know how old he was, whether he was descended from the Huguenots, who his relations were, how well he knew Dutch and if he could write shorthand. On most points Jourdan could satisfy him, but was forced to confess to a lack of shorthand. 'You must learn short-hand,' said Rhodes, and disappeared into the Assembly Chamber. From then on the daily greetings became increasingly friendly.

To say that Jourdan was flattered would be an understate-ment. He was ecstatic. Few accounts of the effect of Rhodes's personal magnetism on an impressionable young man are quite as revealing as that given by Philip Jourdan. 'I became very fond of him,' he wrote. 'I felt that I could do anything for him and developed the strongest imaginable hero-worship for him. I was never happier than when I was with him, even the thought that he was present in the House was a source of happi-ness to me. I loved to watch his face in the House, which I could do by placing the door which led from my room into the Chamber slightly ajar, and I am afraid much of the Government's time was wasted in that way. It was about a year after I first met him that an almost uncontrollable desire took hold of me to be his private secretary and to travel over the world with him. In my own mind I had placed him on such a high pinnacle of fame that such a wish seemed almost impossible of realization. Sometimes

I felt I dared not even think of it. It was my great secret and I did not communicate it to a soul. I delighted to harbour the idea, and sometimes I would lie awake half the night working myself up into a state of delirious excitement, speculating on the joy and pleasure which would be mine when I should be his secretary, when I should always be with him and would go wherever he went. I had not then received the slightest hint that there was even a possibility of my appointment as his secretary. I worshipped him and had an intense desire to work for him and to please him. That was all I wanted.'

When Jourdan's term of service at the House of Assembly had run its course, he was transferred to a Magistrate's court in a small village. For over a year he neither saw nor heard from Rhodes. But, in his besotted way, he went on hoping. 'I used to take long solitary walks,' he says, 'sometimes extending over several hours, into the country thinking of nothing else but Rhodes, Rhodes, Rhodes and my devotion to him.' There was no need for Jourdan to torture himself in this way. His hero had not forsaken him. He was in his twenty-third year and very much on Rhodes's mind. Arrangements were even then being made to set up the Prime Minister's Department and the post of chief clerk had been decided upon.

Jourdan was informed of his appointment in March 1894 and started work there at the beginning of April. On the afternoon of his first day Rhodes sent for him. 'I suppose you thought I had forgotten all about you,' he said. 'Do you know shorthand?' With all that mooning about, Jourdan had neglected to carry out Rhodes's advice. He admitted as much. 'You are a fool,' laughed Rhodes, 'did I not tell you to study shorthand? ... Well, you must acquire a knowledge of it as soon as possible, because I want you to do my private letters.' Until that moment Jourdan had been under the impression that he was to be simply another clerk in the office. Now he could hardly contain himself. 'I went out of that room,' he says, 'treading on air.'

He worked hard to please Rhodes. With the possible exception of Harry Currey, Jourdan was the most efficient of Rhodes's secretaries, conscientious and thoroughly reliable. Rhodes, from the beginning, seems to have placed this ingenuous, doe-eyed boy in a special category. 'I knew he would never abuse my trust or let me down,' he said. In marked contrast to the usual chaff and horse-play which accompanied the initiation of a young man into his service, Rhodes appears to have handled Jourdan with singular tact and tenderness. 'He invariably called me into his office every afternoon to go through his private letters with him,' says Jourdan. 'I looked forward with the greatest pleasure to the half hour or hour with him every afternoon. He was exceedingly kind and tender towards me. He made me draw up my chair quite close to him, and frequently placed his hand on my shoulder. He used to send for me even when he did not have any work for me. On these occasions he talked to me more as a friend than as a chief . . . I never cared to accept money from him, as I told him I was in receipt of an adequate salary as an official of the Prime Minister's Department, but he would have his way and occasionally forced cheques upon me . . . I thought he was the most generous man I had ever met, and was at a loss how to act.'

Despite this growing affection between them, Jourdan had still not realized his ultimate ambition. He was still a civil servant and his position as chief clerk in the Prime Minister's Department fell short of his dream of living with Rhodes as his private secretary. This was a post still held, as something of a sinecure, by the ill-qualified Johnny Grimmer. Nor had Jourdan reason to think that Rhodes's interest in him was exceptional. He was not the only clerk to enjoy special treatment at the hands of the Prime Minister. Few Prime Ministers, in fact, could have paid more attention to the junior clerks in their office than did Rhodes.

In June 1895 Jourdan fell ill with typhoid fever—the first of his many illnesses while in Rhodes's employ—and on the first day he was in hospital, a messenger arrived with the Prime Minister's cheque for £100 to pay his medical expenses. From then on Rhodes sent every day to inquire about his progress.

On returning to his office, however, Jourdan was faced with the most serious set-back of his career. The Jameson Raid was followed by Rhodes's resignation as Prime Minister and his departure for England. It looked as though Jourdan was to be permanently separated from his hero.

And then, quite unexpectedly, on Rhodes's return from England, came the call for Jourdan to join him in Rhodesia. His fantasies were about to come true; those five agonizing years had not been in vain. It was no wonder that he arrived at Rhodes's camp in a dazed state. Somewhat to his surprise, he settled down to life in the open with the greatest of ease. It was true that he was a little alarmed when Rhodes moved away from the military camp in order to meet with the more obstinate Matabele chiefs, but his fear was more than offset by the presence of his beloved chief. In the eyes of Philip Jourdan—or 'Flippie' Jourdan, as he was called by his friends—Cecil Rhodes could do no wrong.

*

The negotiations with the Matabele continued until the beginning of October 1896. Throughout the long discussions, Rhodes treated the chiefs with great tact. 'I do not think,' says J. G. McDonald, who was present at the talks, 'any other man could have done what he achieved at this time, by extraordinary patience coupled with extreme energy.' This judgment is borne out by every other account of the peace consultations. Out in the veld, surrounded by his friends, Rhodes became a different person. It is not surprising that those who knew him at times like these came to regard him with an affection rarely found among his purely political associates.

Rhodes used to claim, probably sincerely, that his greatest desire was to retire from public life to devote himself to farming in Rhodesia. The idea was very much on his mind during the latter half of 1896, the time when he chose the site for his Inyanga estates, some eighty miles from Umtali. Here in the highlands of Rhodesia, he instructed McDonald to buy 100,000 acres of farmland and to construct a dam in order to irrigate them. In years to come, this estate was to be one of his favourite retreats. It was at this time also that he stumbled across a hill in the Matopos which he called 'The World's View'. By African standards the view was by no means remarkable but it captured Rhodes's imagination. On the day he discovered it, he rode back to his camp and insisted on his entire party inspecting it. Walking backwards and forwards on the crest of the hill, he suddenly announced: 'I shall be buried here.' He no doubt appreciated that this isolated spot with its sweeping vistas symbolized his own lonely, far-seeing life. But perhaps it is also appropriate that the view was not the best which Africa had to offer.

When he was not talking to the chiefs or exploring the countryside, Rhodes loved nothing better than to challenge Johnny Grimmer to a shooting match. They would spend the entire day stalking game in the veld, arriving back in the evenings to compare bags and settle debts. These hunting duels, with the stakes sometimes as high as £100, became part of the legend of Rhodes as a sportsman. A great many stories have been told about them; sometimes all the young men in the camp would be divided between the two main contestants and the match would develop into something like a friendly family rumpus. It was all taken in good part and it is said that Rhodes became 'as enthusiastic about it as a high-spirited boy would over a game of marbles'. Never a good marskman, he was often helped by his incredible luck. But he rarely allowed himself to triumph over Grimmer and was even known to cheat in order not to win. This was all part of the strange relationship between Rhodes and his favourite Rhodesian 'Angel'. For of all his friendships with young men, that between him and Johnny Grimmer is surely the most extraordinary.

It has been said that Cecil Rhodes's attitude towards some of his more defenceless victims 'took the form of mental sadism'. And there is evidence to support this criticism. At times he showed a cynical ruthlessness which shocked even his most devoted admirers. An example often quoted concerns his treatment of Lobengula's sons, whom he took into his employ after their father's death. On one occasion, when these Matabele boys were working in the garden of Groote Schuur, Rhodes is supposed to have shouted to them from the stoep: 'Let me see, what year was it I killed your father?' To the scandalized amazement of his guests, this question was followed by an outburst of shrill laughter from Rhodes, in which the youngsters joined.

As is often the case, however, this sadistic streak appears to have been accompanied by its psychological counterpart: a tendency to self-humiliation which can only be described as a form of mental masochism. This became more and more apparent as Rhodes grew older. And nowhere was it more obvious than in his subservient attitude towards Johnny Grimmer.

With the arrival of Philip Jourdan, all pretence that Grimmer was a private secretary vanished. He was now simply a companion for Rhodes. His status in the camp was vague but no doubt more appropriate to his capabilities. Always at Rhodes's side, he exercised a clumsy protectiveness over his employer which was both touching and remarkable. 'He appeared,' it is said, 'to look on Rhodes as a great baby, incapable of being left to himself, and it was amusing to hear Grimmer lecture him on his neglect of precaution in the interests of his health. He cared nothing for politics, nor to identify himself with Rhodes's creations; he was just a sterling, big-hearted, loyal friend, deeply attached to 'the Old Man', and inspired by the very highest motives, unsullied by a mercenary thought, or swayed by the hope of self-advancement.'

At times, however, Grimmer's brusque manner belied his true intentions and made his good-natured concern appear little short of insolent. The way in which Rhodes allowed himself to be ordered about, scoffed at and even openly insulted by his 'secretary' must have caused a good many raised eyebrows. He made no secret of Grimmer's hold over him and frankly admitted that he was terrified of offending the young man. 'Rhodes used to say that Grimmer was the only man he was afraid of,' says one who knew them both well, 'and it is equally certain that Grimmer was by no means afraid of him—in fact, to see them together one might have come to the conclusion that Rhodes was in charge of a keeper.' What is more, far from resenting this treatment, Rhodes seemed to enjoy being bullied by Grimmer. To this, Sir Percy Fitzpatrick bore witness. 'One day,' he said, 'I saw Rhodes get up—it was in camp—and try to do something for himself, so as to spare others. Of course he made a horrid tangle of things. Johnny got up lazily and strolled over; took the things from Rhodes with the growling comment, "Of course you made a mess of it: why couldn't you give me a call?" Rhodes dropped the tangle meekly and with no more than a grunt; but his face was a study. The look of deep amusement and affection in his eyes and the softened expression on his face spoke volumes!' And as the years passed, this strange bond between Rhodes and Grimmer grew even stronger.

When the talks with the Matabele chiefs finally came to an end, Rhodes's party moved on to Salisbury. Here Rhodes was kept busy listening to the complaints of the settlers. The high spirits which had sustained him in the Matopos persisted throughout the Salisbury visit and Philip Jourdan was amazed at the lavish way in which Rhodes met the various requests for money which poured in from individuals and organized charities. During the three weeks they stayed at the Government Residency, Jourdan estimated that he made out cheques for well over £10,000.

Pleasant as this Rhodesian interlude had been, it could not be prolonged indefinitely. The last and most important act of the Jameson Raid had still to be played out in London. All attempts to prevent the British Parliament from formally investigating the South African fiasco had failed. A Select Committee of the House of Commons had been appointed to hold an Inquiry into the affair and Rhodes had given his word that he would attend the hearings. Reasonably confident that Chamberlain would help him safeguard the Chartered Company, Rhodes appears to have been singularly untroubled by the fact that his reputation still hung in the balance. He set off for the Inquiry in something of a holiday mood. At Salisbury he met Bob Coryndon and suggested that he and Johnny Grimmer should both accompany him to London. 'They had passed some strenuous years in the country . . .' explained Philip Jourdan, who remained behind in Salisbury, 'and Mr Rhodes decided to take them with him to England and to give them a really good time.'

*

Before going to London, it was necessary for Rhodes to pay a flying visit to the Cape. The thought of returning to South Africa for the first time since the Raid probably troubled him more than the prospect of facing the Select Committee of the House of Commons. Since leaving for England at the beginning of the year, he had been in close touch with his business and political associates in the south but he was by no means certain as to how he would be received by the population of the Cape Colony. For all his apparent light-heartedness, he could not have approached the country which he regarded as his home with indifference.

The journey to Cape Town started off badly. Shortly after Rhodes left Salisbury, he heard that Groote Schuur had been gutted by fire. When the news was broken to him by Earl Grey (who had replaced Jameson as Administrator of Rhodesia) the colour is said to have drained from Rhodes's face. Then, with a sigh of relief, he said: 'Is that all? I thought you were going to say that Jameson was dead.' It is one of the few references he appears to have made to Jameson since the Raid.

But the fire was to bring the series of catastrophes to an end. From now on things took a turn for the better and the year which had started with disaster ended in triumph. Rhodes had had some idea of the sort of reception which awaited him at the Cape; he had received numerous telegrams and letters asking him to address meetings on his return. But it was one thing to be invited to speak and quite another to be met with what appeared to be universal acclaim and uncritical affection. Far from having to slink home with his tail between his legs, he found himself making a journey which was said to be like 'a triumphal march'.

From the moment he stepped ashore in Port Elizabeth, he was mobbed by his supporters; when he came to address a huge gathering at the Feather Market, his speech was exuberant. 'It is a good thing to have a period of adversity,' he told the cheering crowd. 'You then find out who are your real friends.'

From Port Elizabeth he travelled by train to Kimberley. At every station on the way up crowds gathered to welcome him home. And so overwhelming was his reception on his return to Cape Town that he was reduced to tears. 'I can only say that I will do my best to make atonement for my error by untiring devotion to the best interests of South Africa,' he announced at a private dinner held in his honour.

Many, however, took no part in these noisy demonstrations. Behind the cheering crowds stood a host of bitter and permanently disillusioned opponents. Prominent among them was Jan Hofmeyr who, when he had first heard of Rhodes's involvement in the Raid, declared that he felt as 'a man who suddenly finds that his wife has been deceiving him'. Less surprised, but equally bitter, were those who had long mistrusted Rhodes. In this group was South Africa's most distinguished woman: Olive Schreiner, the brilliant, complex novelist who, as it happened, was booked to sail to England in the same ship as Rhodes. She was travelling to London to arrange for the publication of her latest book, *Trooper Peter Halket of Mashonaland*: perhaps the most passionate denunciation of Rhodes's policies published during his lifetime.

Cecil Rhodes and Olive Schreiner had first met in 1890. Rhodes had read her famous novel, *The Story of an African Farm*, and recognized it as a work of genius. For her part, Olive Schreiner had been so impressed by Rhodes's work and reputation that the prospect of meeting him roused her to an enthusiasm which she rarely displayed for individual South Africans. 'I am going to meet Cecil Rhodes,' she wrote to Havelock Ellis in March 1890, 'the only great man and man of genius South Africa possesses.' For some reason this meeting did not take place and three months later she was still trying to arrange an introduction. She was forever praising him to her friends. 'The only big man we have here is Rhodes and the only big thing the Chartered Company,' she told W. T. Stead, 'I feel a curious and almost painfully intense interest in the man and his career.' She did, however, express the fear that by accepting the Premiership of the Cape, he would compromise the work he had started in the north. At last, she could contain herself no longer and, brushing aside convention, wrote to Rhodes asking him to visit her. Rhodes accepted the invitation. Not long after their meeting, however, Olive Schreiner began to have second thoughts about the man whom she had so recently idealized.

Her fear that the politician in Rhodes would eclipse the man of destiny proved only too well founded. By the time they met, Rhodes was already Prime Minister of the Cape and it was a vote in the House of Assembly which first turned her against him. In 1891 the notorious Masters and Servants Act came before the Cape Parliament. Commonly known as the 'Strop Bill' or, more bitingly, as the 'Every Man To Wallop His Own Nigger Bill', the proposed legislation contained a clause which entitled an employer to administer corporal punishment to his black labourers. To an ardent humanitarian like Olive Schreiner, the idea of legalized brutality was horrifying. She never forgave Rhodes for supporting it. 'The perception of what his character really was in its inmost depths,' she said, 'was one of the most terrible revelations of my life.'

From this time on the gulf between them widened. Olive Schreiner was not a woman to temporize on matters of principle. Headstrong and emotional, she was prepared to oppose Rhodes as fiercely as she had once pursued him. When the occupation of Mashonaland was followed by the Matabele War and the death of Lobengula, the enthusiasm which she had once shown for the Chartered Company changed into a passionate hostility. It was this hostility which inspired her *Trooper Peter Halket of Mashonaland*.

Often described as a novel, the book is a strange mixture of fact and fiction, of mysticism and polemic, and falls into no conventional literary category. What plot there is centres on a lone trooper employed by the Chartered Company, who has been separated from his companions in the Mashonaland veld. A mysterious, Christ-like stranger emerges from out of the night and addresses him in quasi-biblical language. The trooper, Peter Halket—and there was a Trooper Halkett in the Pioneer Corps—is presented as a typical, simple-minded youngster who has been lured to Mashonaland in the hope of making money; he has given little thought to the purpose of the Chartered Company nor questioned the methods used to subdue the Africans. In the course of the long discussion which follows, the Stranger parades the iniquities of the Chartered Company before Peter Halket in harrowing detail. It is a story of theft, murder and torture, behind which looms the sinister figure of Cecil Rhodes.

Many years later, Rhodes was reported to have said that Olive Schreiner produced the book out of pique after he had accused her of writing herself out with *The Story of an African Farm*. But it is unlikely that even he believed this. In any case, as his accusation was supposed to have been made when the two of them were travelling to England at the end of 1896, it could hardly have applied to *Trooper Halket* which was even then on its way to the publishers.

Throughout the voyage, Olive Schreiner studiously avoided meeting Rhodes and was reported to have raised an alarm when she suspected that her luggage had been rifled by Rhodes's agents in an attempt to steal her explosive manuscript. The truth of this is uncertain but there can be little doubt that she and Rhodes made extremely uncomfortable shipboard companions.

*

Rhodes arrived in London at the beginning of January 1897 and was called before the Select Committee on the 16th February. While waiting to attend the Inquiry, he busied himself with preparations for the development of his northern territories. He also had an important interview with Joseph Chamberlain at the Colonial Office when he made a final bid to get the Inquiry stopped. As this was out of the question, Rhodes agreed to face the Select Committee. The telegrams incriminating the Colonial Office, however, would be suppressed. As Chamberlain himself was to be a member of the Committee, Rhodes could count on his support as long as Rhodes played his part in the deception. They were now accomplices. Each clothed his motives in a fine display of patriotism (the truth could only harm national prestige) but each was fully aware of the penalty which would follow any embarrassing disclosures. Both Rhodes's Charter and Chamberlain's career hung in the balance.

Already the two men had experienced a moment of panic resulting from the misguided partisanship of one of Rhodes's supporters. Towards the end of 1896, W. T. Stead had conceived the bright idea of preparing the public for the revelations which were bound to come out at the Inquiry by publishing a semi-fictional account of the Raid. He hoped, by setting the story in a wider context, to suggest extenuating circumstances for Jameson's action. Entitled *The History of the Mystery*, Stead's account hinted at Chamberlain's complicity in the Raid. It included much explosive information contained in the incriminating telegrams. Although Stead had not actually seen these telegrams, he appears to have been informed of their contents by Bourchier Hawksley, and his story was alarmingly accurate. As soon as Rhodes was told about Stead's booklet, he issued firm instructions that nothing concerning Chamberlain and the Colonial Office was to be published. These instructions arrived too late to stop the booklet, but Stead did his best to make amends by blacking out the more damaging references to the telegrams. The suspicious-looking black oblongs now scattered throughout the text merely added to the mystery of the history. To make matters worse, a review of the unexpurgated version appeared in Cape Town before Rhodes could stop it, which included large quotations from the incriminating passages. Stead's unfortunate publication had done more harm than good but at least no vital information had been disclosed. Both Rhodes and Chamberlain were determined to prevent their underlings from making similar blunders at the Inquiry.

Whenever he could spare the time, Rhodes went riding in Hyde Park with Johnny Grimmer and Bob Coryndon. The sight of Rhodes and his two young friends became a familiar one in Rotten Row and they would often be followed by a train of scalp-hunters. One young heiress was particularly attentive and Rhodes liked to joke about the impression she made on Bob Coryndon. 'She used to ride with me in the Park in the morning,' he would say, 'and d'you know, Coryndon thought she came to see him. Of course she didn't. She came to see *me*.'

For another of his friends, however, Rhodes showed a surprising lack of concern. Dr Jameson was ill in a nursing home when Rhodes arrived in London. He had been sentenced to fifteen months' imprisonment for his part in the Raid but no sooner had he been taken to Holloway Gaol than he fell seriously ill. In November 1896 he had been operated on for stone and at the beginning of the following month he was released from prison because of ill health. He had served little more than four months of his sentence. Since his release he had been confined to bed, his sufferings made worse by the thought of the harm he had caused Rhodes. Although Rhodes must have been fully aware of Jameson's illness and anxiety, he made no effort to see him and it was left to Jameson's faithful manservant, Garlick, to bring the two friends together. When, in answer to Garlick's urgent request, Rhodes arrived at the doctor's bedside, he looked down at the sick man and said: 'Both of us have had a rough time, but you have had a rougher time than I.' From then on Jameson began to get better.

Rhodes attended the hearings of the Select Committee twice a week for three weeks. The Committee sat all day, and during the lunch-time sessions Rhodes faced his examiners sipping a glass of porter and chewing a sandwich. At first he seemed nervous and on one occasion he was described as looking 'pitiful'. But he was able to give back as good as he got. He freely admitted his responsibility for the Raid but went on to lecture the Committee on the conditions in South Africa which had led up to it. He evaded the more delicate issues by refusing to answer questions which might incriminate a third party. When pressed about his dealings with the British High Commissioner, for instance, he suggested that the question should rightly be put to Sir Hercules Robinson rather than to himself.

This evasion was accepted by the Committee and used repeatedly by Rhodes in order to get himself out of tight corners. On the subject of the vital 'missing telegrams' he was equally insistent that his refusal to produce them was a point of honour. 'I consider that they were of a confidential nature and should not be produced,' he said blandly. Once again his interrogators shied off. In fact, he was let off very lightly. The various Committee members were divided among themselves; some had their own axes to grind and much of the questioning was irrelevant to the Raid's more serious implications. Nobody appeared over-anxious to delve too deeply into the question of the Colonial Office's involvement in the affair. Elizabeth Pakenham has suggested that this was because the Committee was partly influenced by 'the operations of an impersonal life-force, which by-passed vendettas and party feuds in order to repel the threat to national survival from outside'. If this is true, then it was a force which operated very much to Rhodes's advantage. For, by following his example, Rhodes's subordinates were to exploit this tacit patriotic reluctance by blatantly refusing to supply any significant evidence demanded from them. Under Chamberlain's watchful eye, witness after witness challenged the Committee's authority with remarkable audacity. Thus it was that, at a public investigation, held in the full glare of world-wide publicity, the only facts revealed were those which Cecil Rhodes condescended to supply. It is hardly surprising that the long-awaited Parliamentary Inquiry into the Jameson Raid was wittily dismissed by one of its critics as 'The Lying in State at Westminster'.

After he had given his evidence, Rhodes left England for a short tour of Europe. He took Johnny Grimmer and Bob Coryndon with him. It was all part of the good time he had promised them. As far as Johnny Grimmer was concerned, it was merely an extension of the holiday he had been enjoying ever since he left South Africa. Not for one moment had he attempted to involve himself in his employer's dreary political concerns. 'D'ye know,' Rhodes was later to say, 'Grimmer never showed the slightest interest in the inquiry. He never came into the committee-room.' During this trip, in fact, young Grimmer seems to have surpassed himself in flaunting his independence. There were times when even Rhodes found his impudent behaviour a little too disrespectful. Usually, when the two of them fell out, it led to a flaming row and ended in Rhodes apologizing to Grimmer. This time Rhodes employed more subtle tactics. At the end of the London visit, he presented Grimmer with a photograph of himself. Somewhat mystified, the young man turned it over and found written on the back: 'Your Baas, C. J. Rhodes.'

*

The loyal demonstrations which had greeted Rhodes on his return to the Cape in 1896 were repeated when he arrived back in South Africa after the Raid Inquiry. His ship docked in Table Bay on 20th April, 1897, and he was met by a vast crowd of supporters, led by the Mayors of Cape Town and Port Elizabeth. Replying to an address of welcome, he declared that he had come back to fight for 'equal political rights for every white man south of the Zambesi'. It was later suggested that this statement had been politically inept as it might alienate the Cape Coloureds who then had the vote, and he was persuaded to modify it to 'every civilized man south of the Zambesi'. But as one of his later biographers has pointed out, the distinction, as far as Rhodes was concerned, was purely academic.

Throughout his short stay in Cape Town he was showered with congratulations. Two days after his arrival, a torch-lit procession of artisans and tradesmen marched to Groote Schuur —then in the process of being rebuilt after the disastrous fire of four months earlier—to pledge their loyalty. By the time they arrived at the house, it was estimated that their numbers had increased to 5,000. In the days that followed, deputations from every type of club and organization called on him to assure him of their support.

Included among the stream of visitors to Groote Schuur were members of the staff of the House of Assembly with whom Rhodes had worked as Prime Minister. One of these civil servants was Gordon le Sueur, a twenty-three-year-old South African born clerk, who considered it his duty to follow the lead of his superiors. He went, he said, 'looking on it as a terrible bore [and] hoped to get it over as soon as possible'. Much to his surprise, when he sent in his card, a steward came out and said that Rhodes wished to see him. Le Sueur had had very little contact with Rhodes and was even more astonished when, on finding Rhodes on the back stoep, the former Prime Minister greeted him with: 'Well, I wondered when you were coming to see me.'

'And now,' said Rhodes when tea had been brought, 'what do you want?' Le Sueur was somewhat taken aback. He assured Rhodes that he did not want anything. 'What!' exclaimed Rhodes, 'don't you want to go up country?' The idea of going to Rhodesia was attractive to le Sueur who was a rather feckless young man, ill-suited to his job at the House of Assembly. But although he admitted that the prospect of a more adventurous life appealed to him, he strongly denied that this was his reason for calling. When Rhodes pressed the point, he became rather embarrassed. 'I was beginning,' he says, 'to wish myself well out of it.' The subject was then changed by another of Rhodes's visitors but when le Sueur rose to leave, Rhodes returned to it. He told the young man that if he wanted to go north, he should write him a note that night and he would arrange it. Somewhat bewildered, le Sueur agreed to write. 'Ah, then you did want something?' smiled Rhodes. 'No I did not,' insisted le Sueur, and left.

That evening le Sueur, still smarting from the fact that his well-meant visit had been misinterpreted, wrote a rather stiff letter to Rhodes declining the offer. Rhodes was delighted by this show of firmness. 'He was very angry when he wrote that, wasn't he?' he was later to say approvingly to Johnny Grimmer. He sent for le Sueur immediately, gave him a lecture on controlling his temper, and told him to get in touch with him when he returned from Kimberley. Le Sueur imagined that this had ended the matter. He was soon to discover he was mistaken. A few days later he was walking near Groote Schuur when Rhodes overtook him in a Cape cart, told him to get in and drove him to the house. Rhodes told him he was leaving for Kimberley that night and might possibly be going further north. 'Would you like to go with me and write my letters?' he asked. By this time le Sueur's resistance had been worn down. He accepted the offer. It was arranged that he should hand in his resignation at his office the following day and meet Rhodes later in Kimberley. 'And,' said Rhodes, 'as a young man leaving Cape Town must have a few debts, here is a cheque to clear them off.'

A duty call, reluctantly undertaken, had certainly paid off.

When one considers that he was an unknown young man, by no means remarkable for his secretarial talents, the way in which Rhodes pursued him is astonishing. Le Sueur could hardly believe it himself. He was so suspicious, in fact, that instead of resigning from the Cape service, he merely had himself transferred to the Rhodesian Civil Service. 'I felt I had taken a wise precaution,' he said.

On arriving at Kimberley, he discovered that Philip Jourdan had succumbed to another of his periodic bouts of 'fever' and that Rhodes needed him to take over as secretary. That same day he and Rhodes boarded a train for the first stage of their journey north. It was the beginning of a very different career from the one which young le Sueur had abandoned in Cape Town.

In Bulawayo they stayed at Government House. Here le Sueur discovered that his duties entailed more than simply 'writing letters'. He was expected to act as Rhodes's bodyguard. The first indication of this came one evening when he was following Rhodes into the drawing-room after dinner and one of the guests pulled him back, saying that Lady Lawley, wife of the acting Administrator, wished to speak to Rhodes alone. Late that night Rhodes sent for le Sueur and scolded him for 'leaving him alone with the lady'.

The young man also discovered that his employer had a romantic side to his nature. One evening, taking him out on to the terrace of Government House, Rhodes pointed to the twinkling lights of Bulawayo and said: 'Look at that—all homes; and all the result of an idle thought.' But there were times when Rhodes's attempts to share his vision with his young companion fell flat. When he took le Sueur to the Matopos to show him 'The World's View', the young man's reaction was extremely disappointing. Alive to the drama of the situation, Rhodes had insisted on le Sueur covering his eyes until they reached the top of the hill. Leading him to the summit, he cried: 'Now look: what do you think of it?' To the unimaginative le Sueur, the view was disappointing. 'Oh, I don't know,' he mumbled, 'it's rather fine.' Rhodes was furious. 'I suppose,' he snapped petulantly, 'if Jesus Christ were to ask you what you thought of Heaven, you'd say, "Oh, I don't know, it isn't bad." ' Rhodes's new friend was obviously going to be poor material for the weaving of dreams.

Rhodes visited 'The World's View' on another occasion during this trip. With him this time was Lewis Michell, his banker and future biographer, who was paying his first visit to Rhodesia. They arrived there early one morning, with Rhodes in a sombre mood. Not only did he point out the exact spot where he wished to be buried but lay down on it 'to see how it felt'. Death was very much on his mind at this time. He was in the process of drawing up a new will and persuaded Michell to act as one of his executors. When Michell pointed out that he was older than Rhodes, Rhodes replied that he 'felt like a man under sentence of death'. This preoccupation with death was probably caused by a recurrence of his heart trouble. Riding out from Bulawayo with Gordon le Sueur one day, Rhodes had suddenly reeled and almost fallen from his horse. He had suffered a slight heart attack. Turning their horses, they rode slowly back to the town and on the way Rhodes told le Sueur that he wanted to provide for him 'in case anything happens'. The young man protested but Rhodes replied: 'Don't be a fool; you can't go back to the Civil Service at tuppence a year.' He later gave le Sueur an envelope which, when opened some years afterwards, was found to contain a bequest of £5,000. At that time, they had known each other for a matter of weeks only.

They left Bulawayo on 18th August, travelling to Salisbury in a special coach. At Salisbury they were joined by Johnny Grimmer, who had come over from Umtali to meet them. Grimmer was permanently posted in Rhodesia; his change of occupation made no difference to the relationship between himself and his employer. He still treated Rhodes in that same, high-handed manner, and Rhodes still allowed it.

Grimmer's attitude delighted the indolent le Sueur. In no time he was following his disrespectful example. Between the two of them, Grimmer and le Sueur were to lead Rhodes a lively dance during the weeks ahead.

While they were in Salisbury, Rhodes was asked to occupy the judge's box at the races during the carnival. He accepted with some trepidation. He was not anxious to leave his two irresponsible employees alone at carnival time. His anxiety proved justified. 'Rhodes,' says le Sueur, 'hated riding-breeches and top boots, hunting stocks, and anything loud in the way of dress, and had lectured Grimmer and myself on the subject at Salisbury. He then went off to the races, saying as he went, "I hope you won't come down and make fools of yourselves at the races." Some time after he had gone Grimmer and I arrayed ourselves in riding-breeches, boots, spurs, and the gaudiest ties and loudest checks we had. We then mounted two small ponies belonging to Dr Jameson. When we were mounted, our feet came to within a foot of the ground; and in all our glory we set off to the racecourse. Carefully avoiding the judge's box in which Rhodes was, we made our way to the opposite side of the course, and waited until the horses in the hurdle race had passed us. We then set off and galloped down the course after them. Rhodes was furious . . .' For the rest of the day they wisely avoided a meeting with their indignant employer. Not until breakfast time the next day did Rhodes manage to corner them. He gave them a strongly-worded lecture and forbade them to go out together again. But his annoyance quickly subsided. At a bazaar a few days later, he made a peace offering by going round the stalls and buying 'about a hundredweight of sweets, which he said would do "to feed le Sueur on".'

From Salisbury they went on to Umtali. All the way the young men continued to tease and play practical jokes on Rhodes. He appears to have found their antics far from amusing. 'I suppose you think you are funny,' he would growl as they fell about, convulsed with laughter. But there was no suggestion of his taking any action against them.

Throughout this Rhodesian trip, Rhodes kept in touch with his business and political associates in South Africa, his mail following him in large hampers as he travelled across the veld. His method of dealing with his correspondence in camp followed a set pattern. With the company seated around the fire at night, the hampers would be emptied and the mail sorted. Official and business letters were dealt with immediately while the more personal correspondence was stacked away to be answered when the party returned to civilization. These personal letters often made up the bulk of the mail. They were a motley collection. Requests for work, begging letters and letters from admirers poured in from all over the world. Among them were a great many proposals of marriage. Women from America and New Zealand, Australia and the Cape, wrote to Rhodes telling him that his work would be improved with a wife by his side and offering themselves as suitable partners. According to J. G. McDonald, such letters were promptly put into the fire. While Rhodes's party was encamped outside Umtali, however, there arrived a letter from a female correspondent which was to be carefully preserved. It had been written on the day that Rhodes left England after the Raid Inquiry and was signed 'Catherine Radziwill'. It was the first salvo in a long and intensive campaign.

Like most of Catherine's writings, her first letter to Rhodes was a mixture of apparent outspokenness and assumed familiarity, to which was added an intriguing dash of romantic superstition. She told him that at one time she had regarded him with suspicion, considering him to be a financial adventurer. Since meeting him, however, her views had changed. She now recognized his true greatness and wished to bestow her blessing on him and his enterprises. Her one fear was that something would happen to him and this fear had been heightened by the fact that she possessed second sight. A presentiment told her that an attempt would be made on his life within the next six months and as a safeguard against this danger she was enclosing a small medallion. This talisman, she said, had been given by a gipsy to her cousin General Skobeleff who had worn it throughout his campaigns. She begged Rhodes to keep it with him as a mascot.

Rhodes appears to have been impressed by this unexpected concern for his welfare. The letter, having come from a princess, was considered important enough to keep and le Sueur was instructed to look after the medallion. But no attempt having been made on his life in the stated time, Rhodes seems to have forgotten about the Princess and her presentiment. When next Catherine wrote to him, he had difficulty in remembering who she was.

*

Lewis Michell left the party at Umtali and Rhodes, Grimmer and le Sueur continued on to the farm at Inyanga. Rhodes's love of life in the veld was such that his recent preoccupation with death disappeared and he was soon in the highest of spirits. He adored the rough and tumble of camp life. Sleeping in the open under a sheep-skin and eating game, shot on the way and cooked by his coloured man-servant, Tony de la Cruz, was for him the peak of existence. In only one respect did his camping life differ from that of the hardy Rhodesian pioneers. This was his obsession with hygiene. He would never go a day without shaving and insisted, to their disgust, on his two young companions following his example. 'Grimmer and le Sueur hate water,' he would say. 'I don't believe they'd wash at all if I didn't make them.' Nor could he bear an untidy camp. He would always choose the camping site himself and would insist that it was cleared of all rubbish and well away from the debris left by previous wagons. 'He had an abhorrence of a dirty camp,' says Jourdan, 'and always avoided any place which bore indications of previous camps. His pet aversion was to see old provision tins lying about his camp.' Considering that he was notoriously untidy in appearance and always displayed a great contempt for the niceties of civilization, this concern for cleanliness is somewhat curious.

At Inyanga Rhodes bought more land to add to his already large estate. Le Sueur talks of his exuberant spirits and the energy with which he rode out each day, often climbing hills on foot. He used to refer to Inyanga as the 'sanatorium' of Rhodesia and always claimed that he felt better once he was in the highveld. But the combination of excessive exertion and the high altitude finally proved too much for him. After a few weeks at the farm he suffered another heart attack.

At first Grimmer and le Sueur thought that he was suffering from a fever brought on by his habit of walking about stark naked and exposed to draughts. In their clumsy way, they did their best to nurse him. At times like this he appeared almost childlike in his need for reassurance and comfort. Even the insensitive le Sueur was touched by his helplessness. 'When Rhodes was ill,' he writes, 'he often alternated between periods of peevishness, fretfulness, and loss of temper and periods of despondency; and it was during the latter, when he used to ask one to sit by him and hold his hand, or place one's hand upon his fevered forehead, that one's feeling was perhaps most stirred by him; and one had a peculiar sensation as of an inclination to shield and protect him.' Nothing that they could do, however, seemed to help Rhodes. At last they defied his orders and sent for the local doctor at Umtali, but it was not until Dr Jameson arrived a few days later that the patient began to recover.

Rhodes's main concern, once he was on his feet again, was that the real nature of his illness should not leak out. He was afraid that the truth might affect the stock market. In answer to the stream of inquiries about his health, Rhodes instructed le Sueur to say that he had suffered an attack of fever and was recovering. Similar false reports about his health were to create a great deal of confusion for the remainder of Rhodes's life.

No sooner was Rhodes better than Johnny Grimmer was taken ill. Like his employer, Grimmer was subject to false reports concerning the state of his health. The reasons, however, were very different. It seems that Grimmer had an unfortunate addiction to the bottle and when he was rendered incapable, Rhodes would excuse him by saying that he had a touch of fever. But this time the illness was genuine. A bite on the face from a scorpion or a spider had been followed by a feverish condition, and he and Rhodes exchanged roles as patient and nurse. Dr Jameson had left Inyanga by this time and Rhodes devised his own treatment: it was a mixture of his fetish for hygiene and an old wives' cure. He ordered everything to be cleared out of the sick-room, which was then scrubbed from ceiling to floor with disinfectant, and bathed Grimmer's feet in vinegar.

It all proved too much for le Sueur. Rhodes himself was still not well and the depressing atmosphere of illness and bad temper began to get on le Sueur's nerves. Taking two horses and some servants and without bothering to tell Rhodes that he was going, he set off on a hunting trip to Portuguese East Africa. He was away for ten days. On his return, at midnight on the tenth day, his bravado evaporated. Apprehensive about his reception, he crept into Grimmer's room to find out the lie of the land. 'Hullo,' he said, waking Grimmer. 'How is the "Old Man"?' 'Oh, he is all right,' replied Grimmer, 'but you should have seen his face when I told him that you had gone.' In a whisper Grimmer went on to tell him the tantrums that had followed his departure. To the two youngsters it was all a great joke and they were soon convulsed with giggles. 'Just then,' says le Sueur, 'Rhodes, probably awakened by our talking and laughing, walked in in his pyjamas, and, rubbing himself in front in his characteristic way, he said, with his little whine,

174

"H-e-e-e! I *knew* you'd come back! I *knew* you'd come back! Didn't I say so, Grimmer?" But Grimmer was rolling over with laughter and with a snort the "Old Man" went back to bed.'

They started out on their return journey at the beginning of November. At Salisbury they were met by Philip Jourdan, now recovered from his illness and eager to resume his duties. Any hopes he may have had of replacing le Sueur were soon dashed. Rhodes was still busy planning railway and telegraphic links with the north and, in connection with these schemes, was preparing to visit England the following year. Jourdan had long dreamed of accompanying Rhodes to Europe but found himself, once again, passed over in favour of a less competent but more stimulating member of the Rhodes entourage. 'Le Sueur,' he explains modestly, 'was very anxious to go with him to England, and I was required at Salisbury . . . Mr Rhodes asked me to remain there till his return from England.'

After spending two months at the Cape, Rhodes and le Sueur sailed for England on the *Tantallon Castle* at the beginning of March 1898. It was le Sueur's first visit to London and, like Johnny Grimmer before him, he made the most of it. Given *carte blanche* at fashionable tailors and booksellers, he embarked on a spending spree which startled even his indulgent employer. 'Seems rather a large amount for a secretary,' wrote Rhodes on a copy of a tailor's bill. He nonetheless paid the bill—as well as another for £60, which was what his secretary had spent on books.

Once the day's schedule had been arranged, there was very little for Rhodes's secretary to do on these London visits. 'His private correspondence did not amount to much,' says le Sueur, 'as letters were kept at Groote Schuur to await his return, and my chief duty in London was to attend to his engagements.' Rhodes would often insist on le Sueur accompanying him to social functions and many a startled hostess would find herself forced to adjust her seating arrangements to accommodate the guest of honour's uninvited secretary. Some of the guests found the presence of this gauche young man a trifle disconcerting. 'I wish to God, Rhodes, that you would not bring these African savages over here,' gasped an indignant duke, after one of le Sueur's hearty handshakes. 'He's smashed my fingers.'

Even in these undemanding circumstances, it was apparent

that le Sueur did not have the makings of a private secretary. Rhodes, in fact, seems to have grown a little tired of him. As was his habit when he wished to get rid of an embarrassment, Rhodes began to suggest alternative employment for the young man. At first he tried to persuade le Sueur to remain in England and obtain a medical degree and when this offer was rejected, he suggested the Rhodesian Civil Service. To this le Sueur seems to have agreed. But before the matter could be taken any further, he contracted an ear infection. No doubt glad to have him off his hands for a while, Rhodes left him in a London hospital and returned to South Africa alone.

The next time that Rhodes made this voyage to the Cape, he would find himself saddled with a companion it would not be so easy to discard.

Part Two

CHAPTER EIGHT

The Princess Sails South

SHORTLY after his return to South Africa in 1898, Rhodes celebrated his forty-fifth birthday. He looked a good deal older. His hair was greying rapidly. His face, with its network of broken veins, was flushed and bloated. His eyes had the puffy, watery look of a man who does not get enough rest. He was clumsier, paunchier, more ill-kempt than ever. His breathing was laboured and his manner an odd blend of energy and lassitude. He was clearly a man who had not much longer to live.

Yet there was still a great deal to be done. He had no sooner arrived back at the Cape than he was plunged into the preparations for a general election. As it was the first election since the Jameson Raid, a great deal depended on its outcome.

Rhodes entered the contest in a determined mood. Mustering all his energies, he travelled the country, speaking from the platforms of his supporters, vindicating his past conduct and vilifying his former allies. 'I have been painted very black,' he told a hostile audience, 'and have been represented to you as the embodiment of everything that is bad. The worst acts and the most evil designs have been imputed to me; but gentlemen, I can assure you, although I have my faults, I am incapable of such things.' The meeting ended with a unanimous vote of confidence in Rhodes and his policies. 'I honestly believe,' he declared on another occasion, 'that my years of trouble have made me a better man . . . and I am determined to go on with my work, the work of forming a railway junction with Egypt—and the work of closer union in South Africa.' His words were drowned by cheers. Union was the theme of all his speeches; a union which would include Rhodesia.

It was a bitter fight. It created a hostility between the two

179

white races that was without precedent in the history of the Colony. Rhodes's opponents accused him of perverting his capital to obtain 'objects which conspiracy and violence have failed to compass'. He retorted by claiming that they were financed by the Transvaal and were little more than tools of Paul Kruger. 'I am determined not to leave the South till I see you are clear of the risk of being dominated by Krugerism,' he told the electors of Port Elizabeth. In the midst of the contest vandals broke into the grounds of Groote Schuur, lighting fires, cutting down trees and injuring the animals in his private zoo. Throughout it all Rhodes maintained his resolute stand; he made what are generally considered to be his finest speeches.

But he was defeated. It was a close thing. Rhodes and his party polled the majority of votes in the towns but their opponents won the election on the country vote. Rhodes himself was doubly elected. He had stood in his old constituency of Barkly West, but his friends, apprehensive of the Dutch vote in this rural district, had nominated him for a safer seat. He won both elections and continued to represent Barkly West for the remainder of his life.

He was not cut out to be a Leader of the Opposition. During the new parliamentary session he made a few inconsequential speeches and then gave up. His attempted come-back had been staged too soon. He should have allowed people more time in which to forget the Raid, but time was the very thing he lacked. All efforts must from now on be directed purposefully. He turned his attention once more to the north. At the end of the year he sailed for England to negotiate the extension of the railway through Rhodesia. This time he took the faithful Jourdan with him. For his secretary, at least, the disappointing election result had brought its compensation: after years of being thrust into the background, Flippie Jourdan was to realize his long-cherished ambition of travelling the world with his hero.

They arrived in England in the middle of January 1899. Rhodes was welcomed back with a pre-Jameson Raid enthusiasm. 'Mr Rhodes's presence in England is now becoming a matter of annual recurrence,' commented *The Times*. 'Reverses, obstacles and failures, in which he has openly acknowledged his own share of shortcoming, have but strengthened his determined grip upon the scheme of his life's work. All is not done, but his measure of success has been on the whole remarkable. The end has never been abandoned, and step by step advance is made towards its attainment.'

Throughout his London visit Rhodes occupied a special suite of rooms at the Burlington Hotel in Cork Street. As always, he was pursued by a stream of uninvited visitors. 'Promiscuous callers came to the hotel from early morning till late in the afternoon,' says Philip Jourdan. 'They all wanted something from him—some employment, whilst others asked for monetary assistance. Sometimes my whole morning was occupied in seeing these people . . . Many insisted on seeing him personally, and if told that he was out or engaged, they waited sometimes for hours outside in the hope of catching him as he passed in and out of the hotel.'

One way and another, Jourdan's first weeks in London were fairly hectic. Rhodes, fully occupied with the affairs of the Chartered Company and still very much the social lion, appears to have relied on his secretary much more than usual. This may have been due to the fact that Jourdan was far more dependable than his predecessors. In any case, Jourdan found that coping with swarms of callers, arranging interviews, answering letters and seeing that Rhodes kept his various engagements, left him with little time for the social sprees Johnny Grimmer and Gordon le Sueur had enjoyed. It must have come as a relief to hear that Rhodes was leaving for Egypt at the beginning of February and that his secretary was free to take a month's holiday. Presenting the young man with a handsome cheque, Rhodes advised him to follow his example and travel to Egypt, advice which the devoted Jourdan was only too ready to accept.

Rhodes, accompanied by his two Oxford friends, Sir Charles Metcalfe and Rochfort Maguire, left London on 1st February and, on arriving in Cairo, put up at the Savoy Hotel. Here he was joined, a few days later, by Philip Jourdan and Karri Davies —another of Rhodes's 'young men'. Jourdan was delighted to find that instead of being met by the expected 'pile of work', he was urged by Rhodes to continue his holiday. A sightseeing programme was drawn up and Jourdan and Karrie Davies were despatched on a trip up the Nile.

After leaving Egypt Rhodes paid a flying visit to Berlin where he was warmly received by the Kaiser. These two men, both highly distrustful of others and not a little neurotic, seem to have got on surprisingly well. They joked about the Kaiser's notorious telegram to Kruger after the Jameson Raid and Rhodes came away confident that his telegraph line would be continued through German East Africa. His next meeting with a European monarch was not so successful. Calling at Brussels on his way to London, he had a private interview with Leopold II, the King of the Belgians and the ruler of the Congo. What took place at this interview is not known but Rhodes's reaction to the wily old King left little doubt as to its outcome. 'Satan,' he hissed to the British military attaché as he left the audience room, 'I tell you that man is Satan.'

On his return to London he was once again enmeshed in the affairs of the Chartered Company. The endless negotiations for the financing and building of his trans-continental railway and telegraph system occupied the best part of each day. In the mornings, after his customary ride in Hyde Park, he would drive to the City, leaving his harassed secretary to cope with the inevitable chaos resulting from his absence from the hotel. He did, however, find time for one other important piece of business. This was the redrafting of his will. The thought of this, the seventh version of his will, had been occupying his mind for several months and it was now in the hands of his English solicitor, Bourchier Hawksley. The completing of the document entailed numerous conferences between Rhodes and his legal advisers and the scope of the bequests reflected the lingering glow of his life-long vision. After stipulating that he was to be buried at 'The World's View' in the Matopos, he went on to make a number of personal bequests. Groote Schuur, together with £1,000 a year for its maintenance, he left as a residence for the future Prime Minister of a federated South Africa; his English estate went to his family; his properties in Rhodesia were left in trust for the settlers of that country; and a legacy of £100,000 was bequeathed to Oriel College, Oxford. The most important provision was left until last. This was the extension of his famous Scholarship Foundation. Provision for thirty-six scholarships had been made in a previous will but now Rhodes, helped and advised by W. T. Stead, increased the number of scholarships and clarified the terms of the awards. In effect, education at Oxford was to replace the vague activities he had intended his 'secret society' to perform. Although this will was to be amended by a series of codicils, its broad provisions remained untouched and were put into effect after Rhodes's death.

For Philip Jourdan, the constant discussion of the will was both embarrassing and depressing. He preferred not to think about the possibility of Rhodes's death. His embarrassment became even more acute when, during one of the sessions with Hawksley, he found himself included in the arrangements. 'What shall we do about this young rascal?' Rhodes asked the solicitor. Then, turning to Jourdan, he said: 'I am going to leave you £5,000; will that be sufficient for you?' The young man's resulting confusion greatly amused Rhodes. 'He was very fond of teasing,' says Jourdan, 'and that day he certainly was in a teasing mood. He went on: "No, I think I will leave him £7,000. He has done very good work for me. Yes, put down £7,000. Have you got that?" Hawksley bent down to write, then he interrupted him: "No, wait a bit, make it £10,000, he deserves it. Write it down on a piece of paper as a separate instruction to my executors." I felt horribly uncomfortable whilst all this was going on, and I did think he might have done it differently; but he seemed to enjoy my embarrassment immensely.' As a final mortifying touch, Rhodes had Hawksley produce a slip of paper, dated shortly after Jourdan had resigned from the Civil Service, showing that he had already made provision for a £5,000 legacy for his blushing secretary. This was one of the few occasions on which Jourdan came close to criticizing his hero; but on thinking it over, he considered it an excellent example of Rhodes's fair-mindedness.

During the second half of this London visit Rhodes was once again made aware of the existence of Princess Catherine Radziwill. She wrote to him asking for his advice on an investment. When Jourdan handed him the letter, Rhodes was somewhat puzzled by it. He could not remember the Princess. Turning to Rochefort Maguire, he asked who she was. Maguire thought for a moment and then remembered that they had met her at Moberley Bell's dinner party some three years earlier. He reminded Rhodes that she had sat next to him. Rhodes's face brightened. 'Yes,' he said, 'I remember her; she was quite interesting; a vivacious talker.' He had forgotten her strange letter to him in Rhodesia.

This second letter was quite different. It contained no dire warnings or hints of mystical powers. Occult tactics having failed, Catherine had decided on a more mundane approach. Her appeal was purely financial. She had—or so she said—come in for some £200,000 which she wanted to invest. Could Rhodes help her? Rhodes was constantly being asked to share his financial genius and more often than not such requests met with a polite note of refusal. On this occasion, however, he was prepared to make an exception. 'Being a princess,' says Jourdan, 'he did not instruct me to reply to her note, but sat down and wrote to her personally.' His reply was short and to the point. After apologizing for not having written sooner, he went on to explain that he did not like advising friends on money matters, but he thought she would get a safe return for her money if she purchased Mashonaland Railway debentures. As she had said that she would be away from London at that time, he added a polite postscript saying that he hoped to see her on her return. It was the only letter that he ever admitted writing to her.

*

Rhodes had originally intended to return to South Africa in April. Such was the pressure of business during these busy London months, however, that this was not possible. His financial negotiations on behalf of the Chartered Company and the final drafting of his will made it necessary for him to postpone his departure several times. He had been booked to sail on about five different ships, says Jourdan, before he boarded the s.s. *Scot*, which left Southampton at the beginning of July 1899.

Just before the ship sailed Jourdan learned that Princess Catherine Radziwill was on board. He says he was informed of her presence by an official of the shipping company. It seems that the Princess had been causing the company some concern. According to the official, she had called repeatedly at the shipping office to inquire by which ship Rhodes was leaving and had cancelled an earlier passage in order to sail in the *Scot*. Not knowing how well she was acquainted with Rhodes, the official had thought it wise to warn Jourdan so that he could mention it to Rhodes. Jourdan lost no time in passing on the information. 'Oh! Is she here?' remarked the unsuspecting Rhodes. 'I wonder what takes her to South Africa.'

Her first public appearance was made at dinner that evening. Earlier in the day, Jourdan had reserved a small table in the dining-saloon for Rhodes, Sir Charles Metcalfe and himself; it was a table with sufficient chairs to allow Rhodes to do some occasional entertaining. Most of the other passengers had also booked their places at table. But not Catherine. With skilful timing, she arrived in the dining-saloon ten minutes after the meal had started. Jourdan gives an amusing account of her entrance. 'She glided into the saloon, gorgeously gowned and got up to captivate,' he says. 'She tripped along lightly, only the rustling of her silk garments being audible. As she advanced she looked round the saloon for a seat, but accidentally, I suppose, made a bee line for Mr Rhodes's table. She did not, of course, recognize him till she was at his table. She appeared quite overcome with surprise when she did see him and exclaimed, "Oh! How do you do?" Mr Rhodes rose from his seat and so did Sir Charles and I, and we all bowed to her. She appeared timid, coy and somewhat confused. She nervously placed her hand on the back of a chair at our table and said, "Is this chair engaged? May I have it?" Mr Rhodes gallantly replied, "Certainly, Princess, you are quite welcome to it," and at the same time turned it for her at a convenient angle. Of course she occupied the chair for the rest of the voyage.'

This obvious and over-acted approach served as an introduction, claims Jourdan, to her blatant pursuit of Rhodes. It would seem that her tactics throughout the voyage were so crude as not to have fooled the most unsophisticated of men, let alone the shrewd and cynical Rhodes.

At meal times she was utterly charming. She knew everyone and could talk wittily about anything. Her mastery of the English language and her wide knowledge of English literature astonished Jourdan. There was not a poem nor a book which she could not discuss intelligently and she was quick to inform them that she was even more at home with French than with English. Only one thing spoiled her conversation. This was her tendency to express herself bluntly on 'delicate matters'. Young Jourdan found this outspokenness extremely embarrassing and noticed that on one occasion even Rhodes 'could not suppress a blush'. Sir Charles Metcalfe was quick to reassure his sensitive friends. He told them that this openness in discussing questionable subjects was simply an unfortunate foreign habit.

Jourdan says that quite early in the voyage the Princess made a point of telling them her reasons for going to South Africa. Her husband, she said, was a brute and treated her abominably. She had endured this treatment for as long as she could and was now in the process of divorcing him. As divorce proceedings took a long time in Russia, she had decided to spend a year in South Africa until her divorce was granted. In fact, there is no evidence that Catherine was then contemplating a divorce; in any case, the formalities would have taken much longer than a year. It was to be another seven years before she and the inoffensive Prince Wilhelm were legally separated, and this was merely a preliminary to obtaining a divorce.

The purpose of this divorce story seems only too apparent. The Princess was implying that she would soon be free to marry again. Having thus baited her hook, she proceeded to dangle it brazenly under Rhodes's nose. Jourdan describes how she hung on Rhodes's every word and went out of her way to flatter him. When talking to Metcalfe and himself, says Jourdan, she was inclined to argue and would become so emphatic that her voice could be heard all over the dining-saloon; but there was never a hint of opposition in her discussions with Rhodes. Selecting an agreeable subject, she was all sweet reasonableness and only too anxious that her views should coincide with his. Nor did she confine her attentions to meal times. She would follow Rhodes about on deck, cornering him at every opportunity. She was always complaining of her heart, says Jourdan, and on one occasion when she and Rhodes were sitting beside each other on the main deck, she gave a sudden gasp and lolled over into Rhodes's lap. Trying to support her until help arrived, Rhodes looked the very picture of misery. 'I shall never forget,' says Jourdan, 'the absolutely abject look of helplessness on his face.' Smelling salts were fetched and in no time the Princess was again on her feet; but from that time on Rhodes is said to have avoided the main promenade and confined himself to the captain's deck.

In her role as *femme fatale*, the only thing that Catherine lacked, according to Jourdan, was physical attraction. 'She was not tall,' he reports, 'inclined to be stout, had black hair and black shifting eyes. She could not be called handsome or pretty, and was about forty-seven years of age then.'

This account of Rhodes and Catherine on board the s.s. *Scot* is one of the most vividly described episodes of their strange association. It is not surprising that some of Rhodes's biographers have seized upon it to help present Catherine as a figure of fun. One is left with the impression of a fat, blowzy, middle-aged adventuress, relentlessly chasing an innocent, hapless and extremely eligible bachelor. It is a situation worthy of Gilbert and Sullivan. But the account is suspect.

On the whole, Philip Jourdan is an honest and fairly reliable witness. But in this instance, his accuracy is open to question. The truth is that during this particular voyage, Catherine seems to have made only a slight impression on Jourdan; certainly not enough for him to have remembered her behaviour in such detail. Some months after they had arrived in South Africa, Jourdan had so far forgotten her that he had to ask who she was. It is this, among other things, which makes his lively account of her shipboard antics, written about ten years later, a little difficult to accept. Perhaps he was not being deliberately untruthful. He did, indeed, come to know her much better during her stay in South Africa and his picture may well have been coloured by subsequent knowledge—with a few farcical touches put in for good measure.

In June 1899, when she sailed from England, Catherine was forty-one years of age. A photograph taken of her at this time shows her to have been slim, elegant and still very attractive. It was true that the breathtaking beauty which had once captivated visitors to Berlin and which had impressed W. T. Stead and Maud Gonne in St Petersburg was beginning to fade but she was still a striking-looking woman. With her dark hair piled above her broad forehead, her large, heavy-lidded eyes, her aquiline nose and her mobile mouth, she now had a vivacity and a piquancy of expression that counted for more than mere youth or beauty. Nor was her manner such as would have frightened men off. Jourdan himself talks of her 'bright and versatile' conversation and another passenger, who often dined with Rhodes, was entranced by her 'strange fascination'. Indeed, even the unsusceptible Rhodes was not entirely immune to her charm. By the time the ship docked in Cape Town he had given her an open invitation to lunch or dine at Groote Schuur; one can hardly imagine him doing this had he spent the voyage hiding from her on the captain's deck. He rarely felt it necessary to inconvenience himself for the sake of being polite, and certainly not where women were concerned.

Of Catherine's desire to attach herself to Rhodes there can be little doubt. Whether or not she seriously contemplated marrying him is another matter. For one thing she was not free to marry nor would she be for some time. She might have been content to form a romantic association which would not only have given her a position of influence but, if it became noised abroad, might have accelerated her divorce from Prince Wilhelm. It was decidedly in her interest to have her friendship with Rhodes talked about and this, for the moment, was probably the extent of her ambition. Only a deliberate attempt to court notoriety can explain her shameless behaviour, both on board ship and later in South Africa. Even so, it is doubtful whether her decision to visit South Africa was prompted solely by the hope of creating a *succès de scandale*. Capable of foolishness, she was no fool. It was unlikely that she would embark on a six-thousand-mile voyage without having a few other tricks up her sleeve. Her purpose may well have been twofold. First there was the possibility of ensnaring Rhodes and secondly, the chance of extending her journalistic activities. She was still largely dependent on her writing for her living and at that time South Africa offered considerable scope for an enterprising journalist with influential connections. There was every possibility that the politics of the Cape could provide her with the journalistic opportunities she had lacked since her departure from St Petersburg.

By the middle of 1899 the situation in South Africa was tense. Any hopes of a peaceful solution to the Uitlander problem in the Transvaal had been shattered by the Jameson Raid. The mining community, resenting the way in which their cause had been compromised, had been left with an added sense of injustice, and Kruger, convinced that his self-righteous stand had been vindicated, remained as unyielding as ever. But although, basically, the situation was the same, there had been an important change of focus among the protagonists: the Imperial Factor was now dominant. With Rhodes in disgrace, the Uitlanders had been forced to look to the British authorities for a redress of their grievances and in Sir Alfred Milner, the recently appointed High Commissioner, they had found a dedicated and aggressive champion. Milner, who had assumed office shortly after Rhodes returned from the Jameson Raid Inquiry in 1897, had lost no time in making clear his attitude towards Kruger and the Transvaal. His aim was to assert British supremacy throughout southern Africa and, in his opinion, this could only be done by making the burghers of the Transvaal toe the Imperial line. When a conference between himself and Kruger was arranged in Bloemfontein at the end of May 1899, Milner attended it determined to force the issue. Convinced that the Boers were arguing from weakness, he intended to call their bluff. The conference, which lasted from 31st May to 5th June, ended in stalemate. The Boers showed no sign of giving way. It was no longer a question of whether or not there would be a war, but of when the fighting would start.

News of the abortive Bloemfontein Conference had reached England shortly before the *Scot* sailed. For Catherine, it would have provided a further enticement to visit South Africa. The opportunity of travelling to a crisis spot in the company of a man like Rhodes was not to be missed. But the fact that she arrived in South Africa armed with a letter of introduction to Sir Alfred Milner from Lord Salisbury, seems to indicate that she had more than Cecil Rhodes on her mind when she booked her passage.

That Catherine had a professional, as well as a matrimonial— or at least romantic—interest in visiting South Africa, is something which Rhodes's biographers have ignored. Regarding her as a foolish adventuress, obsessed with the idea of marrying Rhodes, they have tended to exaggerate the comic aspects of her pursuit and to ignore her real interest in politics. This view is derived largely from Jourdan's caricature of her on board the *Scot*. From the very outset she is represented as having no interest other than in trapping the unsuspecting Rhodes. Both actors in this shipboard comedy are made to behave in a manner which is not only out of character but at variance with other accounts of the voyage. Jourdan says, for instance, that Rhodes left London on the 18th June and that the Princess changed her booking 'on several occasions' in order to sail with him. This gives the impression that Catherine had been planning her trip to South Africa as early as April (when Rhodes had originally intended to leave England) and was pestering the shipping office long before the political crisis in South Africa reached a climax. In fact, Rhodes did not set out for South Africa until 1st July, and there is reason to think that the Princess changed her booking only once and that a few days before the *Scot* sailed. This is the story believed by other passengers aboard the *Scot*. 'Rumour,' reports Colin Harding in his account of the voyage, 'said that the Princess was so anxious to travel to Cape Town in the society of Rhodes that she had cancelled a berth which she had taken on a steamer sailing on the previous Saturday to travel now with this illustrious statesman.' Harding, who was travelling to Africa to relieve Bob Coryndon as temporary Administrator of Northern Rhodesia, was invited to dine at Rhodes's table several times during the trip and came to know Catherine well. Both he and his wife were fascinated by her. He says that she and Rhodes 'were very friendly and spent much time in each other's company' but makes no mention of her outrageous behaviour which, if Jourdan is to be believed, must have been the talk of the ship. Everything that Rhodes did during this long and exceptionally calm voyage was carefully observed by the other passengers and one feels that Harding would at least have remembered the fainting episode, claimed by Jourdan to have created such a stir. By the time Harding wrote his version, he had no reason to defend Catherine's by then tarnished reputation.

The truth seems to be that, at this stage of the affair, Catherine's motives were mixed. Having conceived the plan of ingratiating herself with Rhodes, she had been encouraged by events in South Africa to chance following him to the Cape. Her decision had probably been reached on the spur of the moment, in what looked like favourable circumstances, and once embarked on her reckless course, there was no turning back. This appears the most reasonable explanation for many of her seemingly foolish actions. The female Rzewuskas were, as she would have been the first to admit, an impetuous and stubborn lot.

*

There are few places in the world more beautiful than the Cape. June and July, however, are not the best months in which to see it. Sullen clouds mask Table Mountain and the entire peninsula is curtained in a fine, monotonous drizzle. The atmosphere is dull and depressing. But it is not always like this. There are days when the clouds suddenly lift and the sun comes out, bringing the whole scene to brilliant life. The mountain emerges blue and clear, the pine trees shimmer, the whitewash gleams and the long coastline shifts and sparkles.

Such a day was 18th July, 1899. The sun broke through early in the morning, setting Cape Town's harbour aglitter and bringing the promise of a bright and cloudless day. The air was clear and the atmosphere invigorating. The mood of the town matched that of the weather. For the past week the citizens had been preparing for this day. The streets were decked with flags and banners, bunting fluttered from the tram wires and brightly coloured medallions decorated every lamp-post and telegraph pole. Most of the shops and offices had declared a public holiday and crowds had begun to gather in the streets leading towards the docks shortly after daybreak. Once more Cape Town was demonstrating its loyalty to Cecil John Rhodes. This time the welcome was to surpass all previous tributes. 'It was perhaps,' says T. E. Fuller, 'the greatest demonstration ever made in his honour.'

Rhodes knew what to expect. He had received a cable at Madeira from the reception committee, telling him of the arrangements. Nevertheless, when the *Scot* docked and he emerged from the saloon, he was seen to be looking a little irritable. But he quickly brightened when, on walking down the gangway, a tremendous cheer burst forth from the waiting crowd. Accompanied by Sir Charles Metcalfe, and looking unusually spruce in a dark blue suit and black felt hat, he strode to his carriage with, it is said, 'the same boyishness and elasticity of gait as have always been characteristic of him'. When he raised his hat to acknowledge the cheers, however, it was noticed that his hair was considerably greyer than it had been seven months before. He was driven straight to Groote Schuur. All along the route he passed under banners lettered 'Welcome Cecil' or simply 'C.J.R.' and crowds had gathered on every corner to cheer him on his way. Royalty could have expected no more. '*Venit, vidit, vincit,*' declared a local paper. 'He came, he saw, he conquered. His progress through the city was a triumphal procession.'

Throughout the day congratulatory messages poured into Groote Schuur. That night an enormous crowd packed the Drill Hall where Rhodes was presented with over one hundred loyal addresses from admirers. As he entered the hall, the band struck up 'See the Conquering Hero Comes' and the entire audience rose to its feet with a roar of welcome. It was a highly emotional moment.

It is difficult to understand what sparked off such demonstrations. Although Rhodes had been busy negotiating for the extension of his railway and telegraphic systems, these were long-standing projects, unlikely to evoke emotional reactions. It might have been a delayed response on the part of his supporters to his failure to regain the Premiership in the general election. More probably, his return had been seized upon to give expression to the war fever which was gripping the country. But whatever the cause, the effect was regarded as momentous. 'The extraordinary outburst of public enthusiasm with which Mr Rhodes was welcomed . . .' commented the *Cape Times*, 'may fairly be taken as marking another epoch in [his] career.'

There is nothing in the reports of Rhodes's homecoming to indicate whether Catherine attended the demonstrations held in his honour. On the two occasions when he spoke, so many celebrities attended the meetings that it was impossible for the newspapers to list them all. Catherine would not have missed the opportunity of ranging herself among his supporters. She must certainly have been fully aware of his tumultuous reception and any doubts she may have had about Rhodes's standing in Africa since the Jameson Raid would have been dispersed during her first days in Cape Town. There was no need to regret her decision to travel to South Africa.

In the general furore, her own arrival passed almost unnoticed. She was probably gratified to find herself elevated to the rank of Serene Highness in a local newspaper version of the *Scot*'s passenger list. She may, indeed, have been responsible for the designation; local reporters were not *au fait* with the intricacies of the *Almanach de Gotha*, and Catherine was careful to keep the details of her background extremely vague. Even at the height of her subsequent notoriety, the name of her husband was never revealed and none of Rhodes's biographers appear to have known the real identity of Prince Radziwill. But there can be little doubt that, from the time she stepped ashore in Cape Town, it was Catherine's intention to play up her title for all it was worth—and for a great deal more.

For this first part of her South African sojourn, she stayed at the fashionable Mount Nelson Hotel. With her, as fellow guests, were Major and Mrs Harding, the young couple with whom she had become friendly on board the *Scot*. Anxious to observe Colonial formalities, the Hardings lost no time in calling at Government House to sign their names in the Visitors' Book. Catherine went with them. But there was to be no question of her observing such run-of-the-mill conventions. For a princess, the signing of visitors' books was not something to be lightly undertaken. She informed the Hardings that her arrival would be announced to Sir Alfred Milner through her introductory letter from Lord Salisbury. The presentation of this letter was carried out in grand style a day or two later. Arriving at Government House, looking 'perfectly regal' and wearing the enormous collar of pearls which was later to be the subject of much speculation in Cape Town, she had herself announced to the High Commissioner. Seated, stiff-backed and composed, in an armchair in the reception room, she looked, says one over-awed visitor, 'quite a princess'. And she remained quite a princess throughout the visit. When Milner arrived, there was a polite clash of etiquette. 'The Governor came in and spoke to her,' it is reported, 'everyone rising except the Princess. The A.D.C. asked her to rise. This request the Princess refused.' Nonplussed, the A.D.C. explained that Sir Alfred Milner represented the British Crown and, in the absence of the Sovereign, was entitled to the same respect as Queen Victoria. Catherine was unimpressed. She remained seated throughout the interview. In the end, Milner invited her to dine later in the week and Catherine returned to her hotel triumphant.

For all that, her performance may not have been quite as successful as it at first appeared. Milner seems to have had some doubt about her credentials. When Lord Salisbury's son, Lord Edward Cecil, arrived in Cape Town shortly afterwards, the High Commissioner felt obliged to make a few inquiries about

Princess Radziwill. Did Lord Salisbury really know her? Was her letter of introduction genuine? He was told that Lord Salisbury had indeed met Catherine at the Berlin Conference and that the Princess had visited Hatfield a few times. The friendship was slight but the letter was genuine.

Milner might be suspicious, but the Hardings had a great respect for Catherine. To them she was a vivacious, amusing and well informed companion. They saw a good deal of her during their short stay at the Mount Nelson. Not only were they with her when she dined at Government House but, on several occasions, they accompanied her to luncheon or dinner at Groote Schuur. Rhodes made them all welcome. If he had indeed resented Catherine's attentions on board ship, he gave no indication of it once she had arrived in Cape Town. During the first few weeks of her stay he seems to have gone out of his way to make her at home in her new surroundings. He gave her an open invitation to eat at Groote Schuur and, on hearing that she was fond of riding, provided horses for her and Major Harding. It was during these rides that Catherine gave Harding details of the relationship which she claimed was developing between herself and Rhodes. 'She was deeply interested in Rhodes,' says Harding, 'and I thought then, and I still think, that she was in love with the South African statesman. Often she would speak of him in the most affectionate terms.' And she went even further than that. Before long she was confiding to Harding some of the more intimate details of the supposed affair. She told him that Rhodes had shown an interest in her elder son, of whom she was particularly fond, and had promised to arrange for him to come to South Africa if war broke out. To emphasize her point, she read out part of a letter which she claimed Rhodes had written to young Prince Nicholas. According to this letter, Rhodes was contemplating marriage with the Princess. Harding was most impressed.

That Rhodes should have written such a letter and that the Princess should then have read it out to so slight an acquaintance as himself, does not appear to have struck Harding as strange. It says much for Catherine's persuasiveness. In fact, it is the first recorded example of a talent which was to create a great deal of controversy in the days ahead. For the Princess was to employ similar tactics time and again. Reading, and even passing on, what appeared to be personal letters and private documents was to become part of her stock-in-trade and the conviction with which she presented such material was to fool many people. It is impossible to accept the various letters which she produced, in order to win people to her side, as reliable evidence of her own, or her supposed correspondents', intentions. Perhaps the most confusing thing about such letters (of which only copies survive) is that if they were forgeries, they were extremely clever forgeries. In the end, one is forced to ignore them and to turn to independent sources to test the Princess's integrity.

As for this letter which she read to Harding, she almost certainly invented it in order to impress her new friend. Harding was not permitted to read the letter and its contents make it extremely suspect. It takes only a superficial knowledge of Rhodes to realize that, if he had been capable of a romantic association with a woman, he certainly would not have been brought to the point of proposing marriage in so short a time. Although he and Catherine had been friendly on board ship, they do not appear to have been left alone together for long, and since arriving in South Africa, they had seen even less of each other. During the day Rhodes was kept fully occupied with his political concerns (he was often at the House of Assembly) and his spare time seems to have been spent with his guests at Groote Schuur. Indeed, if Rhodes were friendly with any woman during the period that the Hardings were at the Mount Nelson, then it was with a woman very different from Princess Radziwill. This was Lady Sarah Wilson, youngest daughter of the seventh Duke of Marlborough and sister of Lord Randolph Churchill. Of Rhodes's few female acquaintances, Lady Sarah was, perhaps, the only one of his own age who could rightly be called his friend.

Cecil Rhodes had first met Lady Sarah Wilson and her husband, Captain Gordon Wilson, shortly before the Jameson Raid. At that time, the Wilsons had been on their first visit to South Africa. Rhodes appears to have warmed to Lady Sarah immediately. Knowing that the Wilsons were holidaying in Rhodesia, Rhodes had cabled them an invitation to Groote Schuur before he sailed from England on the *Scot*. They had been waiting for him on his return.

Lady Sarah got to know Rhodes well at this period. She says

that her stay at Groote Schuur gave her a fresh insight into 'the many sides of his life, occupations and character'. She would often accompany him on his morning ride, invariably met him at breakfast and in the evening they would play bridge—at which Lady Sarah was an expert and Rhodes an enthusiastic learner.

It is difficult to believe that, with so much of his time monopolized by a woman like Lady Sarah Wilson, Rhodes was simultaneously carrying on an affair with Princess Radziwill. The sight of him in the company of one woman was considered remarkable; for him to have alternated between the two would surely have set every tongue in Cape Town a-wagging. The truth is that Catherine's nose was put somewhat out of joint by the demanding Lady Sarah. The last thing that she could have expected was a female rival for Rhodes's attention. Although they must often have met, Lady Sarah makes no mention of Catherine in her memoirs. This is hardly surprising: they would not have got on particularly well.

To Major Harding, however, the Princess's story appeared more than feasible. There was no reason for him to think that she might be lying. When he and his wife left for Northern Rhodesia, they promised to write to Catherine and were convinced that they would soon meet her again. 'When we said goodbye,' reports Harding, 'I referred to her as the future Queen of Rhodesia.'

*

Rhodes studiously avoided becoming involved in Milner's negotiations with President Kruger. He had no alternative. Since the Jameson Raid his every utterance concerning the Transvaal was regarded with suspicion and his enemies lost no time in twisting his words into evidence of a continuing desire to overthrow the Boer Government. That he still desired the downfall of the Kruger régime there can be no doubt. The unification of South Africa remained essential to his plans and he knew that this could never be achieved while Kruger ruled in the Transvaal. But he was wise enough not to make his enmity towards the Boers too obvious. There was, in any case, no pressing need for him to do so. Milner was doing that part of his work only too well. He could afford to sit back and allow the new crisis in South Africa to develop in the sure knowledge that, for once, the Imperial

Factor needed no prodding from him. With the situation deteriorating rapidly, he maintained his attitude of *attentisme*. 'I keep aloof from the whole Transvaal crisis,' he said in an interview, 'so that no one may be able to say if things go wrong that Rhodes is in it again.'

He did not really expect things to go wrong. He was convinced that with Milner taking a strong line, Kruger would eventually climb down. The thought of the Transvaal standing up to the might of Britain was, in his opinion, inconceivable. When such a possibility was suggested, he dismissed it out of hand. 'I really cannot think about it,' he declared. 'It is too ridiculous . . . There is not the slightest chance of war.' Once again events were to prove how grossly he misjudged the Transvaal burghers whom he was said to know so well.

Instead of listening for the sounds of gunfire, he confined his attention to more constructive interests: to the development of Rhodesia and domestic politics in the House of Assembly. And when he was not occupied with public affairs, he busied himself at Groote Schuur. His house, which Herbert Baker had rebuilt after the fire of 1896, absorbed him more and more in these later years. He had assembled some fine Cape Dutch furniture, glass and china and to it he added items reflecting a more specialized interest. The library at Groote Schuur, for instance, was said to throw 'a singular and most interesting light on Mr Rhodes's literary tastes and studies.' It contained a fair selection of modern books and, at first glance, was in no way remarkable except for the stone figure of a Phoenician hawk which came from the mysterious Zimbabwe ruins in Rhodesia. Closer inspection, however, revealed a set of handsomely bound books which gave the library a peculiar distinction. These were the volumes which formed part of a literary scheme conceived in 1893. After re-reading Gibbon's *Decline and Fall of the Roman Empire*, Rhodes had been so impressed that he had decided to have translations made from the original sources used by Gibbon. He commissioned a London bookseller to obtain these for him and insisted that the translations should be 'absolutely unabridged'. The scheme involved some hundreds of volumes and is estimated to have cost about £8,000. Typewritten and bound in red morocco, it was considered 'the most extensive collection of biographies of the Roman emperors and empresses'.

As Rhodes, since his Oxford days, had been fascinated by the tyrannical powers of the rulers of ancient Rome, his expensive hobby is understandable. There was a facet of this collection, however, which is even more revealing. To add colour to the intimate details of the degenerate lives of the later Roman emperors, the books were illustrated by drawings from coins and medallions, some of which, says le Sueur, were 'of a decidedly erotic nature'. So disturbing were these illustrations that when le Sueur came to catalogue the library, he felt obliged to lock away certain of the volumes. After Rhodes's death, it was found that the books had been tampered with. 'Despite all precautions the illustrations were cut out and removed,' says le Sueur. 'I have,' he adds, 'a shrewd idea as to the culprit.' There were, of course, many books other than these esoteric translations; works on Africa, biographies of Rhodes's heroes—such as Alexander the Great and Napoleon—books of reference and even a few novels. But it is curious to find erotica in any form in the possession of a man who was said to blush at the slightest mention of sex.

Nor were the books the only indication of sexual awareness. In the library there was a cabinet which contained a collection of phallic objects taken from the Zimbabwe ruins where, it is believed, a cult of phallus worship was once practised. According to one of Rhodes's later biographers, this phallic collection caused a good many raised eyebrows among visitors to Groote Schuur and encouraged 'ugly rumours about Rhodes's abnormal sexuality'. The rumours, it is said, concerned Rhodes's bachelor entourage, and the fact that no women servants were employed at Groote Schuur. While there is no independent evidence to support this claim of scandal, the existence of the collection seems to call Rhodes's reputed puritanism into doubt.

An interesting glimpse of Rhodes pottering about Groote Schuur is given by Lady Sarah Wilson. 'After his morning ride,' she writes, 'Mr Rhodes, if nothing called him to town, usually walked about his beautiful house . . . I can often call to mind that tall figure, probably in the same costume in which he had ridden—white flannel trousers and tweed coat—his hair rather rough, from a habit he had of passing his hand through it when talking or thinking. He would wander through the rooms, enjoying the pleasure of looking at his many beautiful

pieces of furniture and curiosities of all sorts, nearly all of which
had a history. Occasionally shifting a piece of rare old glass or
blue Delft china, he would the while talk to anyone who chanced
to come in.' While the rest of the country waited breathlessly
for news of developments in the Transvaal, he remained serene.
Confident that the war scare would blow over, he was able to
relax in the knowledge that any decisions reached at this stage
of the crisis were the responsibility of others. For the first time
in many years, the fate of South Africa did not depend on the
word of Cecil John Rhodes.

In August the Wilsons left for Bulawayo. Colonel Baden-
Powell had arrived at the Cape and was going to Rhodesia to
raise a force to defend the northern borders of the Colony in the
event of a war. Captain Gordon Wilson went with him as his
aide-de-camp and Lady Sarah accompanied her husband. In the
months ahead, the intrepid Lady Sarah was to become involved
in a series of adventures which would make her the most talked-
about woman during the opening stages of the Boer War; her
exploits, in fact, were to be rivalled only by those of her dashing
young nephew, Winston Churchill. But Rhodes refused to be
ruffled even by the mustering of troops in Rhodesia. 'Nothing
will make Kruger fire a shot,' he declared.

With the departure of the Wilsons, the field was cleared for
Princess Radziwill. She had been suffering from flu and, according to Dr Stevenson who attended her, had been obliged to
employ a nurse. During her illness, she had written to Rhodes
asking him to call but there is no evidence that he ever visited
her hotel. Now, with Lady Sarah out of the way and her health
restored, she renewed her attack. Rhodes began to feel vulnerable. 'At first,' says Jourdan, 'when her wires came saying she
was coming to lunch or dinner he did not mind her coming so
much, but afterwards he showed signs of displeasure and tried to
put her off.'

For a while Rhodes was able to plead pressure of work and
fob Catherine off by sending her for rides with Jourdan. But
this excuse soon began to wear thin. As long as Rhodes was in
the house, the Princess was not likely to be content with spending her time with his secretary. She had not travelled six
thousand miles simply to chat to the pleasant but ineffectual
Philip Jourdan. So insistent were her attempts to break in on

Rhodes that he had to look for other means of escape. He would often bolt down his meal and drive off to some mythical appointment in order to avoid meeting the Princess. J. G. McDonald also tells of Rhodes's fear of being left alone with Catherine. He says that one day, as he was about to leave for the beach, he was ordered to postpone his outing and keep Rhodes company during one of Catherine's visits. No matter what the Princess said or did, he was on no account to leave the room. 'Lunch passed pleasantly,' says McDonald, 'but afterwards I had a very uncomfortable time of it till about half past three when Metcalfe arrived and enabled me to get away from the lady's envenomed looks.'

It was not that Rhodes was afraid of being seduced by the Princess. The reason for his alarm was of a more serious nature. 'The Princess,' explains Jourdan, 'had been discussing politics with him too much.' And this, as Rhodes knew only too well, could prove far more compromising than any attempted seduction.

Later, when Rhodes was asked whether he had ever discussed politics with the Princess, he was adamant in his denial. 'No,' he said firmly, 'I discuss politics with very few and certainly not with women.' This is blatantly untrue. Rhodes discussed politics with a great many people, including a few women. Lady Sarah Wilson certainly shared many of his political interests and so, for many years, did the *grande dame* of Cape Town society, Mrs Koopmans de Wet. (It was not until after the Jameson Raid that the elderly Mrs Koopmans de Wet ceased to be Rhodes's confidante.) Moreover, Jourdan claims that Rhodes had political conversations with Catherine and that it was these very conversations that first made him wary of her. Indeed, it is difficult to imagine how politics could be avoided. Catherine had an insatiable appetite for political discussion and Rhodes was incapable of talking for long without making a political observation. They certainly had little else in common. If Catherine was intent on ensnaring Rhodes, the only way she could have hoped to do so was by involving herself in his public career—which meant gaining his political confidence. There is reason to think that, at first, Rhodes spoke quite openly to the Princess on political subjects. Her knowledge of his approach to controversial topics was as informed as that of his closest friends.

There is a letter dated 10th September, 1899, which is supposed to have been written by Rhodes to Catherine. Like the rest of the letters, later produced by the Princess, this may or may not have been a forgery. Its genuineness, however, is not particularly important. What does make it interesting is that its contents reveal a knowledge of the way in which Rhodes's mind was working. Entirely political, it certainly could not have been forged by anyone with whom Rhodes did not discuss politics. While it cannot be relied upon as an expression of Rhodes's views, it shows that, when Princess Radziwill first arrived in South Africa, she was received into the inner circle at Groote Schuur. For whether Rhodes wrote to her or whether she forged the letter—using information which she had picked up in conversation—the letter reflects too detailed a knowledge of Rhodes's political concerns for it to have been manufactured out of thin air.

The letter purports to answer an inquiry made by the Princess. The opening paragraph deals with the mysterious 'missing telegrams'. Rhodes explains that he could not produce these telegrams at the Jameson Inquiry because it would have involved 'the Queen's name' in the affair. The letter then goes on to hint at Chamberlain's complicity in Rhodes's schemes. This is information which Catherine could have picked up at Groote Schuur. Rhodes admitted at the Jameson Inquiry that he often spoke quite openly to his guests. 'You often speak more freely at your dining-table than you would in public,' he said, 'because you do not expect what you say to be reported.' But it is unlikely that he would have committed himself in writing on such a delicate subject; particularly to the Princess, whom he knew to be a journalist. According to Jourdan, it was Catherine's connection with the newspaper world that aroused Rhodes's suspicions. 'He said,' reports Jourdan, 'one never knew what intrigues she might be up to, that most foreign women were disposed to intrigue, that their lives were made up of intrigue, and that they could not live without it.' Rhodes's natural caution alone is enough to make the letter suspect. But if it is a forgery, it is a clever and informed one.

The letter is a good indication of the Princess's own interests. The mystery of the 'missing telegrams' would have fascinated her. She had first met Rhodes when the Jameson Raid furore was at its height. She must have followed the proceedings at the Inquiry closely and have detected the intrigue behind the façade. Her friends on *The Times* might well have supplied her with some snippets of inside information. With her *penchant* for political scandal, she would have found the affair irresistible. It may well have been her all too obvious curiosity concerning the suppressed telegrams which first caused Rhodes to fight shy of her.

*

That Princess Radziwill was determined to make her mark at the Cape was apparent from the moment she arrived. Within no time she had achieved a social prominence and a reputation which bordered on notoriety. She was to be seen everywhere. Soignée, distinctive and voluble, she rarely attended a social function without becoming the centre of attraction. Her name featured high on the lists of guests attending select gatherings and her clothes invariably drew admiring comments from the social columnists of the local papers. At a musical evening at Government House she was described as striking 'a defiant note in colours, with a bright cerise silk gown exquisitely cut. A diamond crown surmounted her dark hair, and an exceedingly handsome necklace encircled her throat.' A few days later, at the annual Bachelors' Ball, it was noted that: 'The gown worn by the Princess Radziwill was composed of the richest of ivory Duchesse satin, the bodice being trimmed with exquisite lace. She again wore that handsome coronet of diamonds.' Added to her striking appearance, her lively conversation—enhanced by a slight but charming foreign accent—always assured her of an audience. Her anecdotes about the royal courts of Europe brought a heady whiff of the *haut monde* into the somewhat flat colonial atmosphere.

A regular visitor to the House of Assembly, she made her presence in Parliament felt by being the only person to remain seated when the Speaker said the opening prayer. She could imbue the most commonplace incident with a sense of drama. 'My pearls!' she shrieked, when her much-talked-about necklace snapped during the Lancers at a fashionable ball. The music stopped immediately, the floor was cleared, and the guests were obliged to scramble about looking for the four missing pearls. Three were found, but of the fourth there was no sign. Reluctantly, she allowed the dancing to start up again. Harry Currey's sister was at the ball, escorted by a subaltern from the local garrison. As the music began her partner whispered: 'They won't find that fourth pearl.' 'Why not?' asked the startled Miss Currey. 'Because,' explained the young man, 'I have just put my foot on it and crushed it.' This was simply one of the many stories that had begun to circulate about the Princess and her magnificent jewels. And not everything that was said about Catherine reflected to her credit. The discerning *élite* of Cape Town were already beginning to eye her with suspicion.

She knew everyone but made few real friends. The only people with whom she established a close friendship were Dr William Scholtz and his wife Agnes. Dr Scholtz was a well-known figure in Cape Town and a close friend of Cecil Rhodes. He and his wife were a socially ambitious couple, and invitations to the lavish entertainments in their charming Cape-Dutch house in the centre of Cape Town were much sought after. Mrs Scholtz was an amusing hostess and William Scholtz's celebrated imitations of Paul Kruger had given him a reputation of being 'an artist to his finger-tips'. Professionally, Dr Scholtz was held in high regard. He was a member of the Colonial Medical Council and had recently abandoned his general practice to specialize in diseases of the ear, nose and throat. He was considered an expert on the effects of varying climates on health and his book *The South African Climate* had earned the rare distinction of a foreword by Cecil Rhodes. It was probably as a result of this publication that Rhodes had appointed Dr Scholtz to the Board of the Kimberley Sanatorium.

It was through Rhodes that the doctor and his wife became friendly with Princess Radziwill. Hearing that Catherine was staying at the Mount Nelson Hotel, Agnes Scholtz had asked Rhodes about her. 'I said,' claimed Rhodes, 'that she was an interesting woman and that she [Mrs Scholtz] might call upon her.' Catherine appears to have got on very well with the doctor and his wife. Dr Scholtz had trained in Berlin and more recently had visited Moscow as the only South African delegate at an International Medical Conference. With Agnes Scholtz the Princess formed an intimate friendship and before long was confiding her pretended matrimonial troubles and very real financial problems to the doctor's wife.

It was probably through the medium of Mrs Scholtz that some intriguing details of the Princess's private life began to circulate in Cape Town. At first it was rumoured that she was secretly engaged to Rhodes and that she had already selected the rooms she would occupy in Groote Schuur. Rhodes was thought to be waiting for a suitable moment at which to announce his engagement. As time went by without the betrothal being made public, the stories concerning the supposed love affair were given a more titillating twist. It was said that, while Rhodes might not be ready to marry the Princess, there could be little doubt that she had become his mistress. Not only was this evident from her frequent visits to Groote Schuur but, according to gossips, Rhodes spent almost every night alone with her at the Mount Nelson. Cape Town's scandalmongers, always on the look-out for an excuse to question Rhodes's disappointing celibacy, began to nod their heads knowingly.

These rumours, started during the early months of Catherine's stay at the Cape, were to be embroidered upon over the years. Many people were to consider that the truth behind them justified Catherine's subsequent behaviour. Hers was the scorned fury, it was thought, which leads women to do foolish and seemingly inexplicable things. It was a feasible explanation and one which the Princess was only too ready to exploit. Rhodes's friends were emphatic in their denials of any secret hotel-room assignations. 'The fact is,' says Philip Jourdan, 'not a servant or anyone else can be found to corroborate this statement, for the simple reason that I can swear that Mr Rhodes had never seen nor entered the Mount Nelson Hotel; moreover, I was acquainted with all his movements from the time that he left his room in the morning until he retired for the night . . . He always had three or four friends staying with him, and they all knew his movements as well as I did; and every one can testify that the Princess's statements about his visiting her at the Mount Nelson Hotel are absolutely false.'

The suggestion that Princess Radziwill started these rumours herself is probably true. She had good reasons for wanting her name linked with that of Rhodes. To be thought of as Rhodes's mistress would strengthen her position with the local politicians whom she was beginning to cultivate. It might have been for this reason, also, that she found it necessary to forge political letters from Rhodes. Whether she hoped to marry Rhodes is not certain—in any case it would not be possible until she had divorced Prince Wilhelm—but to be considered Rhodes's mistress was certainly the next best thing. Her standing—politically—would be enhanced a hundredfold and would far outweigh any considerations of bourgeois morality. It was her first attempt to establish herself in a position of influence at the rough-and-ready Court of Cape Town.

Rhodes soon got to hear about her innuendoes. Very little happened at the Cape that was not reported back to Groote Schuur. They could only have added to his growing suspicions of the Princess. He became more and more impatient with Catherine's inquisitiveness. 'He asked her not to discuss politics with him any more,' says Jourdan, 'but she could not help herself. She could not refrain from the subject, until one day he lost his temper, and told her point-blank that if she refused to comply with his wishes in this respect she had better not speak to him at all. Her visits after that became less frequent, but she still came. There was a strained feeling when she was in the house, and Mr Rhodes appeared uncomfortable.'

But it seems that Catherine did not confine her ferreting activities to asking awkward questions. An incident occurred at about this time which, in view of later events, was very significant. It happened while J. G. McDonald was visiting Groote Schuur. According to McDonald, Philip Jourdan one day told him of his difficulties with the Princess. It appears that when she was unable to approach Rhodes directly, Catherine had the disconcerting habit of wandering into Jourdan's office and there fingering through Rhodes's private papers. On one occasion Jourdan had had to leave her alone in the office for a few minutes and when he returned, he found certain papers missing. Not wanting to worry Rhodes, he was at a loss to know what action to take. McDonald suggested that they should consult Sir Charles Metcalfe. After they had spoken to Metcalfe, it was decided that whenever Jourdan left his room in future, a servant should be stationed by his desk until he returned. McDonald goes on to say that the servant thus stationed later reported another visit from the Princess and that Jourdan then found that the missing documents had been returned.

There is reason to think that McDonald, writing over forty

years later, was not in full possession of the details. He seems to think that the Princess was merely trying to obtain copies of Rhodes's signature. But the only copy of Rhodes's signature used by the Princess came from quite another source. In fact, Catherine was after something far more important than Rhodes's signature, and her search had probably gone a good deal further than fingering loose papers on Jourdan's desk. What is more, it is very doubtful that she returned the documents missed by Jourdan. It is remarkable that Jourdan—who wrote more about Princess Radziwill than any of Rhodes's associates—makes no mention of this disturbing episode.

McDonald says that Rhodes was told about the theft and was supposed to have told Catherine a few days later that she was to come to Groote Schuur only when invited. But at that stage, even Rhodes may not have known the full truth. It was not until some time later that he became really alarmed.

In any case, he did not have to endure Catherine's interference much longer. He was rescued by the march of events. The tension which had been building up since the abortive Bloemfontein Conference reached snapping point at the beginning of October. On the afternoon of 9th October, 1899, President Kruger issued an ultimatum to the British authorities. It demanded that all points of difference between the two countries should be referred to arbitration and that British troops should be withdrawn from the borders of the Transvaal. The British were given forty-eight hours in which to reply. There was no chance of these terms being agreed to and the ultimatum was recognized for what it was—a declaration of war.

That same evening Cecil Rhodes, accompanied by Rochefort Maguire and his wife, Dr Thomas Smartt and Philip Jourdan, left Cape Town for Kimberley.

CHAPTER NINE

The Political Game

RHODES had announced his intention of making for Kimberley some days before he left Cape Town. When it looked as if war was imminent, his thoughts turned to the cradle of his fortunes. Kimberley represented his great beginnings and De Beers Consolidated Mines was still the main source of his continuing wealth. It was, for him, both natural and inevitable that he should take his place among the citizens of Kimberley if the town were threatened. Not everyone regarded his decision in the same light.

As soon as it was known that Rhodes was about to travel north, efforts were made to dissuade him. Friends wrote asking him not to endanger his life and the Mayor of Kimberley sent him a polite telegram suggesting that he postpone his visit. The townsfolk, explained the Mayor, were afraid that his presence among them would induce the Boers to 'rush' the town in an attempt to take him prisoner. There seems to have been good reason for this fear. It was well known that the Boers were anxious to capture Rhodes and it was said that they planned to exhibit him in a cage throughout the Transvaal. The same misgivings applied to the presence of Dr Jameson. When the little doctor arrived in Mafeking hoping to take part in the expected siege, he was peremptorily ordered out of the town. Baden-Powell, in charge of the defence of Mafeking, said that if Jameson stayed in the town, he would need a battery of artillery to defend it and that as he had not so much as a field gun, the doctor must leave. Thwarted at Mafeking, Dr Jim made his way to Ladysmith where he was more successful. Rhodes, however, would not hear of being turned away from Kimberley. He arrived there on 11th October—the day Kruger's ultimatum expired—and two days later the Boers surrounded the town.

Rhodes's conduct during the siege of Kimberley was to become a matter of some controversy. Regarding the town as his own domain, he found it impossible to subordinate himself to the military command. As Kimberley's Great White Chief, he was accustomed to being obeyed and he saw no reason why his authority should now be questioned. A clash between himself and Colonel Kekewich, the commander of the Kimberley garrison, was inevitable; as it happened, the feud between the two men was so intense that, for most of the siege, they were not on speaking terms. The quarrel interfered with the defence of the town and made Kekewich's task of maintaining discipline extremely difficult. Rhodes's most fervent admirers are forced to admit that his conduct during the siege left a great deal to be desired.

Nor was his interference in military matters confined to Kimberley. From the very beginning of the siege he was bombarding Cape Town and the army authorities with demands for immediate relief of the town. He even sent instructions and advice to Baden-Powell in Mafeking. As far as Rhodes was concerned, the fate of the beleaguered towns was of prime importance to the outcome of the war and their relief should take precedence over all other considerations. He could never appreciate that to those outside Kimberley the situation looked very different. The fact that during the opening months of the war the British army encountered a fierce and courageous opposition for which it was blithely unprepared, and that in its march towards Kimberley it suffered defeats that were perhaps without precedent in the history of British colonial warfare—including the disastrous battles of 'Black Week' in December when British casualties were estimated in the region of 3,000—meant little to him. 'Glad to have Kimberley relieved?' he was to say to a reporter at the end of the siege. 'Of course we are all glad, but, in heaven's name, why was it not done sooner? What was the good of all that messing about at Rensburg and Colesberg? Why did they not do at first what was so readily done at last?'

Rhodes's attitude was not appreciated by the army, but to the people of Kimberley he was a hero. Unmistakable in his white flannel trousers, brown tweed coat and narrow-brimmed felt hat, he was to be seen everywhere: chatting to the soldiers, organizing work parties, arranging for the distribution of food and supervising the building of bomb-proof shelters. The very sight of him riding about the town was sufficient to inspire the faint-hearted with confidence. He paid no heed to his personal safety and the way in which he exposed himself to capture by the enemy became a matter of concern among his associates. 'He always wore a pair of white flannel pantaloons,' says Jourdan, 'and it was very easy for the Boers to see him for miles on horseback. He was warned by his friends not to make himself so conspicuous, as the enemy would have loved nothing better than to have captured him, and they soon found out through the medium of traitors in our camp who the individual was who was always riding about in a pair of white flannels.' When, at the height of the Boer shelling, an American engineer constructed a gun with which the town could retaliate, the weapon was immediately dubbed 'Long Cecil'.

It was four months before Kimberley was relieved. Not until 15th February, 1900, did the relieving force enter the town. They were given a tumultuous welcome by the townsfolk and that evening Rhodes entertained the commanding officer, General French, to a 'modest dinner party'.

Rhodes remained in Kimberley until the end of February. He was kept busy answering telegrams of congratulation, receiving loyal addresses from his fellow-citizens and attending to his mining concerns. At the annual general meeting of De Beers on 23rd February, he gave the shareholders his views on the future of South Africa. He stressed the importance of co-operation with the Boers once the war was over and returned once again to his old theme of unity. 'All contention will be over,' he said, 'with the recognition of equal rights for every civilized man south of the Zambesi.' Shortly after this meeting he was approached by a deputation of the coloured community and asked for his definition of a civilized man. His reply was characteristic. 'What is a civilized man?' he wrote on a scrap of newspaper. 'A man whether white or black who has sufficient education to write his own name, has some property or works, in fact is not a loafer.' This was his formula for a lasting peace in South Africa.

Before travelling south, he was interviewed by Julian Ralph of the *Daily Mail*. At the end of their talk, the newspaper correspondent thought it wise to warn him that, among a certain section of the community at the Cape, he was being held responsible for the war and that feeling against him was running high in the Colony.

'I told him,' reports Ralph, 'that I had been told by influential persons in Cape Town that he would be shot if he came there.

'He declared the news "absolutely silly". He said nobody wanted to kill him or would do so.

' "But," said I, "you know they hate you."

' "Some of the leading ones do," said he, "but not the others."

' "They hate you more than they hate England," I replied.

' "Because they see in me the embodiment of English ideas," said he.'

He was quite right in dismissing the threat of assassination. His life was in no danger. When he arrived at the Cape, the greatest threat he had to face came, not from his opponents, but from one who claimed to be his friend. He might have been ready to face the bullets of his enemies, but he was totally unprepared for the dagger thrusts of Princess Radziwill.

*

'It is indisputable,' Catherine was to write long after Rhodes's death, 'that whilst he was shut up in the Diamond City, Rhodes entered into secret negotiations with some of the Dutch leaders. This, though it might have been construed in the sense of treason against his Motherland had it reached the knowledge of the extreme Jingo party, was in reality the sincere effort of a true patriot to put an end to a struggle which was threatening to destroy the prosperity of a country for which he had laboured for so many years.'

There is, of course, no evidence whatsoever for this 'indisputable' statement. On the contrary, everything that is known of Rhodes's attitude at this time seems to point in an opposite direction. Like most people, he thought the war would be short and decisive. Once the Transvaal had been defeated, he imagined that it would be possible to establish racial harmony in South Africa. But not before. A lasting peace could only be achieved after the downfall of what he called 'Krugerism'.

For all its apparent nonsense, however, Catherine's claim is not without interest. For it was not Cecil Rhodes, but Princess

Radziwill who 'entered into secret negotiations with some of the Dutch leaders'.

When Rhodes left for Kimberley, Catherine found herself in a country at war. It was a country, moreover, in which she was resolved to play a prominent part. What could serve her purpose better than to work for a peaceful settlement of the conflict? If she could be instrumental in bringing the opposing sides together, her claim for recognition as a political force in South Africa would be substantiated. Her aim was to achieve a reconciliation between Rhodes and the Afrikander Bond. By doing this, she hoped to create an atmosphere in which negotiations for peace could be started. Convinced that this was what Rhodes himself desired, she planned to start her campaign by dispelling the suspicions of his opponents. In a cursory, unpublished statement which she made some years later, she admitted that this was how she saw her task. 'During those feverish weeks which preceded the war,' she said, 'I saw Rhodes constantly & it was then that I began in observing him in his natural medium, to understand his character & the forces that guided him & made himself often commit some errors. I understood by the same way that from the bottom of his heart he regretted his quarrel or rather his rupture with the Dutch side . . . I began then to work with all my heart to bring a reconciliation between them.'

Once her plan had been conceived, she lost no time in putting it into action. With Rhodes in Kimberley, she was given a clear field. Any pretence that she might make to be acting on his behalf could not easily be repudiated by him. Her social activities were now transformed into a political crusade. Not surprisingly, with the country at war, a good many people regarded her attempts to involve herself in the affairs of the Cape as extremely suspicious. '[She] was inclined to ask questions of all and sundry concerning the disturbed political situation,' it was reported. 'Rumours of all sorts were current about her. It was said she was an agent of the Russian Government, and week by week she was said to despatch lengthy reports to someone in Europe on South African affairs. It was generally assumed, at any rate, that there was some mystery attaching to her, but her activities continued unabated.'

The suspicion with which she was regarded was, for the most part, without substance. There was no question of her acting as a spy for a European power. Her interests were centred in South Africa and her mysterious activities were concerned with nothing more sinister than a bid to further her own political influence. As she saw it, a new political party was needed to surmount the prejudice which divided the two white groups in South Africa. This party should consist of men big enough to ignore petty differences and old animosities and to find a common cause in the greater interests of their war-torn country. For want of a better name, she referred to this projected organization as the 'Anglo-African Party'. She intended, of course, that it should be led by Cecil John Rhodes.

Her first task was to interest the Bond. In order to do so, she wrote to J. W. Sauer, an influential Cape politician who had once been a member of Rhodes's cabinet but who was now one of his most dedicated opponents. Together with another of Rhodes's former colleagues, J. X. Merriman, Sauer was regarded as the principal mouthpiece of the Bond in the Cape House of Assembly. 'What we require here,' she told this experienced politician, 'is a strong party, which has in its ranks all the strong men as well as the powerful ones in South Africa, and which is not hampered by this element of discord and weakness—the Jingos . . . I know you are ready to do and sacrifice a good deal for the welfare of South Africa, and I do not doubt for a single moment that you will not allow personal considerations to sway you.'

How far her overtures succeeded is uncertain. According to Professor T. R. H. Davenport, the historian of the Afrikander Bond, there is no evidence in the Bond papers to confirm the claims she made about her negotiations with Sauer and Jan Hofmeyr. Sauer himself was to maintain that he acknowledged her letter briefly but took no further notice of it, while Hofmeyr claimed that he had 'declined to hold any political communication with the good lady at all'. Consequently, one has only her word for what took place. She is supposed to have recorded her talks with the Bond in a diary which, ostensibly, she started soon after Rhodes left for Kimberley. This diary is one of those questionable documents which she later produced and, as such, is extremely suspect. The fact that the entries in this journal, presumably kept as a personal record of her daily activities, are written in English and slanted to suit her own ends seems to indicate that it was composed for an ulterior purpose. It is even possible that parts of it were written at a later stage. In any case, the Bond leaders, by her own admission, were definitely wary of becoming too openly associated with her at this period and seem to have conducted their side of the negotiations mainly through an intermediary.

But there is no doubt that she was in contact with the Bond leaders. And it seems that the negotiations went further than either Sauer or Hofmeyr was prepared to admit. The *South African News*, an anti-Rhodes newspaper controlled by Sauer, went so far as to announce that Rhodes, 'through a close friend of his, in fact a political agent' (afterwards acknowledged to have been the Princess), was 'making efforts to arrange a new alliance with the leaders of the Afrikander Party'. This announcement was heatedly denied by the pro-Rhodes Press and particularly by the *Eastern Province Herald* which was owned and edited by Rhodes's close friend, Edgar Walton. The Princess certainly made no secret of being in touch with 'the Dutch side'. So open was she in her boasts of being a political agent that the air of suspicion with which she was regarded in South Africa began to spread abroad. 'Everyone in Paris knows that the woman is a Boer agent,' declared Clemenceau.

Perhaps nothing demonstrates Catherine's powers of persuasion better than the way in which she convinced that shrewd political observer, Leo Amery, of her importance. Amery was then chief political correspondent for *The Times* of London in South Africa. He had arrived in the country shortly before the outbreak of war and, having spent some weeks touring the Transvaal and Natal, established himself in Cape Town at the beginning of December. Staying at the Mount Nelson Hotel, he was greatly amused by the odd assortment of guests. 'Not the least conspicuous,' he says, 'was the once lovely, still decoratively imposing, and soon notorious Princess Radziwill, who had conceived an infatuation for Rhodes and had come out in the vain hope of vamping him into matrimony.' Donald Mackenzie Wallace had written to Catherine asking her to be kind to his newspaper colleague and Amery had found a warm welcome waiting for him in Cape Town. Not only did the Princess entertain him to meals at her hotel but she showered him with confidences. Many years later Amery was to remember one of the Princess's colourful stories. She told him that she had arranged a secret meeting with Jan Hofmeyr in the Botanical Gardens. On keeping the appointment, 'Hofmeyr had shown her a letter of Rhodes', very damaging from the Bond point of view. She snatched it and ran down the garden path with old Jan in hot pursuit.' The sight of this elderly and dignified politician panting after the fleeing Princess would have diverted visitors to the Gardens and one regrets that, in all probability, the scene was enacted only in Catherine's lively imagination. However, Amery remained firmly convinced that Princess Radziwill was deeply involved with the Bond leaders.

And there was more to her activities than these peace negotiations. In later years Catherine was to be unstinting in her praise of Sir Alfred Milner. She was to maintain that the High Commissioner had arrived in South Africa at an unfortunate time. Circumstances had made it impossible for Milner and Rhodes to work together. Rhodes's influence was no longer politically dominant and the people frequenting Groote Schuur were determined to poison his mind against Milner. Sir Alfred, she said, was represented to Rhodes as a jealous rival who was determined to crush him and destroy his work in South Africa. 'Incredible as it appears,' she went on, 'Rhodes believed this absurd fiction, and learned to look upon Sir Alfred Milner as a natural enemy, desirous of thwarting him at every step.' What she omitted to say, was that the most active participant in the backbiting campaign against Milner was Princess Catherine Radziwill.

In her attempts to bring Rhodes and the Bond together, she felt it necessary to provide them with a common enemy: Milner fitted the part exactly. The Bond was naturally antagonistic towards the High Commissioner as a result of his treatment of the Transvaal, and the Princess did her best to capitalize on this enmity by persuading Rhodes that Sir Alfred was working against him. All the time that Rhodes was in Kimberley, she plied him with messages warning him against Milner and, at the same time, used her entrée at Government House to set the Governor against Rhodes. It was probably her willingness to sow dissension in high places—more than any desire to be reconciled with Rhodes—that first attracted the Bond leaders towards her.

214

But if she regarded high politics in terms of backstairs manœuvring, she had no intention of keeping her championship of Rhodes a complete secret. Her aim was to become identified with the South African statesman and this could be done only by courting publicity. Already she was writing articles that were designed to place her firmly among Rhodes's intimate friends. In an early one, which she sent to her old acquaintance, W. T. Stead, she compared Rhodes to Caesar, Peter the Great and Cortes. 'When I first arrived in Cape Town,' she wrote, 'I made a stupid joke, and said one found nothing else in South Africa except Mr Rhodes and Table Mountain, and that a fiendish rivalry existed between them. Little by little the glory of the mountain and the genius of the statesman became apparent to me; they seemed to possess a connecting link which bound them to one another. The mountain is steep, and seen from afar seems a barren desert; but when one scans it, with its wonderful wealth of flowers and blossoms, its endless variety of colours . . . one wonders how it is one did not take in all at once this splendour and magnificence. So it is with Cecil Rhodes.' Reading descriptions like these, it would have been difficult to appreciate that Rhodes was doing his best to avoid the Princess.

And she had more ambitious plans than the mere writing of articles. In the public eye, the only woman in any way associated with Rhodes was Olive Schreiner. The author's devastating attack on Rhodes in *Trooper Peter Halket of Mashonaland* had led to considerable speculation about the nature of her feelings for Rhodes; such passion, it was thought, could only be roused by an association which went deeper than politics. It was even hinted that Olive Schreiner had once been engaged to Rhodes. What then could be more significant than another woman entering into this curiously inspired vendetta? By answering Miss Schreiner's attack on Rhodes, Catherine would not only give point to the old rumours but start some new ones: it would be a case of the new love scorning the old love scorned. It was this task which occupied much of her spare time while Rhodes was shut up in Kimberley.

Taking Olive Schreiner's book as her guide, she began writing *The Resurrection of Peter*. Once again the setting is the Mashonaland veld at night. Peter Halket lies dead—as Olive Schreiner had left him. Out of the night come two angels who plead for the Trooper's lost life. They are answered by a voice 'sweet and inexpressibly sad', which declares: 'Take heed that ye not be deceived for many shall come in my name, saying, I am Christ, and the time draweth near; go ye not therefore after them.' Peter Halket rises from the ground. As he stands looking about him, another Stranger appears: a Christ-like figure similar to the Man whom Peter Halket had previously encountered. Once again there follows a long metaphysical discussion. This time, however, it is not concerned with theft, murder and torture, but with blameless ideals and high endeavour; with the noble uses of wealth and the false judgments of an uncomprehending world. Peter Halket is instructed to seek out the man defamed by the false prophet he had met earlier, and to assure him of his loyalty.

'Master, he also won't listen to me. He does not want my encouragement,' says Peter Halket.

'No, he does not want it,' replies the Stranger, 'but he needs it nevertheless, for with all his wealth, with all his power, there are minutes in this man's life when he feels the loneliness of his existence, the solitude created around him by his greatness. He has in his own way always worked for others, always toiled for the fulfilment of a great aim, for the realization of a noble ideal, and he has forgotten himself, until he has got so used to stand alone that he could no longer find strength in another person's encouragement; but nevertheless he wants the help of sympathy, the knowledge that he is understood; he wants to believe in others, and not only in his own genius, as he does now.'

And there was a great deal more in the same vein. Writing to impress the general public, she did not ignore the fact that her book would be read by Cecil Rhodes.

It must have been with some impatience that she followed the slow advance of the relieving column towards Kimberley. One way and another, she would have a great deal to say to Rhodes on his return.

*

When Rhodes learned of her attempts to reconcile him to the Bond he was furious. He dismissed her proposed political party as ridiculous and refused to have anything to do with it. Nor did he listen kindly to her renewed warnings against Milner. In fact, their first few meetings after his return from Kimberley seem to have been disastrous.

Rhodes was in a cantankerous mood; he was not prepared to put up with Princess Radziwill's interference. It took her some time to realize this. For the first few days after his arrival in Cape Town, she bustled about Groote Schuur, full of her new importance and determined to prod him into action. Arriving for luncheon or dinner—sometimes alone and sometimes with Dr and Mrs Scholtz—she would embark on a tirade against Milner until Rhodes became so irritated that even she felt she was on dangerous ground. Years later, she was to tell of the tense atmosphere of these discussions. This is how she describes the close of one such conversation.

' "What can one do with you, Mr Rhodes?" I asked with a smile.

' "Leave me alone," was the characteristic reply, in a tone which was sufficient for me to follow the advice, as it meant that the man was getting restive and might at any moment break out into one of those fits of rage which he so often used as a means to bring to an end a conversation in which he felt that he might not come out as victor.'

This unintentionally revealing picture of herself as an arch, insensitive and infuriatingly presumptuous meddler, provoking the tetchy Rhodes to explosion point, is no doubt accurate. When the Princess came to record it, however, she gave it a deceptive twist by neatly reversing her role: she represented herself as Milner's champion against Rhodes's loudly voiced suspicions. 'Rhodes himself had been persuaded that the Governor harboured the most sinister designs against his person,' she wrote. 'The innuendo was one of the most heinous untruths ever invented by his crowd of sycophants.' By then, of course, she would have had good reason to forget her part in the spreading of this 'heinous untruth' about Milner.

But there can be no doubt about the angry scenes at Groote Schuur. The Princess mentioned them in her 'diary' and later confessed openly to them. So electric did the atmosphere become that she was unable to approach Rhodes personally on a quite different matter—her financial troubles. It was left to her friend Mrs Scholtz to raise the subject. She did so with great tact. 'Mrs Scholtz informed me,' said Rhodes, 'that she thought the

Princess was in pecuniary difficulties. I said: "You can mention it to me and if it is so, let me know the circumstances." ' The circumstances were a good deal more desperate than Mrs Scholtz's polite hints could have suggested.

Since her arrival in Cape Town, Catherine had been living expansively. Leo Amery was not, it would seem, the only one she entertained at the Mount Nelson. In hotel expenses alone, she had spent over £1,000 and still owed £160. Her funds were exhausted and the hotel was threatening to summon her unless she paid her bill by 9th March. Mrs Scholtz brought her Rhodes's reassurance on the day before the time limit expired. She immediately sat down and wrote Rhodes a pathetic letter of thanks. 'To anybody else but you,' she wrote, 'this letter would be impossible to address, but Mrs Scholtz has told me of your kindness, and I won't even thank you for it, because thanks would neither be worthy of you nor me. Allow me to say that in the bitterness of being for the first time in my life obliged to ask anybody for help . . . I put my pride aside, and tell you quite frankly you are the only person from whom I should accept anything, and do so with gratitude.' She went on to explain that her troubles had been caused by her elder son. The boy had been so upset by the shame of her having to work for her living that he had gambled on the stock exchange and had lost money which she had since been forced to repay. 'Now,' she said, 'will you help me out of this muddle, and give me, not your money but your security for a year with the Standard Bank for £3,000? I shall return the money to the bank, and it will enable me to live in peace and earn my daily bread, and go home for a month, to see about the publication of my two books and the removal of my worldly goods and chattels here. I have been left after my divorce with about £1,500 income. I can make about the same with my pen, and have been offered the correspondentship of the *Morning Post* and *Daily Mail*, at the rate of £250 a year for each paper. Then I have got my other work. I can pull through very well here. It is impossible to live in Europe for that money in the way I have been used to live. Besides, I would not have any correspondencies for the papers. So I have decided to take a little house here, and then, later on, go up to Johannesburg and Kimberley with my boy, when he comes out. If I had the sum I mention, I would get through quietly, and not live in dread of the next day, and I could return it in a year. Will you give me this security? . . . May I trouble you to wire a reply, as indeed I am sorely tried, and literally afraid to be turned out in the street.'

Certain claims in this letter, if not obviously untrue, are certainly open to doubt. She was not divorced and there was to be little evidence in the months ahead of a £1,500 income. If she had written two books, only one of them, *The Resurrection of Peter*, was published. Both the *Morning Post* and the *Daily Mail* were adequately represented in South Africa and if there was any chance of her becoming a correspondent for these papers it certainly never materialized. But her letter is not without significance. It represents her first attempt to get Rhodes to act as her financial guarantor and it may well have been his refusal to do so that led her to embark on her subsequent disastrous course. Had Rhodes given his security for £3,000, her career in South Africa might have taken a very different turn.

The fact that Rhodes appears to have ignored her proposition may have had nothing to do with her dubious financial credentials. What most likely frightened him off was one of the few truthful statements in the letter. This was her declared intention of settling in South Africa. To have her permanently established on his doorstep was not an encouraging prospect. During the short period she had been in Cape Town she had caused him more than enough trouble and his only thought now was to get rid of her. Taking full advantage of her plight, he seized the opportunity to send her packing. 'I was subsequently told that she could not pay her bills at the Mount Nelson,' he later said, 'and was in a dire state of impecuniosity. I then said, "Well, I will instruct my attorney [Messrs Syfret] and if she will leave the country I will pay her bills." '

The hotel account was duly paid and Catherine moved temporarily to her friends the Scholtzes'. Whether, in fact, she gave Rhodes a promise that she would leave South Africa is uncertain; if she did, she certainly had no intention of keeping it.

*

On the 22nd March, 1900, Rhodes sailed for England. Like most people at this time, he was confident that the war was almost over and he was determined to play his part in any proposed peace settlement. His public image had suffered in both

England and Europe as a result of the war and his well publicized feud with Colonel Kekewich in Kimberley had done him yet more harm. Articles criticizing his behaviour had appeared in the Press and his opponents were encouraging the idea that he was largely responsible for the outbreak of hostilities. To make matters worse, at the beginning of the year a Belgian newspaper had published some documents, stolen from the office of Rhodes's solicitor, Bourchier Hawksley. These stolen papers were not, as Rhodes's opponents must have hoped, the notorious 'missing telegrams' but they were thought to be sufficiently incriminating for an M.P. to demand that the Inquiry into the Raid be reopened. Chamberlain had rejected this demand in a fighting speech. The Colonial Secretary pointed out that the papers had been stolen by a clerk in Hawksley's office and had then been 'hawked about London to the newspapers . . . and none of them would touch them, even with the tongs'. The papers had eventually been bought by a Boer agent for £100 and their subsequent publication had revealed them to be 'rubbish'. But although Chamberlain had succeeded in averting a fresh Inquiry, Rhodes evidently felt that his own presence in England was necessary.

His visit was brief. He told his friends that he was anxious to get back to Rhodesia. The only important event of his short stay was a long discussion with his old friend and disciple, W. T. Stead. This meeting must have been arranged with some apprehension on both sides. Politically, the two men had drifted far apart. No one had been more disgusted with the outcome of the Jameson Inquiry than Stead. Knowing something of its background, the journalist had fully expected that every aspect of the conspiracy would be revealed to the Select Committee. The fiasco of the Inquiry had filled him with indignation. He considered the proceedings at Westminster to have been a stain on Britain's national honour. He had written piece after piece on the subject in his *Review of Reviews* and had produced special pamphlets demanding that the truth of the Raid be made public. He insisted that Chamberlain be made to acknowledge his share of responsibility in Rhodes's schemes. With the outbreak of war in South Africa, his attacks became more vehement. He considered that there was a definite link between the Raid conspiracy and the fighting in the Transvaal and that it was necessary to expose Chamberlain in order to put a stop to an unjust war. His approach was hardly likely to endear him to Cecil Rhodes.

The meeting between the two men took place on 10th April. Stead and Bourchier Hawksley were Rhodes's guests for dinner at the Burlington Hotel. Stead recorded their conversation the following day. Talking late into the night, Rhodes seemed to capture some of his old enthusiasm. He spoke of his past mistakes and his future plans; he seemed zestful and confident. But in spite of all the efforts of both Rhodes and Stead to create an atmosphere of frankness and mutual trust, they were aware of the differences that had developed between them and which threatened to undermine their relationship. Rhodes's attitude towards Stead was affectionate but disapproving. Stead, on the other hand, considered Rhodes to be a mere shadow of the man he had once known. They disagreed, not only about the war, but about Britain's role in South Africa. The high-minded Imperialism which had once inspired their friendship had by now become a subject of dissension; Stead felt that Rhodes's rift with the Dutch was a betrayal of his former idealism and Rhodes was inclined to dismiss Stead's views as ill-informed and defeatist. One thing that did emerge from their rambling discussion was Rhodes's obvious confidence in Milner. Alfred Milner had once worked under Stead on the *Pall Mall Gazette* and had been regarded as the newspaperman's protégé; Stead, however, had disagreed with his policy in South Africa and there was now a coolness between them; it was Rhodes who championed Milner. He told Stead of Princess Radziwill's attempts to create bad blood between himself and the High Commissioner and said that he had shown Milner the letters which the Princess had written to him while he was besieged in Kimberley. Milner had dismissed her accusations as nonsense and Rhodes had accepted his assurance that they could work together. If anything was needed to disprove Catherine's later assertions that Rhodes distrusted Sir Alfred Milner, this talk with Stead provides ample evidence. Considering Stead's own attitude towards Milner, and the trust he subsequently placed in the Princess, there is no reason to doubt that his report faithfully reflects Rhodes's view.

The two men parted with protestations of friendship. They appreciated that they could not see eye to eye in politics but promised each other that they would not allow this to affect their friendship. So emotional was their parting that Bourchier Hawksley thought that they were about to kiss each other. It therefore came as something of a shock when, less than a year later, Rhodes struck Stead's name from the list of trustees of his will.

Shortly before Rhodes left for South Africa, at the end of April, Catherine arrived in England. They do not appear to have met and there is no reason to think that the Princess's arrival had anything to do with Rhodes's sudden departure. No doubt Catherine was disappointed at not being able to flaunt her friendship with the South African statesman in London but, one way and another, she was able to attract much attention in spite of his absence.

Her London visit started dramatically. Hardly had she arrived when she announced that she had been robbed. Her magnificent pearls and 'various treasures which she had received from her mother and from her cousin General Skobeleff' had, she claimed, been stolen. The jewels were never recovered and there appears to have been some mystery surrounding the alleged robbery. Stories that the pearls were imitations were revived and there were hints that the Princess had disposed of the valuables herself. Whatever the truth, Catherine played up the incident for all it was worth. It was said that the robbery 'made her the talk of the town, and made many familiar with her name who are completely innocent of all knowledge of the political and journalistic sphere in which the Princess moves and enjoys herself'.

Having made herself known to Society, she saw to it that her association with Rhodes was equally well publicized. W. T. Stead had already published the article she had sent from South Africa in *The Review of Reviews* under the heading 'Cecil J. Rhodes: An Impression by Princess Radziwill'. He had introduced it by saying: 'It is of course impossible for her, a foreigner and a stranger, to realize the full sweep of Mr Rhodes's ideals, and it is evident from her paper that she judges him, perhaps of necessity, from what may be called the dinner-table and drawing-room point of view. Nevertheless her appreciation of the great South African is interesting and suggestive.'

This was all very well, but she had no intention of being

written off as an amusing gossip. Her aim was to become known as Rhodes's political helpmate and not as a casual guest at Groote Schuur. As it happened, an opportunity was at hand for her to defend Rhodes. In March the *North American Review* published an attack on Rhodes by an anonymous British officer. Entitled 'The Responsibility of Cecil Rhodes', the article accused Rhodes of misleading the Government as to the fighting capacity of the Boers, and of having deflected the whole plan of the campaign in his own interests. Catherine's long and vigorous reply was published in the same journal in June. 'Mr Rhodes has just left England;' she wrote, 'he left it under a sort of cloud, and it is the fashion just now to abuse him and his conduct during the war. It was the military authorities (previous to Lord Roberts's arrival in South Africa) who started this attack in the hopes of screening their own mistakes . . . [the British officer] accuses Mr Rhodes of having deliberately and wilfully misled the British nation by his solemn assurance that there would be no war. But even admitting that this were true, was Mr Rhodes the only source of information which the British nation had?' She defended Rhodes's conduct in Kimberley and then went on to outline his future role in South Africa.

In her attempts to present Rhodes as the hope of South Africa, the Princess had some revealing things to say about her hero's blighted past. She was particularly anxious to defend his conduct during the Jameson Raid. 'A great future awaits him,' she wrote, 'greater than the one Mr Chamberlain has marked out for himself and obstinately denied to his friend of bygone days, perhaps his accomplice in far-fetched and far-seeking schemes.' She returned to the subject of the Raid later in the article. 'The last word has not yet been spoken with regard to the Raid, and perhaps time will show that Mr Rhodes was in this sad business just as generous as he was imprudent, just as ready as he ever is, when he thinks it necessary for his country's welfare, to sacrifice his person in order to screen its prestige—even when that prestige is embodied in the person of Mr Chamberlain, who is always willing to disavow anything or anybody he believes to be compromising to himself, as he is forgetful of services rendered to him in the past.' If she was trying to overcome Rhodes's distrust, this was hardly the way to go about it.

This provocative article was followed by another, published in the Conservative newspaper, *The Review of the Week*. This time the Princess defended her attempts to reconcile Rhodes to the Bond. She said that her aim had been to form a political organization of 'honest, clever, conscientious men, who put their country before everything else in the world'. She then went on to explain that she had been prevented from achieving this by the reluctance of both Rhodes and the Bond leaders to make the first move.

All in all, it is difficult to imagine a series of statements less likely to endear her to Rhodes. But she appears to have been more interested in presenting Rhodes as she would have him, than in winning his confidence. She was out to create her god before bothering about whether or not he would accept her tribute. She recorded in her 'diary' the confidential political talks she was supposed to have had with the British Prime Minister—her old acquaintance, Lord Salisbury. In these entries the Prime Minister is represented as meeting her secretly and spending most of his time abusing Rhodes. There was, of course, little chance of such meetings being arranged and even less of Lord Salisbury taking into his confidence a woman whom he hardly knew. 'The whole thing,' declared the Prime Minister's daughter-in-law, 'was a cheap fraud.' Nevertheless, it says much for Catherine's inflated opinion of her role that she later produced these 'conversations' and expected politically informed people to accept them as genuine.

If she was unable to interest Lord Salisbury in her schemes, she did find an enthusiastic ally in W. T. Stead. Much of her published writing bears the imprint of Stead's editorial pen. According to Stead's introduction to her article on Rhodes (which she had sent him from South Africa) the editor had not met the Princess since their first encounter in St Petersburg. How true this is, one cannot tell, but they undoubtedly saw a great deal of each other during Catherine's visit to England. Lyttleton Gell, who visited Stead in June to discuss South African affairs, was positively alarmed at the Princess's influence over the newspaper editor. 'He has passed under the sway of Princess Radziwill,' Gell wrote to Sir Alfred Milner. 'It has become absolutely clear to me as we talked . . . that she is an active agent in the policy of getting things in a tangle . . . She has obviously tried to make Rhodes believe you are animated by jealousy of him . . . Well, of course, she has infatuated Stead, and has obviously succeeded in perplexing his whole mind about you.' When, in the same month, Stead reprinted extracts from Catherine's *North American Review* article, his change of attitude towards her was obvious. No longer does he dismiss her as an uninformed social gossip. He points to her close association with prominent British statesmen and claims that Disraeli had been her life-long friend. Her acquaintance with Lord Salisbury, he says, 'has continued down to the present hour'. Naturally, he gives prominence to what he describes as her 'pregnant hint' about Chamberlain's involvement in the Jameson Raid and welcomes her sympathy towards the Dutch in South Africa. 'Princess Radziwill,' he declared approvingly, 'is not a woman who does anything by halves.'

Having created sufficient stir abroad, the Princess was ready to turn her attention to Rhodes and South Africa once more. Her son, Prince Nicholas, had joined her in London and by the end of June they were preparing to leave for the Cape. By this time she was more than ever convinced that she was destined to play an influential part in South African affairs. It was a conviction shared by Stead. 'Her ideas as to the necessity of conciliating the Dutch are sound,' he wrote, 'and she would take a hand in the political game, as if, instead of being Polish and Russian born, she were a native of South Africa.'

Accompanied by her son and her maid, Francine, the Princess set out on her second voyage south.

*

'I paid her bills and she left the country,' said Rhodes, '—but she came back again.'

He was not in Cape Town when she arrived. After returning from England in May, he spent a few days at Groote Schuur and then left for Rhodesia. His idea of visiting his beloved north—of getting back into the veld and relaxing with a few close friends —had probably been at the back of his mind all through the siege of Kimberley. His visit to England had confirmed his need to escape from political concerns. While he was in London, he had visited a heart specialist who had warned him that he was over-taxing himself and that rest was essential. For Rhodes rest meant one thing—Rhodesia.

He found the land route to Rhodesia barred. The war was still dragging on and, although he was convinced that it would not last much longer, he had no intention of waiting for the end of hostilities. He chartered a special steamer, sailed to Beira and went to Salisbury from there. He was accompanied by Sir Charles Metcalfe, Johnny Grimmer, Philip Jourdan and the faithful Tony de la Cruz.

The tour of Rhodesia lasted for five months. Although some of the time was given over to business, it was as much a holiday as anything else. Rhodes was in his element and for a while all was well with his world. It was quite like old times. Never once did he make a concession to his failing health. When his companions pleaded with him not to exhaust himself, he brushed their warnings aside. 'So long as I can keep going,' he said, 'let me continue with my work.' Travelling by horse and mule wagon, the party covered an average of thirty miles a day. Sometimes they would stalk seven or eight miles on foot in search of game; Rhodes would be in the lead and nothing would delight him more than bringing down a bird which one of the others had missed. Only in the towns was he irritable and he would go to extraordinary lengths to eat an extra meal in the open. 'Let us get away, Metcalfe, and have our chops in the veld,' he would say. The wagons would be inspanned and the party would trek a few miles out of the town in order to enjoy a camp-fire meal. 'When he was away from the towns in the country, free from all worry, his true nature presented itself,' says Jourdan. 'He was then bright and cheerful, full of fun, and disposed to chaff everybody, like a schoolboy enjoying his holiday after three months' confinement at a boarding school.'

But he could not entirely free himself from the politics of the south. Shortly after he had left for Rhodesia, there had been a crisis in the Government in Cape Town. The coalition administration that had been formed from the anti-Rhodes groups after the election of 1898 had, as a result of the war, found itself seriously divided. With a large section of the population in sympathy with the Transvaal Boers, rebellion had broken out in some districts of the Cape Colony and the question had arisen of how the rebels should be treated. The Bond and its sympathizers in the Cabinet had been in favour of a general amnesty but, as this suggestion was vetoed by Britain, the more constitutionally minded ministers felt they had no option but to seek a compromise measure. The subsequent proposal that the rebels be disenfranchised for five years, while their leaders were dealt with more severely, was rejected by a caucus meeting of the ruling party and, on 11th June, the Government fell. This, at any other time, would have been the signal for Rhodes's return. He had been kept fully informed of the crisis by his agents in Cape Town but he refused to interfere in any way. His attitude was one of contempt for the pettiness of Cape politics and confidence in Milner's ability to handle the situation. To the appeals sent by his supporters begging him to intervene, his invariable reply, it is said, was: 'You can trust Milner.'

There can be little question of his confidence in Milner. While he was in Rhodesia he was in touch with the Governor concerning the possibility of establishing farming communities in South Africa and Rhodesia after the war. His aim was to attract Uitlanders from the towns in order to balance the Boer vote in the country. It was a scheme which appears to have won Milner's approval. In the course of this correspondence, Rhodes had raised the question of Princess Radziwill's attempts to set Milner against him and had promptly received the Governor's reassurance. Without mentioning her by name, Milner had dismissed Catherine's activities as the meddling of an ill-disposed foreigner and had begged Rhodes not to listen to any of her stories. Both men were to discover that she was not so easily ignored.

To solve the Parliamentary crisis, Milner called upon Sir Gordon Sprigg to form a Government. This shrewd but limited politician had been Prime Minister of the Cape several times before. He was an adroit parliamentarian who inevitably emerged as a compromise candidate for the Premiership. Rhodes gave his blessing to the Sprigg administration more to support Milner in his difficulty than to display confidence in the new Government. Not a few of his supporters regarded his half-hearted acceptance of Sir Gordon Sprigg simply as a means to ensure his own return to office.

When Princess Radziwill arrived back in Cape Town in July, the new Government was already established and she found little in the changed situation to use to her advantage. While the Bond leaders had exercised an influence on the Cabinet, she had hoped to use the power they wielded to attract Rhodes into an alliance with them; now it looked as if she had been deprived of her most important weapon. Sir Gordon Sprigg was not a magnet to attract either side. If Rhodes had acted differently and assumed the Premiership, things might have been arranged otherwise. She could then have reversed her tactics and having failed to lure Rhodes towards the Bond, might have persuaded the Bond leaders to approach Rhodes. 'I believe,' she wrote, 'that if at that moment Cecil Rhodes had become the head of the Cabinet not one voice, even among the most fanatic of the Afrikander Bond, would have objected.' But if she found the situation frustrating, she did not allow it to deter her. The answer to the apparent *impasse* was simple. What had not happened must be made to happen: Rhodes must be prodded into office. It says much for her tenacity that, after all her rebuffs, she could embark on another campaign involving the unfortunate Rhodes. Yet this is what she did. To make Cecil John Rhodes Prime Minister of the Cape now became her main objective.

Her political reputation, if not as influential as she imagined, was by now sufficiently important to warrant public comment. This was largely due to the articles she had published in London. Her account of her attempted negotiations between Rhodes and the Bond had attracted particular attention in the anti-Rhodes press. J. W. Sauer's paper, *South African News*, which had already alluded to her conciliatory efforts, was delighted to have its hint publicly confirmed.

The pro-Rhodes newspapers appear to have been anxious to keep her name out of their columns. There was good reason for this. The gossip of her alleged liaison with Rhodes had spread further afield than Cape Town. Rumours that Rhodes was thinking of marrying her were current throughout South Africa. Inevitably, these rumours began to leak into the Press. In Grahamstown—a somewhat remote, staunchly British town in the Eastern Province—for instance, an enthusiastic columnist could not resist passing on the good news. 'We are informed on good authority,' he wrote, 'that the Right Hon. Cecil J. Rhodes is about to forsake the state of single blessedness, and will shortly be married to a princess, a lady of very high rank in Europe, whose name we cannot at present disclose.' This intriguing little item was ignored by the larger pro-Rhodes newspapers but the opposition press pounced on it and republished it with glee. Catherine was probably delighted. This was the sort of thing that later helped distort the popular impression of Rhodes's relationship with the Princess.

Almost from the moment she arrived back in Cape Town, Catherine started her campaign to have Rhodes accept the Premiership. She was in regular communication with W. T. Stead who appears to have given her his whole-hearted support. Despite his disenchantment with Rhodes, Stead was anxious for a negotiated settlement of the war, and saw in Rhodes's proposed leadership a hope for a peaceful reconstruction of the country. In September, as part of the joint effort being made by Stead and the Princess, the newspaper editor wrote an important letter to Rhodes which he sent to Catherine with instructions that she deliver it to Groote Schuur. The letter has never been published. Later references to it, however, indicate that it contained certain confidential information which Rhodes was to find extremely disturbing. This information was probably supplied to Stead by the Princess. Whatever was in the letter, Catherine appears to have been reluctant to hand it over to Rhodes.

She had an opportunity to deliver the letter not long after she received it. On 8th October, Rhodes returned to Groote Schuur. He was met by a message from the Princess, proposing herself for luncheon the following day. If she took Stead's letter with her, then she did not allow it out of her possession. Some three months later she was to produce it with dramatic effect.

CHAPTER TEN

The Break

WHEN Rhodes left Gordon le Sueur in a London hospital in 1898, it had been arranged that as soon as he had recovered, the happy-go-lucky young man would join the Rhodesian Civil Service. As a secretary, he had proved both inefficient and extravagant and by now Rhodes had lost patience with him. But his disenchantment did not last long. Le Sueur had hardly taken up his post in Rhodesia before Rhodes was once more interesting himself in the young man's welfare and showering him with cheques. And when, predictably, le Sueur left the Rhodesian Civil Service a little while later, it was to Groote Schuur that he made his way. As Rhodes had no employment for him, le Sueur simply joined the rest of the company that drifted in and out of the house. Both Jourdan and Grimmer were there and so was W. D. Fynn—one of the four brothers who were part of Rhodes's 'Queenstown Gang'.

The fact that four young men were now idling about Groote Schuur was not unusual. This is a facet of Rhodes's life which his biographers tend to ignore. But it is impossible to read the memoirs of Rhodes's older friends without realizing that this court of motley young men was a significant feature of his later years. Frank Thompson, for instance, maintains that there were two sides to Rhodes's character. There was the Rhodes whom he knew when they worked together to obtain the famous concession in Matabeleland. 'This,' he says, 'was the Rhodes of the wide vision, the humane temper and unselfish ambition . . . The other Rhodes, with an entourage of fawning sycophants, did not appeal to me.' And there was W. H. Scully, who had once been Rhodes's mess-mate at the diamond fields and who, on a visit to Groote Schuur with Sir Sydney Shippard, was amazed at Rhodes's rudeness in argument. Discussing this on the morning after their visit, Sir Sydney said: 'As a matter of fact Rhodes has been for so long surrounded by men who defer to him in every way, and hang on his every utterance as though it were that of an oracle, that he can no longer brook even a difference of opinion.' Descriptions of an arrogant, choleric Rhodes, surrounded by flatterers and sycophants, were finding their way into print before his death. In 1901, Francis Dormer, a journalist who had known Rhodes in the 1870s, published his book *Vengeance as a Policy in Afrikanderland*, in which he says: 'I have had occasion to discover during the past few weeks, however, that he has ceased to be the Cecil Rhodes that he used to be; that he has come under the influence of new men and an altogether new set of ideas.'

The strange thing about such accusations is that, although they all make mention of a retinue of servile henchmen, it is impossible to discover the identity of those to whom they refer. Who were these toadies? The men with whom Rhodes associated at this time were, for the most part, respectable politicians, journalists and financiers—many of whom had known him for years. Although the opinions of some of them might not have been universally acceptable, these associates hardly warrant the description of 'fawning sycophants'. Of all the men surrounding Rhodes, only one—Dr Rutherfoord Harris—was a likely candidate for the title of a self-seeking adulator. Harris appears to have been universally disliked and there were probably more unpleasant stories circulated about him than about any of Rhodes's other friends. But whatever Harris's shortcomings, Rhodes had known him for almost as long as he had known Jameson and, in any case, one man does not constitute an 'entourage'.

It was the general atmosphere of flunkeyism emanating from Groote Schuur that disturbed Rhodes's old friends. It was an atmosphere often associated with declining power and weakening physique. Princess Radziwill, who had good cause to resent Rhodes's associates, has recorded her own impressions of the frequenters of Groote Schuur; although she was jaundiced and often careless of her facts, she was a shrewd observer and this was an aspect of Rhodes's life with which she was well acquainted.

According to her, Rhodes had an insatiable hunger for flattery. 'This craving continually to have someone at hand to bully, scold, or make use of,' she says, 'was certainly one of the failings of Rhodes's powerful mind. It also indicated in a way that thirst for power which never left him until the last moment of his life. He had within him the weakness of those dethroned kings who, in exile, still like to have a Court about them and to travel in state. Rhodes had a Court, and also travelled with a suite who, under the pretence of being useful to him, effectually barred access to any stranger. But for his entourage it is likely that Rhodes might have outlived the odium of the Raid.' It was natural that Catherine should regard Rhodes's hangers-on in terms of royal favourites, but her description, if apt in certain respects, is open to misinterpretation. Rhodes's spoilt favourites were far removed from those to be found in the scented Courts of Europe.

Of all the hangers-on at Groote Schuur, few were more indolent than Rhodes's rough-and-ready young men. Visitors to the house found these idle employees' presence extremely puzzling. Their status was so vague that they themselves would have found it difficult to explain why they were there. For want of a better term, Rhodes's friends were inclined to refer to them collectively as 'Mr Rhodes's secretaries'. This was an obvious misnomer. Gordon le Sueur, who had, perhaps, some right to consider himself a secretary, makes this quite clear. 'We were all much more companions than secretaries in the ordinary sense of the word,' he says. 'Philip Jourdan was perhaps the nearest approach to the accepted idea of a private secretary, as he wrote shorthand (an accomplishment the rest of us regarded with a sort of awe) and, being rather delicate, his habits were more sedentary than ours.' Le Sueur gives a short list of 'secretaries' who were closely associated with Rhodes and then talks of others who were known simply as Rhodes's 'young men'. This term was not an unusual one for the period. Sir Alfred Milner, for instance, had his famous 'Kindergarten' of budding diplomats and several military commanders cultivated young officers in whom they took a special interest. Where Rhodes's 'young men' differed from the usual run of protégés was in the haphazard manner in which they were recruited and the use that was made of their services. It was not a question of promising talent being recognized and encouraged, but of unknown young men being employed on a whim and often tolerated long after they had proved themselves to be useless. If a young man happened to catch Rhodes's eye, he would be employed without further question and retained despite all justified criticism.

The casual manner in which a young man could enter Rhodes's service can be judged from his impulsive selection of Harry Palk as one of his secretaries. Palk was an officer on one of the Union Castle ships in which Rhodes sailed to England. On the day that Rhodes boarded the ship, the tug conveying him to the steamer took some time in drawing alongside. Young Palk, who was on duty at the head of the gangway, shouted down to inquire 'with much profanity' why the tug was so late. On being told that Mr Rhodes had been late in arriving, Palk launched into another stream of oaths, saying that he did not care who was coming aboard and that he had no intention of allowing the ship to be delayed for anyone. 'Rhodes was highly interested in this emphatic young man,' reports le Sueur, 'and so he became one of the "bodyguard".' His sole qualification, it would seem, was his impertinence.

Having engaged Palk, Rhodes sent him to W. T. Stead for some training and then arranged for him to join one of his treks in Rhodesia. But Palk did not remain with Rhodes for long. Before leaving England he had made the mistake of getting married and when he announced that he wanted to return to Cape Town so that he could be with his wife for the birth of their first child, his career as Rhodes's secretary came to an abrupt end. 'Imagine his leaving me alone at Salisbury with no one to do my letters,' said Rhodes, 'just because his wife was going to have a baby. Why didn't he tell me before he left?'

But no matter how often his bachelor secretaries let him down, Rhodes was always ready to overlook their faults. The inefficiency of Gordon le Sueur is a case in point. Not only was le Sueur unable to write shorthand (which Palk had conscientiously mastered) but he could not be relied upon to carry out the simplest task. It is said, for instance, that when the potential of the newly discovered Premier Diamond Mine was being investigated, le Sueur forgot to post a letter from Rhodesia in which Rhodes had instructed his engineer to examine the property. As a result Rhodes lost his chance of controlling this important mine which later yielded the famous Cullinan diamond. Until they were amalgamated, the Premier Mine was a dangerous rival to De Beers. This shocking gaffe had no effect upon le Sueur's career. 'Oh, I spoilt him,' Rhodes explained to a friend who was amazed at le Sueur's debts, 'and I suppose I've got to pay for it.'

J. G. McDonald tells the story of a certain Percy Ross who arrived unexpectedly at Rhodes's camp one day and asked for a job. Like Grimmer and le Sueur, Ross was heavily built, with a marked aptitude for sport but little inclination for work. Rhodes took an immediate liking to him and he was soon established as a member of the ever-growing entourage. He proved an extremely dubious acquisition. Incorrigibly lazy, he would lounge about the camp all day discoursing on the folly of work and boasting of the fact that he lacked any ambition. His theories on the advantages of evading responsibility were so finely worked out that Rhodes called him 'the Philosopher'. In short, he was the type of youngster whom Rhodes professed to despise above all others: a born loafer. Percy Ross was finally sent to one of Rhodes's farms in Rhodesia where he lived out his purposeless existence. When he died, at the age of sixty-eight, almost forty years after Rhodes's own death, he was still living on his employer's bounty, without having lifted a finger to deserve it. It would seem that any young man who was prepared to give himself over to Cecil Rhodes was set for life.

And there were a great many young men who were prepared to accept this exacting condition. Not all were worthless. Some took advantage of the opportunities offered in order to further laudable ambitions, but such ambitions were not essential to their adoption by Rhodes. All he demanded was an all-consuming loyalty. Where that loyalty was not given voluntarily, he was prepared to buy it. 'What do you want from me?' was his first question to any youngster who approached him. Once he had established his hold over a new acquaintance, he was willing to ignore any subsequent shortcomings. This compulsive desire to possess, to dominate, to secure an unquestioning allegiance to himself was perhaps the most important motivating force in Rhodes's strange psychology. Originating as a deep-seated personal need, it extended to his political, financial and Empire-building activities. The reassurance and sense of security obtained from the knowledge that others were subject to his will—be it expressed as a personal or national directive—compensated for a subconscious psychological deprivation. It explains many of his mistakes as well as his successes and it drew quite a number of unlikely people into his orbit.

Most of his 'young men' were employed in Rhodesia. However varied their abilities might be, Rhodes could always find them work of one sort or another in his northern territories. Whenever they came to Cape Town they were given the run of Groote Schuur. Often ill-at-ease, tongue-tied and socially maladroit, these hefty, weather-beaten lads were to be found as Rhodes's house guests or seated uncomfortably at his dinner-table. He made no attempt to disguise his concern for them. Important business discussions would be interrupted while he disappeared to inquire after the welfare of some youthful stranger and no one could claim his undivided attention until he had settled the problems of a newly arrived young guest. The story is told of one boy who arrived at Groote Schuur for dinner to find himself the only person not in evening dress: Rhodes immediately left the room and came back in his crumpled working clothes. It was a kindly gesture but it must have left the rest of Rhodes's guests feeling extremely uncomfortable.

That some of Rhodes's 'young men' were flattered by his interest is not surprising. Nor is it to be wondered at if they responded at times with what looked liked undue servility. Rhodes enjoyed bullying them. He liked to order their lives, to make them the butt of his jokes and the prey of his temper. They, in turn, grew accustomed to his chaffing and soon learned not to take his tantrums too seriously. Essentially, their role was to act as a buffer for his uncertain moods and to protect him from the unwanted attentions of outsiders. Most of them realized this. While outsiders referred to them as 'Mr Rhodes's secretaries' they were inclined to speak of themselves as the 'bodyguard'. It was an apt description of the services they performed.

No one was more aware of their protecting presence than Princess Radziwill. The more determined she became to pursue Rhodes, the more difficult it was for her to reach him. He was never alone: or if he was then it was not for long. Years later she recalled with bitterness the frustration of her desperate attempts to run him to ground. 'I shall always maintain,' she wrote, 'that Rhodes, without his so-called friends, would most certainly have been one of the greatest figures of his time and generation . . . Unhappily, an atmosphere of flattery and adulation had become absolutely necessary to him, and he became so used to it that he did not perceive that his sycophants never left him alone for a moment. They watched over him like a policeman who took good care no foreign influence should venture to approach . . . A man supposed to have an iron will, yet he was weak almost to childishness in regard to these flattering satellites. It amused him to have always at his beck and call people ready and willing to submit to his insults, to bear with his fits of bad temper, and accept every humiliation which he chose to offer. Cecil Rhodes never saw, never affected to see, the disastrous influence all this had on his life.'

Le Sueur, who now met the Princess for the first time, was well aware of the scorn with which she regarded the secretarial phalanx. 'I am sure,' he reports gleefully, 'she cordially hated not only Jourdan, but Grimmer and myself.'

*

On 15th October, a week after Rhodes's return to Groote Schuur, the Cape Parliament was prorogued. It did not meet again until 20th August, 1902. To all intents and purposes, politics had come to an end at the Cape. This, however, did not deter Princess Radziwill from pursuing her plan to make Rhodes Prime Minister. Anticipating the end of the war, she envisaged Rhodes first as Prime Minister of the Cape and eventually as President of a federated South Africa. The purpose of her campaign was to present Rhodes as the 'one strong man' in Africa.

Once again the Princess became a regular visitor to Groote Schuur. Arriving for luncheon the day after Rhodes's return from Rhodesia, she pestered him with a persistence that made her earlier invasions look tame. Whether she so much as showed him W. T. Stead's confidential letter is uncertain. If she did, he does not appear to have associated her with the disturbing information it contained. At this stage of their relationship, although driven almost to distraction by her relentless pursuit, Rhodes was still trying to be polite to the Princess. He took an interest in her son and even arranged a position for the boy at De Beers; but Catherine's importunities proved too much for him. She admits this herself. It is to this period that much of her dubious correspondence from Rhodes is attributed. While the content of these letters is suspect, certain emphatic phrases that recur have a ring of truth about them. (Catherine may well have been shrewd enough to include a few uncomplimentary remarks to give the correspondence a semblance of authenticity.) Again and again the Princess is told to leave Rhodes alone. She must not meddle in his affairs, he says. She has no idea of the issues involved. Added to these warnings are Catherine's own references to Rhodes's rudeness in letters she wrote to other people. On 27th November, for instance, she reported him as being so angry with her that he began smashing the furniture to emphasize his point.

But for the most part he did his best to avoid her. Stories of his efforts to escape being left alone with the Princess are legion. Some of these stories are amusing, some incredible and not a few have pathetic undertones. They became the talk of Rhodes's supporters and are spoken about in Cape Town to this day. One persistent rumour, for instance, has it that Groote Schuur was organized on the lines of a threatened encampment. 'During the time when the lady was pestering Rhodes,' it is said, 'by appearing at Groote Schuur at all hours of the day and night and wangling an invitation to the next meal, this got on the poor fellow's nerves to such an extent that a servant was left posted on the look-out to warn him of the approaching attack. A horse was left in the stables, saddled, and Rhodes would slink out by a back door and ride away.' According to this story, he would make for Welgelegen—a house he had had restored for his old friend J. B. Currey—and remain there until it was safe to return home.

But flight was not always possible. Shortly after his return to the Cape, Rhodes suffered a bad attack of 'fever' and was confined to Groote Schuur for more than a month. During this period he was very much at the mercy of the Princess and had to be continually rescued by his 'bodyguard'. And in the game of thwarting the Princess, no one was more amused than the irrepressible Gordon le Sueur. Although he had no regular employment, he says that Rhodes had managed to find some 'scratch work' for him at Groote Schuur. Not the least of his duties was that of a bodyguard. In this, as in most things, he could not resist livening the proceedings with his own peculiar brand of devilment. His employer could never rely upon his assistance. 'When Rhodes had to take the Princess over the house,' he says, 'he invariably signalled for one of us to accompany him, as he had a horror of being left alone with the lady, and often to annoy him we would pretend not to see his signal of distress.'

The person to suffer most from the Princess's activities was the unfortunate Philip Jourdan. It was inevitable that Catherine should choose the most vulnerable member of Rhodes's entourage as a likely means of reaching her quarry. The wide-eyed, respectful and conscientious Jourdan must have seemed heaven-sent material for her designs. For a while, she was able to make good use of him. 'She quite took me in,' Jourdan declared.

She started by playing on his devotion to Rhodes. Inviting him to a *tête-à-tête* luncheon she launched into a panegyric of the great man's abilities. She talked on and on but her argument could be summed up in a few words: in the interests of South Africa, Cecil Rhodes must once again become Prime Minister. Having hammered this point home, she then asked Jourdan if he could keep a secret. When he assured her that he could, she went into an adjoining room and returned with a telegram which she said Lord Salisbury had sent her when she was in England. It was an invitation to visit the Prime Minister at Hatfield. 'She then,' says Jourdan, 'mysteriously drew a typewritten document from the pocket of her gown, and holding it up in her hand she said, trembling and quivering with emotion, and with a strange look in her eyes, "Now, would you like to read this?"' The document purported to be an account of an interview she had had with Lord Salisbury. The Prime Minister was supposed to have initialed the document as an accurate transcript of their conversation. She said that she intended sending this to Rhodes and wanted Jourdan's assurance that it would reach his employer. The drift of the alleged interview was, of course, that Rhodes should be made Prime Minister. On returning to Groote Schuur, Jourdan immediately told Rhodes that he had visited the Princess and what had taken place. The typewritten document duly arrived the following day. It had been sent, not by the Princess, but by her friend Mrs Scholtz. Rhodes was not impressed. He told Jourdan to copy it and return it to the

Princess. Later, Rhodes's copy was sent to Lord Salisbury's family and pronounced a complete fabrication.

Shortly after his luncheon with the Princess, Jourdan was taken seriously ill with appendicitis and rushed to hospital. After the operation he was very weak and forbidden all visitors. But the Princess was not to be put off by hospital regulations. Using her title to impress the doctors, she obtained permission to visit the invalid on the strict understanding that she would stay only a few minutes. She was ushered in by a smiling and deferential doctor and poor Jourdan was left at her mercy. 'She walked into my room very slowly and quietly,' he says, 'and when she saw me she rushed to my bedside, seized both my hands, and with tears in her eyes told me how inexpressibly sorry she felt for me. For five minutes she did not give me a chance to say a word, but went on reiterating her deep sympathy for me and asking a hundred questions without waiting for my answers, all the time holding my hands affectionately. The situation was most embarrassing to me, and I felt a glow all over my face . . . She talked incessantly for three hours, until my brain became so confused that at times I lost myself momentarily and could not follow her. When she left me I was on the verge of fainting . . . She called on me regularly every day for three weeks and invariably left me utterly exhausted.' After one or two visits her loudly voiced concern for the sick young man gave way to a more genuine anxiety regarding her relationship with his employer. She wanted to know why Rhodes had changed so much since she had first met him. Why he was so rude to her. What he had thought of the document she had sent him and how seriously he treated her political activities. Weak as he was, Jourdan met the onslaught with commendable resolution. He staunchly refused to give her even a hint of Rhodes's opinions. 'I could see on one or two occasions,' he said, 'when she lost control of her feelings momentarily, by the vindictive look in her eye, that she hated me. She hated me because she could not succeed in her object to make me divulge confidences which my chief had imparted to me.'

His loyalty did not pass unappreciated. When he arrived back at Groote Schuur and told Rhodes what had happened, his chief, he says, 'placed his hand upon my shoulder and said very feelingly, "It is all right, my boy; I have always trusted you and I will always trust you. Do not let the Princess make mischief between us. She has been trying to poison my mind against you . . . she has been playing a double game with each of us, and I expect she hates both you and me with equal venom." '

According to Jourdan, Catherine was so incensed by his rejection of her overtures that she put about a story that he had asked her to marry him and that she had laughed his proposal to scorn.

Many of the accounts which were later written about Catherine's pursuit of Rhodes must be read with caution. Up to a point they are true enough but, more often than not, wildly exaggerated. The conception of Princess Radziwill as a figure of fun was one which appealed to many of Rhodes's admirers. It allowed them to add a little colour to their recollections of her. Had she been quite such an obvious, melodramatic adventuress, it is doubtful whether she would have lasted as long as she did or have impressed and deceived so many people. For, if some politically informed men did eventually begin to suspect her motives, very few regarded her as simply a foolish intriguer. Nor is it possible to overlook her dynamic and persuasive personality. Milner spoke of her with respect, even though he was aware of her intrigues. W. T. Stead was all too ready to trust her. And even Rhodes, for all his wariness of her, responded to some of her arguments.

Much of what the Princess advocated had a very real appeal for Rhodes. His dream had always been that South Africa should become a federated state and, quite naturally, he saw himself as its head. Therefore, when the Princess managed to corner him into a political discussion—and she seems to have done this more often than his champions admit—there were quite a few points which he was willing to concede. Moreover, he was aware of her influence with Stead and other political journalists and may well have been prepared to take advantage of her indiscretions to set up a few hares of his own. Whether he did so or not, is difficult to say. What contact there was between Rhodes and Princess Radziwill before their relationship was completely broken off, was so bedevilled by his basic distrust of her and by her own undoubted duplicity, that the remaining tangle of evidence is impossible to unravel. Consequently, the questions whether Rhodes was planning to seize power after the Boer War;

whether he was ready to cut his losses in the Cape and concentrate on the north; whether he was aiming for an immediate federation of South Africa or indeed, what his actual intentions were, remain a matter for speculation.

It is not merely that the letters produced by the Princess—in which Rhodes is supposed to have discussed these subjects—are suspect. These letters are only one indication of her intrigues. The whole question becomes infinitely more involved when it is realized that her activities were so widespread as to taint even independent-seeming sources of verification. No one was more eager to see Rhodes as the head of a South African Federation than W. T. Stead. But, for a long time, Stead was in league with the Princess. He even sent an agent out to South Africa to assist her. How much of the information which she passed on to Stead came direct from Rhodes, and how much she invented, will never be known. Even after Catherine had been exposed as a fraud, Stead had a sneaking suspicion that much of what she had told him was basically true. Stead was a man of influence and did not hesitate to pass on the information he received from Catherine to those who he thought could further his schemes. One of these was Colonel Brocklehurst who later wrote to Rhodes saying that he had persuaded Queen Victoria that Cecil Rhodes was the only possible leader for South Africa and that immediate federation was the sole solution to the country's problems. Thus, ideas which may well have originated with Catherine were spread and, supported by half-truths, came back to reinforce her arguments. And this was not all. She had other means of propagating her ideas. Although it is unlikely that she was taken on as a regular correspondent by London newspapers, some of her articles seem to have been published in England. The *South African News*, at least, suspected her hand behind the 'phrases which have appeared ad nauseam in several English newspapers as from a "Cape Town correspondent". Mr Rhodes must be Prime Minister, Sir Gordon Sprigg must go . . . the military must be off because—well, for a woman's reason, because they must.'

By the end of 1900 her campaign was well advanced. Though Rhodes was doing his best to avoid her, she had good reason, one way and another, to suppose that with a little more pressure she might be able to break down his opposition. To bring that pressure to bear she took a disastrous step. Not content with being an occasional journalist she decided, with breath-taking audacity and complete disregard for her financial position, to start a newspaper of her own. Hopefully, she told Rhodes of her intention. He gave her not a flicker of encouragement. 'That,' he said emphatically, 'is your own business; you will find it will give you a lot of trouble.' But by now she was used to his rebuffs and was quite prepared to deal with troubles as they arose. She seems to have had no idea of the size of the undertaking upon which she was about to embark. In any case, she was not unduly concerned about her lack of funds. Rhodes had helped her out before; he would probably do so again. This, as later events were to show, was the most grievous error of judgment she ever made.

At the time, however, she was full of confidence. On 3rd January, 1901, she prepared to launch her new enterprise by buying a second-hand typewriter and started a lengthy correspondence with business contacts in both South Africa and England. Not long after she had begun her new career as a newspaper proprietress there was a crisis in her relationship with Rhodes. Uneasy as their occasional meetings had been, they now came to an abrupt end. Catherine never forgave the man responsible for her final rupture with Rhodes. In years to come she was unable to write or speak of him without betraying her bitterness. She always maintained that he alone was responsible for Rhodes's troubles. 'His greatest wrong,' she was to say when speaking of Rhodes, 'has been his affection for a buccaneer —for one cannot qualify him by another name—Dr Jameson.'

*

During the years immediately following the disastrous Raid, the friendship between Rhodes and Jameson was strained. Neither was prepared to admit this: outwardly they seemed as close as ever, but there had been a definite shift in their relationship. They tended to be edgy when they were together and each had become more critical of the other. Rhodes, for instance, had made no effort to see Jameson when he first arrived in England for the Raid Inquiry and when the doctor eventually returned to Rhodesia, he received a very cool greeting from his friend. For his part, Jameson was very conscious of Rhodes's attitude and at times complained bitterly at his friend's half-hearted approach towards South African politics. For, although not essentially a politician himself, Jameson was anxious to justify his conduct in the eyes of the world. Behind his daredevil pose, his was a sensitive nature and he greatly resented the 'music-hall reputation' he had acquired as a result of the Raid fiasco. Instinctively, he wanted to hit back at his detractors, and Rhodes's apparent reluctance to take decisive action left him feeling sullen and restive.

None of this was obvious to the casual observer. On the surface things went on much as before. Rhodes was able to keep Jameson busy by entrusting to him the supervision of the telegraph extension in Rhodesia; they travelled to Europe together and the doctor was a frequent guest at Groote Schuur. Nevertheless, during these years it was Sir Charles Metcalfe who was Rhodes's constant companion and Jameson only flitted in and out of his life for brief periods. It seems to have been the war and Rhodes's rapidly declining health that brought them together again. While Rhodes had been shut up in Kimberley, Jameson had endured the siege of Ladysmith. After the towns had been relieved the two men returned to the Cape and from then on appear to have regained much of their former intimacy. Once again Jameson was to be found at Rhodes's side, both as his friend and his medical adviser.

Although, during Princess Radziwill's early invasions of Groote Schuur, Jameson had paid only brief visits to the Cape, he seems quickly to have taken Catherine's measure. Unlike Rhodes, his attitude towards women was not complicated by psychological conflict and he made no secret of his hostility. 'Dr Jameson took an instant dislike to her from the first,' it is said, 'and took very good care to protect Rhodes against what he regarded as the machinations of a clever and designing woman.' His natural antipathy had been increased by Catherine's dubious flirtation with the Bond leaders. The doctor had no more reason to love the Afrikander Bond than the Bond had to love him. Catherine was quickly aware of this. Many years later, talking of her efforts to reconcile Rhodes with the 'Dutch side', she said: 'That thing only would have been sufficient for me to seem odious in Jameson's eyes who . . . had taken as the [aim] of his life the extermination of both republics.'

Jameson's distrust of the Princess increased when he decided to enter openly into politics. It was a step he had been contemplating for some time. During the general election of 1898, he had been on the point of contesting a seat in Port Elizabeth but it was decided that his inflammable name would do Rhodes more harm than good and he had been persuaded to stand down. At that time he had had little taste for politics and was not unduly disappointed at having to postpone his entry into Parliament. The war, however, had brought a change in the political climate and when, after his return from Ladysmith, a safe seat had become vacant in Kimberley, he agreed to offer himself for nomination. His candidature brought forth a howl of protest from supporters of the Bond. 'What good purpose can be served by selecting "Dr Jim" as a candidate for Parliamentary honours we know not,' declared an opposition newspaper, 'but it ill becomes those who talk about "passing bitterness" to choose the hero of the Raid to send to Parliament to accentuate existing bitterness.' Scorn such as this was as nothing compared to the humiliation he was forced to endure upon taking his seat in the House of Assembly. His introduction to Parliament was greeted by a tense, contemptuous silence. Throughout the gruelling session he sat, says his biographer, 'a little forlorn-looking, hunched-up figure on one of the back benches'. He was constantly attacked by the Opposition and members of the Bond party made him the butt of all their sarcastic remarks and derisory laughter. He made no attempt to defend himself but friends, watching from the visitor's gallery, noticed that he changed colour with each new onslaught. Fortunately he did not have to endure this agony for long. Three months after he had taken his seat, Parliament was prorogued. Once again he was forced to fall back on whatever work Rhodes could find for him.

As it happened, Rhodes had an important mission for the doctor. The interview which he had had with W. T. Stead in April 1900 had done nothing to halt the journalist's demands that the Jameson Inquiry should be reopened. If anything, Stead had become more positive in his attacks on Chamberlain. In September 1900, for instance, he had published a pamphlet, *The Candidates of Cain*, in which he had accused the Colonial Secretary of active participation in the Raid conspiracy. 'The only possible conclusion, at which everyone outside England has long since arrived,' he wrote, '[is] that Mr Chamberlain, although not privy to the financing of the insurrection at Johannesburg, was in the conspiracy up to his neck; that he had a guilty knowledge of Mr Rhodes's designs; that he became not only a passive but an active accomplice in carrying them out; that with his blundering and reckless ignorance he wrecked the conspiracy which he attempted to direct.' The publication of this pamphlet coincided with the writing of the letter which Stead had sent to Rhodes via the Princess. As it is not certain that Rhodes had seen that letter, one does not know whether he was influenced by it. But there can be little doubt that he was perturbed about Stead's attitude towards Chamberlain. This seems to be the reason why he sent Jameson to England at the end of 1900.

Jameson had several discussions in London with Stead. What was said has never been disclosed. The doctor's visit to London is mentioned only incidentally in a letter which Stead wrote to Rhodes. According to this letter, Jameson and Stead appear to have got on well, but there is reason to think that their talks were more disquieting than Stead implies. For Jameson's return to South Africa was followed by two significant events: Rhodes struck Stead's name from the list of trustees of his will—because of the journalist's 'extraordinary eccentricity'—and a decisive move was made against Princess Radziwill.

Matters came to a head at a luncheon at Groote Schuur on 22nd January, 1901. Unfortunately, the only accounts of this significant episode are given by Catherine. However, her statements were never contested and they are supported by subsequent events. Much of what she says is deliberately vague and it is possible to follow the scene only in its broad outline.

During the luncheon, at which Sir Charles Metcalfe and T. E. Fuller were also present, Catherine accused Jameson of spreading lies about her and, she says, 'enjoyed myself by reading loudly a letter from Mr Stead relating them.' This letter appears to have been the one which Stead had sent her the previous September. Apparently Rhodes said nothing during this exchange between Catherine and Jameson. After luncheon Sir Charles Metcalfe left to keep an appointment in town. The Princess left Jameson and Fuller talking on the stoep and went into the house to tackle Rhodes alone. Rhodes immediately lost his temper. 'We had a rather violent quarrel,' she said. 'Mr Rhodes wanted me to do certain things which I positively refused to do . . . One of the things Mr Rhodes wanted me to do was to write on certain points to Lord Milner, and when I got Lord Milner's reply to tell him the text of the reply. I was not in a position to do so and declined. We had a violent quarrel, and I said whatever communications passed I would not communicate them to Mr Rhodes. That was one of the points. Then he wanted me to return certain documents which I possessed, amongst others a copy of a letter from Mr Stead . . . I utterly refused to return it, as they are documents which Mr Rhodes knew I had in my possession.'

This was the account of the quarrel, given in public, by Catherine. In it she tended, for good reasons, to play down the main issue between herself and Rhodes. Her references to Milner and to Stead's letter were of secondary importance: what actually produced Rhodes's outburst was her refusal to hand over certain papers which had been stolen from him. In an unpublished account of her quarrel with Rhodes, the Princess is a little more explicit on this point. 'The first thing to do was to make me return the papers I possessed,' she said. 'I had some [that were] very compromising for certain persons and especially a few of them which, after having been stolen [from] their own proprietors fell into my hands . . . We had, Rhodes and I, a tragic scene about it. He insisted upon my giving him all what I possessed in the matter of letters and papers, I refused vehemently.

' "Very well," said he. "Whatever happens, I will have those papers." '

From the importance which Catherine attached to this quarrel, it would seem that this was the first occasion upon which her 'papers' were openly discussed. She and Rhodes had quarrelled before but never so bitterly or, as it transpired, so decisively. Rhodes may have known for some time that these compromising papers had 'fallen into' the Princess's hands; this would explain his suspicions of her and the chariness with which he treated her. He could not, perhaps, have afforded to be too brusque in his dealings with the Princess. But now that the matter had been forced into the open, he could adopt different tactics.

The circumstances of the violent scene at Groote Schuur must be regarded as important clues to the events which lay ahead. The quarrel occurred shortly after Jameson's return from visiting Stead in England and during the course of it Milner's name and Stead's letter appear to have been mentioned. The last had not been heard of the Princess's mysterious 'papers'. Their contents were such as to threaten the whole of Rhodes's career.

*

The quarrel seems to have put an end to all personal contact between Rhodes and the Princess. There is nothing to show that they met again before Rhodes left for Kimberley in the middle of March. It is unlikely that they did. Rhodes, who was accompanied by Jameson, stayed in Kimberley for two months and then travelled on to Bulawayo where he remained until the end of June. By the time he returned to Cape Town, at the beginning of July, there was no question of his meeting the Princess again.

Catherine did not allow either the quarrel or Rhodes's departure to upset her plans. Despite all that had happened between them, she was determined to make Rhodes Prime Minister of the Cape. Her incredible persistence is a further illustration of what was perhaps the most fatal flaw in her nature: she was quite incapable of abandoning any project. Long after her initial reasons for taking a particular course of action had been forgotten, she continued on the course with dogged and often disastrous resolution. One stage of her progress led to the next, until her original motives became obscure. Her failure to learn from past mistakes had led to her exposure as 'Count Paul Vassili' and to her fall from grace in St Petersburg, and it was a blind refusal to admit defeat which lured her on to her doom in South Africa. She must have realized that there was now no hope of her winning Rhodes's trust. Their relationship had deteriorated into a battle of wits, with each trying to frighten the other into submission. Yet she refused to give up. The game she was playing had become an end in itself: she no longer thought in terms of victory, but merely of using what cards she held.

All her hopes were now centred on her newspaper. She

intended this to be a week-end political review similar to the English *Spectator* and *Saturday Review*. Her first object was to find a capable manager to handle the business side of the enterprise. The man she chose was Frederick Lovegrove, an experienced newspaperman who, at one time or another, had been connected with various newspapers throughout South Africa. At an interview with Lovegrove in March, she outlined her plans for the paper. It was to be published weekly, priced sixpence and avowedly Imperialist in policy. She had decided to call it *Greater Britain*. Its main purpose would be to further her campaign on Rhodes's behalf. Lovegrove agreed to handle the paper for a salary of £35 a month. At the first interview with Catherine he was given £60 to cover his initial expenses and a further £100 to meet the advance required by the printer. He was to receive very little else in the way of payment from the Princess.

It is impossible to assess Catherine's financial state at this period. She was not, as is sometimes supposed, completely penniless. Although it is doubtful whether she received an allowance from her husband, she had a small income from Russia. From time to time money arrived for her from her estate on the Volga. This property did not yield much and was partly mortgaged to a London businessman, but she retained some financial interest in the estate. The payments appear to have come through her London bankers and were inclined to be erratic. For the rest, she had to rely upon her writing, a source from which her income was equally disappointing. At one time she had placed great hopes on her book, *The Resurrection of Peter*. She had received some encouragement from the South African press. 'We understand that Princess Radziwill has a book in the press,' reported the *Eastern Province Herald* in October 1900, 'and, shortly to reach South Africa, is intended as an answer to Olive Schreiner's Peter Halket. This war of women's wit will no doubt be read with some interest by South Africans. The Princess presently writes prose, while her antagonist will no doubt continue to give us political poetry.' But Catherine's prose had been no match for Olive Schreiner's poetry and—an apologia lacking the impact of an attack—the book had been a flop. Only from occasional articles accepted by London newspapers did she receive any payment and this was scarcely enough to meet her daily expenses, let alone finance a newspaper.

Nevertheless, she continued with her plans. She cultivated her political contacts in South Africa and made a great display of her Imperial ardour. Her interest in the Afrikander Bond was now replaced by an expedient championing of Sir Alfred Milner's policies. The suggestion that she was behind the renewed attempts to reconcile Rhodes with the Bond seems ill-founded. She had turned her back on the Bond. She intended *Greater Britain* to live up to its Imperialist title.

Having engaged a manager, she set up offices for the paper. In Cape Town she hired rooms in Anderson's Chambers, at the corner of Long and Strand Streets, and arranged for a firm in Lincoln's Inn Fields to act as her British agents. If she had no money, she certainly had great expectations. After Lovegrove had been working for her for a few weeks, she gave him an indication of what these expectations were. 'I can continue the paper for six months,' she said, 'and we must make it good and sharp. Then I would worm out of Mr Rhodes the money to push it on.' Precisely how she intended to keep the paper going for six months and to worm the money from Rhodes, she did not say.

As it happened, it was neither her political nor her newspaper interests which prompted her first questionable move. The trouble arose from a purely domestic crisis. She needed somewhere to live. This problem had been bothering her for some time. Since her return from England she had had no permanent home. She could no longer afford the Mount Nelson Hotel and to find somewhere cheap but suitable had proved far from easy. At first she stayed with her friends the Scholtzes. But this had proved an uneasy haven. Agnes Scholtz, whom she had once described as 'such a good friend', had apparently proved a little too friendly. Her interest in Catherine's son, Prince Nicholas Radziwill, had become a bone of contention between the two women. 'Mrs Scholtz,' declared Catherine, 'had very undue influence over my son under the pretext of the greatest friendship.' Whether her accusations against Mrs Scholtz were justified or not, she had good reason to suspect the susceptibilities of her twenty-one-year-old son. For the tall, bearded Prince Nicholas had a decided *penchant* for older women and five years later was to marry a widowed Countess, twenty years older than himself and only three years younger than his mother. The ill-feeling which now developed between Catherine and Agnes

Scholtz was to turn into open hostility and to assume an unpleasant significance. At the time, the situation was sufficiently embarrassing for Catherine to leave the Scholtz household. In April 1901 she was living at St John's Villas in the fashionable suburb of Kenilworth; a month later she moved to a local hotel and began negotiations to rent a large house in the neighbourhood.

The house was called 'Crail' and belonged to a Mr Bell who lived in England. Through Mr Bell's attorneys, Tredgold, McIntyre and Bisset, Catherine arranged to take the house, together with a horse and trap, on a year's lease. The inclusive rent was £435 and this the attorney, Mr Bisset, insisted had to be paid in advance. Catherine wrote out a cheque for the full amount and prepared to move into her new house. A week or so later Bisset informed her that her cheque had been dishonoured and that his firm had issued a summons on it. This somewhat exacting attitude on the part of Mr Bisset is hardly surprising. At that time the Princess's bank balance stood at £4 9s 9d.

The threat of Mr Bisset's summons forced the Princess to take action. First, she consulted Mr Charles Howard Kinsley, a law agent. As a result of the negotiations which Kinsley conducted on her behalf, Bisset agreed to accept a note guaranteeing the rent until the Princess received money which, she claimed, she was expecting from Russia. Catherine then faced the problem of getting someone to stand as guarantor for her. She suggested that Dr Scholtz or Mr Lewis Michell, her bank manager, might be prepared to sign a note on her behalf. 'Will you kindly tell me what Mr Bell wants,' she wrote to Kinsley on 22nd May. 'Is it a bill or a promissory note? I want to make it quite clear for the person to whom I want to apply.' Kinsley wrote back saying that he thought Dr Scholtz's signature would be all that was required. But the Princess appears to have had second thoughts about approaching the doctor. Next day she wrote to Kinsley again. 'Just one line,' she said, 'to ask you whether Mr Bell will accept Mr Michell's guarantee. Please reply by return, because I would not like to ask him if it was useless. On the other hand I should like to enter the house on Saturday . . . I am sorry Mr Bell did not tell me earlier about a security, as I could have asked Mr Rhodes before. Unfortunately your letter came when I knew he had left for Bulawayo.' Having switched from Dr Scholtz to her bank manager, the Princess changed her mind once again. Instead of approaching Mr Michell, she launched out in an entirely new direction.

On the 30th May, using the uninspired name of Miss Smith, she pawned a pair of earrings. She then indulged in a little extravagance. At a bookshop in Cape Town's main shopping street, she bought a photograph of Rhodes to hang in the office of *Greater Britain*. It was not an uncommon photograph but it cost more owing to the fact that scrawled across the bottom of it was the signature: *C. J. Rhodes*.

These transactions completed, she wrote to her law-agent. On 3rd June, Mr Kinsley received the note which she had promised to send him. It was a simple typed statement promising to pay an unspecified sum on Princess Radziwill's behalf in four months' time. In the space that had been left blank, Kinsley filled in the sum that was due for the rent and added his own signature to two others at the bottom of the piece of paper. One of these signatures was that of Princess Catherine Radziwill and the other was that of the person endorsing the note—*C. J. Rhodes*.

Part Three

CHAPTER ELEVEN

'I Promise to Pay . . . '

IN THE offices of *Greater Britain* Catherine had a manager, a typewriter, a signed photograph of Cecil Rhodes and very little else. If she tended to avoid her business premises it is hardly surprising. Not only was she busy trying to put a roof over her head but, whenever she did visit the office, Lovegrove was apt to become tiresome by bothering her for money. The original £60 had not gone far and he was badly in need of funds, both for himself and the paper. For a while she had managed to keep him quiet by assuring him that she had financial backing in London: that Burdett-Coutts the banker had shown an interest in *Greater Britain* and was willing to contribute a substantial sum. When no money arrived, this vague promise began to wear thin and Lovegrove became more and more impatient with her evasiveness. His doubts were intensified when, in one stroke, the Princess brought all hopes of obtaining money from Burdett-Coutts to an end.

On the 28th May, Catherine wrote to her manager enclosing a letter, signed by a certain Edward Whistler, which she claimed had just arrived from England. In this letter Whistler told the Princess that Mr Burdett-Coutts was willing to forward £300 to her at once and 'the same sum by instalments every two months'. The only condition was that Burdett-Coutts should have some say in the policy of the paper. According to the letter, the banker objected to her support of Milner and was particularly anxious to avoid the possibility of *Greater Britain* being influenced by big business in South Africa. 'He insists,' said Whistler, 'upon a distinct understanding that you will act in sympathy with Mr Markham, MP, in his campaign against the Capitalist influence which has been so fatal to South African politics, and that whilst supporting the candidature of Mr

Rhodes to the Premiership you should fight De Beers.' The Princess considered this strange request as asking too much. 'It has been a blow to me,' she told Lovegrove. 'I certainly cannot fight De Beers where my son is employed.' She went on to say that she had only one alternative and that was to make a 'violent appeal' to Mr Rhodes and 'endeavour to worm some money out of him'.

A few days later she was able to report success. On 3rd June—the day Mr Kinsley received her letter enclosing the promissory note—Lovegrove received a visit from his employer. 'I have a trump card left,' she announced. 'I have a blank bill here endorsed by Mr Rhodes.' With that she handed the manager a piece of paper bearing Rhodes's signature. She then suggested that Lovegrove fill in the blank space above the signature, making out a promissory note for £3,000, payable to the manager of *Greater Britain*, and that they should take it to the Bank of Africa to get it discounted. With more optimism than common sense, Lovegrove did as he was told and the two of them went to the bank. The bill was handed over. The bank manager told them he would let them know if it was possible to advance money on the note. They did not have to wait long. The following day Lovegrove received a letter from the Princess saying that payment had been refused. 'I am beginning to fear,' she wrote, 'that this bill is a white elephant. However, I have sent it to London.'

In the meantime, the note she had sent to Kinsley was faring no better. Kinsley had sent it to the house-agent, Mr Bisset, who immediately took it to his bank manager, Lewis Michell, whom he knew to be a close friend of Rhodes. Michell had examined the note but had been very dubious about it. He admitted that the signature was like Rhodes's but said that he would need further confirmation before swearing that it was genuine. What he did, in fact, was telegraph immediately to Bulawayo to ask Rhodes whether he had signed such a note. 'I replied "No",' Rhodes was later to declare, 'and that was my first information as to this fact that my name had been used.'

Blissfully unaware of how quickly her activities had aroused suspicion, Catherine called on Mr Bisset to find out whether he was prepared to accept the security she had offered. The house-agent was on his guard. He told her he had shown the note to one of Mr Rhodes's friends. 'What did he say about it?' asked Catherine. 'He did not say it was not Mr Rhodes's signature?' Bisset assured her that the friend—whom he was careful not to name—had said it was like Rhodes's signature. 'Of course,' exclaimed the Princess. 'If one was going to forge, one would forge for a substantial amount, and not a paltry sum like that.' Nevertheless, Bisset was frightened off. Without a more definite guarantee he was unable to accept the promissory note. Once again things looked grim for the Princess. The summons issued by the house-agents was still out against her and there seemed no way of preventing court action. She asked Bisset to give her a few days' grace. She said she would communicate with Rhodes and let him know what happened. In the meantime she wanted Bisset's assurance that neither he nor the friend he had consulted would write to Bulawayo. But by then, of course, it was too late. Michell had already telegraphed to Rhodes.

A few days later the Princess returned to Bisset's office with a bundle of banknotes. She told the attorney that she now intended to pay the rent in cash. It was impossible for her to pay a full year's rent but, if the lease was changed, she could make payment for six months. Bisset agreed to the alteration and Catherine handed over £200 (or slightly more) in notes. The summons was then withdrawn and the Princess was free to move into her house.

By an odd coincidence, the day after Catherine had paid her rent, the sum of £317 arrived for her at her bank. This was the long-awaited remittance from Russia. She was later to explain that she had used part of this remittance to replace the money she had paid Mr Bisset. It was a point of honour upon which she insisted. The notes she had given to the house-agent had come from a completely different source and it was her contention that she had scrupulously avoided using money from that source for her personal requirements. But, considering the source from which she had got the money and the means she had used to obtain it, her arguments were purely hair-splitting. For the money she had given to Bisset was part of a larger amount which she had received in a very shady transaction.

*

The Princess's failure to cash her first two promissory notes was largely due to the type of person with whom she had been dealing. In one case she had been confronted by a reputable house-agent and in the other by an equally respectable bank manager. Catherine was quick to recognize that such people were naturally cautious and rarely took chances. It soon dawned upon her, also, that a promissory note would be more acceptable if it were discounted at a high rate of interest. These two thoughts appear to have led to one conclusion. To raise money on her notes, she would have to find a money-lender who was willing to take a chance on her honesty. As it happened there was no shortage of such speculative gentlemen in Cape Town. One of the less edifying aspects of the war in the Transvaal had been the wholesale flight from Johannesburg of the motley community that had sprung up on the fringe of the gold-mining industry. Small-time money changers, pawnbrokers, dubious insurance agents, dealers in stocks and shares and financial adventurers of every description had packed their bags and fled at the first suggestion of gun-fire. Many of them had settled temporarily in Cape Town. One of these Transvaal refugees was a certain Joseph Friedjohn who now operated a money-lending business in Cape Town's main thoroughfare, Adderley Street. Two days after her second bill had been refused by the Bank of Africa, the Princess called on Mr Friedjohn in his office in Riddelsdell's Chambers. Once again she produced a blank piece of paper bearing Rhodes's signature. She asked Friedjohn whether he would be prepared to discount a promissory note made out on that signature.

Friedjohn was interested but naturally needed a little more evidence to prove that the signature was genuine. He asked the Princess whether she had a letter from Rhodes referring to the promissory note. She said that she thought she had and would go home and look for it. The following day she returned with two typed letters bearing Rhodes's signature. They read convincingly. In one dated: Kimberley, 14th May, 1901, it said: 'How are money matters? Enclosed is a bill; if anything unpleasant happens you will always find a friend who will advance you money on it, as you refuse to take mine. Only don't put it in a bank, and don't write about it; no need for Jourdain [*sic*] to know anything about it. Any friend will do it, Scholtz or another one. I should give you the money to pay it when I come back, sometime in October or November. Don't go further than a thousand for yourself, and again as much for the paper, if you split with Burdett-Coutts.' This was backed up by further references in the other letter dated 20th May which concluded: 'How is the paper getting on? I am sure you will not come to terms with Coutts; he is an awful little beast. You will have to fall back on me. How is the boy? and yourself, any more heart attacks? I am better; Jameson objects to Rhodesia, but I am going nevertheless.' To anyone who knew Rhodes, these letters would have sounded genuine enough but as Friedjohn pointed out, he himself was not acquainted with Rhodes and needed more than two further signatures to convince him of the Princess's bona fides. He told her that it would be necessary to get a friend of Rhodes's to endorse the bill, or at least verify the signature. He suggested that Dr Scholtz—who had been mentioned in one of the letters— might be a suitable person to do this. The Princess agreed.

Dr Scholtz was busy with his morning consulting work when he received a message that Princess Radziwill wished to see him. He was told that she was waiting for him in his drawing-room. Leaving his patients, the doctor went to see her at once. As soon as he entered the room Catherine launched into a long explanation of why she had come. She wanted to know whether he would be prepared to verify Rhodes's signature. Rhodes had given her a bill, she said, but had stipulated that it should not go through a bank and she had found someone in town who was willing to advance her money on it if the signature could be verified. Without giving Scholtz time to reply, she then asked him to read the letter which she claimed she had received from Edward Whistler, written on behalf of Burdett-Coutts. She said that the doctor would see from this that she was sacrificing a considerable amount of money in order to be free to work in Rhodes's interest. If Scholtz would do as she asked, she was prepared to leave this letter with him. She made a point, how-ever, of insisting that the doctor told no one about the transac-tion and particularly not his wife with whom, as he knew, she was not on the best of terms. This does not appear to have bothered Scholtz; nor was he worried by the Princess's reluc-tance to give him the name of the person discounting the bill. She assured him that the gentleman concerned would call at his surgery later that day. 'At this stage,' Scholtz later declared, 'I suspected nothing wrong.'

This display of trust on the part of William Scholtz is an undoubted tribute to Catherine's acting ability. He, better than most, should have known how little Rhodes trusted her in political matters. On several occasions he and his wife had been present when Rhodes had lost his temper over the Princess's incessant meddling. On the other hand, Scholtz was also aware that his wife had persuaded Rhodes to pay Catherine's hotel bills when their relationship was going through a difficult phase and, with the Princess's continual hints at a romantic attachment, the doctor may well have been focled. It is doubtful whether his wife would have been so gullible. Catherine knew this only too well. Hurrying back to the money-lender's office, she told Friedjohn to make out a bill for £1,000 and take it to the doctor's surgery. She said that when he went to Dr Scholtz 'he must be careful that Mrs Scholtz did not see him'.

Two hours later Friedjohn arrived at Scholtz's house with the bill. He did not give his name but said that he had been sent by Princess Radziwill. After comparing the signature on the bill with a signature of Rhodes's which he had in the house, the doctor started to write out a certificate to the effect that the signature was genuine. Friedjohn quickly interrupted him. 'No, Doctor,' he said, 'that won't do, will you endorse it?' Scholtz then endorsed the bill.

The terms of this first loan negotiated by the Princess were extraordinary. They reflect not only Friedjohn's cupidity but the desperation with which Catherine viewed her deteriorating circumstances. The promissory note was made out for £1,000, payable on 8th August—two months from the date of issue— and in return Catherine agreed to accept £700; giving Friedjohn a clear profit of £300. 'That is what she offered me herself,' Friedjohn was later to claim. 'She said, "I do not mind giving you £300." '

Having agreed to these monstrous conditions, Catherine called at Friedjohn's office the following Saturday to collect her money. The money-lender offered her a cheque for the £700 but she refused this, saying that she would prefer to be paid in cash. As Friedjohn had only £50 in notes at his office, she was obliged to return on Monday for the remainder of the loan. Friedjohn then handed her a further £650 in notes and she asked him to accompany her to the Standard Bank where she said she intended to deposit the money. Obligingly, Friedjohn walked with her as far as the bank and watched her enter the building. He then returned to his office.

Once inside the bank, the Princess appears to have waited long enough for Friedjohn to disappear and then to have left, still holding on to the £650. She wanted to give the money-lender the impression that she was behaving correctly, but she seems to have had no intention of putting the money into the bank. Whatever payments were made to her banking account came by cable order from England and for her to have handed over £650 in notes would most likely have drawn unwanted attention to her financial dealings. Moreover, she may well have realized that a time would come when it might be neces-sary for her to deny receiving money from Friedjohn: this would explain why she had refused payment by cheque. Whatever her reasons, there was no record of the £700 being deposited in a Cape Town bank. The money was spent by Catherine in the same way in which she had received it—in notes.

The transaction could not have pleased her. She had received far less than she had hoped for and had been forced to accept cut-throat terms. For all its smallness, however, the loan did give her the immediate capital she needed. Now, at least, she could pay Mr Bisset and get her newspaper into production.

*

The weekly newspaper, *Greater Britain*, appeared on the Cape Town news-stands for the first time on 22nd June, 1901. Printed by the Electric Printing Company, it bore no indication of its proprietors or publishers. There was, however, no mis-taking its policy. 'Another Rhodes organ has made its appear-ance,' remarked the *South African News*, '—this time a sixpenny weekly—with the title *Greater Britain*. It preaches the Gospel according to the Colossus in its entirety; advocacy of the "one strong man", fulsome adulation of Lord Milner, casual sneers at Mr Chamberlain, belittling of Sir Gordon Sprigg, praise of the D[iamond] F[ields] *Advertiser* and the E[astern] P[rovince] *Herald*, and attacks on the Union-Castle Steamship Company— they all find a place in the columns of "Greater Britain".'

There was, in fact, little in the newspaper's content to dis-tinguish it from other pro-Rhodes journals. Apart from one or two obvious personal prejudices of the editor—such as the attack on the Union-Castle Company and a paragraph abusing Cape Town cab-drivers—its tone was much the same as that of its sympathetic contemporaries. It was perhaps slightly more emotional in approach and a little more insistent on the need for a change of Government, but other than that it lacked any originality. The more pedantic reader might, however, have found some amusement in comparing the declared aims of the paper with the performance of its main contributor. In a leading article, the editor had outlined the Imperial, pro-Rhodes policy of the paper for the benefit of would-be subscribers. A prominent feature of this policy was the advocacy of English as the official language of South Africa. Popular as such a measure would have been with the public which the paper was trying to attract, it was an incongruous cause for the editor of *Greater Britain* to champion. For if the opinions expressed in *Greater Britain* were emphatic, they showed little respect for grammar or logic. There can have been few newspapers in South Africa displaying a greater disregard for the language in which they were printed.

The trouble was, of course, that Catherine wrote most of the paper herself. She had very little money with which to pay contributors and the journalists whom she did persuade soon shied off. One such journalist was G. H. Wilson, who was then attached to the parliamentary staff of the *Cape Times*. 'She started *Greater Britain*, and in that connection I met her, as she came to ask if I would be a contributor,' he says. 'With the consent of my editor, I agreed to write short political notes at a certain renumeration, but I regret to say that my requests for payment met with a chilly and entirely negative response.' Lacking a permanent staff and unable to entice voluntary help, she was forced into the combined role of editor and reporter. It presented her with problems which she was ill equipped to handle. She had an undoubted flair for languages and, with concentration or by confining herself to letters and short articles, could write reasonable English. Her talent in this respect has been attested to by W. T. Stead, who published some of her work in his *Review of Reviews*. 'Princess Radziwill,' he said, 'is half Polish and half Russian, but she wields her pen as if she were English born.' And, given time, she could write tolerably well at greater length. Her book, *The Resurrection of Peter*, although far from flawless, is no mean achievement for someone writing in a foreign language and it provides a good example of her ability to imitate another writer's style. But it was quite another matter to bring out a weekly newspaper in which she not only wrote most of the articles herself but collected the news, provided the social gossip, acted as columnist, sub-editor and designer. Dealing with current topics and immediate political issues, she was forced to write hurriedly and to rush her copy to the press without allowing herself time to revise or clarify her articles. The result was often chaotic. In the first issue of *Greater Britain*, for example, she had set out to defend Milner, whose elevation to the peerage had recently been announced. Earlier that year Lord Milner had been appointed Governor of the Orange Free State and the Transvaal and Catherine now rounded on those who disapproved of his new status. She wrote of 'the attitude to which Lord Milner has adhered and remained faithful to'. And went on to say: 'I repeat it again . . . If Lord Milner was not backed by public opinion, or not have the support of the Imperial Government . . . If he is allowed a free hand and the possibility to adjoin himself all these he thinks fit to help . . .' In her paragraph attacking the cab-drivers she declares: 'It is time something was done in the matter of cabs upon which we are dependent for our means of locomotion in Cape Town. Not only are their charges extortionate, but their rudeness surpasses anything ever seen or conceived anywhere else . . . As things stand at present it becomes really dangerous for a lady to confide herself alone to one of our cab drivers, she never escapes being ransomed.' There were many more of these howlers scattered throughout the pages of this first, hastily produced issue.

Her critics were delighted. Pretending not to know the identity of the paper's editor, they used the slip-shod writing of *Greater Britain* as their chief weapon of attack. With the publication of the third issue, the *South African News* ran a long article on the new paper entitled: 'English As She Is Writ!' 'We are not surprised to learn,' it concluded sarcastically, 'that the editor is "a titled personage"!' In a more serious vein, however, it asked, 'if this is a Rhodes organ, started by Mr Rhodes, or his followers, to do what the *Argus* and the *Cape*

Times cannot accomplish; or is it only a gutter journal? If it is the latter . . . should not the third number of the paper be the last?'

But Catherine was not to be discouraged by this sort of criticism. She had not set out to produce a literary review. She was concerned only with political and social questions and felt herself equal to the task of getting her message across. She was greatly concerned about the administration of justice in the Cape. It was a matter upon which she held decided and, at times, quite savage opinions. 'We must congratulate Mr Justice Maasdorp,' she wrote in one issue, 'on the sentence he passed last Wednesday on some coloured boys who had assaulted a shoe-maker in Cape Town. We believe in the cat-o'-nine-tails for crimes of a certain nature, and feel sure that they would not be so frequent if that punishment were inflicted more often.'

Her personal prejudices were very much in evidence throughout the paper. Announcing the birth of the Russian Tsar's fourth daughter, Anastasia, she could not resist taking a long-range swipe at her old enemy, the Grand Duchess Vladimir, whom she described as 'one of the most unpopular Princesses that ever stood in near relation to any throne'. And, when commenting on the award that Edward VII had made to Lady Sarah Wilson for the part she had played in the siege of Mafeking, Catherine assured her readers that the decoration had been given simply because Lady Sarah 'enjoys the honour to be counted among His Majesty's personal friends'.

But the most often repeated theme was that of Imperialism. *Greater Britain* was dedicated 'to uphold firmly the principle of British supremacy all over South Africa and defend the great Imperial ideal'. That ideal, she explained, was 'Imperialism in its aspect as a civilizing element, not as an exclusive factor in politics'. This had been the mission of all great empires —from the Roman Empire to the Russian Empire—and it deserved the support of all men of good will. It did not mean racialism but offered a unity of purpose to all who would adhere to it.

These were philosophic and political opinions of which Rhodes would have approved. They embraced his broad ideals as well as the more practical aspirations of his followers. It is not surprising, therefore, that *Greater Britain*, for all its short-comings, was suspected of being yet another Rhodes organ financed by De Beers. For many it confirmed the suspicion that Princess Radziwill was more deeply involved with Cecil Rhodes than his supporters were prepared to admit.

But if she was willing to toe the party line, she lacked the courage to face Rhodes himself. When, at the beginning of July, Rhodes returned from Rhodesia, she kept well away from Groote Schuur. She was aware that he had arrived in Cape Town and that he was staying only two nights before leaving for England, but she made no effort to see him. Instead, she wrote a short note to Philip Jourdan. 'I send you the last number of *Greater Britain*,' she wrote. 'It may amuse Mr Rhodes to read it on the boat . . . I would so much like to have come over for a moment to Groote Schuur to wish you all goodbye, but my manager is ill, and I am alone at the office, which, added to the fact that it is mail day, makes it almost impossible for me to absent myself. Please give the enclosed to Mr Rhodes . . . I hope you won't think I've been too hard on Sir Gordon.'

She probably hoped that her newspaper would speak for itself. It is possible, also, that she was hoping Rhodes would read between the lines and sense her struggle to keep *Greater Britain* going. For she had recently been forced to reduce the price of the paper from sixpence to threepence. To anyone with a knowledge of journalism, this was an obvious sign that the paper was on its last legs. It had been in existence for little over a month and throughout its short life had battled from one financial crisis to another. The £700 which Friedjohn had advanced on the £1,000 note had soon disappeared. The Princess had no banking account for the paper and a cheque of £150 which she had given Lovegrove for his salary and contributor's fees had been dishonoured at her own bank. When, at last, the manager had insisted that the paper's affairs be handed over to an accountant, it was found that the books were too complicated and badly kept to be sorted out.

For all the seriousness of these business problems, they soon became secondary to an even more pressing concern. The failure of the paper put an end to any hope she may have had of redeeming the promissory note held by Friedjohn. As July drew to a close, the question of repaying the money-lender loomed larger and larger in the Princess's confused calculations. Some-how, before 8th August, she had to find £1,000 or risk complete exposure.

*

August 1901 was a month of grim contrasts for Princess Radziwill. Battling to meet the exigent demands of money-lenders, she was subject to personal anxiety and a deeply felt grief. To add a touch of irony to the wretched state of affairs, she was forced to endure her misery against a background of festivity such as Cape Town had rarely experienced and in which she was obliged to join. Fate was not only engineering her downfall but was laughing in her face.

The month started with a domestic crisis. At the end of July, Colonel Wilson of the recently formed army corps, Kitchener's Fighting Scouts, arrived in Cape Town on a recruiting mission. It was announced that he intended to enrol about a thousand additional men for his regiment which had been 'entrusted to Lord Kitchener with work of a very special nature'. Three days after the Colonel's arrival, recruiting was well under way and all the newly opened depots were reported to be swamped with applications from young men anxious to get to the front. One of the first applicants to receive a commission was Prince Nicholas Radziwill.

Young Prince Nicholas, on sick leave from De Beers, seems to have been staying with his mother at this time. During his illness, he had been treated by Dr Scholtz, and it was Catherine's firm belief that Mrs Scholtz was responsible for her son volunteering for active service. She probably exaggerated the part played by Mrs Scholtz in her son's decision. Nicholas was a high-spirited, impetuous youngster with soldiering in his blood. The young Prince needed no encouragement to answer Colonel Wilson's stirring call for recruits. But Catherine did not see it in this light. Asked why her son had joined the forces, she had only one reply. 'It was distinctly Mrs Scholtz's influence,' she declared emphatically. To all her other worries was now added anxiety for her son's safety.

Nicholas had hardly left for the front when Catherine experi-enced another sorrow. On 5th August, at her castle of Fried-richshof in Germany, the Empress Frederick died. Since the days when she had known her as the Crown Princess Victoria in Berlin, Catherine had regarded the English-born Empress as one of her dearest friends. In September 1898, a few months before she had sailed to South Africa for the first time, she had met the Empress again on the French Riviera. Their meeting had been brief and tragic. Catherine had been shocked at the Empress's haggard appearance. 'Her eyes were quite sunken,' she said, 'and her complexion had assumed a grey hue.' Even so, she had not suspected that her friend's illness would prove fatal. The announcement of her death must have come as a shock. 'I never can think of the Empress Frederick without tears coming in my eyes,' she wrote later. 'What she was to me few can imagine.' Her devotion to her friend's memory remained constant throughout her life. One of the last books Catherine wrote was a biography of the Empress.

When the news reached her, however, she was forced to stifle her grief; there was no time for tears. Events were crowding in on her. Friedjohn would soon be demanding his money and the prospect of her being able to pay it was as remote as ever. Her helplessness was not due to any want of effort. She had been trying frantically to raise the money and, with each new move, had become more and more enmeshed in a tangle of deceit and intrigue.

At first she tried to squeeze more money from Friedjohn. As soon as she had exhausted the £700, she applied to the money-lender for a further loan. She told him that she was in great difficulty and needed an extra £40 or £50. Friedjohn gave her £45 in return for an antique snuff box which she offered him as security. Encouraged by this second success with Friedjohn, she decided to press her luck further by making a much bolder demand. Shortly after Rhodes left for England she arrived at Friedjohn's office with a promissory note for £4,500. This, she said, had been made out for her by Philip Jourdan on the day that Rhodes sailed. Dated, Cape Town, 3rd July, 1901, it read:

'On the third day of April next I promise to pay to Princess Catherine Radziwill or order the sum of £4,500 sterling. Value received. Payable at her house Crail in Kenilworth.
C. J. Rhodes.'

In support of this note she showed Friedjohn a letter addressed to Dr Scholtz and signed with the now familiar C. J. Rhodes signature. According to this letter, Rhodes assured Scholtz that he had given the Princess some bills to help her with her paper. 'Thank you for signing,' it concluded, 'but don't let it get about, as I cannot afford to let people know of it.' Friedjohn accepted this new note and explained that although he had not enough money to discount it, he would see if he could get it discounted elsewhere.

This was all very well, but as the days went by without any sign of Friedjohn obtaining the loan, the Princess grew anxious. She knew that this new note would not stop the money-lender demanding his original £1,000 when it became due and she also needed more money for *Greater Britain*. In desperation she struck out in a new direction. Friedjohn was not the only money-lender in Cape Town: there were other firms who were far more affluent. She now approached the Australian Loan and Discount Company.

At the end of July she called at the firm's offices and met the manager, Mr Meyer Wolff. Once more she reeled off the story of Rhodes giving her a bill to help her with her paper and of his not wanting it negotiated through a bank. The note she produced this time was identical to the one she had left with Friedjohn: it was dated 3rd July and made out to the value of £4,500. Mr Wolff, of course, immediately asked for some proof of the authenticity of the signature. She told him that this was rather difficult as she did not want the bill circulated about the town. After some hesitation, however, she came up with the bright suggestion that they take it to one of the tellers of the Standard Bank for identification. But this was not good enough for Wolff. With so much money involved, he wanted more substantial proof than a bank clerk could provide. Forced into a corner, she had no alternative but to take a risk. She agreed that Wolff should take the bill to the manager of the Standard Bank, on the strict understanding that her own name was to be covered up and only Rhodes's signature shown for verification. She made Wolff promise that the bill would not be seen by any of Rhodes's agents in Cape Town. The fact that Michell, the manager of the Standard Bank, was Rhodes's friend does not appear to have bothered her. This is not as surprising as it at first appears. She herself banked at the Standard and was no doubt aware that

Michell was away and that a Mr Gardiner was acting as manager in his stead. She must, in fact, have been fully prepared to resort to this means of identifying the signature, if all else failed, before she arrived at Wolff's office.

After she left, Wolff took the note to the Standard Bank but Mr Gardiner refused to have anything to do with it. Wolff then showed the note to the manager of his own bank—the National Bank—who also refused to identify the signature. This, however, did not discourage the determined Mr Wolff. Having arranged a generous interest with the Princess, he was as anxious as she that the transaction should take place. His next step was to show the note to Mr Hyman Honikman whom he later described as one of his 'investing principals'. Honikman, a somewhat sinister figure who controlled several financial concerns besides the Australian Loan and Discount Company, was immediately interested. Taking the note from Wolff, he went to consult Mr Allan Wright, who managed the African Banking Corporation of Cape Town. The sight of Rhodes's signature on a bill for £4,500 intrigued Mr Wright as well: he suggested having it identified by the Chartered Company office in Cape Town. Honikman agreed and Wright then took the note to the Cape Town Secretary of the Chartered Company— John Alfred Stevens. Thus it was that, despite all the Princess's precautions, a promissory note bearing Rhodes's signature was again put into the hands of one of Rhodes's close associates. Stevens, of course, refused identification. He gave the note back to Wright, who took it to Honikman, who passed it on to Wolff, who then wired to the Princess asking her to come to his office.

When, after some delay, the Princess turned up, Wolff had a suggestion of his own to offer. He said nothing of the attempts that had already been made to identify the signature but brought forward a new idea. Either by an odd coincidence or by the workings of a money-lender's grape-vine, his suggestion followed the pattern set by Friedjohn. Wolff, it seems, knew Dr Scholtz and thought that he would be just the person to verify the signature. Could the Princess not get Dr Scholtz to endorse the note? This threw Catherine into a quandary. She had assured Scholtz that the note which he had already endorsed was the only one she possessed; to present him with another—

this time for £4,500—would be bound to arouse his suspicions. She needed time to think. Telling Wolff that she would first have to consult Dr Scholtz, she went back to her office.

Her first thought was to reduce the amount in order to make the loan more feasible. She wrote a quick note to Wolff. 'I have just looked over the accounts,' she said, 'and find that £1,500 in cash will be all I shall want at present . . . I shall require a written guarantee that the bill will not be put into the bank until the return to Cape Town of the person who gave it me.' It did not take her long to realize that this meaningless reduction solved nothing. She needed £1,000 to repay Friedjohn and the extra £500 would be swallowed up as quickly as her original loan. In any case, the bill was made out for £4,500 and this was the amount on which it would have to be negotiated; it was no longer possible to make out a note for a lesser amount—to have done so would have cast doubt on all her dealings with Wolff. There was nothing for it but to trust to luck and agree to the money-lender's suggestion. If she could only keep her own name out of the transaction, it might be possible to fool Scholtz a second time. That afternoon she wrote to Wolff again. 'After thinking over the matter of the signature,' she said, 'the thought strikes me that if your client wants to show the signature to Dr Scholtz he may do so provided that part of the bill with my signature was not shown to him. Dr Scholtz is a great friend of mine, and I should not like him to know the bill was in favour of myself . . . I rely on you to do the business without my name being seen.'

This was good enough for Wolff. He took the note to Scholtz, covered up Catherine's signature and asked the doctor to confirm Rhodes's signature. This time Scholtz was wary. He admitted that the signature looked genuine and showed the money-lender Rhodes's signature for comparison but further than that he would not go. The next day the Princess called at Wolff's office to find out how he had fared with Scholtz. Wolff told her. He then went on to say that the only hope now was for her to approach Scholtz herself and get his endorsement. The Princess hesitated. She said that it was a delicate matter but she would see what she could do. It did not take her long. The following morning she returned with the note duly endorsed on the back by 'William C. Scholtz'. It was an audacious move and it was bound to fail. Telling her to come back shortly, Wolff hurried round to Scholtz's surgery and showed the signed bill to the doctor. Scholtz emphatically denied having seen the Princess, let alone having endorsed her note. When Wolff told this to Catherine, she flew into a rage. She said that the doctor's statement was 'simply ridiculous' and, in any case, she no longer needed the money as she had just received some Chartered shares from Rhodesia. She asked for the note back, Wolff gave it to her, and she flounced out of the office.

But she had not heard the last of this little episode. Dr Scholtz, greatly alarmed by Wolff's second visit, now wrote to the Princess demanding to know what was going on. She was unable to help him. His letter arrived the day before Friedjohn's loan was due to be paid back and she used this as a means of confusing the entire issue. She pretended to understand that Scholtz was referring to the first bill he had been asked to sign—the £1,000 discounted by Friedjohn.

'My dear Doctor,' she replied. 'Will you please now explain to me your letter. I rushed to the person with whom I had discounted the bill to which you kindly put your name. It is only due on the 10th [*sic*] and of course he said he had never presented it to you. What do you mean? You say a man brought you a bill; what man? He must have a name. Where is he? If he came back, why did you not stop him? But what is the meaning of this? I thought at first they had presented you the bill we signed, and rushed furious to my friend; but he says he never did it; it is a hideous joke, but I should feel grateful to you for an explanation. We have had heaps of injurious letters threatening *Greater Britain* with I don't know what, and I should like you to tell me what is really the matter. I shall return to you your bill in the course of tomorrow; better bring it myself; you can tear out your signature and return it to me, but please explain. What is it all about and what does it mean? It seems a blackmailing business, but how could they expect you to pay anything on a forged signature, and what have I got to do with it? Please explain as we must pursue this.

'Yours very sincerely, C.M.R.

'Please if they bring you the bill, stop the men and send for the police; it is best.'

In protesting innocence to Scholtz, the Princess felt fairly safe. She had got the bill bearing the doctor's signature back from Wolff and it was now simply a matter of the money-lender's word against hers. If she held Wolff up to be a blackmailer and stuck to her story, there was no way of his disproving what she said. Or was there? Later that day the thought must have struck her that the bill was not the only evidence of her dealings with the Australian Loan and Discount Company. She had written several letters to Wolff and also sent him telegrams. That same day she went to the money-lender's office and demanded that he give back all her correspondence. She now found herself up against the shifty Mr Honikman. Wolff explained that his 'investing principal' had instructed him not to hand over the correspondence until the Princess had paid £25. This money, he said, was for 'out of pocket expenses' and unless it was paid, they would hand the matter over to their solicitors. But the Princess was not so easily frightened. Declaring that she would never submit to blackmail, she refused to hand over a penny. It was, indeed, not only a point of honour but a question of finance. That morning she had drawn £6 from her banking account, leaving the balance at £1 13s 9d.

This was 7th August. It was the day before Friedjohn's promissory note fell due. Her bank account was exhausted and she was expected to pay £1,000 to the money-lender. Incredibly, the money was paid and, what is more, it was paid on the dot.

Even more incredibly, the person responsible for payment being made was not the Princess but Friedjohn himself. That, at least, was how it was made to appear to Catherine.

It is impossible to speak with any certainty about the curious transaction which now took place. There was a mystery about it from the very beginning. It involved a new note for £2,000. For details of how this transaction originated, there is only Friedjohn's word, which is not to be relied on. Later, in court and under oath, the money-lender gave a questionable explanation of what happened. 'Friedjohn said,' reads a court report, 'that on August 4th [sic] the bill for £1,000 became due. [The Princess] then called upon him and said she was not in a position to pay, but she offered him another bill for £2,000. She said that she had got that note also from Mr Rhodes. Witness asked who filled up the promissory note, and she said Mr Jourdan had done so. Witness asked who was present at the time and she said Mr Mitchell. He then asked if it was Mr Michell of the Standard Bank, and she said, "No, another gentleman." She said that she had got the £4,500 and £2,000 notes from Mr Rhodes personally, and that they had been filled in by Mr Jourdan in the presence of a Mr Mitchell.'

That Catherine had presented Friedjohn with another note—this time for £2,000—is true enough. But she denied saying that the bill was filled in by Jourdan and, considering that Friedjohn already held a note for £4,500, made out on the same day, his close questioning of the Princess seems a little superfluous. But his acceptance of this new note is even stranger. The Princess had told him that she could not pay the £1,000; she had already left a note for £4,500 with him and she now produced another note for £2,000. Surely his suspicions should have been aroused? He was no fool and he certainly was not acting out of charity. 'Friedjohn,' said the Chief Justice of the Cape, 'is a man who could be very hard upon debtors who are in distress.' Why then was this hard-eyed man now getting himself more and more involved with promissory notes which bore every appearance of being worthless? And why had he said that the £1,000 note was due on 4th August when it was not, in fact, due to be paid until four days later? He must have had some reason for changing this date. There can be little doubt that Mr Friedjohn was playing a game of his own and, whatever that game may have been, he made sure that he was not the loser.

What happened next is fairly straightforward. On 8th August Friedjohn took the new £2,000 note to 'his attorneys, Messrs Van Zyl and Buissinne'. Here he handed the note to Mr John P. Kayser, a partner in the firm. The note read:

'Cape Town, July 3rd, 1901. On the 23rd day of September next I promise to pay to Princess Catherine Radziwill or order the sum of £2,000 sterling. Value received. Payable at her house, Crail, in Kenilworth. C. J. Rhodes.'

Friedjohn asked Mr Kayser whether he knew anybody who would discount this note. He also gave Mr Kayser his original bill for £1,000 and asked the attorney to put it on record. Mr Kayser told the money-lender to come back after luncheon. When Friedjohn returned to the office he was introduced to

Mr John Frederick Ernest Bernard, an attorney who worked—
or had recently worked—for Messrs Van Zyl and Buissinne.
Mr Bernard told Friedjohn that he was acting on behalf of a
Mr Louw and that his client was prepared to discount the
£2,000 note. Bernard then handed over a cheque for £1,000
and said that a further £850 would be paid to the Princess later
—thus allowing his client an interest of £150. Friedjohn took
the cheque, cashed it, and informed the Princess that she could
have the original £1,000 note back.

By what seemed a miracle, Catherine's debt had been paid on
the very day that it was due. What is more, the money had come
not from another dubious money-lender but from a respectable
Cape citizen acting through the medium of two highly reputable
Cape attorneys. The entire transaction had been concluded in a
matter of hours. There had been no request for verification of
the signature, no attempt to reach anyone willing to endorse the
note. The obliging Mr Louw had paid £1,000 without hesitation
and with the full consent of two legal advisers. It must have
seemed too good to be true.

When she knew the promissory note was safe, the Princess
was elated. She immediately wrote to Lovegrove instructing
him to get a new printer for *Greater Britain* and to promise a
week's payment in advance. 'We shall be rich tomorrow,' she
said, 'send the printer to the devil and get another one.' Then
she wrote to Dr Scholtz. 'Here is your bill returned with a
thousand thanks for endorsement,' she said. 'It was too kind of
you. Mr Friedjohn is taking it to you himself; please tear out
the signature and return it to me—I have not been to the office
today; hope to find a letter from you there tomorrow. I am at a
loss to understand the joke which was perpetrated on you
yesterday—please explain. I am positive no one ever asked you
to pay this bill or any other one . . . Please return me by return
of post the bill with your signature torn out. I must send the
second one to London.' Evidently she did not wait until the
following day but went to her office that afternoon. She found a
letter from Scholtz waiting for her. In it he answered her earlier
queries and explained exactly what happened when Wolff called
to see him with the £4,500 note. She replied at once. 'I am
dumb; don't know what to say or think. I have been to the place
you mention, saw the man you speak of, and he never knew me,

and said only a lady had brought him a bill and taken it away again; put commonsense into the question. Suppose I had been a forger, it is too ridiculous to think of, only should I have forged your name when I might have had your signature easily. I am going to look into the thing quietly and with circumspection, but I assure you I had one bill from Rhodes, for which he sent me the money to pay it, and you have best proof of it in the bill which I returned to you this afternoon. I must proceed to a quiet investigation, and shall do so . . . Rest in peace, and if anyone else comes arrest him and send for me.'

Whether in her jubilation the Princess asked herself how it was that her fortunes had been so providentially changed, it is not possible to say. If she did, she may have provided her own answers. But if she did not question her luck, she most certainly should have done. The circumstances surrounding Mr Louw's loan were, to put it mildly, extremely suspicious.

Why, in the first place, had Friedjohn taken the matter to a firm of attorneys? If he had meant to sue on the note he held, then his action would have been understandable. But he did not mention legal action to Mr Kayser. He asked the attorney to raise money on the £2,000 note. In such circumstances, this surely is not the business of attorneys. They can attend to the legal aspects of a loan but they do not usually act as money-raisers. Their business would have been to approach the Princess about payment; not to help her out by obtaining an even larger sum of money on her dubious credentials. And how was it that they could act so quickly? What made Mr Bernard get in touch with Louw and where precisely did Mr Louw fit into the picture? Who indeed was this Mr Louw who lent money to a person he had not seen and from whom he demanded no guarantees? What attorneys would have sanctioned such recklessness? These are just a few of the questions the Princess could have asked herself. But there was a side to her new-found legal saviours which she could not have discovered at this stage. The firm of Van Zyl and Buissinne had another important client on their books and this client was extremely interested in the doings of Princess Radziwill. His name was Cecil John Rhodes.

With so much happening in one day Catherine could have had little time in which to think carefully about anything. The 8th August had been a day of surprises. But the biggest shock was yet to come. For on that day the *Cape Argus* carried a startling and boldly printed announcement on its cable page. 'MR RHODES: A WARNING: HIS SIGNATURE FORGED:' ran the headlines. 'The London *Times* this morning publishes the following in its money column:

' "We understand attempts have been made to negotiate certain promissory notes purporting to have been endorsed by Mr Cecil Rhodes. We are requested to state that if any such instruments are in circulation they are forgeries." '

Mr Rhodes was moving against the Princess. She would need all her wits about her from now on.

CHAPTER TWELVE

The Princess Under Pressure

AUGUST 1901 was a historic month for the citizens of Cape Town. The Duke and Duchess of Cornwall and York—the future King George V and Queen Mary—visited the city as part of a world tour which they were undertaking. An important event at any time for Cape Town's patriotic English-speaking population, the visit was given added importance by recent events. On 22nd January, 1901, the long Victorian era had come to an end with the death of the eighty-one-year-old Queen. While loyal South Africans mourned the Queen's death, it undoubtedly gave extra lustre to the eagerly awaited royal visit. For the Duke was now heir-apparent to the new King Edward VII and far and away the most illustrious royal person ever to visit South Africa. Cape Town's citizens were determined to make the most of this all-too-brief occasion. Although a bitter war was still dragging on in the north, the city was given over to festive preparations on an unprecedented scale. The whole of Cape Town was transformed into a make-believe city of uncertain period but undoubted splendour. From the imposing medieval gateway at the entrance to the harbour to the elegant classic archway at the foot of Government Avenue, the town was a forest of wooden towers, cardboard turrets, flag-poles, banners and pennants. Every balcony was draped with red, white and blue bunting, Union Jacks fluttered from every roof-top and coloured lights were strung across all the main streets.

To present such a dazzling display meant weeks of hard work. By the beginning of August preparations were well under way and it was through a maze of scaffolding and an army of noisy workmen that Princess Radziwill had to push her way when she visited Mr John Bernard at his office on the afternoon of 9th August. The attorney had sent for her. It was the day after the startling notice appeared in the *Cape Argus* in which Rhodes denied signing any promissory notes that were circulating in his name. A similar notice had appeared that morning in the *Cape Times*. When Catherine arrived at the office she found Bernard waiting for her. With him was Mr John Kayser of the firm of Van Zyl and Buissinne who, the Princess was informed, was representing Friedjohn.

Drawing Catherine's attention to the announcement in the Cape papers, Bernard told her that he was now worried about the loan to which his client, Mr Louw, had agreed the previous day. According to Catherine, it was then proposed that the £2,000 bill should be endorsed by the Hon. Mr Smith of the firm of Smith and Sonnenberg. She claimed that this proposal came from Bernard and that she said it would be impossible to get an endorsement after the announcement that had appeared in the *Argus*. Bernard, however, gave a different version. He was to say that the Princess had already arranged with Friedjohn to get Mr Smith to endorse the note and it was upon this understanding that he had accepted the bill. For once, the Princess's story sounds the more feasible. If there had been an agreement the previous day that the note should be endorsed by Mr Smith, why had Bernard handed over £1,000 to Friedjohn without waiting for the endorsement? Why had he paid out money on a note that did not meet the proposed terms? Friedjohn's £1,000 was due that day, it is true, but Bernard was not responsible for paying it. The attorney's concern should have been to see that all legal requirements were fulfilled before parting with a penny of Mr Louw's money. Why should he take a risk with his client's money, by relying on the word of a dubious money-lender and for no other reason than to pay the Princess's debt when it was due? Friedjohn would obviously have been prepared to wait until the note was safely endorsed. Indeed, why was Mr Bernard so eager to settle with the money-lender?

It is important here to notice the events concerning the payment of this £1,000. Friedjohn called to collect his money shortly after luncheon on 8th August. That afternoon the first edition of the *Cape Argus* for 8th August appeared on the newsstands. Had Bernard waited a couple of hours, he would have been aware of the announcement by Rhodes disclaiming responsibility for any promissory notes bearing his name. That announcement had not appeared in the *Argus* by accident. It was timed to appear when it did. Although it read as if it had been picked up from the London *Times*, the news had not been cabled by the *Argus*'s London correspondent. It had been sent to the Cape papers by Cecil John Rhodes himself. This was inadvertently admitted by Rhodes later. 'He caused a notice to be inserted in the public prints in London,' reads a report of the evidence which Rhodes gave under oath, 'and cabled a similar notice for insertion in the Cape Town papers, disclaiming the alleged signature.' The effect of this notice appearing when and how it did was twofold. It allowed Bernard to pay Friedjohn and gave him good reason for not advancing any more money to the Princess. The result was that the money-lender slipped out of the picture and the attorney was left to deal solely with the Princess. It is interesting to note, also, that even after the notice had appeared, Bernard made no attempt to stop payment of Friedjohn's £1,000.

Whatever the truth about Mr Smith's proposed endorsement of the £2,000 note, it mattered little in the end. Bernard had another proposal for testing the validity of the promissory note. He suggested that the Princess send a wire to Rhodes asking him to confirm the bill. Catherine was evidently ready for this. She explained that Rhodes was reported to be in Scotland at that time and that she did not know how to reach him. Instead, she offered to send a wire to Bourchier Hawksley, Rhodes's London solicitor. Bernard accepted this as a reasonable alternative. A message for Catherine to send was then drafted by the attorneys. It read: 'Please send immediately £1,500. Urgent. Pay discounted bill. People anxious.' The Princess promised to meet the two attorneys again as soon as she had received a reply from Hawksley. She must have left the office a very worried woman.

Bernard was not the only one to tackle her about the announcement in the Cape papers. Lovegrove, the manager of *Greater Britain*, was having some uneasy moments about the £3,000 bill he had made out and which he and Catherine had unsuccessfully tried to cash at the Bank of Africa. He wrote to his employer about the disturbing news-item. 'What does this mean?' he asked. 'Are they pointing their fingers at our bill?' No less worried was Dr Scholtz. The doctor refused to be put off by the Princess's protests of innocence or her hints about black-mailers. When Wolff had visited Scholtz, the £4,500 bill was not the only evidence which he offered to show that he was in contact with the Princess. The doctor had also seen telegrams which Catherine had sent the money-lender. On top of this there was the incidental fact that Catherine had not paid back £20 which Scholtz had once lent her. Considering all the circumstances, Scholtz decided to hand the matter over to the police. He wrote telling the Princess of his decision. She answered him that afternoon. 'Dear Doctor, I have cabled to Hawksley, and must beg you to let the matter drop until we hear from him, and you see me. I should like to have an explanation with you. I certainly think something should be done, but will you kindly not put the matter into the hands of the police until you have seen me. We had better discuss it together quietly, if you will come to my office on Monday. I wish I could have seen this bill. I certainly never telegraphed Wolff, whatever someone else might have done, but will you discuss this with me quietly, and let us concert together about what must be done. I shall send you your cheque tomorrow; I am waiting for a new cheque book. Will you kindly return to me the remains of my bill, the true one? I think you are bound to do so.

'Yours very truly, C. Radziwill.

'Don't think I object to publicity, but I feel I would like to speak to you before embarking on this. I could not reply earlier to your letter, as I had left the office to go down to Muizenberg. Did you see my signature, and how did it look?'

The doctor's attitude was obviously worrying the Princess. Hardly had she posted this letter to Scholtz than she wrote again. 'I have cabled again to Rhodes and Hawksley, and am writing to them,' she said. 'Had done so by the last mail already as soon as I realized what your letter meant. I swear to you I could not understand it at first. This thing must be cleared for all our sakes, but will you do me one favour, and I think I have got the right to ask it, as I am the injured party. Will you talk it over with me and write to Rhodes by the next mail, putting before him the facts whether we should not put the matter in the hands of the police? I have a very special reason to ask you this, and the minute Rhodes gets our letters and says we are to proceed I shall help you with all my might to put the matter in the hands of the police, and bring Wolff to punishment. It is a hideous business, and worse for me than for you. I again repeat to you the wire you saw was a forgery, and I never saw this famous bill—I repeat I would have gone to you had I wanted a signature as I did once, and what I wrote I fulfilled, as you had the proof. My bill was duly paid and returned to you; you cannot deny that. I repeat it again; do me one favour—write to Rhodes. I shall do likewise, and if he cables "Yes", then I shall help you to the utmost to see this thing through to the bitter end, but don't do it until you have received his cable or letter to that effect. Believe me I have good reasons for asking you that, and I know what I am doing, though I am the injured party in this hideous nightmare. I had a wire from the boy; he is safe at Kroonstad. God bless you, dear Doctor and come and see me. We shall and must work together to clear this thing, and I shall help you as much as I can. Good heavens! It is too much awful to think of even!

'Yours very sincerely, Catherine Radziwill.

'Please return me the remains of my bill, or if you have burnt them, do write to me you have safely received them. It is £1,000 after all.'

*

Catherine's repeated assurances that she had wired Hawksley were perfectly true. She knew Rhodes's solicitor well. When she was in England she had seen him several times and had made quite an impression. Since her return to South Africa she had been writing to him regularly. In July, however, her correspondence with Hawksley had taken a more business-like turn. Yet another promissory note, this time for £6,300, in favour of the Princess and bearing Rhodes's endorsement had turned up in London and the solicitor had written to her for an explanation. It was apparently in connection with this note that she now cabled to him: 'Letter received. Astonished no cable. Sending explanation.' For this wire she had paid in cash and had been given a receipt by the clerk in the local cable office. This was not the only telegram she sent that day. After leaving the cable office she went to the telegraph office in Bree Street. Here she sent off her second telegram. It was addressed to—the Princess Radziwill, Crail, Kenilworth.

Hurrying back home, she stopped off to have a word with Mr Alfred Evelyn, the postmaster at Kenilworth. Laughingly, she told him of a prank she was about to play on some friends. She said she was expecting a telegram and she wondered whether 'for a little joke' he would alter the place from which it had been sent when he made out the form. Mr Evelyn was evidently not the type to play little jokes. He told the Princess that he was very sorry but what she was asking was against regulations and it was quite impossible for him to permit such a thing. This pedantic behaviour did not upset the Princess unduly. Once her own telegram had been delivered to her, she went back to the post office. This time she avoided the postmaster and saw the young clerk who wrote out the telegram forms. She told him of the 'big joke' she was playing and showed him the telegram she had just received. In the place where he had written 'Cape Town' as the post office from which the wire had been sent, she had made an erasure. She now wanted him to write in the word 'London'. Mr Evelyn's dour rectitude was apparently not echoed by his junior staff, for the boy entered into the fun of the thing and did as he was asked.

Two days later she called to see Mr Bernard and Mr Kayser at the offices of Van Zyl and Buissinne. She showed them a telegram which was addressed to her from Hawksley in London. It read: 'Say when due. How much? Shall arrange transfer from London. Impossible ask friend now. Would refuse. Write.' Bernard says that he examined this telegram closely and noticed that the word 'London' appeared to have been written over a word that had been erased; he was still able to make out a faint capital C which he thought might have been the beginning of 'Cape Town'.

Now surely was the time for Bernard to call a halt to this highly suspicious business. From the moment he had accepted the £2,000 bill from Friedjohn, everything had pointed to its being false. A warning had appeared in both Cape papers; the Princess could not provide a guarantor for the note; and now she presented him with a very dubious telegram. If Bernard had only his client's interests to protect, he should have confronted the Princess with the erasure on the telegram and taken immediate steps to recover the £1,000 that had already been advanced on the note. He certainly had reason enough to suspect that the

Princess was not acting honestly and that Friedjohn was her accomplice. But Mr Bernard, it would seem, was more concerned with getting the Princess to incriminate herself further than he was with protecting his client's interests. Without so much as consulting Mr Louw—let alone reporting the matter to the police—he and Kayser helped the Princess draft a reply to Hawksley. Writing at the bottom of the telegraph form, they decided on the following message: '£2,000 due 20th September. Holder requests cable confirming. Writing when send.'

The Princess now went through the same procedure as before. She sent a telegram to Hawksley: 'Mailing tomorrow letter explaining documents.' She sent a telegram to herself. She went to explain her second joke to the post-office clerk and gave him a reward of ten shillings 'to buy sweets'. She then returned to Bernard and Kayser with her second telegram from Hawksley and the receipt from the cable office. This time the wire was short and to the point. 'All right,' it read. 'Say confirmed.' As far as Catherine was concerned, this should have settled the matter. She was extremely anxious to get her hands on the £850 balance due to her. 'You will let me have the money today, won't you?' she asked Bernard. But, of course, the attorney had no intention of paying her. Once again he noticed an erasure on the telegram and this, he claimed, confirmed his suspicions. He told Catherine that he would have to make further inquiries before handing over any money. He then went to interview the postal authorities and, he said later, as a result of what he discovered, he refused to make any further payment on the £2,000 note. He does not, however, appear to have made any attempt to recover the £1,000 from Friedjohn. The money-lender, despite all suspicions, was allowed to go unmolested. The only action taken by Bernard was to put pressure on the Princess by threatening to turn the matter over to the Attorney-General. For the moment he was content to confine himself to threats; at no stage did he consult the police.

The loss of the £850 was a serious blow to Catherine. Her finances were in a very poor state. The expense of sending meaningless telegrams had proved a drain on her meagre resources. The day on which she asked Bernard for payment was 15th August. Two days later she again visited the pawn-brokers as the foreign-accented Miss Smith. She pledged a 'watch, chain and trinket' for £4 10s. Soon she would have little left of value to pawn.

*

The Duke and Duchess of York's visit started with a formal levée on 19th August. The Duke first addressed a select male audience in the House of Assembly and then, accompanied by the Duchess, mingled with the large crowd of specially invited guests in the gardens of Government House. Conspicuous among the fashionably dressed women was Princess Catherine Radziwill. Having pawned her watch two days earlier, the Princess was still able to put up a bold front. Accompanying the Duke and Duchess was Catherine's old friend from *The Times*, Sir Donald Mackenzie Wallace, but there is no record of a meeting between them. For the next three days the royal visit was a whirl of receptions, formal dinners and foundation-stone laying. Catherine's name does not appear among the guests at any of the more exclusive gatherings. She was, however, among those presented to the Duke and Duchess at a final reception held in the House of Assembly on 22nd August. Coming when it did, this royal visit provided an almost ludicrous contrast to Catherine's poverty-stricken circumstances. Had anything been needed to underline the depths to which she had now sunk, her presentation to the heir to the British throne must surely have done so. Of all those presented, she was probably the nearest to the royal couple in rank and undoubtedly the furthest from them in fortune. Dropping her practised curtsey, she must have been reminded of similar occasions in Berlin and St Petersburg and of a life which must now have seemed scarcely credible.

No sooner had the royal visitors left than Catherine was once more up to her neck in intrigue. She was still in urgent need of money. Apart from the fact that Friedjohn had been paid off, she had not benefited at all from her dealings with Bernard. Several of the creditors of *Greater Britain* had started proceedings and the rest were threatening to follow suit. Added to the demands of her creditors was the relentless pressure which Bernard was now putting upon her. He would not let her alone. With a ruthlessness which surpassed anything she had experienced at the hands of the money-lenders, he threatened to institute criminal proceedings against her if she did not meet the demands of his client, Mr Louw. To get rid of him became an obsession with her. 'I had one thought and that was to be left quiet by Bernard,' she claimed; 'he came to me night and morning. I wanted peace at any price.' It was to obtain that peace that she made one final attempt to raise money. She wrote to her manager, Lovegrove, telling him that she had received a further promissory note from Rhodes and asking him to find someone who would cash it. Considering Lovegrove's alarm at the notice in the *Cape Argus*, it is surprising that he even entertained the idea. But, strange as it seems, he did. He contacted a Mr Samuel Fox, another refugee from Johannesburg living in Cape Town. It was probably some time during the royal visit that Lovegrove and Fox went to see Catherine at her house in Kenilworth. She then showed them a bill for £6,000 and asked Fox if he could get it discounted for her. Fox was not particularly helpful. He told her that he had not done any business since he left Johannesburg and was not intending to start up again until he returned. The only suggestion he could offer was that she approach a business friend of his who might be willing to help her out. The man he mentioned was Mr David Benjamin, a Johannesburg merchant who, like himself, was temporarily residing in Cape Town. He offered to get in touch with Mr Benjamin on the Princess's behalf.

A few days later, having heard nothing further from Fox, Catherine wrote to him. 'My dear Mr Fox,' she said. 'Excuse me for troubling you, but will you bring Benjamin to see me tomorrow? I really must know something, as Bernard will say I am fooling him, and will not give me time to turn round anywhere else. You forget it is a matter of life and death for me, and I had far better know the worst than be kept in suspense in that way. Will you therefore be kind enough to give me a definite reply, yes or no, and let me know what time you will call here with Mr Benjamin, if you do?—Yours truly, Catherine Radziwill.'

The following evening Benjamin and Fox arrived at the Princess's house. Once again Catherine was to discover that she had drawn a blank. Mr Benjamin turned out to be a very different proposition from his fellow refugees. In Johannesburg he had played a prominent part in the life of the town and had at one time served on a committee with Cecil Rhodes. He was very conscious of his status in society and, as Catherine was to discover, could be infuriatingly pompous in upholding it. Meticulously correct in his behaviour, he was far more concerned with the observance of social conventions than he was with the Princess's distress. Although Fox had shown him Catherine's pleading letter, he refused to allow the promissory note to be mentioned on this first visit. A gentleman did not discuss business when calling on a lady and Mr Benjamin would have been the last person to turn a Princess's drawing-room into a trading mart. Instead, he settled down to a nice sociable chat. When Catherine introduced the subject of *Greater Britain*, he showed no interest in the fact that the paper was bankrupt, but launched into a long discussion of the paper's political opinions. At last Catherine could bear the suspense no longer. She came out into the open and told Benjamin that she needed some financial advice. He was shocked. 'If it is about business transactions,' he said huffily, 'I should prefer that you should see me at my office in Cape Town.' It was then arranged that the Princess and Fox should call on Mr Benjamin in town at eleven o'clock the following morning.

The next day Catherine, trailing Sam Fox, arrived to keep the appointment. The little comedy which was then played out is best described in Mr Benjamin's inimitable account of the interview.

'After a little conversation,' he said, 'the Princess told me she was in embarrassed circumstances in connection with the paper called *Greater Britain*, and after a little while she produced a bill for £6,000, purporting to be made by Mr Rhodes in her favour—by C. J. Rhodes, the late Premier. I am not quite certain about the date of the bill, but I think it was April. It either purported to be made in April 1901, or was due the following April. It was in her favour, payable at her residence at Kenilworth . . . I told her that I thought it was a very remarkable document . . . I said "In the first place, the body of the bill seems to be in a vulgar handwriting." She asked me what other peculiarities there were. I said "The currency of the bill seems strange—nine months. I think it is a peculiar currency, as bills were generally for three or six months at the most." What struck me as more remarkable still was the domicilation of the bill. She asked me what "domicilation" meant and I said it was the place where the bill was payable. I had never seen a bill for so large an amount made payable at a lady's house. Then I did not tell her that I had seen the advertisement Mr Rhodes had put in the paper, but I had that in mind, the bills being for so large an amount, and knowing Mr Rhodes's reputed wealth and position. I thought the whole circumstances were extremely strange and remarkable. I did not tell her this.

'She then said, "I want £3,000." I think at that time she did not ask me [for the money]. She said, "I want £3,000." I said I was not a money-lender nor a bill discounter, and I don't know whether it was at that particular stage that I handed back the bill, but I asked her subsequently whether she was quite sure it was Mr Rhodes's signature. She asked me what I thought. I said if it was not Mr Rhodes's signature, it was a very good imitation. Then I asked her what consideration she gave for the bill, and at this stage she got up rather impatiently, and said I asked too many questions and left the room accompanied by Mr Fox and the bill.'

Unconsciously funny as Mr Benjamin could be, and over-bearingly pompous as he undoubtedly was, his testimony is that of an honest man. His reaction to the bill was refreshingly natural. If Catherine had dealt with a few more men like Benjamin she would never have got into such a frightening mess. Unfortunately, the honest broker appeared on the scene too late.

As she probably realized, the Princess was now nearing the end of the road. The day she invited Benjamin to her house had been publication day for *Greater Britain*: 24th August, 1901. That day's issue of the paper was the last. Its disappearance from the Cape Town news-stands went unremarked. It had been in existence exactly ten weeks. They were ten of the most disastrous weeks of the Princess's life. But there was worse to come.

*

Throughout the months of June and August it is possible to follow the Princess's actions fairly closely. In September the picture becomes obscure. One reason is that she now abandoned all efforts to raise money by means of promissory notes and saw few outsiders. She appears to have enlisted the aid of another attorney—a Mr Fairbridge—but her dealings with him were never fully revealed.

It was probably at this time that she sent urgent cables to her family in an attempt to raise the money she needed to pay Bernard. This was something she should have done long before. As was often the case with her, she left the obvious course until last and then found it was too late. For any hopes she may have had of obtaining assistance from her family—from her brother or from her daughter's wealthy husband, Prince Blücher—were soon to be dashed. She was notified by her bank that her account had been closed and that no further transactions could be conducted on her behalf. Catherine was to claim that the bank deliberately prevented her from receiving money and that on one occasion it had sent back a large sum that was cabled to her account without informing her. A bank official denied this. He said that the account had been closed 'owing to so many cheques being presented when there were not sufficient funds to pay them'. When asked whether any money paid to her account had been returned to the sender, he replied: 'Not to my knowledge.' But it seems strange that the bank should have instructed its London office to decline any monies paid to her. The bank official admitted that such instructions had been issued. And if Catherine was correct in saying that the bank actually returned money that had arrived for her in South Africa, she would have had even greater cause for complaint. She could have been telling the truth. Certain members of her family were far from poor. They would undoubtedly have done something to rescue her and protect the family name. In the end, money did reach her. But it took a long time. The bank's decision to close her account came at a most inopportune moment for the Princess. It was rather like the timing of the notice that had appeared in the *Cape Argus*. Who made this timely decision was not disclosed. But the general manager of Catherine's bank was Lewis Michell: Rhodes's close friend and future biographer.

It was later pointed out that alternative arrangements could have been made for the Princess to receive money from abroad. This is true. But such arrangements would have taken time and money. Catherine had neither. It is something of a mystery how she could cable her family at all. She may have been helped by a friend. At this time a certain Miss Littlejohn appears to have been helping her. Who or what Miss Littlejohn was, it is not possible to say. Her name appears only briefly in Catherine's story. It would seem that she was a local spinster who—probably attracted by Catherine's title—was acting as an unpaid companion to the Princess. Whatever her function may have been, she was evidently a woman with very little money, for it was not long before her funds also were exhausted. Nevertheless, she was to remain faithful to Catherine throughout the harrowing days ahead.

Apart from Miss Littlejohn, and her long-suffering maid, Francine, Catherine was quite alone. The only people who had ever befriended her in Cape Town were Dr and Mrs Scholtz and she could hardly have expected help from them. Yet she wrote a great many letters to the doctor and his wife at this time. The desperate appeal that she made to Mrs Scholtz on 7th October gives some idea of her plight.

'I sent a letter to your husband today,' she wrote. 'Will you out of mercy, open it, read it, and see if you can help me. When the messenger shall have taken this letter, I will be left with half-a-crown in my pocket, no possibility even to cable to anyone. Will you be just, and go tomorrow and see Fairbridge, asking him to tell you how matters stand? Will you speak with Kayser? I don't think you can judge the situation until you know all the details. I have no means of buying food even. I wish you would just come here and see the house. You would realize the position. When I tell you my hair is quite white, you will, perhaps, understand what I suffer. Certainly sorrow does not kill. But for God's sake, for the boy, if not for mine, cable to Stead after you have learned the trouble. His address is Volicen, London. I wish I could see you and show you certain things; you would then have the key to this mystery. It is nothing but blackmailing. If I could come to you, I would, but I daren't move on account of these creditors of *Greater Britain*. Not mine, for not a single personal bill of mine has been pressed upon me. It is all that paper. But for heaven's sake prevent a scandal, lest your business must come out if this thing comes to trial, and R. will suffer just as much as myself. It is that which breaks my heart more than anything else, more than the thought of the boy even. You know how hated he is; what will one say—his ruining a woman who was, who is, his friend, for a small sum, when it will be proved she was the victim of her blind trust, and the money was spent for himself? You quite understand, I cannot, even for him, appear to have taken £1,000. I must prove how it was spent. Do you think this scandal will do good to any of us? My only desire is to pay. I can only do so in going Home; it is impossible from here. Will you do three things for me, which I ask you, as you hope for mercy elsewhere: (1) Read my letter to the doctor; (2) see Fairbridge; (3) speak with Kayser? After this do as you think best, but I am sure a cable from you to Stead and to another person would help. And do not reply to this until you have learned everything. Excuse the bad writing; I am thoroughly unnerved and weakened by want of food. Believe me or not, but Francine and myself have been living on coffee and rice the last few days. Even my wicker chairs are sold. C.R.'

This letter reveals a great deal more than the Princess's poverty. Some of her more obscure references were to have a significant bearing on statements she made later. Of importance at this stage, however, are her instructions to Mrs Scholtz. She tells her former friend to meet with two attorneys: Mr Fairbridge and Mr Kayser of Van Zyl and Buissinne. She also says: 'I wish I could see you and show you certain things; you would then have the key to this mystery. It is nothing but blackmailing.' There seems to be good reason for her saying this. For now it was that a more sinister aspect of the affair began to manifest itself. It concerned the incriminating papers which Rhodes had once demanded from her and which had been responsible for their final break.

Judging from her letter to Mrs Scholtz, it was at about this time that Catherine received a visit from a partner of the firm of Van Zyl and Buissinne. Whether this was Mr Kayser or Mr Van Zyl himself is not clear. The only record of the interview is contained in an unpublished statement which Catherine made many years later. 'First took place the episode of the bill which Rhodes refused to acknowledge,' she was to say. 'Then his solicitor came to me and offered me a certain amount of money if I consented to give him my papers. I resolved to play a game which ought to bring me a few trumps—but to which I ought to lose my best cards. My first was to strain Rhodes's agents to write down their demands. I partly succeeded for my solicitor at last wrote to me in claimant officially all the bills, letters or documents that I could have in my possession relative to Rhodes.'

If one had to rely entirely on the Princess's word for this transaction, it would be necessary to treat what she says with reservation. But she is supported by evidence which was later produced and accepted in a court of law. This is the letter written to her on 11th October, by Mr C. Van Zyl. Part of this letter was published. It reads: 'Will you please give instructions authorizing Mr Lovegrove to give up all letters and papers of yours entrusted to you in regard to pecuniary transactions, and having reference to Mr Rhodes and other parties?' The letter was written with legal discretion but, as she was to point out, 'there is absolutely no matter of false documents, but on the contrary of documents pure and simple.'

The day after Mr Van Zyl wrote his letter the case of Louw *v.* Rhodes and Radziwill came before Mr Justice Maasdorp in the Supreme Court, Cape Town. Mr Bernard had not, as threatened, handed the matter over to the Attorney-General. Instead, his client was suing Mr Rhodes and the Princess on the £2,000 promissory note. It had fallen due on 23rd September and action had been instituted immediately.

*

In the action brought by Mr Louw against the Right Honourable Cecil John Rhodes and Princess Catherine Maria Radziwill on Saturday, 12th October, 1901, neither defendant was present.

The case was opened by Mr Searle, K.C., who appeared on behalf of the plaintiff. He moved for provisional sentence on a promissory note of £2,000. The amount claimed on this note was £1,150. This, presumably, was the £1,000 that Bernard had paid to Friedjohn, plus £150 interest on the seven weeks' loan.

Rhodes was represented by Sir Henry Juta, K.C. Sir Henry moved that the case against his client be postponed. In support of his request, he put in an affidavit by Lewis Michell, the general manager of the Standard Bank. Mr Michell claimed that he held a general power of attorney for Mr Rhodes. 'On hearing of the existence of the document upon which summons had been issued,' it was explained in Michell's affidavit, 'he wrote to Mr Rhodes to inquire if the signature to the document was genuine, and had received a cable in reply stating that Mr Rhodes repudiated having signed any such document and denied all knowledge of it. From a communication received he [Mr

Michell] believed that Mr Rhodes was not indebted to the endorser of the note in any sum whatever. Affidavits were being mailed from England confirming these statements.' Michell then went on to say that Mr Rhodes was in indifferent health and his medical advisers had insisted on his remaining in Europe for the present. He was not expected to return to South Africa 'for some time to come'.

Princess Radziwill was neither in court nor was she represented. The absence of the two defendants gave Rhodes's counsel the grounds he required for requesting a postponement. Now that the signature had been denied, the ordinary procedure would have been to call evidence at once, but as neither party was present, this was not possible. Sir Henry said that in these circumstances he must ask for the part of the case, as against Rhodes, to stand over until the affidavits taken in England had arrived.

Mr Louw's counsel had no objection to a postponement of the case against Rhodes. He insisted, however, that provisional sentence be given against the Princess. Pointing out that notice had been served on Princess Radziwill, 'for whom there was now no appearance', he felt entitled to ask for judgment in her case.

Mr Justice Maasdorp concurred. 'The application as against the defendant Rhodes was allowed to stand over until November 1,' it was reported, 'but provisional sentence was given as prayed against the defendant Radziwill.'

It was on this humdrum note that the first of the many court-hearings in the Rhodes-Radziwill affair was concluded. The only interesting fact to emerge from the dreary legal exchange was that Rhodes denied signing the promissory note. One feature of the case, however, was to become all too familiar. This was the request for a postponement. Similar requests plagued the case until the very end.

When asked later why she had not appeared in court, Catherine said: 'Because I had given my signature. I did not defend it; I was liable for the money. I never denied it. As a fact I did not defend the action.' Indeed, there was little defence she could offer. The action was straightforward. It had been brought simply on the £2,000 promissory note. Payment had been due on the 23rd September and, as an endorser of the note, Catherine was partly responsible for payment. All means of obtaining money having come to an end, there was not the slightest possibility of meeting Mr Louw's demand. She had nothing with which to pay a lawyer, let alone settle a debt of £1,150. As she well knew, judgment would have gone against her whether she appeared in court or not. All she could do at this stage was to keep well in the background and hope that some move would be made to rescue her. She had, it would seem, good reason for hoping that such a move would be made.

A week after the hearing of Mr Louw's action, the Princess received a visit from Agnes Scholtz. The doctor's wife came to demand certain papers. According to Catherine, Mrs Scholtz said 'it was high time to put an end to all this, and that if I consented to give up the papers that were wanted they would try to arrange the whole matter, including Mr Bernard's bill'. There is no record of Catherine's reply. From a letter which she wrote to the doctor's wife at about this time, however, it would seem that she did hand over some papers and then asked for them back. 'I have been anxiously awaiting news from you,' the letter reads; 'please return to me the papers, as I must give them to the lawyer tomorrow. I am ready to do anything if you only tell me what. At present I don't know what to do or how to act. I will do all you tell me.' The papers referred to in this letter were definitely not the ones which Mrs Scholtz had been trying to obtain. No matter how desperate Catherine might have been, she clearly had no intention of surrendering those particular papers. The most important result of Mrs Scholtz's visit, in fact, was that it put Catherine's 'papers' permanently out of reach. For it was now that the Princess sent her mysterious papers to England. 'About the middle of October,' she was later to say, 'when I found people were making violent attempts to get at my papers I sent them Home.' The person to whom she sent them was Mrs Violet Hill of 18 Warren Street, Oxford. Nothing is known of this Mrs Hill except that she was a trusted friend of the Princess and had paid a visit to South Africa earlier that year. But, judging from what followed, it seems reasonably certain that Mrs Hill was now in possession of Catherine's 'papers'.

The Princess could now have had little hope of anyone buying Bernard off. The terms for a settlement of her debts were obvious: she surrendered the documents or she faced the consequences. But there was no guarantee that if she gave up the papers she would be safe. This, apparently, was why she was determined to safeguard her most valuable bargaining asset by sending the papers to England. From now on she would have to rely entirely on threats and on whatever secondary evidence she could get to prove that the documents in fact existed. She had already tried to get Messrs Van Zyl and Buissinne to put their demands in writing and she now attempted to get a similar declaration from Mrs Scholtz. The attorneys' letter had been somewhat evasive and she wanted a more incriminating admission from the doctor's wife. 'I endeavoured to worm out of Mrs Scholtz,' she said, 'the names of the people whose letters they wanted me to give up.' At the same time, she was careful not to reveal that the papers were no longer in South Africa.

The Princess was crafty but she was playing a dangerous game. Powerful forces were ranged against her. She was fully aware of this and was by no means easy about her precarious position. Her main concern seems to have been to escape from South Africa. This, of course, required money. As she had none, her only hope was to force the Scholtzes into a position where they would accept her departure as a convenient way out of the *impasse*. Her flight would be a good compromise solution. She tried desperately to enlist their aid in her plans to flee and there is more than a hint of panic in a long letter she wrote to Agnes Scholtz on 29th October, three days before the second hearing of Mr Louw's suit in the Supreme Court.

'Excuse me if I trouble you again to ask for some news,' she said. 'But my head is simply turning from being kept in that state of anxiety and suspense; I cannot go out, but have to sit alone brooding over my woes, until sometimes I feel it is an effort even to think. I know my reason gives way, and you had better lock me up at once in a madhouse, than leave me like that. I cannot bear it, and there are moments already when I feel my reason has gone. I try to think and cannot. The servants come to worry me; I don't know what to say; indeed death would be a mercy, and I shall end by doing something frightful if I am left like that. For once I say I have no strength left. Shall I be able to leave, and if you have some bowels of mercy in you, reply to the question. I have thought how it could be managed.

If you sent Charles here to fetch my luggage, there is a back way behind the house, which I could show him; he might fetch a cart from Claremont, and enter it, taking it by rail to town, and take on about the same time the steamer was starting. I could slip out too, get to town by tram with Francine, and if you have arranged the permits and met me somewhere, I could board the steamer in the Bay in a tug or a small boat. No one need know, and I could get out at Madeira and go home through Lisbon. For Heaven's sake tell me something definite, or I shall do something desperate. I simply cannot stand this, anything would be better. My brother has left on an inspection tour; will only be back in a fortnight, as I heard by cable. How am I to live if I am left here? If I don't go tomorrow I shall be put in the street or in prison. Suicide is better a thousand times. In the meanwhile for Heaven's sake send me a sovereign or we starve. I have nothing, nothing. I give my last pence to Margaret to carry you this letter. Oh God, what a country this is! Such a thing could never have happened at home. If I had the boy here, so much would have been different, but you encouraged him in his mad scheme, and here I am thrown on the world's mercy. You might at least have sent me a line today, just to say something. One is not made of iron, and no human nerves can stand what mine do. If you cannot do anything, then say so; it is always better to know the worst; this suspense does not kill me, but will kill my reason. One cannot live under such strain, and already at night I see all kinds of things about me. I know I am not sane at present; I know it, and that knowledge only adds to my torment.'

But if she thought that hints of approaching madness, or threats of suicide, would soften Mrs Scholtz's heart, she was mistaken. To this long, hysterical letter Agnes Scholtz replied in two lines. 'Why do you write like this?' she asked. 'What you have done spells the same in any part of the world.' Catherine was later to claim that she did not receive this letter.

The hearing in the Supreme Court on 1st November was, once again, confined to a polite legal exchange. An affidavit sworn by Cecil Rhodes at St Swithin's Lane, London, on 10th October, 1901, had been duly filed. In it Rhodes categorically denied having signed any promissory notes. Mr Louw's lawyer then said that he had been instructed to ask the court to fix a date 'for proof of signature'. He suggested a hearing on the first day of the next term. Sir Henry Juta agreed with this but said that he did not know whether Rhodes would be well enough to return to South Africa by then. If not, he went on, 'they would have to apply for a commission to take his evidence in England'. Mr Louw's counsel had no objections and the first day of the following term was fixed for hearing the matter.

In the meantime Catherine was continuing her battle with the Scholtzes. On 2nd November Dr Scholtz wrote to her. He said that if she would hand over certain letters—written to her by Rhodes and Milner—he would help her and Francine to leave the country. He offered to pay her fare back to Europe and give her an additional £25. Extracts from his letter were later published and read: 'I should assist you to secure food, but on condition that you give up the letters. Now, the moment you place them in the hands of the Rev. Mr Bender, all letters purporting to have been written by Mr Rhodes or anyone else, and declaring these to be the only ones in existence . . . I am asking these letters absolutely on my own account, and on account of my friendship for the people concerned . . . If you do not agree to this I decline to go into further communication with you.'

The doctor's letter was written with discretion. He was careful not to commit anyone but himself. Not only did he want the letters but he wanted a statement from her invalidating any other documents she might later produce. She could not, of course, meet his request. She no longer had the most important of the documents for which he was asking and certainly had no intention of denying their existence. Her reply was as evasive of the main issues as his request had been. 'Sir,' she wrote, 'In reply to your letter of today, all I can say is that I have not in my possession a single letter, whether of Mr Rhodes or of Lord Milner, and if I had letters of Lord Milner's I could not give them up without his authority . . . I am absolutely ready to make an affidavit on that point. I have not the slightest objection to giving details of my visit to you a few months ago asking you to verify Mr Rhodes's signature.'

This little exchange was the first open admission that Milner was somehow or other involved in the affair. Catherine was later to claim that the only reason for her denying that she had any letters from Milner was that she had already entrusted these

letters to a friend in Cape Town. There can be no doubt, however, that she was in communication with Milner. Among her
letters that later came to light was one written to Lord Milner
at about this time. In it she abused Rhodes, claimed that he had
helped her financially with *Greater Britain* and that he was denying signature of the notes because she refused to hand over
letters which Milner had written to her. It was, seemingly, as a
result of her correspondence with Milner that a further attempt
was now made to get hold of her 'papers'. On 11th November,
she had a visit from an officer of the C.I.D. He had been sent by
Milner. She was to describe the incident in typically melodramatic terms. 'One morning,' she said, 'it was Nov. 11 1901
—I heard someone ringing the bell to my door, & an officer in
khaki suit introduced himself for Captain Barns Begg adjunct to
the chief of the secret department of military police at Pretoria.

'He began to ask me a lot of questions about a cablegram
perfectly inoffensive which I had sent a few days before & which
seemed suspect to the authorities. Then after having looked
round about him with heedfulness asked me:

' "Are we alone?"

' "Certainly," I answered, waiting for the continuation.

' "Madam," then said my interlocutor, "the English government knows that you have some documents, interesting for him.
I come to tell you that, if you would give them to me, we should
arrange that you should be largely rewarded." I lost my coolness
in the presence of such a proposition and gave full vent to my
indignation. With vehemence I refused as I had formerly
refused to give away my documents to C. Rhodes. The officer
vexed went away.

'After that memorable visit the persons who in Rhodes' name
[and] absence directed their campaign against me, had resource
to other ways in order to strain me to submit to their desires.
One of them consisted to famish me.'

Like so much of what the Princess had to say, this account was
based on fact without being quite accurate. Milner did send a
C.I.D. man to see her. This man is said to have been Henry
Widdowson, chief of Milner's C.I.D. It is true also that she was
asked to hand over certain documents and at first she refused to
do so. It appears that she told Widdowson that these documents
had been lodged with the German Consul in Cape Town. A few

days later, however, she gave up some letters relating to Rhodes and two documents which she claimed had been written by Rhodes. The letters and one of the documents are mainly concerned with the settlement of South Africa after the war and proposals which Rhodes wanted to make to certain of the Boer leaders regarding this settlement. The other document was a gossipy paragraph which the Princess claimed had been given to her in February 1901 by Rhodes and which he wanted her to insert in *Greater Britain*. But as the paper was not started until four months later, it seems highly unlikely that this snippet originated with Rhodes. In any case, neither the letters nor the documents can be regarded as incriminating and they were not particularly revealing. Certainly, they cannot be accepted as worthy of the drama which surrounded the Princess's 'papers'. It seems, in fact, that this was yet another attempt on Catherine's part to fob off her opponents with a meaningless collection of forged correspondence.

But Milner's intervention poses an interesting question. If his interest in the affair had been aroused merely by Catherine's attacks on Rhodes, why was he bothering with her at all? Earlier, he had agreed with Rhodes that she was simply a foreign meddler and not to be trusted. He was no longer Governor of the Cape. The war was still dragging on and he was extremely busy. Why then was he so interested in the hysterical outbursts of a foreign adventuress? How could Catherine have letters of his which were of vital importance to Cecil Rhodes? But there can be no question that he was interested. He not only investigated the matter but detailed one of his top men to carry out the investigation. There was obviously much more to the Princess's intrigues than anyone was prepared to admit.

Hounded, desperate and starving, Catherine must have felt that she had now suffered the worst that fate could inflict. But the bitterest blows were yet to come. The first was probably the hardest to bear; it was certainly the most unexpected. For once it had nothing to do with Cecil Rhodes. On 14th November, she received a wire telling her that her son, Prince Nicholas, had been 'dangerously wounded' at Tweefontein in the Transvaal. In a fit of abject despair she wrote a savage letter to Mrs Scholtz, accusing the doctor's wife of killing her son. 'I will have my revenge,' she declared, 'and I will show you no mercy.'

But Prince Nicholas was not dead. After being released from the field hospital, he was sent back to Cape Town to convalesce. On his arrival at the Cape, the first person he went to see was Agnes Scholtz. Of all Catherine's humiliations, none wounded her more than this act of treachery. 'I appeal to any mother and to any father what their feelings would be,' she was later to cry. 'The first person he went to see when he came down from the front wounded was that woman, and not me, his mother, and I appeal to any mother whether she would not feel it bitterly hard.'

Six days later, on 20th November, J. A. Stevens, of the Chartered Company, wrote to Rhodes to tell him that the Princess had been arrested. If this was true, her arrest was kept very quiet, for there is no report of it in the Cape papers. The authorities, in fact, appear to have taken no action against her in regard to the judgment passed by the Supreme Court. Indeed, her arrest may well have been connected with the first visit of Milner's C.I.D. officer and kept secret for security reasons. After giving her account of this visit, Catherine said: 'It is then that I have been arrested.' It could have been as a result of her arrest that she gave up those two innocuous documents which were later discovered in the Milner papers. In any case, the matter was quickly settled. A week later Stevens wrote to Rhodes again to say that she had been released; he assumed that she had been set free after receiving a large remittance from abroad. But his explanation seems unlikely. As later events were to show, she still had no substantial funds and was not able to settle Louw's debt until much later.

*

If the Cape papers were silent about her arrest, it was not for lack of interest in her affairs. By now Cape Town was alive with rumours about Cecil Rhodes and the Princess. It was the first time that the august name of Cecil John Rhodes had been linked publicly with that of a woman, and the scandalmongers were making the most of it. Whatever the courts might or might not say, Princess Radziwill had already been judged by the knowing citizens of Cape Town. On 22nd November, two days after her rumoured arrest, the *Owl*, a scurrilous weekly magazine, published a full-page cartoon of the Princess. In the cartoon

Catherine, squat and dowdy-looking, is depicted clutching a copy of *Greater Britain*, with a batch of promissory notes fluttering to her feet. It was captioned:

'This lady of high rank
Holds bills signed "Rhodes" galore
All cancelled by the bank:
We'll soon hear something more.'

In another column it was more explicit. 'Before many days are over we shall hear something more of Princess Radziwill and those pro notes for £20,000 alleged to have been signed by Cecil Rhodes,' it declared. The charge against her in the Supreme Court concerned only the £2,000 note. The *Owl* apparently had inside information.

At the end of November Catherine was again faced with the problem of finding somewhere to live. The lease on her house in Kenilworth—to obtain which she had produced her first dubious bill of security—had run out. There was no hope of her renewing it by the same method; she had to move. How she managed to do this is a matter of conjecture. She may have been helped by new friends. Some people seem to have sympathized with her. Among them was a prominent Cape Town civil engineer, James Flower, and his daughter. Miss Flower was one of the people with whom Catherine later claimed she had left Lord Milner's letter and Mr Flower was of great assistance to her in the days ahead. There may have been other friends. However it was arranged, she managed by the beginning of December to move from Kenilworth to Kalk Bay.

She may have had this refuge in mind for some time. Kalk Bay was a small fishing village some seventeen miles along the coast from Cape Town. At that time the nearest railway station was at the seaside resort of Muizenberg, a couple of miles away. Rhodes had a cottage at Muizenberg and if he returned to the Cape during the summer he was bound to spend a good deal of his time there. It was the only place where he could hope to find relief from the heat of the city. Kalk Bay had other advantages for the Princess. Living there removed her from the immediate attentions of her numerous and persistent creditors. In the subsequent drama surrounding the promissory notes, her other debts were sometimes overlooked. But they were very real. It was later disclosed, for instance, that between 31st January and 21st October, 1901, no less than five writs for civil imprisonment were issued against her in one magistrate's court alone. Things had reached a stage where she dared not leave the house for fear of a new summons being presented. For this reason alone it had become imperative to leave Cape Town.

Her departure did not go unremarked. She could not hope to obtain peace by a simple change of address. Her every move was being watched. 'It is really time we heard something more about those alleged forged pro-notes held by the Princess Razzledazzle and signed Cecil J. Rhodes,' declared the *Owl* on 13th December. And many other people thought the same.

CHAPTER THIRTEEN

Rhodes Returns

'I FEEL that neither I nor any living man will ever really "know" him,' Harry Currey once wrote of Rhodes. 'His life and interests seem mapped out into squares; and the man who is concerned with Square No 6 must know nothing of Square No 7.'

This observation—true of most of Rhodes's projects—was never more applicable than to his final dealings with Princess Radziwill. There can be no doubt that he had a great many subordinates working for him in this business, but none of them appears to have known precisely what part he was playing or what the others were doing. Rhodes gave the instructions and they were fulfilled without further questions. Only one man appears to have shared his full confidence—Dr Jameson, and for once Dr Jim was as circumspect as his friend. The entire affair was conducted with such secrecy that one suspects that the few surviving clues that have been found in Rhodes's correspondence are either irrelevant or deliberately misleading. It is, in fact, the end results of Rhodes's actions that are revealing rather than the seemingly conflicting references to the 'Radziwill affair' which he allowed to filter through. As a solitary young digger in Kimberley he had adopted the maxim: 'Do a good day's work and keep your own counsel.' This appears to have stood him in good stead until the end of his life.

His outward reactions to the Princess's intrigues are easy enough to follow. He first heard of the promissory notes when Michell had wired him in Bulawayo, in June 1900, concerning the original £435 note with which Catherine had hoped to pay her rent. He replied denying signature. When he returned to Groote Schuur at the beginning of July he did not see the Princess. He stayed at the Cape for two nights only before leaving for England and, much to Philip Jourdan's relief, Catherine allowed him to leave with only a farewell letter. 'I dreaded a meeting between them,' says Jourdan, 'as I felt sure a scene would have occurred that might have injuriously affected his heart. I was therefore glad when her note came.' As far as the £435 promissory note was concerned, Rhodes claimed that he was no longer bothered about it. 'I was informed,' he said, 'that the note had been withdrawn in England.'

The next news reached him when his ship touched at Madeira. Here he had received a wire from Hawksley, telling him of a note for £6,300 that had turned up in England. Again he wired back denying knowledge of it. When he arrived in London, he instructed his solicitor to write to the Princess about this second note. It was in answer to this inquiry that Catherine, a few weeks later, sent her genuine cables to Hawksley while she was dealing with Kayser and Bernard. A few days after she sent the cables, she wrote to Hawksley saying that his suspicions were ground-less and that she did not need money as she had been given some bills by a woman friend, whose name she did not give. Appar-ently the £6,300 note was then returned to the Princess's attorney and no more was heard of it.

For the month that he was in London, Rhodes was kept busy with the affairs of the Chartered Company and De Beers. He rode in Hyde Park every day and paid an important visit to his English heart specialist, Dr Kingston Fowler. The doctor pro-nounced him to be seriously ill and recommended 'a long rest and constant change of surroundings'. For once Rhodes was pleased to follow his doctor's instructions and leased Rannoch Lodge in Scotland for two months' shooting. Before leaving London, however, he had two or three meetings with Lord Milner, who was also on a visit to England. One of the results of these meetings was that he now made Milner a trustee of his will in place of W. T. Stead, whose name he had deleted the previous January. Another result of these meetings may well have been the interest which Milner showed in the Princess's activities on his return to South Africa. This seems a more likely explanation of the C.I.D. officer's visits than the suggestion that Milner had merely responded to Catherine's hysterical letters.

Accompanied by Jameson, Metcalfe, Mr and Mrs Maguire and Philip Jourdan, Rhodes travelled to Scotland in August. He must still have kept in touch with Hawksley who, in turn, was in contact with J. A. Stevens of the Chartered Company in Cape Town. This is probably how Rhodes came to hear of the £4,500 note that Honikman had shown Stevens. And, either before leaving London or as soon as he arrived in Scotland, he arranged for the notice to be inserted in *The Times* and in the Cape papers. In Scotland he entertained several visitors, including Alfred Beit, Lady Warwick and the young Winston Churchill. Jourdan reports him as enjoying the open air, where 'he was always in good spirits and forgot all about his heart trouble'.

At the beginning of October the party returned to London, where they spent two weeks before going on a tour of the Continent. While in London Rhodes made an affidavit denying signature of Mr Louw's £2,000 bill, an affidavit sworn in response to a request from Lewis Michell who was obviously keeping Rhodes informed of developments at the Cape.

The Continental tour lasted a little over a month. Jameson, Metcalfe, Alfred Beit and Jourdan travelled with Rhodes and they visited Paris and Lucerne before continuing through Italy. Rhodes had by no means forgotten the Princess. Michell had sent him the correspondence on Louw's Supreme Court action and is said to have told Rhodes that he was uneasy about Dr and Mrs Scholtz. He seems also to have suggested that it would be a good thing to get the Princess away from South Africa. From Italy Rhodes wrote to Hawksley, on 2nd November, instructing him to get in touch with Lord Salisbury about the dubious extracts from the Princess's 'diary'. Lord Salisbury's daughter-in-law, on the other hand, says it was Dr Jameson who sent the diary to Hatfield. In any case, it is obvious that Rhodes was now preparing to take action against the Princess.

In Egypt Rhodes and his party stayed for some time at the Savoy Hotel in Cairo and then travelled up the Nile. The heat made Jameson decide that Rhodes should abandon the tour. 'He acted on Dr Jameson's suggestion,' Jourdan says, 'and we left Egypt sooner than we had anticipated.'

Before they sailed for England, Rhodes again heard from Hawksley. The solicitor told him that Lord Salisbury's son had repudiated the 'diary' extracts but, at the same time, Hawksley suggested that it might be necessary for Rhodes to return to the

Cape to give evidence in the Louw case. This is said to have been the first time that the question of Rhodes's return to South Africa had been put forward. How true this is depends largely upon the extent to which Hawksley was in Rhodes's confidence.

When Rhodes arrived back in England at the beginning of January, 1902, he looked desperately ill. Gordon le Sueur, who had just come from Rhodesia and met the party at the docks, was shocked at his employer's appearance. He had not seen Rhodes for four months and found him completely changed. 'His face was bloated, almost swollen,' he says, 'and he was livid with a purple tinge in his face, and I realized that he was very ill indeed. I mumbled something about being glad to see him when I shook hands, but I felt too shocked to say much.'

It came as an even greater shock when, a few days later, Rhodes announced that he intended to return to South Africa in order to confront the Princess. All his friends were staggered at his decision. As they well knew, the climate at the Cape during January and February could be vicious. There were times when the heat could equal anything that he had fled in Egypt. Every-one tried to get him to change his mind. He was warned by his medical friends that his heart would not stand the strain. Dr Jameson, who was preparing to accompany Rhodes, was told that he was sending his patient to 'his death'. A friend pleaded with Rhodes to meet the forged bills rather than expose himself to such danger. 'What is £24,000 to you,' he said, 'compared with the risk avoided?' Rhodes would not listen. 'It is not the money,' he replied, 'but no risk will prevent me clearing my character of any stain in connection with that woman.' This was the refrain that he repeated over and over again. 'I must go and defend my honour,' he insisted, 'and I can only do it by upsetting the bona fides of the Princess.' J. B. Taylor, who had known Rhodes in his early Kimberley days, tells of a dinner party that Alfred Beit gave at this time. Throughout the meal Rhodes complained of having to return to South Africa. He said that the heat of Egypt had bowled him over and that the thought of going back to the Cape was more than he could stand. He asked them to look at the way his pulse was throbbing. 'It will be far worse in the heat of the Cape,' he said. Alfred Beit became so alarmed that he asked for a cable to be sent to Stevens of the Chartered Company in Cape Town instructing him to see whether Sir

Henry de Villiers, the Chief Justice, could postpone the case. They then sat down to play bridge until the reply came through. Hawksley eventually came in with a message from South Africa. He said that the Chief Justice had advised against a postponement as it might be thought that Rhodes was afraid to face the music. 'When the sentence "to face the music" was read out,' says Taylor, 'Rhodes jumped from his chair. "Face the music," he cried, "of course I'll face the music; damn the woman." ' It was strange advice for a responsible judge to have given to a sick man. There appears to have been no legal objection to the case being postponed and the expression 'face the music' was nothing more than a cliché used by Rhodes and his associates. However, the incident impressed Taylor. It was probably intended to.

This, in fact, is how all Rhodes's friends were made to view the situation. A sick man was being hounded by a fiendish adventuress and was determined to safeguard his honour whatever risks might be involved. It presents Rhodes in a tragic light and—considering his exhausted condition—is a seemingly valid interpretation of the last few months of his life. His biographers have accepted it without question. But it leaves a great many questions unanswered.

*

Reading contemporary accounts, one has the impression that Rhodes's decision to return to the Cape was reached quite suddenly. Gordon le Sueur, for instance, says that the news of the Princess's intrigues 'came like a bombshell'. Philip Jourdan more or less supports the same theory. He says that shortly after Rhodes returned to England from Egypt, 'he received news to the effect that the prosecution of the Princess had been decided upon, and that his presence was urgently required. This upset him very much. He felt that, in view of the false statements that were being circulated in reference to his relations with her, it was imperative, in order to safeguard his good name, that he should return to South Africa to give evidence against her if necessary, otherwise it would immediately be said by his enemies that these libels were true, and that he knew them to be true.'

Both Jourdan and le Sueur are inaccurate in their accounts of

Rhodes's dealings with the Princess. Nevertheless, they were both with Rhodes in England and the versions which they (and others) have given of their employer's sudden and reluctant decision to return to the Cape have usually been accepted as reliable. From them, Rhodes emerges as the Princess's hapless victim and there has been a tendency to make any later facts fit this image. Rhodes is pictured as ignoring the Princess for as long as he could and of taking action against her only as a last desperate resort. In a way, this is true. What must be questioned, however, are the circumstances which led him to make his fatal decision.

From the time that he left South Africa in July 1901, Cecil Rhodes had been very much concerned with the Princess's intrigues. This much can be gathered from what is known of his own activities. Throughout the latter part of the year he was in constant communication with Hawksley, Michell and Stevens concerning the Princess. In July he had instructed Hawksley to write to the Princess. In August he had had a notice inserted in *The Times* and the Cape papers denying signature of any promissory notes. In October he had sworn an affidavit repudiating the Princess's charges in the Louw case. That same month he had received full details of the case from Michell. At the beginning of November he had started collecting evidence to use in a defence which he was obviously preparing. In December he was still corresponding with Hawksley and Michell concerning the Princess. Far from ignoring Catherine, he was actively working against her.

But, of course, he was still more deeply involved in the affair. When his attorneys, Van Zyl and Buissinne, demanded the Princess's papers in October, they did so on Rhodes's instructions. 'What right had you to demand those letters?' Kayser was later asked in a court of law. His reply was unequivocal. 'We were acting for Mr Rhodes,' he said. The attorney's demand for the papers was followed by similar demands from Dr and Mrs Scholtz. It is admitted that Mrs Scholtz was writing to Rhodes at this time and it is unlikely that she and her husband were acting without Rhodes's authority. When these two attempts to get the papers failed, the Princess received a visit from Lord Milner's C.I.D. officer. Milner had recently met Rhodes in London. Is it possible that Milner was acting independently in this matter which concerned Rhodes so deeply? It would have been a strange coincidence. And there are other coincidences that must be questioned. Not the least amongst them are the activities of Mr Bernard and his client Mr Louw. How was it that these two appeared on the scene when they did? Why were they so quick to arrange the loan that the Princess needed to free her from the clutches of Friedjohn? Was it another coincidence that this vital loan was made a few hours before the notice in the *Argus* put an end to any further loans being made? Was it also simply a matter of chance that the transaction had been managed by Mr Bernard who had recently been employed by Rhodes's attorneys? Above all, how did it come about that Mr Louw had been prepared to advance £1,000 on the Princess's dubious security? To attempt to answer any of these questions, it is necessary to know a little more about the obliging and somewhat mysterious Mr Louw.

In December, while he was in Egypt, Rhodes had written an angry letter to Lewis Michell. He wanted to know why Louw was insisting on payment of what was obviously a forged note. It is impossible to take this show of annoyance seriously. If the only thing that was worrying Rhodes was Louw's action in the Supreme Court, his remedy was simple. All he had to do was pay Louw £1,150 and that particular action would have been dropped. For any other man the payment of such a large sum would have been a serious consideration. But Rhodes would hardly have felt it. He had recently paid £2,000 to hire Rannoch Lodge in Scotland for two months' shooting. To have safeguarded his health for £1,150 would have been a cheap investment. It would have enabled him to postpone his return to the Cape and to deal with any further intrigues of the Princess at a more convenient time. Why then should he have been angry with Louw? For this £1,150 was the only money outstanding on any of the Princess's bills. It was not a question of £24,000, as Rhodes's friends seemed to think. All the other bills had been withdrawn by December and only Mr Louw's promissory note remained to be settled. Set against the risk to his health, Rhodes's complaint to Michell seems trivial indeed.

Nevertheless, the question he asked needs to be answered. Why was Louw demanding immediate payment? As far as is known, he at no stage approached Rhodes directly on the matter. Having parted with his money so easily, he had immediately started proceedings to recover it and had pressed on with his action without showing the slightest concern for Rhodes. Considering that his own attorney, Bernard, was in constant touch with Rhodes's attorneys, it seems astonishing that no agreement could be reached between them to postpone the matter. This apparent *impasse* seems even more incredible when the identity of Mr Louw is made clear.

To discover his identity is no simple matter. Of all the people concerned in the 'Radziwill affair', the man whose action brought things to a climax was to remain the most elusive. At no stage did he enter a witness box. His occupation was never stated. His dealings with the Princess were discussed only through the medium of his attorney. To know that his name was Louw does not help matters much. Louw is a very common name in South Africa. Various persons named Louw appeared in the court every day. To identify himself distinctly, anyone by the name of Louw needed to give his full initials. In most of the actions to come before the courts Mr Louw was referred to simply by his surname or as T. Louw. There was, however, an exception to this abbreviated form of address. This was in the original action which came before the Supreme Court in October 1901. On this occasion, the plaintiff was reported as T. A. J. Louw. And, in the course of one examination, Bernard referred to his client as Tom Louw. Further clues to Mr Louw's identity were later provided by Jourdan and le Sueur. Philip Jourdan describes him as 'a prominent Member of Parliament and citizen of Cape Peninsula'. Le Sueur says that he was 'an ex-member of the Legislature'. Who then was Thomas A. J. Louw the parliamentarian, and why had this distinguished citizen turned money-lender?

Tom Louw was an old friend and loyal follower of Cecil John Rhodes. They had known each other for many years, having first met when Rhodes was supported by Hofmeyr and the Bond. Louw, a Member of Parliament for Malmesbury, had been one of the original members of Hofmeyr's organization. Unlike most Bond members, however, Tom Louw had remained faithful to Rhodes after the Jameson Raid. He had done more; he had come out in open support of the ex-Prime Minister. At the Jameson Inquiry in London, only two Dutch-speaking colonists had given evidence. They had both spoken in Rhodes's favour and it was suspected that Rhodes had brought them to London in order to impress the Select Committee. One of them was Tom Louw. At the time of the Supreme Court action, Louw was mayor of the predominantly English-speaking suburb of Claremont; one of the Rhodes strongholds in the Cape. As mayor of Claremont, Louw had been chairman at the tumultuous welcome-home meeting given to Rhodes on his return to South Africa in July 1899. There is no evidence to show that the mayor of Claremont had ever acted as a money-lender before. His wealth came largely from his farming interests. One can only assume that if Mr Louw had embarked on a new profession, it was at the instigation of his first debtor and old friend, Cecil Rhodes.

There is no need to labour the point. Unless one is prepared to accept a series of extraordinary coincidences, it seems obvious that, far from being forced to take action, Rhodes had deliberately engineered his return to the Cape. The money for which he and the Princess were being sued had been advanced by his friend. His own attorneys had arranged the transaction. The people who were bringing pressure to bear on the Princess were all linked with him in one way or another. He could, if he had wanted, have called the whole business off, when and as he liked. Why did he not do so? Was he really afraid of the effect it would have on his 'good name'? It seems highly unlikely. Rhodes did not care what people said about him. 'Newspapers!' he once shouted. 'Do you think I care a continental fig what the newspapers may say? I am strong enough to do what I choose in spite of the whole pack of them.' And if he was not worried about newspaper hostility, he was even less concerned about petty gossip. Scandalmongers were always trying to link his name with some vice or other. There had been attempts to associate Groote Schuur with licentious drunken orgies and he had only to speak to a woman to set tongues wagging. Such talk did not bother him. He ignored it just as he had ignored the rumours concerning his brief relationship with Olive Schreiner. When his friends urged him to sue the novelist for libel after her attack on him in *Trooper Peter Halket*, he had refused to take any action. He was wise enough to know that the publicity of a court case only added substance to slander. Why should he now be so concerned about 'the old Princess', as he contemptuously called her? She was already discredited in Cape Town. It was being openly said that the notes she held were forged. If he could survive Olive Schreiner's attacks, he could certainly afford to ignore innuendoes about Princess Razzledazzle. As long as he did not interfere, the gossip would die of its own accord. There was no longer any chance of the Princess cashing promissory notes in his name. It is not credible that he would have endangered his life simply to silence malicious tongues.

There was a more tangible reason for his fear. It would seem that Catherine's persistent claim to be in possession of certain 'incriminating documents' was well founded. The pressure that was being brought to bear on her had nothing to do with forged promissory notes; her persecutors' sole concern was to obtain the papers she held.

First her debts were taken over by Mr Bernard. The notice in the Cape papers allowed him to threaten Catherine with prosecution for forgery by the Attorney-General. She was also effectively prevented from obtaining any more money on her notes. It is possible that, at this stage, it was hoped that she would hand over the papers voluntarily in order to escape public exposure. If this was the case, such a hope showed little appreciation of the Princess's astuteness. She must, of course, have quickly realized what was happening. She was far too canny not to have been suspicious of Bernard's timely intervention. But she may not, at first, have appreciated the role the attorney was playing. In fact, it seems likely that she saw Bernard as an agent of Rhodes's who was trying to buy her off. There was definitely a triumphant note in the letters which she wrote to Dr Scholtz and Lovegrove at this period. 'I assure you I had one bill from Rhodes,' she said in her letter to Scholtz, *'for which he sent me money to pay it.'* This might also explain why she was bold enough to attempt negotiating the £6,000 note with Mr Benjamin. If this was how she saw things, she was quickly disillusioned. When the 'papers' were not forthcoming, the pressure increased. Louw instituted his Supreme Court action and Van Zyl and Buissinne openly demanded that she hand over the papers. She refused to do so. Mr Louw's counsel asked for and obtained judgment against her in court. She then received a visit from Agnes Scholtz. Again the papers were asked for and again she refused to give them up. She was now penniless; the bank had closed her account and she was desperately in need of money to buy food. Dr Scholtz wrote to her offering to relieve her distress and to pay her passage to Europe if she would hand over the papers. When this failed, Milner sent his C.I.D. officer to visit her and it is possible that she was then arrested. By now it must have been obvious that she would not, or could not, part with the documents she held.

It was at about this time, also, that Rhodes showed signs of changing his tactics. Hitherto there had been no suggestion of his returning to South Africa. In court, Louw's counsel had raised no objection to his evidence being taken on commission in England. There was therefore no legal ruling which demanded his presence in court. Rhodes, however, now began to collect evidence to use against the Princess and the suggestion was made that he might have to return to the Cape. What was the reason? One can only surmise. Having failed to get the papers, Rhodes's only alternative was to discredit the Princess decisively and publicly. If it could be proved in court that the Princess was a forger, then any documents she might produce would—at the very least—be suspect. 'It was necessary,' Catherine was later to claim, 'that I should be punished and besides disgrace me so that anything I should say later on should be disreputed.' In doing this, it was important that Rhodes display his innocence by voluntarily facing Catherine in court. Nobody else could do this for him. He must have known that it would eventually come to this. He must also have known that he had not much time in which to act. His doctors had warned him that his heart condition was serious. If he left it much longer, he might be too ill to fight the matter out. If things were held up until the weather was cooler at the Cape, he might be dead. It was now or never.

On 18th January, 1902, he left England for South Africa. Whatever hold Princess Radziwill had over him, Cecil Rhodes considered it important enough to gamble with his life in order to silence her.

*

The voyage to the Cape did nothing to improve Rhodes's health. The ship was not very crowded but bookings for Rhodes and his party had been made late and the only cabins available were below the main deck and very hot. When Rhodes saw his cabin, he flew into a rage and refused to occupy it. In desperation, Gordon le Sueur sought out the Chief Officer, who generously offered to give Rhodes his own cabin which was on the boat deck and equipped with an electric fan. So delighted was Rhodes that, typically, he presented the officer with a cheque for £50. But the change of cabin did little to alleviate the agonies of that fateful voyage.

Rhodes was accompanied by Dr Jameson, Sir Charles Metcalfe and Gordon le Sueur. Philip Jourdan had been sent on a week or so earlier. Throughout the voyage, Rhodes's friends were beset with anxiety about his health. Not only did he catch a severe cold but one night, when sleeping on a writing table in his cabin in an attempt to catch a cool breeze, he fell and badly bruised his nose and shoulder. 'It is a marvel he was not killed,' says le Sueur. By the time the ship reached Cape Town, Rhodes's condition had considerably deteriorated.

Every effort had been made to keep his arrival as private as possible. As soon as the ship anchored, on the morning of 4th February, a tug drew alongside and Rhodes, Metcalfe and Jameson disembarked and were taken ashore. A carriage was waiting on the quayside and the three men were driven hurriedly to Groote Schuur. A photograph of Rhodes and Metcalfe walking to their carriage on the dockside shows Rhodes looking a puffy-faced and worried old man. It is almost impossible to believe that he was only forty-nine.

Nothing concerning his ill-health was allowed to appear in the newspapers. As always, he was afraid of the adverse effect of the news on the stock market. A newspaperman had been waiting for Rhodes's party on the quay and his report was obviously written under instruction. After noting that Mr Rhodes looked in 'capital health', he said that 'the distinguished traveller . . . expressed himself as having derived much benefit from the voyage'.

As far as the general public was concerned, political considerations were not uppermost when the former Prime Minister's return was announced. By this time it was widely known that Rhodes's presence in South Africa was only incidentally concerned with politics. Catherine had not been idle during the past two months. Cape Town was seething with rumours that Princess Radziwill was in possession of incriminating documents which she was threatening to produce in court. A notice had already appeared in the press announcing that the case of Louw *v.* Rhodes and Radziwill had been postponed until later that week to allow Mr Rhodes to appear in person. Now that Rhodes had arrived, it was confidentially expected that the whole intriguing affair would get a public airing and that the Princess's papers would reveal some titillating pieces of information. At last, it seemed, the misogynistic Mr Rhodes was about to be unmasked.

Rhodes was fully aware what was being said. He had no intention of allowing it to interfere with his case against the Princess. As soon as he arrived at Groote Schuur, the resources of his financial and political empires were brought into play. A messenger was despatched to Worcester in the Cape, where Philip Jourdan was staying with his family, in order that the file of 'Radziwill Papers' (which included his slight correspondence with the Princess) could be prepared for court. He then sent for James Rose-Innes, the former Attorney-General, and Victor Sampson, the legal adviser to De Beers. Rose-Innes was unable to come but Victor Sampson arrived immediately.

As soon as Sampson arrived Rhodes gave him his briefing. 'He called me into the sitting-room at Groote Schuur,' reports the attorney, 'and told me that I ought to know "he had never had anything to do with the woman".'

*

For the crowd packing the public benches of Cape Town's Supreme Court on the morning of 6th February, 1902, the day started disappointingly. They had hoped to witness the first public confrontation of Mr Rhodes and the Princess. On the two previous occasions when the case had come before the court, neither of the principal figures had appeared. This hearing seemed likely to prove more rewarding. Rhodes, the defendant, was known to be in Cape Town and Princess Radziwill was expected to appear as principal witness for the plaintiff, Mr Louw. But when the Chief Justice, Sir J. H. de Villiers, and Mr Justice Maasdorp took their places on the Bench, neither defendant nor chief witness was to be seen.

Mr Gardiner, counsel for the plaintiff, was quickly on his feet to explain the absence of the Princess. Although she had been subpoenaed and he had seen her himself the previous afternoon, she had not arrived at the court that morning and had sent word that she was unwell and could not attend. 'We have had no time to get a medical certificate, and I have to ask that the case might be postponed until this day fortnight. I *was* going to ask, but I understand that Mr Sampson would prefer a postponement until this afternoon, only we have no information to show how bad she is or anything to show whether she would be able to attend in the afternoon.'

To this, Victor Sampson replied heatedly: 'Of course I objected very strongly. Mr Rhodes has been brought out here for this case, and there is no affidavit that the Princess cannot come. I submit that a postponement should not be granted.'

The Chief Justice agreed with Sampson. 'We will go on with the case,' he announced firmly.

This was not the last that the courts were to hear of illnesses and medical certificates. Like the repeated postponements, bad health, doctors' certificates and eventually deaths became part and parcel of the Radziwill case.

After it had been established that the plaintiff was suing for provisional sentence on a promissory note for £2,000, purporting to have been signed by Mr Rhodes in favour of Princess Radziwill, the court adjourned until later that morning. Victor Sampson explained that as it had been arranged that Rhodes should come in after the Princess had given evidence, he could not be expected in court before eleven o'clock.

Rhodes drove into town later that morning in a small Cape cart. He had been sleeping at his cottage on the sea-front at Muizenberg. Although most of his days were spent at Groote Schuur, he returned every evening to this little cottage in the hopes of catching a cool breeze from the sea. The heat that February was intense. All day Rhodes would pace the great rooms at Groote Schuur in an attempt to find relief from the stifling atmosphere. With his shirt unbuttoned, his hair matted and the sweat pouring from his brow, he would slump, panting, on to a couch in the darkened drawing-room, soon to get up again and drag himself to an open window upstairs in the hope of finding a breath of air. But there was no breeze. The heat pressed down on the huge white house, the garden shimmered in the scorching sun and the trees were still. The great heads of his beloved hydrangeas hung limply down. Only at night, sitting on the veranda of his cottage, listening to the crash of the breaking surf, could he hope for a temporary respite; and even that was by no means certain.

When he appeared in court at 11.45 that morning—a mere two days after his arrival at the Cape—the effects of his hopeless struggle against the climate were already apparent. Even so, the Press, alive to his touchiness about reports on his health, was cautious in its comments. 'The Rt. Hon. gentleman was evidently suffering from a cold,' it was noted, 'and frequently coughed.' The ordeal was not as bad as it might have been. The Princess had not appeared and he faced a largely sympathetic audience. Before coming into court, he had sat in his tented cart and fortified himself with a packet of sandwiches and a medicine bottle of whisky-and-water. When giving his evidence some of his old forthright manner returned; at times he was almost jaunty.

'You are sued in this case,' Victor Sampson told him, 'as the maker of a promissory note dated July 3rd, 1901, for £2,000. The body of that note says that "on September 23rd I promise to pay the Princess Catherine Radziwill or order £2,000 for value received at Kenilworth. C. J. Rhodes". Will you tell me if this is your signature or not?'

Taking the note, Rhodes replied emphatically: 'No, it is not.'

He then went on to tell the court how he had first heard of the notes in Bulawayo and how later, when he arrived in England, he had heard of further bills bearing his name.

'From your information and the documents that have come before you it would appear that forgeries amounting to £23,000 were attempted to be put forth and discounted,' prompted Victor Sampson.

'I do not know the exact amount,' Rhodes replied, 'but I was informed in continuation before this note was discounted which is being sued upon today.'

Pressed to be a little more precise, Rhodes became impatient. When Sampson produced Friedjohn's £1,000 note and asked him whether it was a forgery, Rhodes waved it aside. 'They are all forgeries,' he gasped. 'I have signed no promissory notes.'

'But you must look at it,' said Sampson.

'All absolute forgeries,' Rhodes repeated testily, as he glanced through the papers which Sampson handed him.

His high-handed impatience with the promissory notes was in contrast to the guarded way in which he replied to questions concerning Agnes Scholtz. There was no waving away of questions here. Sampson introduced Mrs Scholtz's name into his examination without any explanation of how the doctor's wife was involved in the case.

'Now,' he said, 'when the Princess arrived here you introduced her to Mrs Scholtz.'

'No,' said Rhodes, 'I met Mrs Scholtz. I think she mentioned the Princess. I said she was an interesting woman and she might call upon her.'

'Did you tell the Princess that if the Princess wanted anything she was to refer to Mrs Scholtz?'

'No, I certainly did not.' (After a pause.) 'One moment. Wanted what?'

'If she wanted advice or anything. Did you not put it in that way? Those are my instructions.'

'Certainly not. Mrs Scholtz informed me once that she thought the Princess was in pecuniary difficulties. I said "You can mention it to me and if it is so, let me know the circumstances".'

Rhodes then went on to explain how he had paid Catherine's bills at the Mount Nelson on condition that she should leave the country. His statement: 'I paid her bills and she left the country, but she came back again,' was greeted by a burst of laughter. This was evidently the sort of thing his audience had been waiting to hear. But Rhodes was quick to rectify the impression that he was merely the Princess's dupe. He pointed out that Catherine had once been 'one of the maids of honour of the German Empress', and had been a hostess at the Berlin Conference. He said that this had been confirmed to him by Lord Rowton, who had been Disraeli's secretary at that time. This, he considered, justified his original trust in the Princess. Once again he was brought back to the question of Mrs Scholtz.

'Some time in 1901,' he was asked, 'did the Princess write to you and inform you that she had received certain bills from Mrs Scholtz with your name?'

Rhodes's answer was an emphatic 'No'.

At this stage, Victor Sampson put in a tracing of Rhodes's signature and showed that it matched the name signed on all the documents before the court. It was obvious that the scrawled *C. J. Rhodes* on every paper had been copied from a single signature. They were as exact as if they had been photographed.

'It is a very good imitation, isn't it, Mr Rhodes?' remarked the Chief Justice with a smile.

'I think so,' grunted Rhodes.

The cross-examination by Mr Gardiner was very tame and revealed nothing. Rhodes claimed that he had never discussed politics with the Princess. His correspondence with her had been slight and he had given her no encouragement with *Greater Britain*. He said he had placed the notice in the Cape papers in case 'some innocent person might be injured'. This concluded the cross-examination.

There then followed a polite exchange between the lawyers. Victor Sampson said that he had several other witnesses but he did not think it necessary to call them. He pointed out that the signatures had all been taken from one copy. Mr Gardiner replied that he thought there was some variation in the signatures but he was not prepared to argue. The evidence was before the court and he left the matter in its hands. If provisional sentence was refused he would 'ask the Court to allow him to go into the principal case'.

In giving judgment, Sir Henry de Villiers explained why he had refused to grant a postponement of the case that morning. He said that an earlier application for a postponement had been made on behalf of the defendant and that this had been 'strongly objected to'. As the Princess had submitted no affidavit as to the state of her health he had not been prepared to grant a postponement to the plaintiff. This was the first mention to be made of Rhodes's lawyers having applied for a postponement. One cannot help wondering what Mr Louw's 'strong objections' were and why an affidavit as to Rhodes's state of health had not been submitted. Considering Louw's friendship with Rhodes and the ease with which he had originally parted with his money, his 'objections' seem most unreasonable. It is not without significance that no mention was made of this earlier application for a postponement until Rhodes was actually in court. One wishes that Sir Henry had been a little more explicit in his reference to that application. But then, before the 'Radziwill affair' was over, there were several things that required further explanation from the Chief Justice.

However, Sir Henry had no hesitation in refusing provisional sentence. 'The defendant has now been called and positively denies these signatures,' he said. 'In my opinion they are not the signatures of the defendant, and it is clearly an absolute forgery.' Having expressed himself decisively on this point, he went on to say that it was competent for the plaintiff to go into the principal case. 'I say it is competent for him to do so,' he concluded, 'but I think that after this expression of opinion about the case, we shall probably hear no more about it. Provisional sentence must be refused with costs.'

Thus ended the case for which Cape Town had waited so eagerly. It had certainly not come up to expectations. There had been no sign of the Princess or her mysterious papers. Rhodes had said nothing to suggest that he and Catherine had been on intimate terms. The impression left by the case was that Princess Radziwill was no more than a tiresome and rather comic adventuress who had tried to take advantage of an eligible bachelor. It was entertaining, but hardly the stuff of which romantic intrigues are made. After their long wait, the gossips had been rewarded with nothing more than a good laugh.

Rhodes, however, must have been well satisfied. Things had worked out much better than he could have expected. By not appearing in court, Catherine had played right into his hands. Not only were all the documents bearing his name declared 'absolute forgeries' but it looked as if the Princess was afraid to meet him face to face. Anything she might subsequently say or do was bound to be dismissed out of hand. He had put an end to the Princess's intrigues in a couple of hours. He was now prepared to let the matter rest.

The entire affair might have ended here. Rhodes was not intending to take further action nor, strangely enough, were the Cape authorities. This is another curious aspect of the 'Radziwill affair'. In widely publicized court proceedings, Sir Henry de Villiers, Chief Justice of the Cape, had declared that the documents with which the Princess had tried to obtain money were forgeries. In other words she had clearly committed a criminal act. One would have thought that, having given this judgment, Sir Henry would have handed the papers in the case over to the Attorney-General so that criminal proceedings could be instituted against the Princess. This was not done. Later, Sir Henry said: 'It is not clear to me that any criminal proceedings would have been taken, because it is not usual to take criminal proceedings until someone makes an affidavit charging a person with an offence.' But in this case he had declared Catherine to be a criminal in the Supreme Court of Cape Town. If the Attorney-General required an affidavit, he should have had little difficulty in obtaining it.

The fact remains that no action against the Princess was contemplated. Had she wanted, she could have left South Africa after Sir Henry had given his judgment and no attempt would have been made to stop her. The law, it seems, was not interested in her. But, unfortunately, she was interested in the law. In the end, it was not Rhodes but her own extraordinary behaviour that brought about her downfall.

*

If the move to Kalk Bay did not remove Catherine from the public eye, the sea air seemed to have revived some of her old spirit. She had not been living long in her new house—'a house with huge gables, that reminds one of a Swiss cottage on a large scale,' is how it was described—before she started hitting back at her opponents. She turned her attention first to the Scholtzes. Having threatened to have her revenge on Agnes Scholtz, she now put her threat into effect in a particularly vicious manner.

In the days of *Greater Britain*, William Scholtz had been conducting a slanderous campaign against a Dr Gregory, one of his colleagues on the Colonial Medical Council. He had done this anonymously. In several Cape papers, letters attacking Dr Gregory had appeared under various pseudonyms. One of these letters, signed 'Old Colonist', had been published in *Greater Britain*. The original had, of course, been signed by Dr Scholtz and remained in Catherine's possession. She now sent the letter to the Colonial Medical Council and informed Dr Scholtz that she had done so. The Council seems to have been reluctant to interfere in a dispute between two of its

Committee members but, once Dr Scholtz's identity had been disclosed and Dr Gregory had lodged a complaint, it had a statutory obligation to hold an inquiry into the matter. As a result Dr Scholtz was found guilty of 'disgraceful conduct in professional respect' for having degraded a brother practitioner and his name was struck from the Medical Register. Actually, the Council had not intended this to be a permanent measure and meant to reinstate Scholtz after three months. Only after the Council's verdict had been announced was it discovered that the medical body's rules did not allow for temporary punishment. Subject to Government confirmation, therefore, William Scholtz's name had been permanently erased from the Register of Medical Practitioners in the Cape. It is doubtful whether Catherine appreciated how drastic the results of her action would be. Nor could she have realized that she would eventually be blamed for the tragic consequences of Dr Scholtz's professional disgrace. At the time, it was enough to know that she had successfully scored off her old enemies.

Having partly settled her account with the Scholtzes, she started pursuing her former law agent, Mr Kinsley. Of all the promissory notes which she had presented only three were no longer in her possession. One was Mr Louw's note for £2,000, another was the £4,500 note which Friedjohn had failed to negotiate and the third was the original bill for £435, which she had tried to use as security for her rent and left with Mr Kinsley. When Mr Louw started his action against Rhodes for 'proof of signature', Catherine was subpoenaed to produce all the notes involved in her transactions. There was nothing she could do about those held by Friedjohn but she seems to have been determined to prevent Mr Kinsley from handing the £435 bill to the lawyers. When she first demanded this bill from Kinsley, he refused to give it to her. He said that he believed it to be a forgery and would only surrender it if he himself were subpoenaed. His refusal made Catherine desperate. She set siege to Kinsley's office and eventually invaded his home. 'One night she went up to my private residence,' he was to say, 'about nine or ten o'clock. I was not in, but she said she would stay there all night until I came home. I came home about half-past ten o'clock, and she had already gone. Next morning she came to see me. I was so much annoyed that I told her, "You know very well this note is a forgery, and if you annoy me any more, I will tell the police; I have nothing more to do with you!" '

Frustrated in this direction, she made frantic efforts to get the case (which was still pending at that stage) dropped. She wrote hysterical letters to Rhodes, who was still in England, threatening to reveal the documents she held if the action was not called off. It must have been at this time also that rumours concerning her incriminating papers first began circulating in Cape Town. When Rhodes did not respond, she began to look for money with which to buy back Mr Louw's note. In this, incredible as it seems, she almost succeeded. At the very last moment her new friend Mr James Flower agreed to accept a second mortgage on her estate in Russia in return for the £1,150 demanded by Louw. On the morning of the hearing which Rhodes attended, Mr Flower rushed to Bernard's office with a bill guaranteeing payment of the note. This Bernard refused. He said later on that he did not know Mr Flower was a rich man and could therefore not accept his guarantee. It is difficult to believe that Bernard really had doubts about Mr Flower's financial standing. The firm of James Flower and Sons was one of the biggest civil and mechanical engineering concerns in Cape Town. One suspects that Bernard had no intention of allowing his client's note to be settled at this stage.

Although she had avoided attending court, Catherine awaited the outcome of the day's proceedings with great anxiety. When she learned what had been said in court—probably by reading a report in the *Argus*—she appears to have been beside herself with anger. She immediately sat down and wrote a furious letter to the editor of the *Argus*.

'Sir,' she wrote, 'I was taken ill today as I was about to start for town to attend the sitting of the Supreme Court. I am more than sorry I was thus prevented from challenging some of the most extraordinary statements made by Mr Rhodes in court this morning. One of them alone would have made me jump to my feet. It is the curious one that he had at one time wished me to leave the country. What interest could he have had in my going or staying in South Africa if his acquaintance with me was so slight? The real truth of the case is that, far from things being as Mr Rhodes describes them, I was a regular visitor to Groote

Schuur after my return here, as I can prove by letters which I have in my possession, as well as the evidence of the people who wrote them. I am etc., Catherine Radziwill.'

She obviously intended this as a further threat to Rhodes. The letter she was hinting at was evidently the one which Stead had asked her to deliver to Rhodes, the letter which had led to their most violent quarrel. However, this particular threat did not reach Rhodes until some days later; the editor of the *Argus* held up publication for a little while.

Meanwhile she was able to settle her debt with Mr Louw. Exactly how was never disclosed. The only person ever questioned about it was Bernard and his answers were extremely vague. At first he said: 'I do not know whether the bill was paid or not; I know some arrangement was come to.' When asked whether he had ever discussed the matter with his client, he admitted that Louw had spoken to him about it. 'But,' he said, 'he did not tell me what the definite arrangement was; he told me that it had been compromised.' Considering the pressure that Bernard had once put on Catherine for payment of this bill, his lack of interest in the final settlement is not without significance. It is also worth noting that Mr Louw—who was once represented as being so eager to get his money back that he was supposed to have forced Rhodes to return to South Africa—was now willing to compromise on the settlement. However, a settlement was reached. On 13th February, seven days after Rhodes had appeared in court, the following notice appeared in the *Cape Times*: 'We are asked by Mr Michau, the legal adviser to the Princess Radziwill, to state that the amount of the bill in the case of Louw *v.* Radziwill and Rhodes has been paid to the plaintiff by the Princess Radziwill.'

This is the first mention to be made of the Princess's new legal adviser. How long Mr Michau had been assisting Catherine it is not possible to say. He may have entered into the affair only after Rhodes had appeared in court, for it is doubtful whether he would have advised the Princess to absent herself during that vital hearing. Mr Michau's name was well known in Cape Town and the announcement that he was now acting as the Princess's attorney must have aroused considerable interest.

J. J. Michau was a former resident of Kimberley. He was well known on the diamond fields and was described as 'one of

Kimberley's leading Afrikander citizens'. During the siege of Kimberley there had been a sensation when Michau was suddenly arrested for treason. Immediately after the siege he was sent to Cape Town where he was kept in prison for some weeks and then, for some unknown reason, sent to De Aar in the northern Cape. Still under arrest, he was transferred to a prison at Modder River and finally despatched to Hope Town, near Kimberley, where he was released on bail. At the end of March 1900, it was announced that Mr Michau had been 'released unconditionally, the Attorney-General declining to prosecute on the evidence produced.' The announcement had come as a shock, particularly to some of the Cape papers which had been openly calling Michau a traitor. One of the first things the attorney did on being released, was to start proceedings against these papers for libel. All of this had brought Mr Michau a considerable notoriety. What made his association with the Princess particularly interesting, however, was not his experiences in gaol but his politics. For, besides being a prominent attorney, Mr Michau was the secretary of the Afrikander Bond.

Whether Michau's interest in the Radziwill case was that of an ambitious attorney seeking to associate himself with a *cause célèbre* or whether, as most people suspected, he was anxious to oppose Rhodes in his capacity as Bond secretary, is uncertain. Catherine was to admit that there had been some suggestion of the 'Bond people' offering her £10,000 for her correspondence. But she said: 'I should certainly have not sold Mr Rhodes's letter.' She also admitted that she had received a hint from a friend in England that J. W. Sauer was prepared to defend her for nothing. This, she maintained, was only a hint. 'It was never mentioned actually as an offer,' she says. Whatever Michau's motives, his assistance must have been very welcome.

It may well have been the acquisition of this valuable ally which restored Catherine's confidence and prompted her next fatal step. With fantastic audacity, she launched a fresh attack on Rhodes.

On the day the announcement of her settlement with Louw appeared in the papers, Dr Jameson received a letter from the Princess. 'Dear Dr Jameson,' she wrote. 'As you will have learned through the papers, I have paid Mr Louw's bill. Had you done me the pleasure of calling on me as I requested you to do I would have told you that all I desired was for Mr Rhodes to counsel not to oppose the request for postponement of the trial. The money was paid on Monday, but after the abominable lies Mr Rhodes told in court neither he nor you will wonder when I tell you that I mean to take strong measures to prove he repeated in the Supreme Court his experiments before the Select Committee of the House of Commons. In one case he perjured himself to save Mr Chamberlain, in the second he did so to dishonour a woman who had fought his battles and been his friend. Well, the woman will show she can bite. Yours truly, Catherine Radziwill.'

Precisely what she meant by 'strong measures' was made clear a few days later. Rhodes was served with a summons—the Princess was suing him for payment of the £2,000 bill.

'Damn that woman!' exploded Rhodes when le Sueur presented him with the summons. 'Can't she leave me alone?' What am I to do?' In his simple way, le Sueur told him that he had no alternative but to prosecute the Princess for forgery. This, Rhodes seemed reluctant to do. 'It seems like persecuting a woman,' he is supposed to have said. Le Sueur pointed out, quite sensibly, that as he had already declared the bills to be forgeries, he had no alternative. Apparently still reluctant, Rhodes agreed. Sending for his lawyer and a magistrate, he drew up an affidavit accusing the Princess of forgery. His affidavit was in support of a similar one signed by Dr William C. Scholtz. A warrant was issued for the Princess's arrest.

On the morning of 25th February, 1902, Inspector George Easton of the Criminal Investigation Department called at the Princess's house in Kalk Bay and read to her the warrant charging her with forgery and uttering a forged document. The Princess was equal to the occasion. After she had been duly cautioned, she answered loftily: 'I cannot say anything to incriminate myself, and in a sense I am glad that proceedings have been taken. I will have an opportunity of saying where I got the bills from.'

CHAPTER FOURTEEN

A Criminal Charge

CATHERINE was charged at Wale Street Police Station, Cape Town, a few hours after her arrest. The police asked for a three-day remand of the case and Mr Michau applied for bail on behalf of the Princess. Both applications were granted: Catherine was admitted to bail on two sureties of £1,000 each, she being responsible for one and James Flower standing surety for the other. (Mr Flower was probably responsible for the full £2,000.) The Princess left the police station with her attorney. It was Michau's thankless task to prepare her defence.

From this time on Catherine took to haunting the vicinity of Rhodes's cottage at Muizenberg. Many years later, local residents were to recall her 'standing in the roadway staring up at the cottage'. The sight of her lurking in the road is said to have preyed on Rhodes's nerves to such an extent that at times he became almost hysterical. On one occasion, having passed her on the beach road while driving home, he dashed into the cottage and instructed le Sueur to stand at the gate and drive the Princess away—even if it meant using brute force. 'She passed, however, without a glance or sign of recognition,' says le Sueur. Whether Catherine was deliberately waging a war of nerves against Rhodes or was drawn to the cottage by some perverse fascination, her continued presence outside the cottage unquestionably added to the torture which Rhodes was suffering from his heart.

Rhodes was not the only recipient of Catherine's unwanted attentions. Her attempts to minimize the incriminating evidence that could be produced against her were now intensified. Not only did she make a last desperate but unsuccessful effort to obtain the £435 note from Mr Kinsley but she tried to influence

Frederick Lovegrove to keep silence. Her dealings with her former manager were conducted mainly through her loyal companion, Miss Littlejohn. They met with no success. Lovegrove later said that Miss Littlejohn wrote suggesting 'that very likely the Princess would pay me if I did not say nasty things'. For Lovegrove, who was badly out of pocket after his disastrous time as manager of *Greater Britain*, it was a tempting offer. He seems to have toyed with it. A few days after the Princess's arrest, he replied to Miss Littlejohn but made it quite clear that he did not want to see Catherine. He said he would come to Muizenberg 'where I should wish to meet you alone, and not in a house but, say, two or three yards along the road to Kalk Bay. I don't care to see the Princess until things are settled.' He did not keep the appointment. That same afternoon he saw Michau who appears to have told him that there was little chance of his being paid the back salary due to him. This made him abandon all further negotiations with the Princess and her companion.

The first preliminary examination of the case against Princess Radziwill took place at Burg Street Police Court on Friday, 28th February, 1902. Catherine, wearing pink and a large hat crowned with black ostrich feathers, answered her bail and was given permission by the magistrate, Mr Fleischer, to sit next to her attorney in the front row of benches.

The first witness for the Crown was Dr William Scholtz. The doctor's appearance, when he entered the witness box, shocked everyone who knew him. Not only was he weighed down by the worry of his fight against the decision of the Medical Council but he was suffering from severe influenza. He was allowed to remain seated while giving evidence. After telling the court that he had known the Princess for about two years, he went on to explain how he had endorsed the £1,000 promissory note that Friedjohn had brought him, and told of his subsequent dealings with Catherine and Meyer Wolff. When he had finished, Michau announced that there would be no cross-examination. 'I think it only fair to my client,' he said, 'to intimate to the Court at this stage that she has a complete answer to the charge and is anxious at once to go into the defence, but on my advice she has decided not to do so at this stage, and therefore there will be no cross-examination.'

Scholtz was followed by Friedjohn. The money-lender made a

shockingly poor witness. He had too much to hide to give a direct answer to any question. He denied being a money-lender and described himself as 'a broker and general agent'. On being asked how much he had advanced on the £1,000 note, he became evasive. At first he refused to answer and only after ten minutes of persistent questioning and an assurance that he would not incriminate himself, did he admit giving the Princess only £700. At this point Michau felt obliged to intervene. 'The witness has the receipt for the amount, given to him by the Princess,' he said. 'Why he does not now tell the Court I cannot understand. It was not £700. It was a good deal more.' To have admitted having accepted a mere £700 would, of course, have been extremely damaging to Catherine's defence. It implied that she had entered into the transaction with little concern for the debt she was incurring. From now on she was to claim that she had received £950 from Friedjohn but the money-lender denied this throughout the case.

A further point of interest arose during the questioning of Friedjohn. Referring to the payment of his note by Mr Louw's attorney, the money-lender said that the cheque for £1,000 had been given to him by 'Mr Bernard, of Messrs Van Zyl and Buissinne'. For those who were trying to keep Mr Louw's transaction separate from the dealings of Cecil Rhodes's firm of attorneys, this slip of Mr Friedjohn's tongue was evidently disturbing. So much so, in fact, that in later reports of the case, it was considered necessary to make the following correction: 'In the above report of the proceedings in this case, the following phrase occurs: "Mr Bernard, of Messrs Van Zyl and Buissinne". This phrase was inadvertently inaccurate, Mr Bernard having set up business for himself some little time ago.'

After Friedjohn had given his evidence, the Crown Prosecutor, Mr Howel Jones, moved that the Court be adjourned to Groote Schuur that afternoon. He explained that it would be necessary to take Mr Rhodes's evidence at his house as he was not well enough to come into town that day. Michau had no objections.

When Catherine arrived for what was to be her last visit to Groote Schuur, she was met by an old acquaintance. Waiting for her in the drawing-room of Rhodes's house was Mr Kayser of Van Zyl and Buissinne; he was there as Rhodes's legal adviser. (Kayser was also acting for Rhodes in the case where the Princess was suing him on the £2,000 note.) By now, Catherine could have had little doubt about the trap into which she had fallen.

A journalist later described this last meeting between Cecil Rhodes and the Princess. 'After the magistrate had taken his seat at a table, the like of whose magnificence was never seen in a Police Court,' he said, 'a messenger went out for Mr Rhodes. The great man entered by the door furthest from the front of the house, and immediately took a seat on a couch just within . . . He gave his evidence, I think, from his seat on the couch, and never once looked at the Princess as she sat with her solicitor at the back of the little circle of people in front of the Magistrate's desk. But the Princess never took her eyes off him. He was dressed in a grey jacket coat, white flannel trousers, and black boots.' Rhodes's evidence was a prepared statement to the effect that he had never signed any of the documents then before the Court. He gave a list of his movements between 14th January, 1899, and the 4th February, 1902, and submitted the letter that the Princess had written to Jourdan before they had sailed to England in July 1901. It was noticed that while giving his evidence 'Mr Rhodes looked very ill' and was coughing badly. 'Almost immediately after he had signed his statement,' says the journalist, 'he left the room by the door through which he had entered . . . But before he went from the room, the Princess was asked if she had any question to put.

' "No," said her solicitor, speaking for her.

' "But I will speak," insisted the Princess in a dramatic stage whisper, as she half rose.

' "No, no; sit down," peremptorily ordered the solicitor and the lady obeyed him.'

With this, Catherine lost her last opportunity to speak to Rhodes. Afterwards she caught only occasional glimpses of him during her continued vigils outside his cottage. She was always convinced that if she had not been prevented from speaking the last time they met, she could have broken through the barrier which separated them: 'I only saw him occasionally,' she wrote a few years later; 'the others were always there, ready to make use of every opportunity to bring about a quarrel between us. At last he was goaded to the last pitch of exasperation, and did what he had threatened he would do—that is, ruin me. But he suffered whilst doing so, and had I, the last time we met, stooped to implore his pity, I believe he would have tried to undo what he had done.

'I went home, and wrote to the medical man who attended him, and who I knew well—asking him to tell Rhodes that I forgave him, and prayed for him night and morning. I do not know whether the message ever reached him. I suppose it did not; and yet I believe that, had he got it, the poor Colossus would have died happier.'

This defensive, one-sided interpretation of their relationship entirely ignores the fact that she alone was responsible for goading Rhodes into the final step which he took against her. Nevertheless, her profession of pity for the desperately ill man may well have been genuine. Despite all that had happened between them, many people remained convinced that she cared deeply for Rhodes. One was the doctor who attended Rhodes during his illness and to whom she says she wrote at that time. 'That she became fond of Rhodes I have no doubt,' said Dr Stevenson. 'I met her often and found her very clever. She was not, as was said at first, an adventuress, and in the matter of forgery, I firmly believe that she intended to settle this . . . As I have said, she fully intended to return the money, but things were against her.' Another person who refused to believe that she deliberately intended to harm Rhodes was Major Colin Harding, who had sailed with her on her first voyage to South Africa. 'She was deeply interested in Rhodes,' he wrote many years later, 'and I thought then and still think that she was in love with the South African statesman . . . I could never believe all the terrible scandal I read about this strange and fascinating creature.'

*

Her first appearance in court and the hearing at Groote Schuur proved too much for Catherine. When the court met again, four days later, Michau had to ask for a postponement on the grounds that his client was 'extremely ill and unable to appear'. A postponement until 10th March was granted.

Before the next hearing, however, the case took an unexpected and dramatic turn. On Friday, 7th March, exactly a week after

he had appeared as a witness, Dr Scholtz died, his influenza
having turned to pneumonia. He was forty-three. The Governor
of the Cape sent a special representative to his funeral, which
was also attended by Gordon le Sueur on behalf of Rhodes. A
few days before his death it was announced that: 'The Government has refused to confirm an order of the Medical Council
removing Dr Scholtz's name from the register of medical practitioners.' This did not prevent people from saying that Catherine's vindictive action had 'hastened Dr Scholtz's end'. Nor
was his death the only fatality to be laid to the Princess's
account before the case was over.

When the court met on 10th March, Michau had to apply for
another postponement. He produced a medical certificate signed
by the Princess's doctor saying that she was confined to bed and
would have to stay there for some days. But by this time the
Crown Prosecutor had had enough of adjournments and
demanded that the Princess's doctor should appear in court to
give a more detailed explanation of her illness. Next day the
doctor told the court that he had examined the Princess the
evening before when she had been very weak and depressed.
'I feel anxious about her,' he said. She was suffering from
diarrhoea and a haemorrhage and was not in a fit state to travel.
When asked to comment on a report that the Princess had been
seen at Muizenberg station, he said: 'I do not think she could
have been there. Another lady, I think, was mistaken for her.'

The Crown Prosecutor was still by no means convinced of the
Princess's ill-health and suggested that if she could not travel the
court should move to Kalk Bay to take evidence. The magistrate
agreed, provided that a suitable hall or room could be found.
Michau said that it might be possible to use the Princess's
drawing-room which was 'very big' but he did not know whether
the Princess would agree. To this the Crown Prosecutor replied
that he did not want to thrust the court into the Princess's
drawing-room. In the end the magistrate said he 'would leave it
to the parties concerned to find a suitable room which could be
open to the public'.

While the Princess was delaying the law in one direction, it
was proceeding at her own instigation in another. The suit in
which she had impulsively summoned Rhodes for £2,000 was
due to be heard. The day after her doctor had declared her too ill

to attend the criminal court, the case came up for hearing in the Supreme Court. In the excitement of the past few weeks it had almost been forgotten by the public; but it was very much in the minds of both the plaintiff and the defendant. Once again the Chief Justice, Sir Henry de Villiers, was on the Bench. Rhodes was represented by a Cape advocate named Benjamin and the Princess by Mr Roland Wilkinson, an elderly lawyer who had been in South Africa for only two years, having come out from the English Bar. Since his arrival at the Cape, he had appeared in a few minor cases without particularly distinguishing himself; he seems to have been a competent lawyer but not equal to the complicated task of defending his new and far from co-operative client.

As soon as the case opened in the Supreme Court, Mr Wilkinson asked for a postponement. 'It would,' he claimed, 'be highly prejudicial to the interests of justice—the highest interests of justice—if this action were tried before the criminal proceedings have concluded.' But Rhodes, having been forced into court, was evidently determined that the question of the £2,000 bill should be thrashed out. He had provided his lawyer with an affidavit and instructed him to oppose any attempt at postponement. When the Chief Justice pointed out that Mr Rhodes could not attend court and that therefore a postponement was in the defendant's own interest, Rhodes's lawyer said that he was prepared to go ahead on his client's affidavit. His apparent attempt to force the issue failed. 'As criminal proceedings have been taken in respect of the very note now in suit,' concluded the judge, 'it is only fair that a postponement should take place.' Before leaving court, however, Wilkinson made a final comment on the case. 'Will your lordship allow me to make one observation,' he asked, 'on the very anomalous nature of the proceedings of taking criminal proceedings on the document that is being sued upon?'

'Ah well,' replied the Chief Justice, 'we cannot discuss that.'

*

The month of March saw no alleviation in the sweltering weather. Rhodes's health continued to deteriorate. He was now confined to his cottage at Muizenberg and reports of his worsening condition appeared daily in the local press.

Rhodes read the newspapers every evening but in order not to alarm him, a special issue of the paper was struck off, in which the bulletin merely stated: 'Mr Rhodes has passed a somewhat restless night.' But he knew the end was near, and responded by sending for Lewis Michell to make certain amendments to his will. One was to include Jameson's name as one of his executors. 'It is an extraordinary thing,' remarked Gordon le Sueur, 'that, in view of the years of friendship between the two men, Rhodes did not make Jameson one of his executors until 12th March, 1902.'

Both Jameson and Dr Stevenson did all that could be done to lessen his suffering. Jameson was at the cottage all day and Stevenson called in every evening. 'He was unable to leave his bed,' Stevenson remembered, 'and owing to his being unable to breathe when lying down, he was kept sitting on his bed. A contrivance was made which kept him suspended. Then to help the breathing, a double ceiling was made, into which oxygen gas was pumped.' But nothing seemed to freshen the still, hot air. Even after a hole had been knocked in a side wall of his bedroom in order to create a cross draught, Rhodes continued to gasp for breath. 'It was most heartrending,' says Jourdan, 'to see him sit on the edge of his bed with one limb resting on the floor and the other akimbo in front of him on the bed, at one moment gasping for breath, and at another with his head sunk so low that his chin almost touched his chest. Sometimes in the early morning and towards evening it became quite chilly, but he did not heed the cold. He could not get sufficient fresh air, and, even when those around him were in their overcoats, he sat in front of the open window with his thin pyjamas as his only covering. He was always asking for more fresh air.'

Catherine was wrong when she said that Rhodes was alone 'with only a few servants around him'. All his friends were in constant attendance at the cottage; Jameson, Metcalfe, Michell, Edgar Walton, Rhodes's younger brother, Elmhirst, Gordon le Sueur, Philip Jourdan and finally Johnny Grimmer, sat by his bedside in turns. Of them all, Jameson was the most constant and tireless in his devotion. 'Jameson,' says le Sueur, 'was indefatigable, and one marvelled at his endurance. He would be with Rhodes for hours, and then steal away for a few moments' much-needed rest, when Rhodes would miss him, and on his

"Where's Jameson?" the doctor would reappear for another spell. Towards the end Jameson sometimes almost went to sleep where he stood.' Of equal importance to Rhodes was the presence of Johnny Grimmer. Among the last to arrive, Grimmer remained steadfast to the end. He had travelled down from Rhodesia, having been specially sent for by Gordon le Sueur. 'Not long before Rhodes died,' says le Sueur, 'he expressed a wish to see Grimmer, and I then told him that Grimmer would arrive the following day. Always devoted to Grimmer, he was as pleased as possible, but pretended to be extremely annoyed at my wiring on my own initiative. Until his death he hardly allowed Grimmer out of his sight.'

Others wrote asking to be allowed to see Rhodes for the last time, but few were given permission. Among those who were refused were Rhodes's old friend from his early Kimberley days, J. X. Merriman, and Harry Currey. It was almost ten years since Rhodes had quarrelled with Harry Currey. Since then, they had drifted apart politically and had seen nothing of each other. Currey had joined Merriman who had long since been one of Rhodes's dedicated political opponents. Now, when Merriman and Currey wrote asking 'if they might come to say farewell', they found that the political barrier was stronger than their personal affection for Rhodes. 'Jameson,' says Currey's son, 'with whom all decisions now lay, was obdurate in his refusal to allow this. So the quarrel was not to be made up in this world.'

Everyone now knew that Rhodes was dying. There was no longer any question of keeping the news from the public to safeguard the stock market. Crowds began to gather outside the cottage every day and Philip Jourdan despaired of keeping the windows free from intruders. Nothing could keep them away. Standing in silent groups, they stared at the cottage where occasionally one of Rhodes's friends would appear on the veranda to breathe in the sea air. There was little else to see. Writing a few months later, one of the women in the crowd remembered the cottage as it was at this time, with its 'wooden gate opening on to the little garden where white marguerites and pale blue plumbago bloomed at the edge of the grass. The homely simplicity of the cottage arrangements were in accordance with Mr Rhodes quiet tastes; an extra window, with unpainted shutters, had been hastily made in his room, looking towards Simon's Bay, to admit the sea breezes. At the end of the stoep would be seen one of the servants silently and ceaselessly working the punkah through the other window, the veranda blinds being drawn down in front.'

*

On the morning of 14th March, while every effort was being made to ensure silence round Rhodes's cottage, a rather boisterous crowd collected a short distance along the road. From early in the morning an ever-growing group of people had been waiting to gain admission to the Kalk Bay police station. It was the day set down for the adjourned hearing of the Radziwill case. As soon as the doors of the police station were opened, there was a stampede for places on the only two benches provided in the tiny court room. The crowd consisted mainly of fashionably dressed women and, in order to accommodate as many of these inquisitive ladies as possible, 'the village was ransacked for chairs'. Even so, there was an enormous overflow and by ten-thirty, when the magistrate and witnesses arrived from Cape Town, it was almost impossible to get near the police station. The only persons missing were the Princess and Mr Michau.

As soon as the magistrate took his place on the Bench, a policeman was despatched in a buggy to fetch the Princess. He came back with a message from Catherine saying that she was too weak to attend the police station but had made arrangements for the court to sit in her drawing-room. Somewhat put out by this high-handed attitude, the magistrate then sent a detective to interview her. This second messenger was no more successful than the first. The Princess adamantly refused to move from her house, so the magistrate had no alternative but to announce that the court would adjourn to Princess Radziwill's residence.

The announcement produced a second stampede among the spectators. Clutching their hats and hoisting their skirts, the ladies set off down the road 'in indecent haste' and as many as were able pushed their way into the Princess's drawing-room. A newspaper reporter who had followed the panting women described the scene: 'Here we found her [the Princess] in bed—a small stretcher bed—looking very pale and almost uninterested. But now and again her eyes gave her away in spite of her profession of illness. She was anxious—but she was an actress. One could see the powder on her cheeks, put on to give her a ghostly look. Criminal though she was I felt more regard for her than I did for the well-dressed women of Muizenberg and St James and Kalk Bay, who, when the front door was opened, hurried and scrambled into this half Court half bedroom to secure the best seats on sofas and chairs, and when they had secured them, sat hungrily and greedily gazing at the powdered face on the pillows.'

The ladies did not long occupy their hard-won seats. The moment the magistrate arrived, he ordered the room cleared of everyone except officials, witnesses and newspaper reporters. Protesting volubly, the women, it was reported, were turned out into the street.

At this late stage Mr Michau arrived, full of apologies for having mistaken the time that his train left Cape Town. But even now, with the Court assembled and everyone present, the Princess's doctor once again intervened. He said that his patient was still not well enough to sit through a court hearing and he could not permit her to do so for at least another week. After a great deal of discussion, it was agreed that the court would meet again in the Princess's drawing-room the following Friday.

Thus, after three adjournments, the second preliminary examination of the Radziwill case was heard at Kalk Bay on 21st March. This time things were a little better organized. Although the general public were excluded from the Princess's drawing-room, an 'elegant screen' was placed in the doorway and those who could stand the crush followed the proceedings from the passage outside. On this occasion Catherine was reported to be 'up and looking well' and to display 'no small interest' in the proceedings.

The first witness was Philip Jourdan. He affirmed that certain letters which the Princess claimed had been written to her by Rhodes, could not, in fact, have been sent from Groote Schuur as they were typewritten and there was no typewriter at Rhodes's house. Asked whether he had ever typed any of the letters or documents before the court, he replied: 'No, for the simple reason that I don't understand typing.' Jourdan was followed by Meyer Wolff and Charles Kinsley. The evidence of both men was straightforward; they explained their dealing with the Princess and Kinsley told of Catherine's last attempt to get the £435 note from him the day before the trial started. 'I told her I didn't want to have anything to do with the matter,' he said, 'but that if I was subpoenaed I should produce the bill.'

After Kinsley's evidence, it was noticed that the Princess was 'feeling the strain of the proceedings'. According to Gordon le Sueur, whom Rhodes had sent to report on the hearing, 'she sat like a tigress at bay, and assumed such an attitude, finally pretending to faint, that it was impossible to continue'. The effect of facing the law in her own drawing-room had proved even more devastating for Catherine than attending court. She requested Michau to ask for adjournment so that the case could continue at the police court. 'It is only the second day that I am out of bed,' she told the magistrate. 'I really do not feel I shall be fit enough for the strain of hearing further evidence. Perhaps you may adjourn till tomorrow in Cape Town.' But the Crown Prosecutor had had enough of the Princess's ailments. 'Adjourn now!' he exploded. 'Why we have several witnesses down here and since they are here we might as well go on . . . It is not necessary for the Princess to strain herself at all. She has her legal adviser with her, and she might go to sleep for all that.' But that afternoon she sat as alert as ever listening to the evidence of Mr Bisset, the house-agent, Fred Lovegrove, her former manager, and Sam Fox, who had introduced her to the pedantic Mr Benjamin. The session ended late in the afternoon when it was agreed that the Court would meet again in Cape Town the following Thursday.

At the final session of the preliminary examination—held at Burg Street Police Court on 27th March—the first witness was John Frederick Ernest Bernard. When the court met at ten o'clock in the morning, Catherine arrived promptly with Mr Michau and 'appeared to be in very much improved health and took a keen interest in the proceedings.' At first, Bernard's evidence roused little interest. His statement that, without knowing the Princess, he had had no hesitation in advancing £1,000 on her promissory note went unremarked. It was only when he told of his suspicion that the 'Hawksley telegrams' had been tampered with that the Court became interested. When the Postmaster from Kenilworth and officials of the Cable and

Telegraph departments of the Post Office supported Bernard's evidence, the attention of the crowd packing the public benches was riveted. Here was undeniable evidence of the Princess's duplicity: all else was forgotten and the significance of Bernard's earlier statement was lost amid Princess Radziwill's more obvious intrigues in Cape Town's post offices. The aura of melodrama surrounding false telegrams provided a useful camouflage whenever Mr Bernard took the stand. It was not thought necessary to ask how the attorney had entered into his dealings with the Princess when those dealings were so colourful in themselves. The day's final evidence came from Mr Benjamin. The self-important merchant could add nothing to what was already known, except a confirmation of the Princess's audacity in trying to cash a further £6,000 note.

Catherine, who had reserved her defence, was then committed for trial. Her bail was increased to £5,000. She was made responsible for £2,500 and the rest came from two sureties of £1,250 each. This increase in her bail came as a shock to the Princess. 'The pledge fixed was so enormous,' she declared, 'that nobody could even remember such a colossal thing. But I found a friend to provide it to me.' The friend, needless to say, was the ever-generous Mr James Flower.

The reports of this final examination give no indication of the tense atmosphere in which it was conducted. The case ostensibly concerned a charge of forgery, but in the eyes of many of those present the accused appeared in court as a far more dangerous criminal. Princess Radziwill was, in fact, considered by many of the public to be little better than a murderess. For the drama enacted at the Burg Street Police Court was overshadowed by the tragedy of the day before.

When the *Cape Argus* reported the trial that evening, its front pages were encased in thick black borders. It was recording the fact that, at three minutes to six on the evening of 26th March, 1902, Cecil John Rhodes, former Prime Minister of the Cape and South Africa's most esteemed statesman, had died.

*

He had been more or less unconscious for three days. Most of the time he lay dozing, hardly aware of those around him. On the day before his death he had managed to surmount his first serious crisis. It had left him weak but by the following day he had become calm and it was thought that there was no immediate cause for alarm. Late that afternoon, Lewis Michell was sitting in the cottage at Muizenberg. Jourdan and le Sueur had returned to Groote Schuur and Jameson was taking a short rest. From the bedroom Michell could hear Rhodes singing softly to himself; then, suddenly, the singing stopped and he called for Jameson in a loud, clear voice. When the doctor arrived, Michell decided to follow the others' example and slip away for a short break. Leaving the cottage, he returned to his own home a few miles away, intending to come back later that evening. Within an hour of arriving home, he received a telegram informing him that Rhodes was dead.

Jameson had quickly realized the seriousness of his patient's condition. He summoned a group of Rhodes's friends from a neighbouring cottage. Sir Charles Metcalfe, Edgar Walton, Dr Thomas Smartt, Colonel Elmhirst Rhodes and Johnny Grimmer arrived and stood with Jameson, waiting for the end. A few minutes before six, Rhodes stirred and muttered the names of his friends before he died.

The others were quickly sent for. Among the first to arrive were Gordon le Sueur and Philip Jourdan. 'Jameson took us in, in turn,' says le Sueur, 'to have a last look at him, and for a moment I stood there trying to realize the loss, while Jameson turned and fumbled with the window curtains that he might hide his own emotion.'

Earlier, Jameson had performed another duty. Going out on to the veranda of the cottage he had announced Rhodes's death to the waiting crowd. According to the doctor, his friend's last coherent words were: 'So little done, so much to do.'

CHAPTER FIFTEEN

The End of the Affair

THE trial of Princess Catherine Maria Radziwill, on twenty-four counts of fraud and forgery, started in the Criminal Sessions of the Supreme Court at Cape Town on Monday, 28th April, 1902. It was obvious from the outset that the trial was no ordinary criminal proceeding. Both the public and the police displayed exceptional interest in the case. Long before the doors of the Criminal Court were opened, a huge crowd had gathered in the hopes of gaining admittance. Most of them were to be disappointed. 'The approaches to the Court were guarded by constables,' it was reported, 'and only a limited number of spectators were allowed to witness and listen to the proceedings.' Even so, every seat in the room was occupied long before 10 a.m., when the trial was scheduled to start. Prominent among the spectators was Mrs Agnes Scholtz. Swathed in black, the doctor's widow is said to have been 'the object of general sympathy'.

At ten minutes past ten, the ushers' cry, 'Silence in court,' announced the arrival of the judge, Sir Henry de Villiers, Chief Justice of the Cape. The fact that Sir Henry was allowed to preside at this important trial must be regarded as extraordinary. The Chief Justice had first entered the 'Radziwill case' when Cecil Rhodes had returned to South Africa to give evidence: until that time the case had been heard by Mr Justice Maasdorp. Sir Henry had been on the Bench when the Princess's action against Rhodes had been dismissed. Now he was about to hear the criminal proceedings which the Crown was bringing against Princess Radziwill. Giving judgment when Rhodes appeared in court in the earlier proceedings, he had said: 'The defendant has now been called and positively denies these signatures. In my opinion they are not the signatures of the defendant, and it is clearly an absolute forgery.' But it was for forging those same signatures that the Princess was now being tried. Sir Henry was therefore presiding at a trial in which he had already pronounced the accused to be guilty. It is perhaps equally astonishing that his presence on the Bench was not questioned. Neither the Attorney-General, Mr T. L. Graham, who was in charge of the prosecution, nor the Princess's counsel, Mr Wilkinson, raised any objection to Sir Henry rehearing the case. This legal irregularity was not the only remarkable aspect of the proceedings.

The case opened with the usual request for a postponement. On behalf of the Princess, Mr Wilkinson said that he wished to call certain witnesses who were not at present in South Africa. The application was refused by the Chief Justice 'in rather summary fashion'. The accused was then called.

Wearing a grey costume and a black ostrich feather hat, Catherine entered the court accompanied by the matron of Roeland Street gaol. She was given permission to sit next to her legal advisers and 'chatted pleasantly' to her wardress. She was obviously presenting a bold front. After the indictment had been read and she was called upon to plead, she showed herself to be nervous and confused. 'Are you guilty or not guilty?' she was asked. 'Yes,' she replied and looked nervously at her attorney for assistance. Michau whispered something to her and she quickly turned to face the judge. 'Oh, no; not guilty,' she said hurriedly. Her nervousness is hardly surprising. Things had not gone well with the Princess since she had been committed for trial a month earlier.

The day before the last preliminary hearing, a notice had appeared in *The Times* in London: 'Mr Burdett-Coutts, M.P., asks us to state,' it read, 'with reference to the case of Princess Radziwill, in which his name was mentioned, that he has never had any communication with Princess Radziwill or with anyone acting on her behalf.' This had been followed by an attack in the Edinburgh newspaper, *The Scotsman*, which had described Michau as a 'rebel attorney'. Michau had immediately threatened to sue the paper for libel. In Cape Town, the deaths of Rhodes and Dr Scholtz had turned public opinion firmly against the Princess and she could have no hope of any witnesses speaking on her behalf. With widespread hostility building up against her and the slight defence she could offer being systematically undermined, her one thought had been to escape. There was a report that she had got as far as the docks in Cape Town but had been recognized and turned back. This is probably why the police stationed a detective in her house. It was claimed that the close watch which was being kept on the Princess was to safeguard Mr James Flower, who was acting as her surety. But the detective appears to have carried his duties to excess. He not only followed Catherine about but examined her letters and tore one from her typewriter as she was writing it. (When this letter was offered as evidence, the Chief Justice refused to allow it: 'It was a document got by treachery,' he said, 'and it should not be read.') After keeping her under surveillance for three days, it was decided that the Princess would be safer behind bars. Mr Flower was asked to withdraw his surety. 'The police went to his house,' said Catherine, 'and forced him to take back the said pledge to be able to keep me in prison till the case was in court and so deprive me of any ways of defence.' She had remained in Roeland Street gaol until she appeared in court.

The evidence given at the trial was, as the *Cape Times* pointed out, 'practically a recapitulation of that which has already been given in the Magistrate's Court, though some new facts were elicited.' The most interesting of these 'new facts', as far as the public was concerned, were those provided by the Princess.

She took the stand on the afternoon of the second day. Once again her nervousness was evident. Throughout the first day she had kept up her show of aplomb and, during the afternoon session, had taken 'a keen interest in her surroundings, and stood erect for some time, calmly scrutinizing through her lorgnette the people who were crowded in the back of the court'. She attempted to keep up this aloof attitude when she entered the witness-box. Asking for a glass of water, she calmly sipped it and then turned smilingly to face the judge. Before long she was faltering. To many questions she replied: 'I don't remember, I forget.' On occasions the Chief Justice had to pull her up sharply to prevent her from rambling from the point. She had difficulty understanding some of the questions and her answers were often followed by roars of laughter. Even on the simplest points she became confused. Trying to establish her financial standing, for instance, she spoke of her Russian estate.

'Where is that?' she was asked.

'In the west of Russia. If you take a map you will find it there.'

'Well, be good enough to describe it a little more accurately, the exact geographical position, and I would remind you that you are on your oath.'

'Oh, that estate is in the east. Oh, now if I only had a map . . .'

No further attempt was made to locate the estate. Few believed that she had one. In reports of the trial Simbirsk is given as St Biersk and her estate is called Kitchivsky. She found herself defeated by her farcical reputation as much as by her guilt.

A sensation was caused when she was asked to explain the history of the bills. She embarked upon a long, irrelevant discourse and had to be pulled up by the judge.

The Chief Justice: 'The question was in regard to the bills.'

Witness: 'I will come presently to the point.'

The Chief Justice: 'No, you must come to it now.'(Laughter.)

Witness (continuing): 'Well, upon that point . . . a friend of mine who was a great friend of Mr Rhodes, an intimate friend of Mr Rhodes, came to me and said that he had some bills.'

The Attorney-General: 'Who came to you?'

Witness (deliberately): 'Mrs Agnes Scholtz, widow of Dr Scholtz of Riebeek Square.' (Sensation.) 'She told me she had these bills from Mr Rhodes to use for *Greater Britain* . . . Of course if I had thought that the things were not genuine, if I had had the slightest doubt, I certainly should not have taken them to the Bank of Africa. It is the very last place I should have gone to.'

The prosecution made much of her accusation of Mrs Scholtz. The Attorney-General claimed that until the Princess went into the box, the court had no idea that this was to be her defence. This is not strictly true. From the beginning of the case there had been clear indications that the Princess was going to make this claim. Rhodes had been specifically questioned on the point. Moreover, shortly before the Princess was examined, the Attorney-General had said: 'I do not propose to call certain witnesses, for instance, Mrs Scholtz, as to whom no relevant evidence has been given; but if the accused is put in the box and a certain line of defence is foreshadowed, I shall ask your Lordship to call Mrs Scholtz to rebut the evidence.'

The Chief Justice also rejected Catherine's introduction of Mrs Scholtz's name. 'I need not read all the letters written by the accused,' he said in his summing up, 'because all her correspondence to Mrs Scholtz, which in many respects is very painful to read, contains no suggestion that Mrs Scholtz handed any of these notes to the accused, and certainly I think you will agree with me that they are somewhat inconsistent with the accused having received the alleged forged notes from Mrs Scholtz.' But again this is not strictly true. In her letter to Agnes Scholtz of 7th October, 1901, Catherine had written: '. . . But for Heaven's sake prevent a scandal, lest your business must come out if this thing comes to trial, and R. will suffer just as much as myself. It is that which breaks my heart more than anything else . . . Do you think this scandal will do good to any of us?' While this does not prove that Mrs Scholtz gave her the notes, it is not inconsistent with her having done so. It certainly seems to point to an intrigue in which Rhodes and Mrs Scholtz were involved as well as the Princess. Mrs Scholtz was called as a witness after the Princess left the box. Her examination was brief. She denied giving Catherine the bills. She was not questioned about the papers she had demanded from the Princess. There was no cross-examination. Wilkinson probably thought that to cross-examine a recently widowed woman would do more harm than good. As a result, the part played by Agnes Scholtz was never properly investigated. It is doubtful whether she gave the bills to the Princess, but she was certainly more involved in the affair than was revealed in court.

But the Attorney-General's contention that the Princess had kept her defence a secret was true up to a point. Her instructions to her lawyer appear to have been extremely vague and Mr Wilkinson was left to flounder about as best he could. Often his efforts to establish an effective defence were disastrous. One of the few leads he had been given was that Rhodes had made out the promissory notes while drunk. When Wilkinson put this suggestion to Philip Jourdan, there was another sensation. 'No,' replied Jourdan indignantly, 'that is a gross libel.' Jourdan's protest was supported by many of Rhodes's friends. There was later to be a heated correspondence in the newspapers on the subject, another of those red herrings which distracted attention from the real issues.

The background of the case was never explored. In many ways the trial was as big a farce as the Jameson Inquiry. Rhodes was dead but his interests were being guarded by his friends. Only what Rhodes would have allowed to come out was admitted as evidence. The Attorney-General kept a close watch on the questioning. Friedjohn was badgered unmercifully about his rate of interest but his dealings with Mr Bernard and Mr Kayser were glossed over. Bernard was questioned extensively about the Princess's false telegrams but he was not asked why his client, Mr Louw, had entered into such a rash financial transaction. Mr Louw was never put into the witness-box. The coincidence of Mr Kayser acting for Friedjohn and of his firm representing Rhodes, was allowed to pass unremarked. The Chief Justice did question the right of Van Zyl and Buissinne to demand the Princess's papers.

'What right had you?' he asked Mr Kayser. 'I cannot understand what right you had to do so. I don't see how it affects the case. She was not bound to give them up.'

Mr Wilkinson: 'Tremendous pressure has been brought to bear upon her.'

Mr Graham (the Attorney-General): 'I object to my learned friend making speeches of that kind to the jury.'

When the question of Lord Milner's letters was raised, the Attorney-General again prevented the interrogation from going too far.

Chief Justice: 'You are referring now to letters about Lord Milner. From whom was that letter addressed?'

Mr Wilkinson: 'I am referring to a letter received from Dr Scholtz.'

Mr Graham: 'How can the witness know anything about that letter? What has a letter from Dr Scholtz referring to Lord Milner got to do with this case?'

The Chief Justice: 'Precisely.'

The Attorney-General was no doubt technically correct. But only by a thorough investigation into all the seemingly irrelevant aspects of the case could the Princess's actions be properly understood. Once again Rhodes was saved by a debatable technicality. At the Jameson Inquiry he had evaded awkward questions by refusing to answer anything that involved a third party. At the Radziwill trial similar evasions were allowed by the refusal to accept any questioning not immediately connected with the forged promissory notes. If justice is concerned with the circumstances of a crime as well as with the act committed, then Princess Radziwill fared badly at her trial. In some ways it was just as well that she did.

The third day of the hearing was devoted mainly to the prosecuting and defence counsels' addresses to the jury and to the judge's summing up. Before the Attorney-General rose to speak, Mr Wilkinson asked permission to put in two belated pieces of evidence for the defence. One was an answer to a cable that had been sent to W. T. Stead. The newspaper editor had been asked whether he had written to Rhodes and sent his letter to the Princess to deliver in September 1901. Stead wired back: 'Yes.' The second item was a statement from the printer of *Greater Britain*, showing that the Princess had paid him £3,837. As Catherine had obtained only £700 in cash for her various bills, most of this money must have been paid out of her own pocket. The Attorney-General had been at great pains to prove that the Princess was penniless throughout her stay in South Africa and the judge had accepted his arguments. How Catherine obtained the money to pay the printer is uncertain. The new evidence arrived too late to be debated.

In his address to the jury, the Attorney-General dismissed all references to the Princess's 'papers' as an 'attempt to mystify the jury by reference to mysterious telegrams from hare-brained individuals like Mr Stead and others, by allegations that she had in her possession certain important incriminating documents—the ordinary armoury of the blackmailer—from various persons'. With Stead being unpopular because of his opposition to the war, this argument must have gone down well with the English-speaking jury. When he came to deal with the documents relating to Rhodes, the Attorney-General was able to dismiss the Princess's vague claim with another slanted argument. 'Incriminating documents from a dead man, which had been carefully sent to England before this case!' he declared contemptuously.

When Mr Wilkinson tried to take up these points in his address, it resulted in a heated exchange between the lawyers.

Mr Wilkinson: 'My learned friend warned you not to be mystified by what I should say to you. Gentlemen, that is very suggestive. It is suggestive that he himself knows that there is something in the background; whatever it may be.'

Attorney-General: 'I did not say so.'

Mr Wilkinson: 'No, I did not say you did.' (To the jury) 'I am drawing inference from the way in which my learned friend spoke to you. I say he possibly suggests to you that he himself may have seen that there was something in the background.'

Attorney-General: 'Oh, no; nothing of the sort.'

Mr Wilkinson: 'I think that an improper observation for you to make.'

But Wilkinson could not pursue the point; he had to admit to the jury that he knew no more about the Princess's 'papers' than the Princess had hinted at in the witness-box. He did, however, draw attention to the pressure put on her. 'There is,' he concluded lamely, 'something behind the whole matter that has not seen the light.'

In his summing up, the Chief Justice refused to comment on the papers. 'Much comment has been made by the counsel for the defence about demands made upon the prisoner to hand over letters and other documents purporting to come from Mr Rhodes and Lord Milner,' he said. 'I confess I do not see what those letters really have to do with the case.' He did, however, go on to point out that the Princess had been justified in refusing to hand over the letters to those who had demanded them.

The jury was out for thirty-five minutes. They returned to find the Princess guilty on all counts. Catherine kept up her show of confidence to the end. During the jury's absence, she was seen spinning a coin with her legal advisers 'with the apparent object of divining what the verdict would be'. In passing sentence, the Chief Justice allowed for the fact that all the bills had been redeemed by the Princess and that nobody had been out of pocket by her criminal action. But he went on to point out that: 'The offence of forgery is a serious one, and it is impossible for me to pass it over lightly . . . In passing sentence I shall relieve you of sentence of hard labour, but the least sentence I can pass on you is that you be imprisoned in the House of Correction and be subject to the discipline of that institution, or such other place as His Excellency the Governor shall be pleased to appoint, for the term of two years.'

The Court was then adjourned. Catherine shook hands with her two legal advisers and was led away.

*

'If that is justice,' Catherine declared, 'I pity those who are administered by people having such a peculiar idea of it.'

But if she did not get a fair trial, it was partly her own fault. She deliberately withheld vital information from her counsel and made it impossible for him to conduct a proper defence. To a certain extent she had ensured her own conviction. There seems little doubt that she forged Rhodes's name on the promissory notes. It was proved that all the signatures had been traced from the autograph on the photograph of Rhodes which she had bought at the time the forgeries began. If the court proceedings were suspect, it was not because Princess Radziwill was penalized. What must be questioned is the reluctance of all concerned to probe too deeply into certain aspects of the case.

Why, for instance, did the Princess not produce her 'incriminating documents'? She could have got them back from England in time. The documents would not have saved her but they would have helped to explain some of her actions. They would have proved that others besides herself were guilty of double-dealing. She had continually threatened a complete exposure; why did she hold back and allow her persecutors to escape? It was certainly out of character for her to shield her enemies.

And why were the activities of Friedjohn, Bernard, Kayser and Louw not questioned? Everyone concerned in the case must have been aware of the suspicious circumstances in which the important £2,000 note was negotiated. This was not immediately apparent in reports of the trial, but any lawyer engaged on the case must have had doubts about this transaction. Yet the conduct of Rhodes's attorneys went unchallenged. Mr Louw was not even called as a witness. Why was the Chief Justice allowed to preside at a trial in which he had already judged the accused guilty? Why were criminal proceedings not instituted after he gave his original verdict? Was there any truth in Mr Wilkinson's suggestion that the Attorney-General knew there was 'something in the background'?

The questions are endless. They involve almost everyone who had anything to do with the case. If there was a conspiracy to prevent certain facts from emerging during the trial, it was widespread, and many eminent and respectable men were included among the conspirators. How could such a thing come about? The answer seems to lie in the contents of the Princess's mysterious documents.

There can be little doubt that the papers which Catherine held were connected with the Jameson Inquiry. She repeatedly threatened to expose Rhodes's conduct before the Select Committee. In her letter to Dr Jameson, she said: '. . . he repeated in the Supreme Court his experiments before the Select Committee . . . he perjured himself to save Mr Chamberlain.' And later she said that Stead's disturbing letter 'proved the complicity of Mr Chamberlain in the raid'. This points to one conclusion: somehow or other, the Princess had got her hands on the notorious missing telegrams. Only documents of such outstanding importance could have made Rhodes go to the lengths he did to get them back.

No one is quite sure what happened to the telegrams. Alfred Beit claimed that the Rhodes Trustees had destroyed them at Joseph Chamberlain's request. If this is true, it is strange that Chamberlain did not destroy the copies of them which he allowed to survive in his own papers. Rhodes's most recent biographer suggests that the telegrams might have been disposed of by Bourchier Hawksley's son. In any case, there was probably more than one copy of the telegrams. It may have been copies of them held by Rhodes that had 'fallen into' the Princess's hands. This would explain his decision to get her convicted as a forger. If her 'papers' were not the missing telegrams, they were undoubtedly something equally incriminating connected with Chamberlain and the Raid.

The question of Chamberlain's complicity in Rhodes's schemes is an intriguing one. In recent years it has been fully discussed in two excellent books on the Jameson Raid. A conclusive answer to the problem remains elusive. Today the question is of importance primarily to students of the Raid. In those April days of 1901, however, the picture was very different. The Princess's intrigues were not to be regarded in an academic light. The effects of any disclosure would be tremendous.

The Anglo-Boer War, still torturing the country, was regarded as a 'capitalist war', for which Rhodes was largely responsible. It was said that big business interests were trying to obtain by violence what they had failed to achieve by way of the Jameson Raid conspiracy. The war had been instigated by Rhodes and his friends, and these financiers were actively supported by the British Government. In Britain, this was a minority view, but it was shared by influential and responsible opinion abroad. Rhodes was looked upon with grave suspicion and, after his death, no secret was made of his unpopularity. In France, for instance, *Le Temps* had been scathing in its obituary. 'He was without religion,' said the French newspaper, 'without love, and without ideals; he lived only for his schemes, and enjoyed life only as a cannon ball enjoys space, travelling to its aim blindly and spreading ruin on its way. He was a great man, no doubt—a man who rendered immense services to his country, but humanity is not much indebted to him.' If it could be shown that the British Government was in any way implicated in Rhodes's schemes, national prestige—already at a low ebb— would have suffered immensely. Even though the notorious telegrams might not be conclusive evidence of Chamberlain's complicity, to have produced them at all would have been catastrophic.

It is not difficult, therefore, to understand how so many upright citizens could have entered into a conspiracy of silence. For, although some of them were politically opposed to Rhodes, they were for the most part patriotic Imperialists. What is more, they may have had no option in the matter. The Cape was governed by martial law and to have refused to co-operate with the authorities would have been tantamount to treason. This would also explain Catherine's hesitant behaviour. She must have realized that she was playing with dynamite. Two years' imprisonment for forgery would have been preferable to the more serious charges she would have faced had she overplayed her hand. At the very least, she would have had theft and blackmail added to her list of crimes. Perhaps she had been warned of this.

From the very beginning, Rhodes had realized that it might be necessary to call on the Imperial Factor for assistance. According to Catherine, and she was probably telling the truth, Rhodes, in the course of their violent quarrel over the 'papers', had asked her to write to Milner, and to let him see Milner's reply. Rhodes may have said this as a threat. If the Princess had written to Milner, informing him that she had the telegrams in her possession, there can be little doubt of what Milner's reply would have been. She realized this herself. From this time on, she began treating Milner with greater respect. Instead of continuing her abuse of the High Commissioner, she came out squarely in support of his policies.

Rhodes appears to have taken Milner into his confidence when they met in London in July 1900. It was after Milner returned to South Africa that the Princess received her visit from the C.I.D. officer. But before sending this officer to see her, Milner may have written demanding that she hand over the documents. This seems the most likely explanation of Catherine's claim to hold 'incriminating letters' from Lord Milner. Again it was evidence too explosive to use at her trial.

Everything seems to support the theory that Princess Radziwill had gained possession of the missing telegrams. The intrigue would have been very much in the nature of Catherine's activities in Berlin and St Petersburg, and it would explain Lord Milner's intervention. So accustomed was she to cloak-and-dagger schemes that she probably did not fully appreciate how dangerous a game she was playing. She would certainly have seen little morally wrong about it. Only by holding such a powerful weapon would she have been bold enough to embark on her career as a forger of promissory notes. She imagined that as she was using the money to help Rhodes gain the Premiership, he would not dare move against her. She mistook the man with whom she was dealing. The practised way in which he forced her into a corner exemplifies the ruthlessness with which he always crushed an enemy. He was as skilled in subterfuge as she. His determination to call her bluff by facing her in court was also typical. But he would not have taken this trouble for anything less than the telegrams. For Rhodes, the telegrams involved more than Britain's prestige: everything he had ever worked for was at stake. He could not have survived another Inquiry. The Princess had to be silenced, even at the risk of his own life.

Not the least remarkable aspect of the 'Radziwill affair' is the way in which it has been overlooked by Rhodes's biographers. This is not because Rhodes's career has lacked critical examination. If anything, there has been a tendency to emphasize his failings at the expense of his achievements. But, for the most part, the last years of his life have been dealt with summarily. His great days ended with the Jameson Raid; after that the rot set in. The fact that Princess Radziwill entered his life during these declining years has made her part seem unimportant. There seemed no reason to connect her with earlier events.

This neglect of the Princess is understandable. For a long time the 'Radziwill papers' were carefully guarded by the Rhodes Trustees. When they were eventually released, they seemed to contain little of importance. The only other clues to her activities were contained in reports of her trial. At first glance these reports reveal little but her attempts to cash forged promissory notes. Indeed, it seems likely that the newspaper reports of the trial were subjected to a certain amount of censorship. All references to her 'incriminating documents' are obscure and are buried among tedious descriptions of her monetary transactions. Few, if any, have felt it worthwhile to reconstruct her crimes and thus discover the forces at work beneath the surface of the legal proceedings. The Princess has been regarded simply as a foolish, husband-hunting adventuress: a tragi-comic footnote to Rhodes's controversial career. Much that was written about her by Rhodes's friends and associates deliberately underlined this comforting view. Rhodes, himself, certainly did not look on her in this light.

But she was as responsible as anyone else for her comic reputation. It was she who started the rumours that Rhodes intended to marry her, who hinted at secret assignations in hotel rooms and who broadcast the fact that Rhodes was paying her bills. The result was that her later claim to hold 'incriminating letters' from Rhodes was misinterpreted. Inevitably, it was assumed that her famous documents were merely evidence of a romantic liaison. Even today, there are those who are convinced that Princess Radziwill was Rhodes's mistress.

*

'So it came to pass that he who had never harmed a woman in his life met his death in clearing his name from the aspersions of a woman whom, out of sheer good-heartedness, he had befriended in time of need.' Thus wrote W. T. Stead piously, shortly after Rhodes's death.

The accusation that Princess Radziwill was responsible for Cecil Rhodes's early death was to be repeated by many of his friends. Lord Castlerosse, who claimed to have learned all about Rhodes from Dr Jameson, wrote in 1934: 'Cecil Rhodes, though he never cared for women or allowed himself to be influenced by them in the slightest, was nevertheless killed by a woman.' And Lady Milner, who had known Rhodes when she was Lady Edward Cecil, said in 1951: 'In the end Princess Radziwill killed Mr Rhodes.'

This was all part of the Rhodes legend: the innocent bachelor persecuted by the fiendish adventuress. It fitted in with the other stories that were spread about Cecil Rhodes and the Princess. For Rhodes to have returned to South Africa against all medical advice seemed to imply a deep emotional reaction to Catherine's threats. It suggested that there was more to this strange relationship than politics. Why else should a man wish to silence a woman? But, like much that was said of Rhodes, the obvious explanation seemed the most unlikely.

Rhodes's lack of interest in the opposite sex has been a source of embarrassment to some of his admirers. They have been prepared to accept his arrogance, his probable dishonesty, his questionable dealings and his ruthlessness, but are horrified at the suggestion that his sexual responses were in any way out of the ordinary. (This is an approach to morality of which Rhodes himself would have approved.) Yet there seems no escaping the fact that—whatever Rhodes's attitude to sex might have been—he was not heterosexual. At no stage in his life did he display sexual awareness of women. Outside the realms of uninformed gossip, his name was never seriously linked with a woman's.

During his life, he was commonly regarded as a 'woman hater'. This rather quaint Victorian expression was used to explain much of his otherwise inexplicable behaviour. But his friends went to great lengths to rebut the charge that he hated women. After his death, the South African papers were full of letters and articles denying his hostility towards women. 'True, he had no female servants at Groote Schuur,' wrote one of his more indignant champions, 'but he would chat pleasantly to a lady or to a roomful for matter of that, without the slightest indication of his so-called hatred of their sex.' In memoirs written by his friends and associates, the same point is made. But in all that has been written, there is nothing to show that Rhodes's approach to women was anything other than social. The most conclusive argument to dispel the accusation that Rhodes was a misogynist is missing. His friends—with one exception—have never so much as hinted at a heterosexual attachment.

The exception is Gordon le Sueur. In his book on Rhodes, le Sueur says that Rhodes proposed several times to a certain young woman (whom he does not name) but his suit was rejected. This statement was later embroidered on—without any corroborating evidence—by one of Rhodes's more colourful biographers. It seems most unlikely. Not one of Rhodes's more intimate associates mentions this supposed romance in defending his attitude towards women and had Rhodes wished to confide the secret of a love affair to anyone, it most certainly would not have been to the irresponsible Gordon le Sueur.

Whenever Rhodes was asked why he never married, his reply was the same. 'I cannot get married,' he would say. 'I have too much work on my hands. I shall always be away from home, and should not be able to do my duty as a husband towards his wife. A married man should be at home to give the attention and advice which a wife expects from a husband.' This trite evasion, which hardly warrants serious consideration, has been widely accepted by his biographers. But marriage is not something in which men indulge if they have the time to spare. For most men, it is the answer to a basic need. It has not been left to busy bachelors to shape the destinies of the world. Rhodes's wife would have wanted for nothing; like the wives of other great men, she would have accommodated herself to her husband's career and could well have proved an asset rather than a liability. Moreover, Rhodes was not always away from home and he certainly found time to spoil and indulge the various young men whom he adopted. An intelligent wife would have been more useful to Cecil Rhodes than some of his more irresponsible protégés.

And Rhodes admired intelligent women. Most of his female acquaintances were strong-minded, forceful characters. There was nothing frivolous, for instance, about Olive Schreiner or Sarah Wilson—nor, for that matter, can Catherine Radziwill be described as scatter-brained. The personalities of these women are in marked contrast to those of some of the young men on whom he lavished so much attention. This is surely a reversal of the usual male attitude: to choose women as strong-minded companions and to indulge frivolous young men.

'We were all much more companions than secretaries in the ordinary sense of the word,' said le Sueur. But they were hardly companions in the ordinary sense of the word. Very little real friendship existed between them and Rhodes. With the exception of Neville Pickering and, to a certain extent, Harry Currey, Rhodes had little in common with his 'young men'. He did not share his thoughts, his schemes, his hopes or his politics with them. Rhodes's real companions were men like Dr Jameson, Sir Charles Metcalfe and Alfred Beit. After the departure of Harry Currey, what existed between Rhodes and his 'secretaries' was an almost adolescent relationship: banter, horse-play and practical jokes, interspersed with moods of fierce jealousy and possessiveness. They provided Rhodes with a means of relaxation rather than companionship. It was in his dealings with these young men that his emotions were most obviously engaged— the tears, the sulks and the tantrums. He treated them rather as another man might treat a skittish mistress. He indulged their whims, pandered to their exuberance, spoilt them, teased them and amused himself with them: but never took them into his confidence. It is impossible to imagine his making any of these young men a trustee of his will or handing on to them the responsibility he had entrusted to Neville Pickering.

The theory that Rhodes was homosexual is not new. At least one of his more responsible biographers has hinted at it and another has felt it necessary to make an emphatic denial. In the most recent biography of Rhodes, J. G. Lockhart dismisses the suggestion as a 'fashionable calumny' of our vindictive generation. But he offers no alternative explanation of Rhodes's sexual peculiarities. He bases his rejection of the homosexual theory on two arguments. In the first place, he says, such an accusation was not made in Rhodes's lifetime. It is difficult to say whether this is true or not; all sorts of rumours, which rarely found their way into print, about Rhodes's sex life were current during his lifetime. In any case, the argument is purely negative and proves nothing. Mr Lockhart's second argument is more tangible. He cites a woman who offered her services to Rhodes as a secretary and was told: 'I don't want a secretary. Can't you find me a nice English boy?' According to Mr Lockhart, no homosexual would dare to say such a thing unless he was a 'flagrant exhibitionist'. And Rhodes was not that. It would be utterly out of character for him to behave in such a way. But would it? Rhodes was never over-concerned with what people thought of him. Much of what he said when talking of his young men was equally revealing. If this unguarded remark seems to indicate innocence, it is probably because Rhodes was not guiltily conscious of his homosexual tendencies.

For, if Rhodes was homosexual, his aberration, like so much else about him, was far from straightforward. His involvement with young men appears to have been purely emotional. There can be little doubt that those who played the most prominent part in his life were ordinary heterosexual youngsters. It is extremely unlikely that any of them were conscious of anything untoward in Rhodes's feelings for them. They were all uncomplicated and well-adjusted in their attitudes to sex. It seems, in fact, to have been their obvious masculine normality that attracted Rhodes. He would never have associated with homosexuals. His horror of the slightest suggestion of effeminacy was so excessive as to be suspect. 'He liked a man to display the attributes of a man,' says Jourdan, 'and despised indecision, weakness, and effeminateness in the male sex.' And le Sueur says that he was so suspicious of jewellery on a man that he would not even wear a watch. Such traits are not uncommon in repressed homosexuals. They indicate both sexual inhibitions and the attractions of aggressive masculinity.

To be surrounded by young men, to be looked up to and admired by them and to exercise a control over their lives was, it would seem, sufficient for Rhodes. But this was a definite emotional force in his life. Women could never arouse similar emotions in him. On one point all his biographers agree: Rhodes did not hate women but he was decidedly happier in the company of men.

*

'So little done, so much to do.' According to Dr Jameson these were Rhodes's last coherent words. One would like to believe the doctor. But it seems that Rhodes's last words were less heroic. Those who stood at his bedside have said that he murmured several names and then, addressing Johnny Grimmer, whispered: 'Turn me over, Jack.' Even this is doubtful for he always called Grimmer, Johnny. But it would have been appropriate if Grimmer was the last person to whom he spoke.

No one came nearer than Johnny Grimmer to filling the emotional void created in Rhodes's life by the death of Neville Pickering. Of all Rhodes's 'young men' Grimmer was the favourite until the end. Their relationship was turbulent; they quarrelled incessantly. It was sometimes days before they could bring themselves to speak to each other. 'They were not unlike two schoolboys,' says Philip Jourdan. 'Each was anxious to make up his differences with the other but each was too proud to make the first advances.' Once the breach was healed—and Rhodes usually made the first move—they were all over each other. 'For some days afterwards,' says Jourdan, 'each was most attentive to and could not do enough for the other.' Others have left similar descriptions of these temperamental tiffs. There was no escaping the intensity of their friendship.

For, if Rhodes was devoted to Johnny Grimmer, it was a devotion which the younger man returned in full. Grimmer had little time for his employer's grandiose schemes. He had no outstanding talents and was bored by politics. But his loyalty to Rhodes is undeniable. 'He was,' says Sir Percy Fitzpatrick, 'the kindliest, most loyal and staunchest of men.' When Rhodes was shut up in Kimberley, Grimmer made a desperate attempt to break through the enemy lines to reach his chief. And throughout Rhodes's last illness, his attentiveness was equalled only by Jameson's. It was for Johnny Grimmer that a stretcher was placed in Rhodes's room during those last tortured days.

So close in life, death separated them by only a few months. Johnny Grimmer was among those who accompanied Rhodes's coffin to Rhodesia. At Bulawayo he was taken ill with a bout of malarial fever and was unable to attend the impressive ceremony at which Rhodes was buried at the summit of his beloved 'World's View'. Immediately after the funeral Grimmer returned to the Cape. He and Philip Jourdan had arranged to spend part of the £10,000 legacy which they had each been left by Rhodes on a world tour. By 29th May Grimmer appeared to be fully recovered from his malarial attack and went to spend a few days at Caledon before setting out with Jourdan. Hardly had he arrived at the small Cape village than he caught a chill which 'developed the dreaded "blackwater" fever'. He died a week later, after being unconscious for three days. His funeral was attended by both Philip Jourdan and Gordon le Sueur. He was thirty-five.

Seven years later another of Rhodes's friends died. In June 1909, T. A. J. Louw, the elusive figure in the 'Radziwill case', died at Kissengen in Germany. In his obituaries he was remembered mainly for the support he had given Rhodes at the Jameson Inquiry.

It was to Dr Jameson that Rhodes's political supporters looked after his death. Jameson served them well. The Raid had chastened the high-spirited doctor. He was to commit no more rash acts. A friend is said to have warned him that if he took a certain course of action he would be making the greatest mistake of his life. 'No,' said Jameson; 'it may be a mistake but it won't be my greatest. I have made that.' After Rhodes's death, Dr Jim lived on at Groote Schuur and became the acknowledged leader of the Rhodes party in the House of Assembly. Overcoming much of the hostility that had been apparent when he first entered Parliament, he went on to achieve the seemingly impossible. Less than ten years after the Raid, he became Prime Minister of the Cape Colony. He held office from 1904 to 1908. Three years later, King George V conferred a baronetcy on him and it was as Sir Leander Starr Jameson that he was elected President of the Chartered Company, after the death of the Duke of Abercorn in 1913. For the last five years of his life he lived with his brother in England. He died there, during the First World War, on 26th November, 1917. Eighteen months after the war, his body was taken to Rhodesia for burial on the summit of 'World's View'. Appropriately Dr Jameson was buried on the right-hand side of Cecil Rhodes.

In the same year that Jameson was buried in Rhodesia, Gordon le Sueur died, aged forty-six. Since Rhodes's death he had led a foot-loose life. For a while he had remained on at Groote Schuur with Jameson 'arranging and codifying' Rhodes's library. In 1904 he appears to have invested his legacy from Rhodes in an exploration company which he founded in Portuguese East Africa. The venture came to nothing, although perhaps it was the cause of his being elected a Fellow of the Royal Geographical Society. Two years later it was announced that he was 'engaged in writing personal reminiscences of his deceased master'. This task also proved fruitless. When the Rhodes Trustees heard what the indiscreet le Sueur was up to, they bought his materials on condition that he abandoned the project. The only really interesting document among his papers was the transcript of a communication which he had received from Princess Radziwill. Written in the most appalling English, it reveals many interesting sidelights on the Radziwill affair and has been quoted extensively in this book. Le Sueur does not say how he came to receive it from the Princess but there can be no doubt that his record is authentic. Many of the facts he gives could have come only from Catherine. His introduction to the Princess's statement is full of mistakes but contains one interesting observation. 'Catherine Radziwill came out of prison when Cecil Rhodes died,' he writes. 'Today she appears on that empire founder's tomb as a stray, as a riddle. She bring an action against the executors of Cecil Rhodes asking a restitution of £1400,000. One says that she is armed of redoubtable & terrible secrets and her process wouldn't be of a man only but that of an epoch. It seemed to us very interesting to rise a veil that covered it . . .'

In 1910, le Sueur returned to Rhodesia where he was said to have 'entered journalism'. One can only hope that by then his English had improved. Three years later he went back on his promise to the Rhodes Trustees and published his book, *Cecil Rhodes: The Man and His Work*. It contained none of the information he had obtained from the Princess and, except when outlining his own association with Rhodes, is completely unreliable. His portrait of Rhodes is far from flattering. Sir Herbert Baker, Rhodes's architect, has dismissed the book as the product of a spoilt secretary with a 'valet mind'. Some of his observations, however, are unconsciously revealing. By the time of his death in 1920, he was practically forgotten in South Africa.

Of all Rhodes's secretaries it was probably Harry Currey who achieved the greatest distinction in later life. That independence of mind which had led to his break with Rhodes was apparent in his subsequent career. He was often attacked for his opposition to his former chief. 'Young Harry Currey is singing small lately,' commented the *Owl* on one occasion, 'and in future we shall hear little from him of the way Mr Rhodes treats old friends . . . it would be nothing short of filial outrage for the young gentleman to denounce Mr Rhodes.' But Harry Currey did not allow sneers of this sort to deter him. His differences with Rhodes were political and he was prepared to make a stand on matters of principle. His family remained friendly with Rhodes. At the Radziwill trial his father, J. B. Currey, gave evidence that he had been in Rhodes's company continually during the two days he was at the Cape in July 1901, and swore that Rhodes had then had no contact with the Princess. J. B. Currey was also one of the pallbearers at Rhodes's funeral. After Rhodes's death the Curreys lived on at Welgelegen, the Cape-Dutch house which Rhodes had had restored for them, and two of Harry Currey's sisters—very much personalities in their own right—live there to this day. Harry Currey, however, continued on his independent course and formed a close political association with J. X. Merriman. He refused to discuss his final quarrel with Rhodes and firmly resisted attempts made by Rhodes's biographers to obtain information from him. Ten years after Rhodes's death, his son was elected to a Rhodes Scholarship. When Harry Currey died in 1945, at the age of eighty-two, he was a highly esteemed old gentleman, noted for his adherence to liberal political principles.

Philip Jourdan outlived them all. Rhodes's often ailing and 'delicate' secretary died at the venerable age of ninety-one. His life had been as exemplary as le Sueur's had been dissolute. After Rhodes's death he went back to the Civil Service and in 1905 was appointed senior public prosecutor in the little town of Boksburg in the Transvaal. The following year he married a Kimberley girl. They had three children. His book, *Cecil Rhodes: His Private Life by His Private Secretary*, published in 1910, is dedicated: 'To Julian. My two-year-old son and all contemporary little British subjects . . . In the hope that they will continually and strenuously strive to emulate the lofty ideals of the subject of these reminiscences.' The title of Jourdan's book is more provocative than that of le Sueur's but its contents are decidedly tame. It is simply a eulogy of the man he adored. His hero-worship is apparent on every page. He remained discreet to the end of his life. 'I knew he would never abuse my trust or let me down,' Rhodes had said. He was proved right.

Though Philip Jourdan did not marry until he was thirty-six, he lived on to celebrate his golden wedding, surrounded by his children and their families. He ended his public career as the Magistrate of Volksrust in the Transvaal. Although he was once threatened with murder by a dangerous criminal against whom he had issued a warrant, his later life was relatively uneventful. He died on 12th May, 1961. By an odd coincidence his death occurred on the twentieth anniversary of that of another important person in Rhodes's life.

*

On 15th April, 1941, Mrs Charles Kolb-Danvin, an elderly American widow, was admitted to St Clare's Hospital on West Fifty-first Street, New York. She had slipped and fractured her hip. She was by no means an easy patient. Throughout her illness, she kept the hospital staff busy fetching and carrying for her. The Second World War was raging in Europe and the old lady had much to say about how it was being conducted. Despite the pain of her injury, she sat up in bed writing article after article on European events. An American newspaper reported that she insisted 'that her knowledge of European politics could be of great use to this country in the present world crisis'. Her articles were written under the name by which she was slightly better known: Princess Catherine Radziwill.

Things had not gone well with Catherine. After her trial she was taken to Roeland Street gaol to serve her two-year sentence. Philip Jourdan later claimed that she was released after serving only nine months. Like so much written about the Princess, this —although it has been accepted without question by Rhodes's biographers—is incorrect. In fact, she served sixteen months, until 13th August, 1903. When she came out of prison she was completely without friends in South Africa. Even her attorney, J. J. Michau, appears to have turned against her. Michau told the editor of the *Cape Argus* that she had been released early because she had made life unbearable for the prison authorities. He said that she had mastered the prison regulations so thoroughly and demanded their observance so often that the prison governor was on the verge of a nervous breakdown and insisted on her being deported from South Africa. According to Michau, Catherine objected vigorously to the idea of being deported and would not agree to be released until she had been promised a first-class passage to England, with sufficient money to enable her to live for some time in a decent English hotel. The authorities were so much afraid that she would not keep this agreement that Michau had to accompany her to the ship on a tug and was allowed to hand over the hotel money only when the ship, a German steamer, was about to sail for Europe. Another informant, who told the editor of the *Argus* that he had been a passenger on this ship, said the Princess had kept herself aloof from the rest of the passengers and communicated only with the bar where she ran up large bills for drink. How true any of this is, it is not possible to say.

The official reason given for reducing Catherine's sentence was ill-health. This may well be true. A few months earlier, the unhappiness of her captivity must have been accentuated by the news that on 1st March, 1903, her younger son, Michel-Casimir, had died in St Petersburg at the early age of fifteen. Although not an ideal mother, she was not completely devoid of feeling.

On returning to Russia her first concern was to write her memoirs. She intended these to be an account of her life in Berlin and St Petersburg. At the end of the book, however, she included a chapter on Cecil Rhodes. She only hinted at her association with him and tried to give her sketch the appearance of impartiality, but she was unable entirely to disguise her bitterness. The book, *My Recollections*, was published in 1904 and the chapter on Rhodes concludes: 'Of all he did, planned, achieved, nothing will soon remain but the evil, for according to Shakespeare's famous words, the good he ever did "is interred with his bones". In Europe his name is seldom mentioned, in South Africa it is already half forgotten; even the attempt to raise a public monument has failed. The *Sic transit gloria mundi* has never been more forcibly illustrated than in the case of Cecil Rhodes.' Nevertheless, South African reviewers were surprised at her moderation. 'Her chapter on Rhodes,' commented the *African World*, 'will only whet the appetite of those who would learn more of the events which culminated so unhappily in the Cape Town trial . . . That calamity, merited or not, would excuse any prejudice she might now cherish regarding the illustrious man who sleeps in the Matopos. Yet her estimate of him, saving here and there a blemish, is superlatively fair . . . We are content to read this chapter as a profoundly pathetic human document upon which it is not for us to pronounce judgement. Some day, perhaps, what now is obscure may be made clear.'

Whether, as le Sueur suggests, Catherine ever contemplated suing the Rhodes Trustees is not certain. The unpublished document in the *Le Sueur Papers* says that the Princess hoped to obtain £1,400,000 from her action but, in his book, le Sueur says: 'She commenced an action for damages against the Rhodes Trustees for £400,000 damages.' Whatever the truth, Catherine was never in possession of any large amount of money after her return to Europe.

Two years after the publication of her memoirs she was involved in a legal action. In 1906—in proceedings at Warsaw, which lasted from 20th May to 2nd June—she and Prince Wilhelm were finally separated. This separation was said to be a preliminary to divorce, but there is no evidence that any divorce was granted. It was not until after Prince Wilhelm's death in Vienna, on 22nd August, 1911, that Catherine married again. Her second husband was Charles-Emile Kolb, a business man from Alsace, who was living in Stockholm at the time of their marriage. He is described as 'an exporter engaged in trade with English and Dutch concerns'. Apart from this and the fact that Catherine later changed her name to Kolb-Danvin, the Princess's second husband remains a shadowy figure. The marriage does not appear to have lasted long and M. Kolb played no significant part in Catherine's later life.

After Prince Wilhelm's death, Catherine continued to live in St Petersburg. She never seems to have regained her position in Russian society, but her love of intrigue was as strong as ever. Her past experiences had taught her nothing. Incredibly enough, a deadly mixture of all her past mistakes caused her last disaster in Russia. Involved in this episode were the mischief-making pseudonym of Count Paul Vassili and a vital State secret.

Catherine's dislike of the Emperor Nicholas II and the

Empress Alexandra had not been alleviated by her absence from Russia. The Russian sovereigns fared badly in her memoirs. Nevertheless she continued to take a great interest in the Court of St Petersburg. Like the rest of Russian society she was intrigued by the mysterious illnesses of the young Tsarevich Alexis. It was commonly known that the heir to the Russian throne was prostrated for weeks at a time by crippling attacks. He was carefully guarded by two sailor attendants and allowed to play with other children only under strict supervision. St Petersburg was alive with rumours as to what was wrong with the little boy, but official bulletins on the Tsarevich's health gave no indication of the precise nature of his illness. This was the great secret of the Russian Court and Catherine was determined to discover the truth. She did. As is now well known, the boy was a victim of haemophilia—the incurable 'bleeding disease' which manifested itself in many royal courts of Europe. In 1913, Catherine published this fact in a book written under her old pseudonym. The book created a stir and speculations about Count Paul Vassili's identity were revived. In the English edition, *Behind the Veil of the Russian Court*, it was announced that the book was being published post-humously. 'The Count,' said the publisher's note, 'passed away a few months ago.' In the *Washington Post*, the Marquise de Fontenoy accredited authorship to the joint efforts of Eli de Cyon and the unfortunate Auguste Gerard, who had suffered from Catherine's earlier efforts. The only people to have no doubts about the matter were the Russian authorities. Once again Catherine was visited by the police. This time she was deported from Russia. She took her exile philosophically. 'It is no stigma,' she said, 'to have been ostracized by the Russian police under the old régime, so I did not mind or care.'

She went to live in Stockholm. For the next few years, books from her pen appeared almost every month. Written sometimes under her own name and sometimes under the pseudonym of the resurrected Count Vassili, they covered a multitude of royal subjects, fact and fiction. In a review of her book, *Germany under Three Emperors*, an astonished reviewer remarked: 'Her rate of production of books for readers who enjoy the society of royalty has been more than one a year; and she is still catering for them.' But this took no account of her many novels or of the productions of 'Count Vassili'. What is surprising about these hastily compiled works is that they have been taken seriously by many historians. Books by Princess Radziwill and Count Vassili are referred to in many reputable studies of the nineteenth century.

At the outbreak of the First World War, Catherine was living in Stockholm. Her son, Prince Nicholas Radziwill, was an early casualty, killed fighting in the Russian army at Lodz in December 1914. Catherine claimed that the bullet which killed him had been fired from a rifle of the Radziwill Fusiliers—a regiment named after her father-in-law. She was heartbroken by his death. Although she had been disappointed by his marriage to a forty-seven-year-old Polish widow in 1906 and regretted his sympathy with the Polish cause, there can be no doubt of her love for her elder son. Throughout her life she kept his photograph proudly on display.

In 1916 she published a book dealing with the Swedish royal family's contribution to the work of the Red Cross. That same year she arrived in England, ostensibly to lecture on the Red Cross, and was still there when Dr Jameson died in 1917. His death prompted her to write a book on Cecil Rhodes. Like most of her writing, it was hastily put together, confused and evasive. It says nothing of her association with Rhodes but here and there contains some shrewd observations. In effect, it is an extension of the chapter on Rhodes in her earlier book. She is loud in her praise of Milner and more charitable than before in her summing up of Rhodes. 'The years that have gone by since his death,' she said, 'have proved that in many things Rhodes had been absolutely mistaken. Always he was an attractive, and at times even a lovable personality; a noble character marred by small acts, a generous man and an unscrupulous foe; violent in temper, unjust in his view of facts that displeased him, understanding chiefly his personal interests, but implacable towards the people whom he wronged. He was a living enigma to which no one ever found a solution; because he presented constantly new and unexpected sides that appeared suddenly and shattered the conclusion to which one had previously arrived.' All in all, a reasonable and not unjust assessment of a man whom nobody has ever fully explained. The book, *Cecil Rhodes: Man and Empire Maker*, was her last published comment on Rhodes.

She left England to continue her lectures in America. Her arrival in the United States was well publicized. When her ship reached New York, she was detained for some time on Ellis Island. No reason was given for this. But her detention did her no harm. 'Mrs Kolb-Danvin,' said the *New York Times*, 'started a lecture tour with considerably more publicity than she might have had if she had not been detained.'

Catherine's career in America is something of a mystery. In 1932 she wrote her last autobiographical work, *It Really Happened*, in which she outlined her life in Europe and the United States. The title seems to have been a misnomer; it is unlikely that much of what she describes ever really occurred.

According to this book, she had learned in New York that, as a result of the Russian revolution, she had lost her fortune. She does not refer to having earlier been deported from Russia. As the result of her loss, she had to look for work and describes how she tramped the streets of New York, answering advertisements and visiting employment agencies. Always she was faced with the same objections; she was too old and too inexperienced. She says that she was then 'forty, and a few years added to it'. In fact she was sixty. She took a room in a tenement house on the Bowery. Here she was befriended by the inevitable prostitute with the heart of gold. The other tenants were similar stock characters: a little dying Jewish girl, a neglected child beaten by his drunken father, and 'old Sally', a toothless, raggedly-dressed crone who later turns out to be very rich and pays for the little Jewish girl's funeral. The prostitute, of course, gives up the streets for a decent Italian shoemaker, and Catherine accompanies them to City Hall for their wedding. They live happily ever after. It reads like a bad film scenario of the 1930s.

Her account of her own career is equally predictable. By a stroke of luck she was offered a temporary job as a switchboard operator. She had never operated a switchboard before but was given a quick lesson by a girl who worked in a large hotel. She did so well that when the girl whom she was replacing returned, Catherine was kept on and her salary raised to fourteen dollars a week. She was then spotted by a businessman who offered her a job in a stockbroker's office. In no time she mastered the intricacies of stocks and shares, dividends and interest, rose to great heights and became indispensable to her new employer. Unfortunately, the office was moved to Chicago and she wanted to remain in New York. Her attempts to find a new job were not so successful and when she did find one, her employer turned out to be a crook. But by this time she had made enough contacts to earn her living by writing newspaper articles.

One does not know how true any of this is. But whatever the other circumstances, she certainly continued churning out books and articles. She wrote on anything and everything. Her talent for discovering secrets and exposing frauds stood her in good stead. Among other things, she claimed to have unearthed a marriage certificate which proved that old King Ludwig of Bavaria had actually married the notorious Lola Montez. When it was suggested that the film actress, Elissa Landi, was the daughter of the Empress of Austria, it was Catherine who threw doubt on her pretensions. Mr Ernest V. Heyn, who edited *Modern Screen* in which Catherine's refutation was published, was to remember his unusual contributor. 'Her English was not particularly good,' he says, 'but she was able to put together some fascinating facts about her associations in Europe . . . she wrote for me a rather sensational article about a movie star . . . and [it] made quite a stir . . . I recall Princess Radziwill as quite short and plump with bright, highly intelligent eyes. Although her English was rather poor, I was always amazed at the trenchant and searching observations that she made . . . I took a great deal of pains to get whatever I could from her recollections and was able to turn them into readable stories; I believe she was having some trouble making ends meet.'

Her most outstanding *coup* was her exposé of the infamous, anti-Semitic *Protocols of the Elders of Zion*. She claimed that the Protocols had been forged in the Bibliothèque Nationale and that she had seen the manuscript when she was in Paris. She was able to offer 'direct evidence' that the document was a forgery. Her claim was given the distinction of being hailed by *The American Hebrew* as conclusive proof that the Protocols were false. But later, when Professor Norman Cohn, the historian of the Protocols, examined her findings, he was unable to accept them. 'Unfortunately,' he says, 'the dates and other particulars given in this account are so manifestly wrong, that this particular effort to discredit the Protocols did more harm than good.'

A few other facts are available about Catherine's later years. After a lifetime of opposition to the religion of the Radziwills, she was converted to the Roman Catholic faith. When the weekly publication, *The Commonweal*, was started in America by a group of Catholic laymen, Catherine became one of its regular book reviewers and later claimed that its editor, Michael Williams, was one of her dearest friends. She also became a proud American citizen. Her one-time fervour for Russian and British Imperialism was replaced by a whole-hearted devotion to democratic principles and the American way of life. 'I really became an American in heart;' she said, 'I cannot conceive of living anywhere else.'

Whatever one may think of Catherine's dubious activities, there is no gainsaying her courage and tenacity. Crushed time and again as a result of her intrigues, she was never daunted. She was always able to pick up the pieces and start again. Her twenty-odd years in America were not the least remarkable of her eventful career. Arriving at the age of sixty in a strange land without money, influence or connections, she set out to make a new life for herself and, though she rose to no great heights, and was always poor, she managed to carve a niche for herself. Towards the end of her life, Sir Newman Flower of Cassell, her British publishers, visited her in New York. He found her 'an old lady, sweet with the years that lay upon her'. They met in a restaurant which she claimed was one of her favourite haunts. After dinner, she took the publisher and his son back to her flat for coffee. It was a well-furnished apartment, full of souvenirs of her life in Europe. The walls were covered with signed photographs of the great figures of her life and in the centre of her desk was a large portrait of her beloved son, Prince Nicholas. She was as lively as ever: full of interesting talk and fascinating anecdotes. To listen to her was, says Sir Newman, 'a privilege'.

But it is unlikely that her gallery of illustrious portraits included that fatal signed photograph of Cecil Rhodes. She never spoke of South Africa to her American friends. There was no mention of Rhodes in her obituaries. Her ability to blot out the unpleasant past was perhaps the most beneficial of her many gifts. In South Africa, nobody knew what happened to her. Biography after biography of Rhodes appeared during her life-time; often they contained vicious references to her. She made no attempt to reply. So adept at lifting the veil on other people's lives, she kept her own past discreetly covered.

She died on 12th May, 1941, aged eighty-four.

Epilogue

IN AUGUST1967, the South African newspapers announced the death of Princess Louise Blücher. The Princess had once lived at the Cape and was well remembered by her South African friends. It was stated that Princess Blücher had been born 'Princess Louise Radziwill', but there was nothing to indicate that she was in any way connected with the more notorious Princess Radziwill who had known Cecil Rhodes. In fact, she was Catherine's eldest daughter.

Catherine saw little of her family after she left Europe. Old Prince Blücher died in 1916, leaving his wife Wanda and three children. Catherine's youngest daughter, Ella, never married but became well known in Geneva where she worked for the League of Nations. The eldest of the Radziwill girls, Louise, appears to have been the most remarkable. An attractive, witty young woman, she lived for a long time with her aunt in Vienna. If Louise inherited none of her mother's failings, she had much of Catherine's sophisticated charm. 'Well known for many years as Loulou Radziwill,' says Lady Norah Bentinck, 'she had a reputation of being one of the cleverest people and most attractive talkers in Vienna.'

Her marriage in 1913 caused some surprise. Reversing the pattern set by her brother and sister—who had both married much older partners—Louise chose a husband considerably younger than herself. This was not the only unusual thing about the marriage. For the man she married, at the age of thirty-seven, was Prince Lothair Blücher, twenty-three-year-old son of old Prince Gerbhard Blücher. Louise thus became the step-daughter-in-law of her younger sister Wanda. Contrary to all predictions, the marriage was happy. It lasted fifteen years and ended with Prince Lothair's death in 1928.

Louise had three sons. Nicholas, the second son, was killed while serving in the R.A.F. in 1943. The eldest boy, Tommy, died at the Blücher estate in Czechoslovakia, shortly before the communist *coup* of 1947. Louise was then living in Czechoslovakia and is said to have escaped from the country 'on the last train'. A few years later she joined her youngest son, Alec, who had recently emigrated to South Africa.

She lived on a farm at Bot River in the Cape for some sixteen years. Popular and unpretentious—she thought her title too grand and called herself Countess Blücher—she amused her neighbours with her witty descriptions of life in Vienna and St Petersburg. Only her closest friends were aware of her mother's connections with South Africa. She knew little of Catherine's turbulent association with Rhodes and her sympathies were for her unfortunate father, Prince Wilhelm.

When, three years before her death, she left South Africa to live in Jersey with her son, few were aware that she represented the last tenuous link between Cecil Rhodes and the Princess.

Acknowledgments

IN WRITING this book I have been helped considerably by having had access to the Rhodes Papers (from the Library of Rhodes House, Oxford) which are now on micro-film at the Cape Archives, Cape Town. I would like to thank the Rhodes Trustees for making these papers available and for allowing me to quote from the statement by Princess Radziwill which is contained in the *Le Sueur Papers*.

I am greatly indebted to Miss Judy Scott of Kimberley for her invaluable assistance in tracing details concerning her great-uncle, Neville Pickering, and for supplying me with copies of a letter and photograph from her family papers. My thanks are due also to Dr Ronald Currey of Grahamstown for his interesting anecdotes of Princess Radziwill's stay at the Cape and for allowing me to quote from his account of the association between Cecil Rhodes and his father, Henry L. Currey.

Among the many people who have assisted me in tracing details of Princess Radziwill's activities in Cape Town, I am particularly grateful to the Hon. Leslie Blackwell, who kindly allowed me to read an unpublished manuscript which was a useful guide to various legal aspects of Princess Radziwill's trial. I owe thanks to Mr Ernest V. Heyn, editor of the *Popular Science Monthly*, New York, for his recollections of Princess Radziwill's journalistic career in America and to Professor Norman Cohn, of the University of Sussex, for answering my queries about Princess Radziwill's 'exposé' of the *Protocols of the Elders of Zion*. In Port Elizabeth I was given valuable and much appreciated assistance by Mr Brocas Harris, who provided me with details of Neville Pickering's birth, and Mr S. E. Edkins, Rector of the Grey High School, who sent me extracts from the school records relating to the Pickering family. I am most grateful to Mrs F. J. Rozwadowski, of Somerset West, Cape, for supplying me with clues to the background of Princess Radziwill's children in later life and for interesting information concerning Princess Louise Blücher's life in South Africa.

For answering queries, offering advice and assistance, I would like to record my very warm thanks to Major and Mrs V. Rozwadowski of Mbabane, Swaziland; Mrs Elisaveta Williams-Foxcroft of the Russian

373

Department, University of South Africa; Miss Elizabeth Dey of Johannesburg; Miss Esther Roberts of Durban and Mr Eric Rosenthal, Mr Peter Tomlinson and Mr Alfred Vital of Cape Town.

I have been fortunate in receiving valuable co-operation from many public institutions in South Africa and would like, in particular, to express my thanks to the following: Miss J. H. Davies and the staff of the Cape Archives; Miss A. T. Hadley and the staff of the State Library, Pretoria; Miss A. H. Smith and the staff of the Africana Library, Johannesburg; Dr A. M. Lewin Robinson and the staff of the South African Library, Cape Town; and Mr P. M. E. van Zyl and the staff of the Durban Public Library.

My final, and undoubtedly my greatest debt, is to Mr Theo Aronson whose advice, encouragement and constructive criticism have aided me every step of the way.

B.R.

Bibliography

(I) RHODES: BIOGRAPHICAL

Baker, H., *Cecil Rhodes by his Architect*. Oxford University Press. 1934.

Clark, G. N., *Cecil Rhodes and his College*. Oxford University Press. 1953.

Currey, R., *Rhodes: A Biographical Footnote*. Carmelite Press, Cape Town (n.d.).

Fuller, T. E., *The Right Honourable Cecil John Rhodes: A Monograph*. Longmans Green, London. 1910.

Gross, Felix, *Rhodes of Africa*. Cassell, London. 1956.

Hensman, H., *Cecil Rhodes: A Study of a Career*. Blackwood, Edinburgh. 1901.

Hutchinson, G. S., *Cecil Rhodes: The Man*. Oxford University Press. 1944.

'Imperialist', *Cecil Rhodes: With a Personal Reminiscence by Dr Jameson*. Chapman & Hall, London. 1897.

Jourdan, Philip, *Cecil Rhodes: His Private Life by His Private Secretary*. The Bodley Head, London. 1910.

Le Sueur, Gordon, *Cecil Rhodes: The Man and His Work*. John Murray, London. 1913.

Lockhart, J. G., *Cecil Rhodes*. Duckworth, London. 1933.

Lockhart, J. G., and Woodhouse, C. M., *Rhodes*. Hodder & Stoughton, London. 1963.

McDonald, J. G., *Rhodes: A Life*. Chatto & Windus, London. 1941.

McDonald, J. G., *Rhodes: A Heritage*. Chatto & Windus, London. 1943.

Maurois, André, *Cecil Rhodes*. Collins. 1953.

Michell, Lewis, *The Life of the Right Hon. Cecil John Rhodes* (2 vols.). Edward Arnold, London. 1910.

Millin, S. G., *Rhodes*. Chatto & Windus, London. 1933.
(Revised edition: Central News Agency, Cape Town. 1952.)

Plomer, W., *Cecil Rhodes*. Nelson, London. 1933.

Radziwill, C., *Cecil Rhodes: Man and Empire Maker*. Cassell, London. 1918.

Stead, W. T., *The Last Will and Testament of Cecil John Rhodes*. London. 1902.

Stent, Vere, *A Personal Record of Some Incidents in the Life of Cecil Rhodes*. Cape Town. 1925.

'Vindex', *Cecil Rhodes: His Political Life and Speeches*. 1881–1900. George Bell & Sons, London. 1900.

Williams, B., *Cecil Rhodes*. Constable, London. 1921.

(II) BOOKS BY PRINCESS RADZIWILL

The Resurrection of Peter: A reply to Olive Schreiner. Hurst & Blackett, London. 1900.

My Recollections. Isbister & Co., London. 1904.

Memories of Forty Years. Cassell, London. 1914.

The Royal Marriage Market of Europe. Funk & Wagnall, New York. 1915.

Sovereigns and Statesmen of Europe. Funk & Wagnall, New York. 1916.

The Black Dwarf of Vienna. W. Rider & Sons, London. 1916.

The Austrian Court From Within. Cassell, London. 1916.

Because It Was Written. Cassell, London. 1916.

'Furstinnor i Röda Korsets tecken'. A. Bonnier, Stockholm. 1916.

Germany Under Three Emperors, Cassell, London. 1917.

Cecil Rhodes: Man and Empire Maker. Cassell, London. 1918.

Russia's Decline and Fall. Cassell, London. 1918.

The Firebrand of Bolshevism. Small, Maynard, Boston. 1919.

Those I Remember. Cassell, London. 1924.

The Intimate Life of the Last Czarina. Longmans, Green, Toronto. 1928.

Child of Pity (in collaboration with Grace A. Catherwood). Sears, New York. 1930.

Nicholas II: The Last of the Tsars. Cassell, London. 1931.

The Taint of the Romanovs. Cassell, London. 1931.

It Really Happened. Dial Press, New York. 1932.

The Empress Frederick. Cassell, London. 1934.

UNDER THE PSEUDONYM: COUNT PAUL VASSILI

Berlin Society. Sampson Low, Marston. 1885.

La Société de Saint-Pétersbourg (in collaboration with Yuliana Glinka). Nouvelle Revue. 1886.

Behind the Veil at the Russian Court. Cassell, London. 1913.

France From Behind the Veil. Cassell, London. 1914.

Rasputin and the Russian Revolution. Bodley Head, London. 1918.

Confessions of the Czarina. Harper & Bros., New York. 1918.

The Disillusions of a Crown Princess. Bodley Head, London. 1919.
Secrets of Dethroned Royalty. Bodley Head, London. 1920.

UNDER THE PSEUDONYM: HILDEGARDE EBENTHAL

The Tragedy of a Throne. Funk & Wagnall, New York. 1917.

TRANSLATION

They Knew the Washingtons: Letters From a French Soldier Etc. Bobbs-Merrill, Indianapolis. 1926.

(III) GENERAL

Amery, L. S., *Days of Fresh Air*. Jarrolds, London. 1939.
Anon, *Letters From a Man of No Importance* 1895–1914. Cape, London. 1928.
Beet, George, *Grand Old Days of the Diamond Fields*. Maskew Miller, Cape Town. 1931.
Bentinck, Lady Norah, *My Wanderings and Memories*. T. Fisher Unwin, London. 1924.
Bismarck, Prince, *Reminiscences*. Smith, Elder, London. 1898.
Blackwell, Leslie, *Of Judges and Justice*. Howard Timmins, Cape Town. 1965.
Blücher, Princess Evelyn, *An English Wife in Berlin*. Constable, London. 1920.
Blücher, Princess Evelyn, *Memoirs of Prince Blücher*. John Murray, London. 1932.
Buchanan, Meriel, *Recollections of Imperial Russia*. Hutchinson, London. 1923.
Bülow, Prince von, *Memoirs* (4 vols.), Putnam, London. 1932.
Cartwright, A. P., *Gold Paved the Way*. Macmillan, London. 1967.
Castlerosse, Viscount, *Valentine's Days*. Methuen, London. 1934.
Chilvers, Hedley, *Out of the Crucible*. Cassell, London. 1930.
Chilvers, Hedley, *The Story of De Beers*. Cassell, London. 1939.
Churchill, Lord Randolph, *Men, Mines and Animals in South Africa*. Sampson Low, Marston, London. 1892.
Cloete, Stuart, *African Portraits*. Collins, London. 1946.
Cohen, Louis, *Reminiscences of Kimberley*. Bennett & Co., London. 1911.
Cohn, Norman, *Warrant for Genocide*. Eyre & Spottiswoode, London. 1967.
Colvin, Ian, *Life of Jameson*. Edward Arnold, London. 1922.
Cronin, Vincent, *Four Women in Pursuit of an Ideal*. Collins, London. 1965.

Davenport, T. R. H., *The Afrikander Bond*. Oxford University Press, 1966.

Dormer, F. J., *Vengeance as a Policy in Afrikanderland*. John Nisbet, London, 1901.

Doughty, O., *Early Diamond Days*. Longmans, London. 1963.

Dufferin & Ava, Dowager Marchioness of, *My Russian and Turkish Journals*. John Murray, London. 1916.

Emden, Paul H., *Randlords*. Hodder & Stoughton, London. 1935.

Field, Julian Osgood, *Uncensored Recollections*. Eveleigh Nash, London. 1924.

Flower, Newman, *Just As It Happened*. Cassell, London. 1950.

Froude, J. A., *Two Lectures on South Africa*. Longmans, Green, London. 1880.

Green, G. A. L., *An Editor Looks Back*. Juta, Cape Town. 1947.

Guthrie, Frank, *A Frontier Magistrate*. Stewart, Cape Town (n.d.).

Halecki, O., *A History of Poland*. J. M. Dent, London. 1955.

Hamilton, Lord Frederic, *The Vanished World of Yesterday*. Hodder & Stoughton, London. 1950.

Hamilton, Mary Agnes, *Remembering My Good Friends*. Cape, London. 1944.

Hammond, John Hays, *Autobiography*. Farrar & Rinehart, New York. 1935.

Harding, Lt.-Colonel Colin, *Far Bugles*. H. R. Grubb Ltd., London. 1933.

Headlam, C. (Ed.), *The Milner Papers*. Cassell, London. 1933.

Hesekil, J. G., *Life of Bismarck*. James Hogg, London. 1870.

Hofmeyr, J. H., and Reitz, F. W., *The Life of Jan Hendrik Hofmeyr*. Van de Sandt de Villiers, Cape Town. 1913.

Hunt, Herbert J., *Honoré de Balzac*. Athlone Press, London. 1957.

Hutchinson, G. T., *Frank Rhodes: A Memoir*. Privately printed. 1908.

Innes, James Rose, *Autobiography*. Oxford University Press. 1949.

Johnson, Frank, *Great Days*. G. Bell, London. 1940.

Kiewiet, C. W. de, *The Imperial Factor in South Africa*. Cambridge University Press, 1937.

Kleinmichel, Countess, *Memories of a Shipwrecked World*. Brentanos, London. 1923.

Kruger, Rayne, *Goodbye Dolly Gray*. Cassell, London. 1959.

Le May, G. H. L., *British Supremacy in South Africa*, 1899–1907. Oxford University Press. 1965.

MacBride, Maud Gonne, *A Servant of the Queen*. Gollancz, London. 1938.

MacNeill, J. G. Swift, *What I Have Seen and Heard*. Arrowsmith, London. 1925.

Massie, R. K., *Nicholas and Alexandra*. Gollancz, London. 1968.

Meintjes, J., *Olive Schreiner*. Hugh Keartland, Johannesburg. 1965.

Milner, Viscountess, *My Picture Gallery*. John Murray, London. 1951.

Moneypenny, W. F., and Buckle, G. E., *The Life of Benjamin Disraeli*. John Murray, London. 1929.

Mossolov, A. A., *At the Court of the Last Tsar*. Methuen, London. 1935.

Paget, Walburga, Lady, *The Linings of Life*. Hurst & Blackett, London (n.d.).

Pakenham, Elizabeth, *Jameson's Raid*. Weidenfeld & Nicolson, London. 1961.

Pearson, Hesketh, *The Whispering Gallery*. John Lane The Bodley Head, London. 1926.

Poel, Jean van der, *The Jameson Raid*. Oxford University Press. 1951.

Ponsonby, Sir Frederick, *Recollections of Three Reigns*. Eyre & Spottiswoode, London. 1951.

Reischach, Hugo Baron von, *Under Three Emperors*. Constable, London. 1927.

Rouillard, Nancy, *Matabele Thompson*. Faber & Faber, London. 1936.

Sampson, Victor, *My Reminiscences*. Longmans, Green, London. 1926.

Sauer, Hans, *Ex Africa*. Geoffrey Bles, London. 1937.

Schreiner, Olive, *Trooper Peter Halket of Mashonaland*. T. Fisher Unwin, London. 1897.

Schreiner, Olive, *Letters*. T. Fisher Unwin, London. 1924.

Scholtz, W. C., *The South African Climate*. Cassell, London. 1897.

Schwering, Count Axel, *The Berlin Court Under William II*. Cassell, London. 1915.

Scully, W. C., *Reminiscences of a South African Pioneer*. T. Fisher Unwin, London. 1913.

Scully, W. C., *Further Reminiscences of a South African Pioneer*. T. Fisher Unwin, London. 1913.

Sherard, R. H., *My Friends the French*. T. Werner Laurie, London (n.d.).

Stead, W. T., *The Truth About Russia*. Cassell, London. 1888.

Stephens, W., *Madame Adam*. Chapman & Hall, London. 1917.

Stevenson, E. S., *Adeventures of a Medical Man*. Juta, Cape Town. 1925.

Tanser, G. H., *Founders of Rhodesia*. Oxford University Press, 1950.

Taylor, J. B., *A Pioneer Looks Back*. Hutchinson, London. 1939.

Waddington, Mary, *Letters of a Diplomat's Wife* 1883–1900. Smith, Elder, London. 1903.

Walker, Eric A., *Lord de Villiers and His Times.* Constable, London. 1925.

Whyte, F., *The Life of W. T. Stead.* Cape, London. 1925.

Williams, A. F., *Some Dreams Come True.* Howard Timmins, Cape Town. 1948.

Williams, G. F., *The Diamond Mines of South Africa.* Macmillan, London. 1902.

Wilson, Lady Sarah, *South African Memories.* Edward Arnold, London. 1909.

Wrench, J. E., *Alfred, Lord Milner.* Eyre & Spottiswoode, London. 1958.

Zetland, Marquis of, *Letters of Disraeli.* Ernest Benn, London. 1929.

(IV) NEWSPAPERS AND PERIODICALS

South African: Cape Argus, Cape Times, South African News, Eastern Province Herald, Diamond Fields Advertiser, Natal Advertiser, Natal Witness, Johannesburg Star, Rand Daily Mail, Greater Britain, The Owl, The Cape, South Africa, African World.

English: Times, Telegraph, Review of Reviews, Review of the Week, Pall Mall Gazette.

American: New York Times.

GENERAL REFERENCE

Almanach de Gotha, South African Who's Who, South African Dictionary of National Biography, Prominent Men of the Cape 1902, Men of the Times, Current Biography (U.S.A.).

References

CHAPTER ONE

p. 4. 'A slender . . .' Michell. *Life*; girl at gate, Williams B.
Cecil Rhodes.

p. 8. 'very quiet and a great reader'. *Natal Advertiser*, 30th
May, 1936.

p. 9. 'could always be sure . . .' *Natal Witness*, 3rd May, 1902.

p. 10. 'The lads . . .' Michell. *Life*.

p. 11. 'Mr Rhodes came close . . .' and (p. 12) 'Captain Bond
proposed . . .' *Natal Advertiser*, 30th May, 1936.

p. 12. 'Diggers from America . . .' Froude. *Two Lectures*.

p. 13. 'A tall gaunt . . .' Williams B. *Cecil Rhodes*; 'A compound
of . . .' Michell. *Life*; 'I received . . .' Scully. *Reminiscences*;
'The silent self-contained . . .' Cohen. *Reminiscences*.

p. 14. 'I can very clearly . . .' Scully. *Reminiscences*; 'As I
search . . .' Michell. *Life*.

p. 15. 'I do not believe . . .' Cohen. *Reminiscences*.

p. 18. 'I know that Father . . .' Williams B. *Cecil Rhodes*.

p. 19. 'a slender stripling . . .' Michell. *Life*; 'he was a fresh . . .'
G. Beet. *Cape Argus*, 4th April, 1902.

p. 20. Rhodes's first will. Lockhart & Woodhouse. *Rhodes*.

CHAPTER TWO

The best source for Princess Radziwill's childhood and youth
is her first and most reliable autobiography *My Recollections*.
Unless otherwise stated the quotations in this chapter are taken
from this book. For confirmation of details concerning the
Rzewuski family and life at Pohrebyszcze see also: Kleinmichel.
Memories; Hunt. *Balzac*; Cronin. *Four Women* and appropriate
editions of the *Almanach de Gotha*.

p. 24. 'a happy reign'. Cronin. *Four Women*.

p. 28. 'matrimonial agent'. Field. *Uncensored Recollections*.

p. 32. 'I was not given a chance . . .' Radziwill. *It Really Happened.*

p. 34. 'Berliners had always . . .' Hamilton F. *The Vanished World.*

CHAPTER THREE

p. 41. 'They were full . . .' Michell. *Life.*

p. 42. 'a shy solitary . . .' MacDonald. *Rhodes: A Life*; 'He belonged to a set . . .' Michell. *Life*; 'Shouldn't do that . . .' Williams B. *Cecil Rhodes.*

p. 43. 'Now, Mr Butler . . .' Williams B. *Cecil Rhodes*; Rhodes to Stead: Whyte. *Life of Stead.*

p. 49. 'right-hand man'. Maurois. *Cecil Rhodes*; 'probably the closest . . .' MacDonald. *Rhodes: A Heritage*; 'more confidence . . .' Gross. *Rhodes of Africa*; 'For him Rhodes had . . .' Williams B. *Cecil Rhodes*; David and Jonathan. Lockhart & Woodhouse. *Rhodes.*

p. 50. 'All this to be painted . . .' Williams B. *Cecil Rhodes*; 'Pickering was delicate . . .' MacDonald. *Rhodes: A Heritage.* 'Beloved by both men . . .' Miss J. Scott. *Private Information.*

p. 51. 'strict probity . . .' *Eastern Province Herald*, 18th October, 1886; details of Pickering family. Miss J. Scott. *Private Information*; Pickering's birth. *Baptismal Register St. Paul's Church*, Port Elizabeth; Pickering's schooling. *Records of Grey Institute*, Port Elizabeth.

p. 52. 'exile'. Letter in possession of Miss J. Scott, Kimberley.

p. 53. 'We have dinners . . .' and 'Our club . . .' Letter. Miss J. Scott; 'They shared the same . . .' Colvin. *Life of Jameson.*

p. 54. Different generations. Lockhart & Woodhouse. *Rhodes*; 'frank, sunny . . .' Colvin. *Life of Jameson.*

p. 55. Rhodes's third will. Michell. *Life*; 'a most undeniable Godsend . . .' Letter. Miss J. Scott.

p. 56. 'I'm still in . . .' Williams B. *Cecil Rhodes*; 'I went down . . .' Vindex. *Speeches.*

p. 57. 'I look upon . . .' and 'We want to . . .' Vindex. *Speeches.*

p. 58. 'Blood must flow . . .' and 'That young man . . .' Williams B. *Cecil Rhodes.*

p. 59. 'What is your game . . .' Millin. *Rhodes.*

p. 60. Pickering's accident. *Diamond Fields Advertiser*, 28th June, 1884, and 29th July, 1884.

p. 61. 'certainly one of the best . . .' *Diamond Fields Advertiser*, 10th May, 1884.

pp. 62–3. Rhodes on reef and Pickering's illness. Sauer *Ex-Africa* and Chilvers *Out of the Crucible*.

pp. 63–4. Pickering's death and funeral. Colvin. *Life of Jameson*; *Eastern Province Herald*, 18th October, 1886; *Diamond Fields Advertiser*, 18th October, 1886.

p. 64. Rhodes and William Pickering. Cloete. *African Portraits*; 'There seems . . .' Plomer. *Cecil Rhodes*.

p. 65. Recent study of Rhodes. Cartwright. *Gold Paved the Way*.

p. 66. 'Ugly rumours'. Gross. *Rhodes of Africa*.

pp. 66–7. Pickering's engagement. *Private information*. 'Everyone knew he was engaged . . .' Johnson. *Great Days*.

CHAPTER FOUR

Quotations from Radziwill, *My Recollections*, except as follows:

p. 68. 'But to me . . .' Radziwill. *It Really Happened*.

p. 69. 'For the most part . . .' Vasili (pseud.). *Berlin Society*; 'it was nothing but rank . . .' Radziwill. *It Really Happened*.

p. 70. 'They were all . . .' Paget. *Linings of Life*; Princess Marie Radziwill. Schwering. *The Berlin Court*.

pp. 71–2. 'I retain very pleasant . . .' and 'Princess Wilhelm (William) Radziwill . . .' Hamilton F. *Vanished World*. Bismarck and Kulturkampf. Bismarck. *Reminiscences*.

p. 73. 'Doubtless under the pretence . . .' Radziwill. *Memories of Forty Years*.

p. 74. 'By some miracle . . .' Radziwill. *It Really Happened*.

p. 76. 'Never has a political . . .' Vasili (pseud.). *Berlin Society*.

pp. 76–7. 'He represented to my . . .' and 'I am not thinking . . .' Radziwill. *Memories of Forty Years*; 'Austria feasted us . . .' Zetland. *Letters*.

p. 78. 'hearing that Princess Radziwill . . .' Dufferin. *Journals*. 'I had a little talk . . .' Waddington. *Letters*.

p. 80. Mme Adam. Stephens W. *Madame Adam*; Sherard. *My Friends*; Vasili (pseud.). *France From Behind the Veil*.

pp. 83–4. M. Gerard and 'Berlin Society'. Bülow. *Memoirs*; Vasili (pseud.). *Confessions of the Czarina*.

pp. 84–5. Radziwill and Duke of Clarence. Radziwill. *Memories of Forty Years*; Radziwill and Empress Augusta. Radziwill. *It Really Happened*.

pp. 85–6. Collaboration on *La Société de Saint Petersbourg*. Vasili (pseud.). *Confessions of the Czarina*; Exile of Yuliana Glinka. Cohn. *Warrant for Genocide*.

p. 87. 'The Empress disliked me . . .' Radziwill. *It Really Happened*.

CHAPTER FIVE

p. 91. 'come in here like wolves . . .' Williams B. *Cecil Rhodes*.

p. 94. Concession signed by Lobengula. Rouillard. *Matabele Thompson*; De Beers Trust deed. Williams B. *Cecil Rhodes*.

p. 96. 'Mr Rhodes is my man . . .' Whyte. *Life of Stead*.

p. 97. 'Everything in the world . . .' Millin. *Rhodes*; 'pure philanthropy . . .' Williams B. *Cecil Rhodes*; 'Money is power . . .' Vindex. *Speeches*.

p. 99. Rhodes and Jameson. Colvin. *Life of Jameson*.

pp. 100. 'I must not only have you . . .' Johnson. *Great Days*.

p. 101–2. Rhodes and Johnson. Johnson. *Great Days*.

p. 105. 'Mr Rhodes first made . . .' *Cape Argus*, 10th June, 1902; 'That boy has . . .' Williams A. F. *Some Dreams Come True*; 'undemonstrative' and 'I only want men . . .' Le Sueur. *Cecil Rhodes*.

p. 106. 'When at last . . .' Williams B. *Cecil Rhodes*; 'You've got back . . .' Johnson. *Great Days*; 'Johnson was lost . . .' Ibid.

p. 107. 'I'll take their——' Johnson. *Great Days*.

p. 110. 'Let's try on £250 . . .' Currey. *Rhodes*.

p. 111. 'Whom Rhodes's quick eye . . .' Currey. *Rhodes*.

p. 112. 'One morning Rhodes . . .' Currey. *Rhodes*; Rhodes and Victoria. MacDonald. *Rhodes: A Life*, and Ponsonby. *Recollections*.

p. 113. 'We only live once . . .' and 'I feel that . . .' Currey. *Rhodes*.

p. 114. 'Can't you square . . .', 'I am very jealous . . .' and 'Rhodes was . . .' Currey. *Rhodes*.

p. 116. 'Mashonaland, so far . . .' Churchill. *Men, Mines and Animals*; Telegram to Jameson. Colvin. *Life of Jameson*.

p. 118. Naming of Rhodesia. Plomer. *Cecil Rhodes*.

p. 120. Kruger and Rhodes. Williams B. *Cecil Rhodes*.

p. 122. Rhodes and Hammond. Hammond. *Autobiography*.

p. 125. 'Newspapers, do you think . . .' Williams B. *Cecil Rhodes*.

p. 126. 'I received so many messages . . .' Lady Sarah Wilson. *South African Memories*.

p. 127. 'Old Jameson . . .' Williams B. *Cecil Rhodes*.

CHAPTER SIX

Quotations from *My Recollections* except as follows:

pp. 128–9. 'I was related . . .' Radziwill. *It Really Happened*.

p. 132. 'She was then . . .' *Review of Reviews*, December 1899.

p. 133. 'certain political documents . . .' Vasili (pseud.). *France From Behind the Veil*; 'It was certainly against . . .' and 'Princess Radziwill . . .' MacBride. *A Servant of the Queen*.

p. 134. 'I had to warn . . .' MacBride. *A Servant of the Queen*; 'Madame Adam . . .' Vasili (pseud.). *France From Behind the Veil*.

p. 135. 'Amongst my father's . . .' Blücher. *Memoirs*.

p. 136. 'And we thought it . . .' and 'Personally I love England . . .' Radziwill. *Memories of Forty Years*.

p. 139. 'Tradition says . . .' Radziwill. *Memories of Forty Years*.

p. 140. 'He never got used . . .' Radziwill. *It Really Happened*; 'A brute', Jourdan. *Cecil Rhodes*; 'she treated him . . .' *Private Information*.

p. 141. 'I was supposed . . .' Radziwill. *It Really Happened*; 'would not look', Anon. *Letters From a Man*.

p. 142. 'but also with socialist . . .' Gross. *Rhodes of Africa*; 'was obsessed', Blücher. *Memoirs*.

p. 144. 'Moberley Bell went . . .' Radziwill. *Memories of Forty Years*.

CHAPTER SEVEN

p. 145. 'It's rare sport . . .' Pearson, E. Hesketh. *The Whispering Gallery*.

p. 146. 'I was a naughty . . .' Williams B. *Cecil Rhodes*.

p. 148. 'Mr Rhodes as a rule . . .' Fuller. *Cecil Rhodes*.

p. 150. Rhodes and Indaba. Stent. *A Personal Record*, and MacDonald. *Rhodes: A Life*.

p. 151. 'Mr Rhodes's physical . . .' Jourdan. *Cecil Rhodes*.

p. 152. 'That's not my . . .' MacDonald. *Rhodes: A Heritage*; Grimmer's letter. Le Sueur. *Cecil Rhodes*.

p. 153. 'On one occasion . . .' Guthrie. *A Frontier Magistrate*.

pp. 154–6. Rhodes and Jourdan. Jourdan. *Cecil Rhodes*.

p. 157. 'I do not think . . .' MacDonald. *Rhodes: A Life*.

p. 158. 'as enthusiastic . . .' Jourdan. *Cecil Rhodes*; 'mental sadism' and Lobengula's sons. Gross. *Rhodes of Africa*, and Radziwill. *My Recollections*.

p. 159. 'He appeared to look . . .' and 'Rhodes used to say . . .' Le Sueur. *Cecil Rhodes*; 'One day I saw Rhodes . . .' Introduction to Stent. *A Personal Record*.

p. 160. 'They had passed:. . .' Jourdan. *Cecil Rhodes*.

p. 161. 'Is that all?' Millin. *Rhodes*; 'I can only say . . .' Fuller. *Cecil Rhodes*.

p. 162. 'I am going to meet . . .' and 'The only big man . . .' Schreiner. *Letters*; 'The perception of what . . .' Plomer. *Cecil Rhodes*.

pp. 163–6. Chamberlain and Rhodes and Select Committee. van der Poel. *The Jameson Raid*, and Pakenham. *Jameson's Raid*.

p. 166. 'D'ye know Grimmer . . .' Le Sueur. *Cecil Rhodes*.

p. 167. 'equal political rights . . .' Michell. *Life*.

pp. 168–70. Rhodes and Le Sueur. Le Sueur. *Cecil Rhodes*.

p. 170. 'to see how it felt', Michell. *Life*.

p. 172. The Princess's letter. Le Sueur. *Cecil Rhodes*, and Lockhart & Woodhouse. *Rhodes*.

p. 175. 'Le Sueur was very anxious . . .' Jourdan. *Cecil Rhodes*.

CHAPTER EIGHT

p. 179. 'I have been painted . . .' and 'I honestly believe . . .' Michell. *Life*.

p. 180. 'objects which conspiracy . . .' and 'I am determined . . .' Michell. *Life*.

p. 181. 'Promiscuous callers . . .' Jourdan. *Cecil Rhodes*.

p. 182. 'Satan, I tell you . . .' Williams B. *Cecil Rhodes*.

p. 183. 'Yes, I remember her . . .' Jourdan. *Cecil Rhodes*.

p. 184. 'Being a princess . . .' Jourdan. *Cecil Rhodes.*

pp. 184–7. Jourdan's account of voyage. Jourdan. *Cecil Rhodes.*

p. 190. 'Rumour said . . .' Harding. *Far Bugles.*

p. 191. 'It was perhaps . . .' Fuller. *Cecil Rhodes.*

pp. 191–2. 'the same boyishness . . .' and 'Venit, vidit . . .' *Cape Times*, 19th July, 1899.

p. 193. The Princess at Government House. Stevenson. *Adventures of a Medical Man.*

p. 194. Lord Salisbury's letter. Milner. *My Picture Gallery;* 'She was deeply . . .' Harding. *Far Bugles.*

p. 196. 'The many sides . . .' Wilson. *South African Memories;* 'When we said . . .' Harding. *Far Bugles.*

p. 197. 'I keep aloof . . .' and 'I really cannot think . . .' MacDonald. *Rhodes: A Life.*

pp. 197–8. Rhodes's library and phallic collection. Fuller. *Cecil Rhodes,* and Le Sueur. *Cecil Rhodes.*

p. 198. 'ugly rumours about Rhodes's . . .' Gross. *Rhodes of Africa.*

p. 199. 'At first . . .' Jourdan. *Cecil Rhodes.*

p. 200. 'Lunch passed . . .' MacDonald. *Rhodes: A Life;* 'The Princess had been . . .' Jourdan. *Cecil Rhodes;* 'No, I discuss politics . . .' *Cape Argus Weekly,* 12th February, 1902.

p. 201. Letter of 10th September, 1899. Lockhart & Woodhouse. *Rhodes.* 'He said one never knew . . .' Jourdan. *Cecil Rhodes.*

p. 202. 'a defiant note . . .' *Owl,* 8th September, 1899; 'The gown worn . . .' *Cape Argus Weekly,* 27th September, 1899; 'My pearls . . .' R. Currey. *Private Information.*

p. 203. Dr and Mrs Scholtz. *The Cape,* 29th January, 1909; and *Prominent Men of the Cape,* 1902.

p. 204. 'The fact is . . .' Jourdan. *Cecil Rhodes.*

p. 205. 'He asked her . . .' Jourdan. *Cecil Rhodes;* The Princess and Rhodes's private papers. MacDonald. *Rhodes: A Heritage.*

CHAPTER NINE

p. 209. 'He always wore . . .' Jourdan. *Cecil Rhodes;* 'All contention . . .' and 'What is a civilized . . .' Michell. *Life.*

p. 210. Interview with Julian Ralph. *Cape Times,* 6th April, 1900; 'It is indisputable . . .' Radziwill. *Cecil Rhodes.*

p. 211. 'During those feverish weeks . . .' Rhodes House. *Le Sueur Papers*; '[She] was inclined . . .' *Eastern Province Herald*, 2nd May, 1902.

p. 212. 'Anglo-African Party' and 'What we require . . .' *South African News*, 14th July, 1900; No evidence in Bond papers. T. R. H. Davenport. *Private Information*; 'declined to hold . . .' *South African News*, 14th July, 1900; Princess's diary. Lockhart & Woodhouse.

p. 213. *Rhodes*; 'through a close friend . . .' *South African News*, 14th July, 1900; 'Everyone in Paris . . .' Milner. *My Picture Gallery*; 'Not the least . . .' Amery. *Days of Fresh Air*.

p. 214. 'Incredible as it appears . . .' Radziwill. *Cecil Rhodes*.

p. 215. 'When I first arrived . . .' *Review of Reviews*, December 1899.

p. 217. Arguments at Groote Schuur. Lockhart & Woodhouse. *Rhodes*; 'What can one do with you . . .' Radziwill. *Cecil Rhodes*; 'Mrs Scholtz informed me . . .' *Cape Argus Weekly*, 12th February, 1902.

p. 218. 'To anybody else but you . . .' *Cape Times*. Trial of Princess Radziwill.

p. 219. 'I was subsequently told . . .' *Cape Argus Weekly*, 12th February, 1902.

p. 221. Talk with Stead. Stead. *Last Will and Testament*, and Millin. *Rhodes* (revised edition).

p. 222. 'various treasures . . .' and 'made her the talk . . .' *Review of Reviews*, June 1900.

p. 224. 'The whole thing . . .' Milner. *My Picture Gallery*; 'He has passed . . .' Headlam. *Milner Papers*.

p. 225. 'I paid her bills . . .' *Cape Argus Weekly*, 12th February, 1902.

p. 227. 'Let us get . . .' and 'When he was away . . .' Jourdan. *Cecil Rhodes*.

p. 228. 'I believe that if . . .' Radziwill. *Cecil Rhodes*. 'We are informed . . .' *South African News*, 25th July, 1900.

p. 229. Stead's letter. *Cape Times*. Trial of Princess Radziwill; Princess calls at Groote Schuur. Lockhart & Woodhouse. *Rhodes*.

CHAPTER TEN

p. 230. 'This was the Rhodes . . .' Rouillard. *Matabele Thompson*.

p. 231. 'As a matter of fact . . .' Scully. *Further Reminiscences*; 'This craving continually . . .' Radziwill. *Cecil Rhodes.*

p. 232. 'We were all . . .' Le Sueur. *Cecil Rhodes.*

p. 233. Story of Harry Palk. Le Sueur. *Cecil Rhodes.* Le Sueur's inefficiency. Colvin. *Life of Jameson.*

p. 234. 'Oh, I spoilt him . . .' Le Sueur. *Cecil Rhodes*; Story of Percy Ross. MacDonald. *Rhodes: A Heritage.*

p. 235. Dinner guest at Groote Schuur. Lockhart & Woodhouse. *Rhodes*; 'I shall always . . .' Radziwill. *Cecil Rhodes.*

p. 237. Rhodes's anger with Princess. Lockhart & Woodhouse. *Rhodes*; 'During the time . . .' R. Currey. *Private Information.*

p. 238. 'When Rhodes had to . . .' Le Sueur. *Cecil Rhodes*; The Princess and Jourdan. Jourdan. *Cecil Rhodes.*

p. 241. 'phrases which have appeared', *South African News,* 5th July, 1901.

p. 242. 'That is your business . . .' *Cape Argus Weekly,* 12th February, 1902; 'His greatest wrong . . .' Rhodes House. *Le Sueur Papers.*

p. 243. 'That thing only . . .' Rhodes House. *Le Sueur Papers.*

p. 244. 'What good purpose . . .' *South African News,* 29th May, 1900; 'a little forlorn . . .' Colvin. *Life of Jameson.*

p. 245. 'enjoyed myself . . .' Rhodes House. *Le Sueur Papers.*

p. 246. 'We had rather a violent . . .' *Cape Times,* Trial of Princess Radziwill; 'The first thing to do . . .' Rhodes House. *Le Sueur Papers.*

p. 248. Princess and Lovegrove. *Cape Times,* Trial of Princess Radziwill; 'We understand . . .' *Eastern Province Herald,* October 1900.

pp. 249–50. *Greater Britain* and negotiations for house. *Cape Times,* Trial of Princess Radziwill.

CHAPTER ELEVEN

Details of Princess Radziwill's business and financial dealings, together with extracts from her letters, were reported in the South African papers at the time of the preparatory examinations for her trial and during the trial itself. The most comprehensive account of these legal proceedings is given in a booklet, *The Trial of Princess Radziwill*, published by the *Cape Times* in May 1902. Unless otherwise stated the quotations in this chapter are taken from this booklet. As the booklet omits certain interesting aspects of the trial, see also for a full understanding of the events, the accounts given in the *Cape Argus, Eastern Province Herald,* and *Diamond Fields Advertiser.*

p. 256. 'I replied, No . . .' *Cape Argus Weekly,* 12th February, 1902.

p. 261. 'Another Rhodes organ . . .' *South African News,* 29th June, 1901.

p. 262. 'She started *Greater Britain* . . .' Wilson G. H. *Gone Down the Years*; 'Princess Radziwill is half . . .' *Review of Reviews,* June 1902.

pp. 263–4. Quotes from *Greater Britain. Greater Britain,* 22nd June, 1901, to 24th August, 1901; 'We are not surprised . . .' *South African News,* 5th and 6th July, 1901; 'entrusted to Lord Kitchener . . .' *Cape Times,* 25th July, 1901.

p. 267. 'Her eyes were . . .' Radziwill. *My Recollections*; 'I never can think . . .' Radziwill. *It Really Happened.*

p. 274. 'We shall be rich . . .' *Cape Argus Weekly,* 30th April, 1902.

p. 276. Notice in Cape papers. *Cape Argus,* 8th August, 1901, and *Cape Times,* 9th August, 1901.

CHAPTER TWELVE

Quotations from *Trial of Princess Radziwill* except as follows:

p. 279. 'He caused a notice . . .' *Cape Argus Weekly,* 5th March, 1902.

p. 281. Hawksley and £6,300 note. Lockhart & Woodhouse. *Rhodes.*

p. 282. Faint capital C. *Cape Argus Weekly,* 2nd April, 1902.

p. 283. 'You will let me have the money . . .' *Cape Argus Weekly,* 2nd April, 1902.

p. 284. The Princess at royal receptions. *Cape Times,* 19th–23rd August, 1901.

p. 290. 'First took place the episode . . .' Rhodes House. *Le Sueur Papers.*

pp. 291–2. Louw's action in Supreme Court. *Cape Times,* 14th October, 1901.

p. 295. Second hearing and Rhodes's affidavit. *Cape Times,* 2nd November, 1901.

p. 297. 'One morning, it was November 11th . . .' Rhodes House. *Le Sueur Papers*.

pp. 297–8. Henry Widdowson's visit and documents. Lockhart & Woodhouse. *Rhodes*.

p. 298. 'dangerously wounded', *Cape Times*, 18th November, 1901.

p. 299. J. A. Stevens and Princess's arrest. Lockhart & Woodhouse. *Rhodes*; 'It is then that . . .' Rhodes House. *Le Sueur Papers*.

p. 300. 'This lady of high rank . . .' *Owl*, 22nd November, 1901.

p. 301. 'It is really time . . .' *Owl*, 13th December, 1901.

CHAPTER THIRTEEN

Quotations from *Trial of Princess Radziwill* except as follows:

p. 303. 'I dreaded a meeting . . .' Jourdan. *Cecil Rhodes*; 'I was informed . . .' *Cape Argus Weekly*, 12th February, 1902; Princess to Hawksley. Lockhart & Woodhouse. *Rhodes*; 'a long rest . . .' Jourdan. *Cecil Rhodes*.

p. 304. Rhodes in contact with Michell and Hawksley. Lockhart & Woodhouse. *Rhodes*; Lord Salisbury's daughter-in-law. Milner. *My Picture Gallery*.

p. 305. 'His face was bloated . . .' Le Sueur. *Cecil Rhodes*; Dr Jameson and 'What is £24,000 . . .' Stead. *Last Will and Testament*; 'I must go and defend . . .' Le Sueur. *Cecil Rhodes*; Dinner party. Taylor. *A Pioneer Looks Back*.

p. 306. 'came like a bombshell . . .' Le Sueur. *Cecil Rhodes*; 'he received news . . .' Jourdan. *Cecil Rhodes*.

p. 307. Mrs Scholtz's letters to Rhodes and Rhodes's letter to Michell. Lockhart & Woodhouse. *Rhodes*.

p. 309. 'a prominent member . . .' Jourdan. *Cecil Rhodes*; 'an ex-member . . .' Le Sueur. *Cecil Rhodes*; Rhodes and T. A. J. Louw. Davenport. *The Afrikander Bond, Men of the Time, South Africa*, 17th July, 1909, *Cape Times*, July 1899 and July 1909.

p. 311. 'the old Princess', Stead. *Last Will and Testament*.

p. 312. 'It was necessary that I . . .' Rhodes House. *Le Sueur Papers*.

p. 313. 'it is a marvel . . .' Le Sueur. *Cecil Rhodes*; 'capital health . . .' *Cape Argus*, 4th February, 1902.

p. 314. Sent for Rose-Innes. Innes. *Autobiography*; 'He called me into . . .' Sampson. *My Reminiscences*.

pp. 316–18. Rhodes in court. *Cape Times*, 7th February, 1902, *Cape Argus Weekly*, 12th February, 1902, *Eastern Province Herald*, 10th February, 1902.

p. 320. 'a house with huge gables . . .' *The Cape*, 29th January, 1909.

p. 321. The Princess and Dr Scholtz. *Cape Argus Weekly*, 28th May, 1902; *Diamond Fields Advertiser*, 2nd May, 1902, *The Cape*, 29th January, 1909.

p. 322. Bernard and Flower. *Cape Argus Weekly*, 30th April, 1902; 'Sir, I was taken ill . . .' *Cape Argus*, 13th February, 1902.

p. 324. Michau's arrest. *Cape Times* and *Cape Argus*, March 1900.

p. 325. 'Damn that woman! . . .' Le Sueur. *Cecil Rhodes*; 'I cannot say anything . . .' *Cape Argus*, 25th February, 1902.

CHAPTER FOURTEEN

Quotations from *Trial of Princess Radziwill* except as follows:
p. 326. 'She passed, however . . .' Le Sueur. *Cecil Rhodes*.

p. 327. Preliminary examination of 28th February, *Cape Argus*, 28th February, 1902, and *Cape Times*, 29th February, 1902.

p. 329. 'After the magistrate . . .' *The Cape*, 5th February, 1909; 'I only saw him . . .' Radziwill. *My Recollections*.

p. 330. 'That she became fond . . .' Stevenson. *Adventures of a Medical Man*; 'She was deeply . . .' Harding. *Far Bugles*.

p. 331. Death of Scholtz. *Cape Argus*, 7th March, 1902; 'The Government has refused . . .' *Cape Argus Weekly*, 12th March, 1902; 'hastened Dr Scholtz's end . . .' *Diamond Fields Advertiser*, 2nd May, 1902; 'I feel anxious . . .' *Cape Times*, 11th March, 1902.

p. 332. Supreme Court hearing. *Cape Argus*, 19th March, 1902.

p. 333. 'Mr Rhodes has passed . . .' and 'It is an extraordinary . . .' Le Sueur. *Cecil Rhodes*; 'He was unable . . .' Stevenson. *Adventures of a Medical Man*; 'It was most heartrending . . .' Jourdan. *Cecil Rhodes*; 'Jameson was indefatigable . . .' Le Sueur. *Cecil Rhodes*.

p. 334. 'Not long before . . .' Le Sueur. *Cecil Rhodes*; 'if they might come . . .' and 'Jameson with . . .' Currey. *Rhodes*; 'wooden gate opening . . .' *Review of Reviews*, August 1902.

p. 335. 'indecent haste . . .' *Cape Argus*, 19th March, 1902; 'Here we found her . . .' *The Cape*, 29th January, 1909.

p. 336. Hearing at Kalk Bay on 21st March. *Cape Argus*, 21st March, 1902, and *Cape Times*, 22nd March, 1902.

p. 337. 'she sat like a tigress . . .' Le Sueur. *Cecil Rhodes*; Final preliminary examination. *Cape Argus*, 27th March and *Cape Times*, 28th March, 1902.

p. 338. 'The pledge fixed . . .' Rhodes House. *Le Sueur Papers*.

p. 339. Rhodes's death. Le Sueur. *Cecil Rhodes*; Jourdan. *Cecil Rhodes*; Michell. *Life; Prominent Men of the Cape*, 1902.

CHAPTER FIFTEEN

Quotations from *Trial of Princess Radziwill* except as follows:

p. 340. 'The approaches to the court . . .' *Diamond Fields Advertiser*, 2nd May, 1902; 'In my opinion . . .' *Cape Argus Weekly*, 12th February, 1902.

p. 341. Mr Burdett-Coutts, M.P. *The Times*, 26th March, 1902; 'rebel attorney', *Cape Argus*, 9th April, 1902.

p. 342. Attempt to flee. *Diamond Fields Advertiser*, 2nd May, 1902; 'The police went . . .' Rhodes House. *Le Sueur Papers*.

p. 347. 'There was something . . .' *Cape Argus Weekly*, 7th May, 1902.

p. 348. 'If that is justice . . .' Rhodes House. *Le Sueur Papers*.

p. 349. 'proved the complicity . . .' Rhodes House. *Le Sueur Papers*.

p. 350. 'He was without . . .' Quoted in *Natal Witness*, 3rd May, 1902.

p. 352. 'So it came to pass . . .' Stead. *Last Will and Testament*.

p. 353. 'Cecil Rhodes, though . . .' Castlerosse. *Valentine's Days*; 'In the end . . .' Milner. *My Picture Gallery*. 'True, he had . . .' *Cape Argus*. 11th April, 1902; 'I cannot get married . . .' Jourdan. *Cecil Rhodes*.

p. 356. 'I don't want . . .' Lockhart & Woodhouse. *Rhodes*; 'He liked a man . . .' Jourdan. *Cecil Rhodes*.

p. 357. 'Turn me over, Jack', Millin. *Rhodes*; 'They were not unlike . . .' Jourdan. *Cecil Rhodes*; 'he was the kindliest . . .' Introduction to Stent. *A Personal Record*.

p. 358. Grimmer's death. *Cape Argus*, 10th June, 1902; *Cape Times*, 6th July, 1902; Louw's death, *South Africa*, 17th July,

1909; *Cape Times*, July 1909; 'No, it may be . . .' Colvin. *Life of Jameson*.

p. 359. Le Sueur's career and death. *Men of the Time*, Rosenthal. *South African Dictionary of National Biography*.

p. 360. 'Young Harry Currey . . .' *Owl*, 29th September, 1899; Currey's career and death. Currey. *Rhodes*.

p. 360–1. Jourdan's career and death. *Cape Argus*, 13th May, 1961, and *Rand Daily Mail*, 22nd May, 1961.

p. 361. Mrs Kolb-Danvin admitted to hospital. *New York Times*, 13th May, 1941; 'that her knowledge . . .' Ibid.; Princess's release from prison. *Cape Argus*, 14th August, 1903, and *Cape Times*, 14th August, 1903; Account by editor of *Argus*. Green. *An Editor Looks Back*.

p. 362. Death of Prince Michel-Casimir. *Almanach de Gotha*, 1910; 'Her chapter on Rhodes . . .' *African World*, 10th December, 1904.

p. 363. Separation from Prince Wilhelm. *Almanach de Gotha*, 1910; 'an exporter engaged . . .' *New York Times*, 13th May, 1941.

p. 364. 'It is no stigma . . .' Vassili (pseud.). *Confessions of the Czarina*; 'Her rate of production . . .' *Times Literary Supplement*, 12th July, 1917.

p. 366. 'Mrs Kolb-Danvin . . .' *New York Times*, 13th May, 1941.

p. 367. 'Her English was not . . .' E. V. Heyn. *Private Information*.

p. 368. 'An old lady . . .' Flower. *Just As It Happened*.

EPILOGUE

p. 370. Death of Princess Louise Blücher. *Star*. Johannesburg, 1st August, 1967; Death of Prince Blücher. Blücher. *Memoirs*; Ella Radziwill. Hamilton M. *Remembering My Good Friends*; 'Well known . . .' Bentinck. *My Wanderings*.

p. 371. Princess Blücher at the Cape. Mrs. F. J. Rozwadowski. *Private Information*.

Index